Where to Wear 2006

FASHION SHOPPING FROM A–Z

D1392718

Fairchild & Gallagher

NEW YORK • LONDON

PUBLISHERS
Jill Fairchild, Gerri Gallagher & Julie Craik

SERIES COPY EDITOR
John Graham

SERIES DESIGN/PRODUCTION ARTIST
Jeff Baker & Cynthia Roberts
at Bookmechanics

WRITERS
ROME Agnes Crawford
FLORENCE & MILAN Jasmine Serrurier

PREVIOUS WRITERS
Heidi Baravalle, Jane Fox Cappuzzello,
Michelle Hough, Enid Pinder, Helen Richards,
Jennifer Robinson, and Valerie Waterhouse

FACT CHECKER
Simone Muzza

COVER DESIGN
Richard Chapman

CARTOGRAPHER
Candida Kennedy

DISTRIBUTION SALES AND MARKETING
The Julie Craik Consultancy

Where to Wear, Italy, 2006 Edition
ISBN 0-9766877-6-3

Copyright © 2005 Fairchild & Gallagher
Printed and bound in China.

Table of Contents

Introduction	v
Clothing & Shoe Size Equivalents	vii
Italy Map	viii-ix
Where to Wear Rome 2006	1
Rome Best Picks	2
Rome Store Directory	3
Rome Stores by District (and Maps)	91
Rome Stores by Category	103
Rome Restaurants	115
Rome Services	121
Where to Wear Florence 2006	127
Florence Best Picks	128
Florence Store Directory	129
Florence Stores by District (and Maps)	193
Florence Stores by Category	201
Florence Restaurants	215
Florence Services	221
Where to Wear Milan 2006	227
Milan Best Picks	228
Milan Store Directory	229
Milan Stores by District (and Maps)	339
Milan Stores by Category	353
Milan Restaurants	365
Milan Services	371
Fashion Speak	379

Introduction

Dear Italy Shopper,

Welcome to *Where to Wear*, the world's most detailed and authoritative directory of clothing and accessory stores.

Written by a team of international fashion journalists, *Where to Wear* tells you what ordinary guidebooks don't: where to find out-of-the-way boutiques and designer discount outlets; the best places for vintage, for wedding dresses, for childrenswear; where to go for budget-busting extravagance or bargain-basement trophies. From the globally famous names of the Via del Babuino and the Piazza della Repubblica to hidden treasure-houses, *Where to Wear* shows visitors where to begin and Romans, Florentines and Milanese where to go next. Each of our guides is updated annually, to give you the latest lowdown on shopping hotspots.

If we wouldn't go there, we don't recommend it. If the merchandise is hot but the staff are frosty, we let you know. If the changing-room mirrors make you look more like a supertanker than a supermodel, we're not afraid to say so.

The directories for each city are organized alphabetically, with two indexes at the back (by category and by neighbourhood). Our favourite stores are marked with a star (☆)—see page 2 for more details. To make life even easier for you, we've included ten pages of user-friendly maps. And because we know that a shopping trip involves more than just shops, we list the chicest lunch spots, the best day spas, where to have your Jimmy Choos repaired, and much else besides.

Shopping has never been easier! So rev up your credit card and get going, and make sure to keep *Where to Wear* in your handbag, briefcase or backpack.

—Jill Fairchild, Gerri Gallagher & Julie Craik

p.s. We love feedback! Please e-mail us on uk@wheretowear.com or usa@wheretowear.com

Jill Fairchild, daughter of fashion world legend and *W* magazine founder John Fairchild, worked as an intern at *Glamour* magazine, *GQ* and *Vogue*. Ms Fairchild has also worked for Ailes Communications, a television production company, and in the late Eighties she founded and ran her own accessories company.

Gerri Gallagher is a Condé Nast editor who has lived in Europe for 20 years. She was the managing editor of Fairchild Publication's *W Europe* from 1990 to 1993 and is currently associate editor of *Tatler* magazine in London.

Julie Craik, *Where to Wear* partner and director of sales, marketing and distribution has worked in publishing for 20 years. Before joining *Where to Wear* she was associate publisher of *Tatler* magazine and had previously worked for the National Magazine Company.

Clothing & Shoe Size Equivalents

Children's Clothing

American	3	4	5	6	6X
Continental	98	104	110	116	122
British	18	20	22	24	26

Children's Shoes

American	8	9	10	11	12	12	1	2	3
Continental	24	25	27	28	29	30	32	33	34
British	7	8	9	10	11	12	13	1	2

Ladies' Coats, Dresses, Skirts

American	3	5	7	9	11	12	13	14	15
Continental	36	38	38	40	40	42	42	44	44
British	8	10	11	12	13	14	15	16	17

Ladies' Blouses and Sweaters

American	10	12	14	16	18	20
Continental	38	40	42	44	46	48
British	32	34	36	38	40	42

Ladies' Hosiery

American	8	8.5	9	9.5	10	10.5
Continental	1	2	3	4	5	6
British	8	8.5	9	9.5	10	10.5

Ladies' Shoes

American	5	6	7	8	9	10
Continental	36	37	38	39	40	41
British	3.5	4.5	5.5	6.5	7.5	8.5

Men's Suits

American	34	36	38	40	42	44	46	48
Continental	44	46	48	50	52	54	56	58
British	34	36	38	40	42	44	46	48

Men's Shirts

American	14	15	15.5	16	16.5	17	17.5	18
Continental	37	38	39	41	42	43	44	45
British	14	15	15.5	16	16	17	17.5	18

Men's Shoes

American	7	8	9	10	11	12	13
Continental	39.5	41	42	43	44.5	46	47
British	6	7	8	9	10	11	12

Italy Map

Italy Map

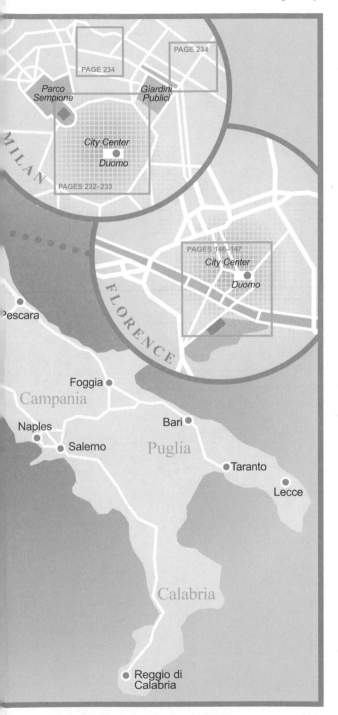

Where to Wear Rome 2006

Best Picks

Rome Best Picks

Here are our particular favourites (marked ☆ in
the Directory)

244 Panisperna Via
Abit Art
Abiti Usati
Alberta Ferretti
Alexander
Arsenale
Battistoni
Bonpoint
Borsalino
Brugnoli
Cambalache
Claudio Sanò
Corner
Dal Co
Davide Cenci
Degli Effetti
De Grillis
Edo City
Eleonora
Fabindia
Fendi
Fornarina
Gallo
Giuseppe Messina
Josephine de Huertas
Laltramoda

L'Anatra all'Arancia
Leam (San Giovanni)
Le Gallinelle
Loco
Loro Piana
Luna & L'Altra
Maga Morgana
Malo
Mandarina Duck
Marisa Padovan
Molly Bloom
Nia/Nia & Co
Nuyorica
Only Hearts
People
Pure
Rubinacci
SBU
Scapa
Sole by Soledad Twombly
TAD
Thé Verde
Valentino
Verso Sud
Vestiti Usati Cinzia
Vittoriana

Rome Store Directory

Newcomers to Italy's proudest cities may be amazed to discover that many stores close during the lunch hour, and in some cases the "hour" is in practice two or two and a half hours. Don't despair, they will re-open! It's just that having invented one of the world's greatest cuisines, they see no reason why they shouldn't enjoy it. Our advice is to join them, and for each of the cities in this book we have provided a select list of restaurants, sidewalk cafés, salad bars, pizzerias etcetera, ideal for your shopping excursions.

We have also listed the opening hours for each store, though these may vary considerably; to avoid frustration, we recommend checking by telephone if in doubt. And finally, while Italian fashion and Italian clothing stores are among the most stylish in the world, you may be disappointed if you plan your shopping in August. The Italians have a special relationship with August (which is often fiendishly hot), and are happy to forsake retail in favor of the beach. To the regular astonishment of workaholic Protestant-ethic northern Europeans and Americans, many Italian stores happily close for weeks—yes, weeks!—at a time. It's a Mediterranean thing…

☆ 244 Panisperna Via

After a change of address in September 2004, this is the shop previously known as Via degli Zingari 10. Ebullient owner Mauro Gagliardini has taken advantage of the larger stockroom to increase his range of shoes in this tiny wood-beamed red cube with a distinctly retro feel (think black Fifties flooring, kitsch chandelier and battered armchairs). If you're one of those hard-core fashion hounds who loves to sniff out fresh new design talents, this is the store for you. Collections change every couple of weeks; last time we popped by Greek designer Erotokritos' retro print dresses and Milena's floaty ephemeral skirts caught the eye. Heels with a retro feel from Stephen and floral ballet slippers by Ras finish off the look.

Expensive   MC/V

Via Nazionale area

Via Panisperna 244   **06 478 23889**
00184 Rome   Mon-Fri 10-10, Sat 10-7:30

☆ Abit Art

Blue and green should never be seen? Swirls and stripes should never go together? Those who live by fortune-cook-ie fashion wisdom should avoid this store. The green and yellow carpet and bright orange and turquoise furnishings are only the first indication that in Abit Art-land, black defi-nitely isn't back. In fact, owner Vanessa Foglia's mantra is to abolish black in all forms. She challenges with clashing colours and styles—in mixes of silk, lace and Lycra—which are just a little bit tongue-in-cheek. Bootleg jeans for instance, are livened up with a scarf belt and two mid-calf circles of patterned silk, while miniskirts, if turned upside down, look like the brightly coloured court jester hats you see at carnival time. Men will find a few (mostly small-fitting) shirts at the back of the store. If you fall in love with some-thing here, snap it up; it won't be there the next time you go back.   *abitartworld.com*

Affordable   Amex/MC/V

Piazza di Spagna area

Via della Croce 46/47 (boutique)   **06 699 24077**
00187 Rome   Mon-Sat 10:30-8, Sun 11-8

Trastevere

Via della Scala 7 (outlet)   **06 977 46383**
00153 Rome   Tues-Sun 10:30-10

☆ Abiti Usati

Delve into this musty cave-like shop and around the piles of vintage jeans and you could stumble across treasures like Seventies Burberry coats, cashmere sweaters by Braeman or Ballantyne, YSL and Hermès ties, Gucci bags, and leather biker jackets. If you can't find what you're looking for just ask; the staff are helpful and you might even get to to pick owner and vintage expert Michele Salvatore's brains. There are occasionally funky kids' pieces, including new Converse

All-Stars. Feel a *Cabaret* moment coming on? Look no further than the wide selection of bowlers and top hats decorating the rafters.

Affordable   *Amex/MC/V*

Piazza Navona area

Via del Governo Vecchio 35   **06 683 07105**
00186 Rome   Mon-Sat 10-8, Sun 2-8

☆ Alberta Ferretti
Follow the stars—most notably Nicole Kidman—to Alberta Ferretti, the feminine but decisive designer who founded the Aeffe group (which now includes Moschino and Jean Paul Gaultier's prêt-à-porter line) in the Seventies. The Rome store is unhurried, minimalist and hushed; you get the impression that loud noises might break the delicate clothes. Dresses and skirts are ephemeral and delicate, and in the summer there's a bewilderingly exciting selection of sandals, from snakeskin through pink and black to gold evening shoes.   *aeffe.com*

Luxury   *Amex/MC/V*

Piazza di Spagna area

Via dei Condotti 34   **06 699 1160/679 7728**
00187 Rome   Mon-Thurs 10-7, Fri-Sat 7:30
                                        Sun 11-1:30, 3-7

☆ Alexander
Not for the timid, Alexander is a big hit with Middle Eastern women (who rarely wear their purchases in public) and the helpful staff speak every language under the sun including Japanese, Arabic and Russian. Styles are classily flirty and European designers producing in LA with one eye on the Hollywood set are a favourite, including distressed, embroidered, beaded denim by the LA-based French label Goa. There's a special denim collection in all colours for Alexander by jeans meister Adriano Goldshmied, Transit crumpled silk tops and more than a few spangly belts.

Moderate   *Amex/MC/V*

Piazza di Spagna area

Piazza di Spagna 49   **06 679 1351**
00187 Rome   Mon 12-7:30, Tues-Sat 9:30-7:30

Alternative
True to its name, Alternative's spirit (and setting) is off the beaten track. Tucked away on the edge of the old Jewish ghetto, it was opened in July 2004 and designed by owner Maurizio Catalioti. The metallic grey interior drips with cascades of sparkling chandeliers, and slinky feminine style dominates. Lines by Alessandro Dell' Acqua and Valentino are accompanied by Grimaldi Giardina's shimmering catwalk gems, while light-knit and floaty silk dresses from Missoni's M line provide alta moda at a fraction of the price. You'll find cashmere by Matilda and strappy shoes by Strategia and Rochas. If you're all shopped out, take advan-

tage of the Bartaruga opposite and admire the splendid Fountain of the Turtles with a drink in hand.

Expensive   *Amex/MC/V*

Largo Argentina area

Piazza Mattei 5   **06 683 09505**
00186 Rome   Mon-Sat (and most Sundays) 10-7:30

Alviero Martini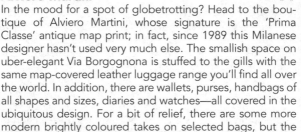

In the mood for a spot of globetrotting? Head to the boutique of Alviero Martini, whose signature is the 'Prima Classe' antique map print; in fact, since 1989 this Milanese designer hasn't used very much else. The smallish space on uber-elegant Via Borgognona is stuffed to the gills with the same map-covered leather luggage range you'll find all over the world. In addition, there are wallets, purses, handbags of all shapes and sizes, diaries and watches—all covered in the ubiquitous design. For a bit of relief, there are some more modern brightly coloured takes on selected bags, but the antique print comes back on jackets and trousers in cotton and suede with sections of coastline picked out in beading. Why not give in and splash out something? At least you won't lose your way.   *alvieromartini.it*

Expensive   *Amex/MC/V*

Piazza di Spagna area

Via Borgognona 4/G   **06 699 23381**
00187 Rome   Mon 12-7:30, Tues-Sat 10-7:30
                                          Sun 11-2, 2:30-7:30

Angelo di Nepi

Roman designer Angelo di Nepi is the last person you'd go to if you wanted to buy a little black dress—or anything black for that matter. Boy, does he like his colours. His small store is packed with a rainbow palette of warm reds, burnt oranges, chirpy turquoises, emerald greens and shocking pinks. He uses linens, taffeta, raw silks and cotton—tweed in winter—and decorates his designs with brightly coloured beads and sequins. Clothes are generously cut so they look good and don't pinch even if you overdo the pizza and ice cream. The inspiration for his designs wavers between Africa and the East, but the feel-good factor is constant.   *angelodinepi.com*

Moderate   *Amex/MC/V*

Campo de' Fiori area

Via dei Giubbonari 28   **06 689 3006**
00186 Rome   Mon 12:30-8, Tues-Sat 9:30-8

Piazza di Spagna area

Via Frattina 2   **06 322 4800**
00187 Rome   (opening hours as above)

Via del Babuino 147   **06 360 04299**
00187 Rome (opening hours as above)

Via Cola di Rienzo area

Via Cola di Rienzo 267/A   **06 322 4800**
00192 Rome   (opening hours as above)

Arli Cashmere

Only the most determined will uncover this fabulous cashmere workshop near the Teatro Olimpico, in the most unlikely of streets, behind an unpromisingly industrial-looking shopfront near the river. But when you get there, it's like finding the treasure at the end of the rainbow. An ex-auto repair shop hung with industrial-style aluminium lamps, this anonymous location is home to a cashmere 'production line' (four people and their roaring knitting machines) crafting super-soft cashmere sweaters, baby clothes, polonecks, capes and T-shirts in all colours. Prices for 100% cashmere pieces start at about 150 euros for irresistible baby clothes, 300 for women's jerseys and 400 for men's sweaters. In the summer, there are more affordable pieces in linen. These magical creations are neatly stacked in the entrance area on shiny glass tables and shelves. Sabrina, who does the designing, is usually on hand for advice, and you can order any style in any colour and size; it'll arrive in about five weeks.

Expensive   *Amex/MC/V*

Flaminio area

Via Giorgio Vasari 10   **06 360 04107**
00196 Rome   Mon-Sat 8:30-7:30

Armani Jeans

Armani's most accessible line has its flagship store on Via Tomacelli. The Via del Babuino store is a bit smaller but still filled to bursting with those metal-eagled jeans in all shapes, sizes and colours. There are also ribbed jerseys for weekends, dark blue linen jackets, stripey T-shirts and leather jackets. If you're drained of inspiration after a hard day's shopping, the Via del Babuino store has shelves stacked with style books showing the way beautiful people should live, Armani style.   *armanijeans.com*

Moderate   *Amex/MC/V*

Piazza di Spagna area

Via Tomacelli 137   **06 681 93040**
00187 Rome   Mon 3-7:30, Tues-Sat 10-7:30, Sun 2:30-7

Via del Babuino 70/A   **06 360 01848**
00187 Rome   (opening hours as above)

☆ Arsenale

Roman designer Patrizia Pieroni opened this New York loft-style space in the early Nineties, and it's still a favourite with theatre actors looking to keep up their boho-chic images. The most extravagant among them walk off with one of Pieroni's own-design evening dresses, perhaps finished off with a pair of Emma Hope's shoes. Signora Pieroni justly prides herself on being a craftswoman producing niche clothes, but they're definitely at their best on the relatively tall and slim. However, there are easier looks in dark, ultra-sophisticated, recherché fabrics, and Patrizia Pieroni's own attractive range of chunky jewellery completes the look.

Moderate to expensive   *Amex/MC/V*

7

Piazza Navona area

Via del Governo Vecchio 64   **06 686 1380**
00186 Rome   Mon 3:30-7:30, Tues-Sat 10-7:30

AVC by Adriana V. Campanile

Adriana Campanile started off with a footwear store in Parioli, but now her empire has spread far and wide. The flagship store on the Piazza di Spagna is an address which proves she's truly arrived. In fact, the Piazza di Spagna store is where the largest variety of new items is to be found, including a capsule collection of clothing. Last time we dropped by there were summer dresses and light suits from Sonia Fortuna and Christina Gavioli. The AVC range of shoes offers splendid value—prices start at 89 euros for leather thong sandals and average around 140. You'll find everything from gold ballet slippers to 9cm stilettos; believe us, there aren't many other places in the Tridente where you'll find so much choice for so little. The children's range is housed upstairs at the Piazza di Spagna store. Once again, variety is the name of the game: there's everything from elegant party shoes and loafers by AVC to trainers from Gola. The narrow (but well stocked) Via Frattina store opened in spring 2004, while the Testaccio and Campo de' Fiori stores are discount outlets for goods from previous seasons: bargains abound.   *avcbyadrianacampanile.com*

Moderate to expensive   *Amex/MC/V*

Piazza di Spagna area

Piazza di Spagna 88   **06 699 22355**
00187 Rome   Mon-3:30-7:30, Tues-Sat 10:30-7:30
                              Sun 10:30-2:30, 3:30-7:30

Via Frattina 141   **06 679 0891**
00187 Rome   (opening hours as above)

Parioli area

Viale Parioli 178   **06 807 0951**
00197 Rome   (opening hours as above, but closed Sun)

Testaccio area

Via Mastro Giorgio 66/68 (outlet)   **06 572 50493**
00153 Rome   Mon-Fri 9-2, 3:30-6:30, Sat 9-2

Campo de' Fiori area

Largo del Pallaro 1 (outlet)   **06 682 10670**
00186 Rome   Daily 10-7:30

Bagheera

This is the place where Parioline—the female residents of this studiedly smart district—replenish their insatiable wardrobes. At the more casual level, there are jeans by Just Cavalli and hip bikinis from Vanda Catucci, while for evening there is suited elegance from Armani and colourful young dresses by Chloé. But the store's real coup is the seriously hip boho-chic Jorando line from Francesca Jori (the daughter of the store's owner). Feminine minidresses, cropped tops and tie-dyed T-shirts are made from Italian fabrics, and hand-decorated in Asia with sequins, crystals and ribbons. Beautifully exotic. *jorando.com*

Moderate to luxury *Amex/MC/V*

Parioli area

Via G. Antonelli 26 **06 807 4401**
00197 Rome Mon 4-8, Tues-Sat 9:30-1, 4-8

Bagheera Accessories

This little jewel box of shoes and bags follows the main store's style line—garnering key looks from international designers, mixed with boho styles from Jorando by Francesca Jori. This is the place to come for Miu Miu's low suede slip-ons, Marc Jacobs silver sandals with butterflies attached, or grown-up red heels. They sit side-by-side with Jorando's more off-beat beaded and sequinned sandals, espadrilles and string-knit bags in glorious colours, plus darker, more sober beaded evening bags from Jamin Puech of Paris. For moments of extravagance there are also some of Rene Caovilla's extraordinary Venetian creations. *jorando.com*

Moderate to luxury *Amex/MC/V*

Parioli area

Piazza Euclide 30 **06 807 0046**
00197 Rome Mon-Sat 9:30-1, 3:30-7:30

Bally

Bally's Swiss founders sold their shoe company to the multi-national Texas-Pacific Group in 2000, and after a couple of wobbles it is now back on track. With the help of a design group in part pilfered from Gucci, it has come a long way from the days when it was a staple for smart and sensible school shoes. The Gucci link (subconscious, no doubt) is particularly noticeable on the horse-bit style snaffle that crops up on loafers, sandals and bags. Shopping bags are available in both patent leather and suede, and there are also handbags of all shapes and sizes including slim document cases—all with elegant design twists. *bally.com*

Expensive *Amex/MC/V*

Piazza di Spagna area

Via dei Condotti 38-40 **06 699 0236**
00187 Rome Mon-Sat 10-7, Sun 2-7

Barbara Gregori

This local boutique, run by Barbara Gregori for the best part of the last 20 years, caters to the smart Italian woman of a certain age who favours chic understatement over fashion victim. Lines are all Italian and include Allegri's splendid raincoats, sweaters from Rivamonti, trousers and skirts with a slight ethnic twist by Peserico and colourful summer linen dresses and palazzo pants from Abitificio. Among accessories are hats in various materials from Grevi in Florence (particularly elegant are the finely woven straw ones) and scarves by Altea. The decor is as simple and elegant as the clothes, with white walls, parquet, and pale wooden cabinets and shelves.

Moderate to expensive   *Amex/MC/V*

Piazza di Spagna area

Via Vittoria 37/A-38   **06 322 1818**
00187 Rome   Mon 3:30-7, Tues-Sat 9:30-7

Barrilà Boutique

Just down the road from the super-chic Hotel de Russie is one of the scruffier stores on Rome's hippest street. But pop in anyway: it's one of the only places you'll find fashionable shoes for less than 100 euros, and you could walk out with a real bargain. In the Eighties, the Marche-based Barrilà factory produced shoes for Chanel amongst others, but this shop focuses on their own less expensive line. They're just the thing on days when your Manolos have rubbed blisters on your feet and you need something cheap, good-looking and comfortable to give yourself a break. If their own line doesn't convince, you'll also find Tuscan-made heels from Luciano Barachini, sportier styles from the northern Italian Keys, and espadrilles from Spain. There's also a selection of bags for 50 euros with some real gems to be had, including Tuscan leather bags at a fraction of the price they go for when sporting big brand labels. Staff are helpful and speak English.

Affordable   *Amex/MC/V*

Piazza di Spagna area

Via del Babuino 33   **06 360 01726**
00187 Rome   Mon-Sat 9:30-8, Sun 10-8

☆ Battistoni

There's nothing as vulgar as a street entrance for this bastion of the Roman establishment. A family tailoring business since its foundation in 1946, Battistoni is reached through a splendid courtyard—which adds to its cachet. Once you've tracked down the boutiques for both ladies and gentlemen, get ready for some seriously stylish service—all done in the old-fashioned way. Instead of the standard black-clad shop assistants, sophisticated ladies greet you at the door of the women's boutique, a teak-lined affair with high ceilings that you have to crane your neck to see. In the historic men's store, distinguished gentlemen await you behind their desks, in an elegant space furnished with rare works of art and antiques. The undoubted stars are the glorious but ruinously expensive made-to-measure suits for both men and women, but there is also a vast selection of off-the-peg trousers, skirts and jackets. The service is understated and excellent, and the after-sales service (alterations and repairs) even better. You'll also find shoes, ties, shirts and accessories as well as a range of classic-chic casualwear, in the very best materials: silk, cashmere, linen and leather.

Expensive to luxury   *Amex/MC/V*

Piazza di Spagna area

Via dei Condotti 60-61/A
00187 Rome

06 697 6111
Mon 3-7, Tues-Sat 10-7

BBC (Bassetti Brothers Corporation)

This upper-crust designer emporium is where you get your uniform to join the tribe of highly fashion-conscious Pariolini, the younger inhabitants of this smart residential area. This large store sprawls off the main drag of Viale Parioli, and is reached by descending a hard-to-spot ramp: blink and you'll miss it. Boys can toy with BBC's own line of shirts with and without collars, suits and ties, and Messagerie's unstructured jackets. For the weekend there are trousers by Dockers and Mason's, T-shirts and sweaters by Urca and sneakers by Nike; Paul Smith cologne and Zippo lighters complete the package. For girls, there's denim by Notify, T-shirts and jackets by Vanessa Bruno, and Ungaro's diffusion line Ungaro Fever. Look out for Hervé Chapelier's nylon bags in a variety of colours, and Car Shoe's flat suede classic moccasin—the ultimate in bourgeois-chic.

Expensive   *Amex/MC/V*

Parioli area

Viale Parioli 122
00197 Rome

06 808 3680
Mon 4-8, Tues-Sat 10:30-2:30, 4-8
Sun 10:30-2:30, 4-8

Belsiana 19

No longer at number 19 but at number 94, this small, mirrored store is perfect for chaps who like fashion but loathe excess. Lines are modern and high-quality but never showy. Crisply classic suits by Exté and Alberto Aspesi are anything but stuck-in-the-mud. Knitwear by Ballantyne is so nicely understated it goes with everything, while the cotton shirts, long-sleeved polo-shirts, gym shoes and flip-flops by Polo by Ralph Lauren will make you want to head immediately to your best friend's Tuscan country house. The staff are friendly and genuinely interested in clothes. Bet you can't avoid glancing in the mirrors to admire your newly revamped reflection on the way out.   *belsiana19.com*

Moderate   *Amex/MC/V*

Piazza di Spagna area

Via Belsiana 94
00187 Rome

06 678 0529/678 5423
Mon 3:30-7:30, Tues-Sat 10-7:30

Benetton

Years after those adverts, the Treviso-based company is still everywhere. With branches in every possible corner of Italy and beyond, you'll be hard-pressed to find an Italian who hasn't entered a store at some point—even if many of them keep quiet about it. Benetton is still best for basics, although if you object to being a walking advertisement it's becoming harder and harder to find classic T-shirts without the ubiquitous logo. The Via del Corso store is the most comprehensive: be patient and you'll probably find what you're looking for in its meandering sequence of rooms. *benetton.com*

Affordable   *Amex/MC/V*

Piazza di Spagna area

Via del Corso 423   **06 681 02534**
00187 Rome   Mon-Sat 10-8, Sun 11-8

Piazza di Spagna 67-69   **06 675 8241**
00187 Rome   (opening hours as above)

Campo de' Fiori area

Corso Vittorio Emanuele II 77-79   **06 688 03577**
00186 Rome   Mon 12-8, Tues-Sat 9:30-8

Via Nazionale area

Via Nazionale 174   **06 679 1555**
00184 Rome   Mon-Sat 10-8, Sun 11:30-8

Termini Station Concourse

Via Giolitti 9   **06 478 25258**
00185 Rome   Daily 8-10

Via Cola di Rienzo area

Via Cola di Rienzo 193-209   **06 322 7171/320 2802**
00192 Rome   Mon 11-7:45, Tues-Sat 10-7:45
                                          Sun 11-1:30, 4-7:45

Pantheon area

Piazza Fontana di Trevi 91-94   **06 691 90919**
00187 Rome   Mon-Sat 10-8, Sun 12-8

Blumarine

Anna Molinari is particularly big in Southeast Asia, but the Rome store for the Emilia-Romagna designer's feminine and floatily ephemeral creations only opened in summer 2003. On a very fashionable street in the Tridente, the metallic-grey Blumarine store is lit by spotlights that show off the spangly wall details. As well as the more upmarket Anna Molinari and Blumarine lines (light-as-a-feather dresses of the palest pink, beaded dressy vest tops, and colourfully floral summer dresses), there is the younger and more playful diffusion line Blugirl; discreetly distressed jeans and leopardskin sandals are par for the course. *blufin.it*

Expensive   *Amex/MC/V*

Piazza di Spagna area

Via Bocca del Leone 24   **06 679 0951**
00187 Rome   Mon-Sat 10-7:30

Blunauta

Since the Seventies, the Roman Greco family have been making the most of trade links with China, ordering clothing to their specifications crafted from cotton, cashmere and silk. Styling is distinctly 'Made in Italy' but, fortunately, prices aren't. Floral-print summer silk dresses start from 65 euros, silk T-shirts hover around the 45 mark, and you can pick up an embroidered bag for just 20. Other popular lines are the Chinese-style high-collar jackets and Chanel-style tweed suits. The main Piazza di Spagna store is reached through a charming internal courtyard, and contains both men's and women's collections; the Via dei Condotti store only stocks womenswear. There's also a discount outlet near Campo de' Fiori, where some real bargains are to be found. If the airline ever loses your luggage, this is the place to head. *blunauta.it*

Affordable   *Amex/MC/V*

Piazza di Spagna area

Piazza di Spagna 3	**06 678 0110**
00187 Rome	Mon-Sat 9:30-8, Sun 10-7:30
Via dei Condotti 29 (W)	**06 693 80556**
00187 Rome	Mon-Sat 10-7:30

Cola di Rienzo area

Via Cola di Rienzo 303-309	**06 397 37336**
00193 Rome	Mon 4-8, Tues-Sat 10-8

Campo de' Fiori area

Largo del Pallaro 19/A (discount outlet)	**06 687 6671**
00186 Rome	Mon 4-8, Tues-Sat 10-8

☆ Bonpoint   🛉

Bonpoint is the label to be seen in at the smartest nursery schools. But the Parisian brand caters for all kids, from new-borns right up to 14-year-olds. The Rome store—with its gilded mirrors and crystal chandeliers—is the immaculately elegant boutique one would expect. It stocks everything from formal party dresses to ever-so-slightly smocked linen summer dresses in neutral colours, plus teensy flared pink cords, T-shirts and jerseys. There is a small and seasonal selection of shoes.   *bonpoint.com*

Expensive to luxury   *Amex/MC/V*

Piazza di Spagna area

Piazza San Lorenzo in Lucina 25	**06 687 1548**
00186 Rome	Mon 3:30-7:30, Tues-Sat 10-2, 3:30-7:30

Borini

This unassuming shop (think crumbling walls and graffiti) has been owned by the Borini family since 1940. Don't be put off by the setting, this is one of Rome's most affordable shoe treasure troves. Store owner Franco Borini puts his sketches onto paper and the family sends them off to the factory. The result is everything a footwear fan could ever dream of—from pointed slingbacks, mules, flats and stilet-tos to over-the-knee or cowboy boots, platforms and glad-iator sandals. There's also a small selection of men's shoes and footwear from lines other than Borini's own, with Kallisté's pointy coloured suede heels marking the upper end of the price range. You'll have to pick your way through piles of shoes and punters fighting for attention to actually find what you want, but the quality and price will make it worth the bruised elbows.

Affordable/Moderate   *Amex/MC/V*

Campo de' Fiori area

Via dei Pettinari 87   **06 687 5670**
00186 Rome   Mon 3:30-7:30, Tues-Sat 9-1, 4-8

☆ Borsalino

If you're looking for a hat for a wedding, to keep your head warm, or just to beat the sunshine—this is the spot for you. Here you'll find everything from real roll-up-and-put-it-in-the-can panamas for chaps who are looking for that Great-Gatsby-in-Rome look, to soft cloche hats for boho girls who can stuff them in their bag when not needed. Classics are the staple, but there's also a variety of amusing reworkings of favourite styles. There are Thirties golfers' caps in suede with coloured material inserts, and woven straw hats with lively trims—ideal for stylish women with a sense of fun. And if you ever get a chance to see the Seventies spoof grangster movie *Borsalino*, with Jean-Paul Belmondo and Alain Delon wearing the hats, don't miss it. Why, you're only one purchase away from looking just like them… *borsalino.com*

Moderate to expensive   *Amex/MC/V*

Piazza di Spagna area

Piazza Fontana di Trevi 83   **06 678 1015**
00187 Rome   Mon 3:30-7:30, Tues-Sat 10-2, 3:30-7:30

Piazza del Popolo 20   **06 326 50838**
00187 Rome   Mon-Sat 10-2, 3-8, Sun 10:30-2, 3-7:30

Pantheon area

Via di Campo Marzio 72/A   **06 679 6120**
00186 Rome   Mon 3-7:30, Tues-Sat 9:30-1:30, 3-7:30

Bottega Veneta

The enormous store on the ultra-chic Piazza di San Lorenzo in Lucina was once part of a 17th-century convent. Its thick carpets, low lighting and attentive assistants all whisper money—and add up to just the kind of setting you'd expect for the luxurious leather bags from this 50-year-old Gucci-owned brand, now under the creative direction of Tomas Maier. One of the undoubted stars of the collection is the handwoven, limited-edition Kabat, which famously takes two craftspeople two whole days to make. Also perennially popular is the fringed Veneta shoulder bag in suede or velvet. There is a range of wallets and key-rings, plus a small selection of leather jackets, some colourfully beaded sandals, and children's loafers in the brand's signature woven leather—this time in child-friendly colours. If woven leather's not your thing, don't miss the large floppy men's bags in leather so soft it almost melts in your hand.   *bottegaveneta.com*

Luxury   *Amex/MC/V*

Piazza di Spagna area
Piazza San Lorenzo in Lucina 9   06 682 10024
00186 Rome   Mon-Sat 10-7

Braccialini

Startling white walls make Carla Braccialini's brightly coloured bags stand out like strips of blue in a cloudy sky at the Italian chain's Rome flagship. Bags in vibrant pink, red, turquoise and yellow—in fact any colour that will get you noticed—enhanced with floral appliqués and ornate buckles are the perfect antidote to the chic but serious black, brown and beige you'll find in other places. This thriving Italian chain is apparently beating the slump that has been hitting bigger names with the opening of new stores in London and Hong Kong along with a planned second store in Shanghai and another in Hangzhou, China. Whichever store you visit, remember to take your sunglasses: individually, these bags look great, but stacked up on the shelves together, their dazzling colours get a little too much.   *braccialini.it*

Expensive   *Amex/MC/V*

Piazza di Spagna area
Via Mario De' Fiori 73   06 678 5750
00187 Rome   Mon 3-7, Tues-Sat 10-2, 3-7

Brioni

Since 1945, this Rome-based family firm has been suiting Italian gents as well as foreign stars: John Wayne, Clark Gable and, more recently, 007 Pierce Brosnan have all had their inside legs measured here. Suits are tailored from the highest quality natural fibres, and beautifully finished with great attention to detail. Get measured up at Brioni and they'll send your suit anywhere on the planet, an essential service given that each takes a minimum of two months to finish. They also keep measurements on record, and send out fabric samples from the thousands on offer to international clients who have their suits made-to-measure in Rome from all over the world. Don't have time to hang around waiting for your suit to be made up? The Roman men's stores contain an enormous selection of ready-to-wear shirts, ties and suits, plus pyjamas, shoes, belts, fountain pens, cufflinks and more. The original marble-floored store on Via Barberini includes a large women's department, with suits (of course) as well as summer dresses—perfect for a day at the races.   *brioni.it*

Luxury   *Amex/MC/V*

Piazza di Spagna area
Via Barberini 79-81   06 484 517/485 855
00187 Rome   Mon-Sat 10-1:30, 3:30-7:30
Via dei Condotti 21/A   06 678 3635
00187 Rome   Mon-Sat 10-7:30
Via Veneto 129   06 478 22119
00187 Rome   (opening hours as above)

☆ **Brugnoli**

This pleasingly old-fashioned firm has been cladding smart Roman feet since 1969. The newer Parioli store, with its masculinely solid brown cloth sofas, opened in 2003 and is just for men. Classic handmade lines like Church's, Allen Edmonds, and Brugnoli's own label provide the core, but there is a selection of accessories including ties by Milan-based Petronus, high-quality leather belts, and bags by Neapolitan company Tramontana. The original store on Via del Babuino caters to both men and women with Brugnoli's own-brand heels and sandals, plus more casual Moma boots and driving shoes by Prada-owned Car Shoe. Don't miss the racy styles by Sabelt, originally designed for Formula 1 drivers. *brugnolishoes.com*

Moderate to expensive Amex/MC/V

Parioli area

Viale Parioli 108 (M) **06 807 0751**
00197 Rome Mon 3:30-7:30, Tues-Sat 10-7:30

Piazza di Spagna area

Via del Babuino 57 **06 360 01889**
00187 Rome (opening hours as above)

Bruno Magli

The Opera group snapped up this Bologna-based family company in 2002 but, despite the altered logo and new look, stock is still made in the Magli factories. Decor at the Via dei Condotti store is elegantly spare; walls are wood-panelled with beech, floors are in pale marble strewn with the occasional beige rug and leather chair. Of course, shoes are the thing (remember all that talk about O.J. Simpson's Bruno Maglis?) and for both men and women there are classics as well as sportier styles. For women, pale green leather heels are inlaid with tartan prints and strappy sandals have appliqué butterflies. For men there are suede and nylon sneakers, and homage is paid to the velcro-strapped Puma Mostro in black leather. There's also a good selection of jackets in jewel-coloured leathers for both men and women, plus briefcases, handbags, belts, ties and silk scarves. *brunomagli.com*

Expensive Amex/MC/V

Piazza di Spagna area

Via dei Condotti 6-6/A **06 692 02264**
00187 Rome Mon 3-7, Tues-Sat 10-7, Sun 2-7

Bulgari

A home-grown big name, Bulgari's vast flagship store opened on the Via dei Condotti in 1905. It's had more than its fair share of jewel-hungry celebrities: throw a stone at any Oscar ceremony and you'll hit a Bulgari-wearing star. As well as the jewellery, there is room after room of elegant bags, wallets, ties and scarves. There's also a museum section dedicated to the Bulgari family's personal collection, including a gold-plated age-old picnic set, plates and pictures. Worth a look around even if you aren't about to emulate Elizabeth Taylor by starting a jewellery collection of your own. If you do splash out you'll receive invites to the launch parties and Christmas cocktails which have the passing throngs peering curiously past dark-suited bouncers talking into their lapels. Just the thing to feel in the thick of things if you happen to find yourself back in the Eternal City. Service is, of course, exquisite. *bulgari.com*

Luxury *Amex/MC/V*

Piazza di Spagna area

Via dei Condotti 10 **06 679 3876**
00187 Rome Mon 3:30-7:30, Tues-Sat 10:30-7:30

Burberry Prorsum 👤👤
When Thomas Burberry set about producing an ever-so practical waterproof coat in the mid-19th century, little did he know that stick-thin models would be tramping up and down runways in it 150 years later. Its deep back yoke, epaulettes, buckled cuff straps and storm pockets heightened the dashing reputation of World War 1 fighting men, and once the famous checked interior was added everyone wanted a 'trench coat'. Over the past decade Burberry has revitalised its image and expanded its product range, most recently under former Gucci designer Christopher Bailey. The Burberry Prorsum line—the store's newest and smartest innovation—moves way beyond the trench coat into the highest levels of fashion. *burberry.com*

Luxury *Amex/MC/V*

Piazza di Spagna area

Via dei Condotti 61 **06 675 0101**
00187 Rome Daily 10-7:30 (Sun 11-7:30)

Calvin Klein 👤👤
The mega griffe, gobbled up by the vast Phillips-Van Heusen Corporation in 2002, opened Rome's first dedicated Calvin Klein store on the super-smart Via Borgognona a year and a half ago. The decor is pale slate minimalism on all three floors, the ground floor being given over to the ubiquitous range of watches, jewellery, perfume, sunglasses and so forth. The first floor menswear selection reflects both the Jeans line and the more formal collection of suits, ranging from sober dark grey to more adventurous shiny numbers. On the larger second floor, womenswear is similiarly divided between casual and classic formal and eveningwear. *cku.com*

Moderate to expensive *Amex/MC/V*

Piazza di Spagna area

Via Borgognona 42/B **06 692 00837**
00187 Rome Mon 1-7.30, Tues-Fri 10-7.30, Sat 10-8

CK Jeans

Exactly what you'd expect: minimalist stores with jeans in various levels of distress, tees and vest tops, belts and accessories and the ubiquitous logo. Pick up a pair of casual cotton trousers for that just-arrived-from-the-beach-house look.

Moderate   *Amex/MC/V*

Piazza di Spagna area

Galleria Colonna   **06 678 1904**
00187 Rome   Mon-Fri 10-10, Sat 10-9, Sun 10-8

Via Cola di Rienzo area

Via Cola di Rienzo 151-153   **06 321 11881**
00192 Rome   Sun-Mon 2-8, Tues-Sat 10-8

☆ Cambalache

East meets West at Cambalache, and you can kit yourself out as an Indian princess in clothes that offer a taste of the Orient without ever forgetting that quality counts as much as style. The designs are based on traditional ethnic items and while some materials come from abroad, the clothes are actually made in Italy. The colour palette whirls through golds, rich browns and oranges to mustards and purples in glorious silks, velvet and chiffon. The occasional tie-dye T-shirt may crop up, but the collection is mostly made up of more interesting pieces like the wrap-around silk skirt which can be worn three different ways and the long, floaty embroidered silk dresses—perfect for a night at the theatre. To complete the look, there are silk bags and scarves and a range of Argentinian jewellery. It's a favourite destination for brainy-girls-who-shop and models looking for original outfits at unbelievably friendly prices.

Affordable   *MC/V*

Campo de' Fiori area

Via dei Chiavari 30   **06 686 8541**
00187 Rome   Mon-Sat 9:30-8

Camiceria Albertelli

How can you go wrong if you have your shirts made by the man who personally tailors Valentino? Piero Albertelli has been making shirts for men and women near the Pantheon since 1967, and he and his family have, at various times, served Henry Fonda, Kirk Douglas, Catherine Deneuve and Robert De Niro. The fabrics, from top-notch Italian companies like Alumo, Riva, Albini and Ortolina, are first cut to measure, then washed to test eventual shrinking, and finally fitted to the customer on two different occasions to guarantee an impeccable and lasting fit. There's also a collection of sweaters. They deliver worldwide, a splendid souvenir.

Expensive   *Amex/MC/V*

Pantheon area

Via dei Prefetti 11   **06 687 3793**
00186 Rome   Mon 3:30-7:30, Tues-Sat 9:30-1, 3:30-7:30

Carla G

Bolognese designer Carla G has set herself up as the saviour of uptown girls on a budget, and her look has certainly caught on—the stores are cropping up right across Italy. Eminently wearable essentials in pale neutral colours are the core of the collections, and lines are crisp and body-skimming; trouser suits, jackets and coats have a Prada-esque lean silhouette. The Via del Babuino store is the flagship in Rome, and all the elegant shops reflect the neutral colours she prefers. Amongst these subdued tones, the occasional forays into pinks and blues are all the more striking. Once in a while you'll also spot nicely cut jean jackets and skirts with spangly collars and bodice fastenings adding a tasteful touch of glitz to the proceedings.

Affordable to moderate   *Amex/MC/V*

Piazza di Spagna area

Via del Gambero 24   **06 679 1210**
00187 Rome   Mon 3:30-7:30, Tues-Sat 10:30-7:30

Via del Babuino 121   **06 679 3158**
00187 Rome   Mon 3:30-7:30, Tues-Sat 10:30-7:30

Via Cola di Rienzo area

Via Cola di Rienzo 134   **06 324 3511**
00192 Rome   Mon 3:30-8, Tues-Sat 9:30-8

Parioli area

Via Salaria 66   **06 854 6688**
00197 Rome   Mon-Sat 10:30-7:30

Carpisa

If you haven't come across this ubiquitous Neapolitan company with the turtle logo yet, it might be time to pop in and take a look. This is the place for youthfully colourful (and youthfully priced) wallets, bags, luggage and accessories in hard plastic, nylon or leather, many in pretty colours with decorative appliqués. If you've still got a few last-minute gifts to pick up for begrudging teenagers back home, it's well worth looking for them here. With wallets starting at 13 euros, the value's hard to beat.   *carpisa.it*

Affordable   *Amex/MC/V*

Piazza di Spagna area

Via Belsiana 59   **06 678 6101**
00187 Rome   Daily 10-7:30

Celine

Initially rescued from oblivion by Michael Kors, the French label Celine is now part of the multinational monster LVMH. In 2004 the line's artistic direction was turned over to Italian stylist Roberto Menichetti (partly responsible for saving Burberry with the ultra-cool Prorsum line). The recently refurbished two-storey store is a refreshingly cool refuge from the swarms of hot tourists on the Via dei Condotti, with pale floors and walls set off by dark wood shelving. Menichetti has now moved on, and as we went to press LVMH were about to name a new designer-in-chief for Celine. Whoever is chosen, he or she will take over a classic heritage.   *celine.com*

Luxury   *Amex/MC/V*

Piazza di Spagna area

Via dei Condotti 20/A   **06 678 7586**
00187 Rome   Mon-Sat 10-7

Centoventi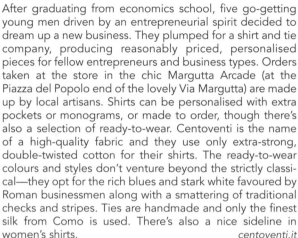

After graduating from economics school, five go-getting young men driven by an entrepreneurial spirit decided to dream up a new business. They plumped for a shirt and tie company, producing reasonably priced, personalised pieces for fellow entrepreneurs and business types. Orders taken at the store in the chic Margutta Arcade (at the Piazza del Popolo end of the lovely Via Margutta) are made up by local artisans. Shirts can be personalised with extra pockets or monograms, or made to order, though there's also a selection of ready-to-wear. Centoventi is the name of a high-quality fabric and they use only extra-strong, double-twisted cotton for their shirts. The ready-to-wear colours and styles don't venture beyond the strictly classi-cal—they opt for the rich blues and stark white favoured by Roman businessmen along with a smattering of traditional checks and stripes. Ties are handmade and only the finest silk from Como is used. There's also a nice sideline in women's shirts.   *centoventi.it*

Moderate   *Amex/MC/V*

Piazza di Spagna area

Margutta Arcade   **06 324 2655**
Via Margutta 3   Mon 3:30-7:30, Tues-Sat 10:30-7:30
00187 Rome

Cesare Paciotti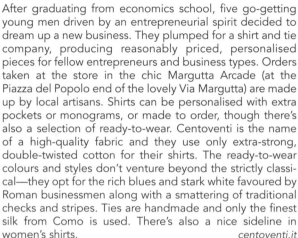

This minimalist boutique has entrances both on super-exclusive Via Bocca di Leone and on the busier Via Frattina at number 118. Marble floors and white leather Mies Van der Rohe stools set off Paciotti's menacing shoes perfectly. Not by chance is the label's logo a dagger and these are stilettos in the truest sense—you can just imag-ine a 21st-century Bond girl whipping one off to despatch a growling Russian. Understated isn't part of the vocabu-lary here: recent collections have featured leopardskin prints, blinding neon and bondage black—with tie-me-up ankle straps that are more sexily aggressive than elegant. The store also has a small range of shoes for men featur-ing sabre-sharp pointy twists on classic brogues and loafers.   *cesarepaciotti.it*

Expensive   *Amex/MC/V*

Piazza di Spagna area

Via Bocca di Leone 92   **06 679 6245**
00187 Rome   Mon 3-7, Tues-Sat 10-7

Chanel

Tired of holding her handbag, Coco Chanel hung it from a gilt chain, and thus the classic black patent-leather padded bag was born. Coco, of course, never looked back, and today Chanel boutiques worldwide are approached with the kind of reverence that lesser labels can only dream of. The Rome store is no exception. Inside you'll find racks of Chanel's chic jackets and suits, shelves stacked with the latest bags and, of course, the enduring No. 5 perfume. A view onto a charming internal courtyard complete with palm tree renders the Roman outpost unique. *chanel.com*

Luxury   *Amex/MC/V*

Piazza di Spagna area

Via del Babuino 98-101   **06 692 0701**
00187 Rome   Mon-Sat 10-7

☆ Claudio Sanò

Cult artisan Claudio Sanò dropped out of college to follow his passion for working with leather, and aren't we glad? Whether you want a briefcase with a huge keyhole through the middle, a bag with a chunk bitten out, or a fire-engine-red handbag in the shape of a pouting fish, Claudio is the man for you. He uses the finest leather and only vegetable dyes on his ironic, traffic-stopping sculptured creations. He also does made-to-measure. *claudiosano.it*

Moderate   *Amex/MC/V*

San Lorenzo area

Largo degli Osci 67/A   **06 446 9284**
00185 Rome   Mon 4-8, Tues-Sat 10-1, 4-8

Coin

Coin is a rare example of a Roman department store, though believe us, it's no Bloomingdale's. The Via Cola di Rienzo outpost of the Veneto-based, mid-market chain is where Romans buy sensible skirts and bed linen that lasts—but you'll have a hard time finding anything to take your breath away. On the ground floor, in cosmetics and perfumes, look out for worthwhile lines by Make-Up Forever and MAC. Upstairs, amongst the lingerie and conservative womenswear, you may find the occasional funky little piece from Dolce & Gabbana's diffusion line '&', as well as some decent and affordable kids' clothes. In the basement at the Cola di Rienzo store there's a supermarket—a lifesaver on days when you've been too busy shopping for clothes to think about anything so banal as bread and milk. *coin.it*

Affordable to moderate   *Amex/MC/V*

Cola di Rienzo area

Via Cola di Rienzo 173   **06 360 04298**
00192 Rome   Mon-Sat 10-8, Sun 10:30-8

San Giovanni area

Piazzale Appio 7   **06 708 0020**
00183 Rome   Mon-Sat 9:30-8, Sun 10-8

☆ Corner

As we've mentioned elsewhere, Alberto Aspesi from Milan has a cult following amongst the numerous well-dressed Romans who go for that clean-cut, classic look, and this store is one of few that stocks all his eight ranges for women, from elegantly colourful sportivo styles right up to eveningwear. There are strappy summer dresses which you could wear in just about any situation, linen and cotton suits for the summer and tweed, wool and velvet co-ordinates for winter. In the cooler months, some menswear is also stocked, though male clients are best off heading round the corner to the dedicated Aspesi Uomo boutique on Via Mario de' Fiori.

Moderate to expensive   *Amex/MC/V*

Piazza di Spagna area

Via Belsiana 97   **06 679 5020**
00187 Rome   Mon 12:30-7:30, Tues-Sat 10-7:30

Costume National

One of that rare breed, a southern Italian label. Designer Ennio Capasa has spread his empire way beyond his native Puglia and his classy styling is a favourite of those in the know. Recent designs have loosely taken their inspiration from African tribal dress, using plain and printed silks accessorised with pearls—a gravity-defying midnight blue silk sheath is held up with a pearl choker in a free interpretation of Masai body ornamentation. The long, narrow store also stocks the ever-so-slightly eccentric shirts, tailored jackets and the elegant flatties for which the label is reknowned. For men, there are chunky loafers, sandals and handbags for the brave.   *costumenational.com*

Luxury   *Amex/MC/V*

Piazza di Spagna area

Via del Babuino 106   **06 692 00686**
00187 Rome   Mon 3-7, Tues-Fri 10-2, 3-7, Sat 10-7

Custo

The decor of the Italian flagship of the hip Barcelona label takes its cue from the young and wittily colourful clothes. The round entrance hall is bright orange, and a fuchsia tunnel leads from here into a white-walled room where the latest collections are displayed. The next room has red wood walls and giant screens showing Custo's catwalk shows, while the final chamber is a hall of mirrors. Custo's distinctive T-shirts, vest tops and dresses are decorated with Sixties-style prints or tie-dye designs and many incorporate original vintage fabrics. You may notice a couple of items strewn about on the floor as you walk in. Don't ask; that's fashion, darling.   *custo-barcelona.com*

Moderate to expensive   *Amex/MC/V*

Piazza di Spagna area
Via Tomacelli 101   **06 681 35842**
00186 Rome   Mon-Sat 10-8, Sun 2:30-7:30

☆ Dal Co

The tiny Via Vittoria is fast becoming one of *the* shopping streets in Rome. Although it's just around the corner, it's seemingly a million miles away from the heaving crowds sporting T-shirts and trainers at the Spanish Steps. It's also just the spot to cultivate a shoe dependency: Dal Co's women's shoes are handmade in their own workshop and cover all bases from low-key to drag queen, though you certainly won't find anything remotely sporty here. This is one of those rare places where an artisan wearing a white smock comes downstairs to measure your foot—the experience alone is worth the price if you've never indulged before in the luxury of made-to-order. Fortunately, the store's calm interior, beige marble floors and original brick vaulted ceilings will put you in a choosing frame of mind, as will the helpful staff. Just as well, as at a minimum of 400 euro per pair you wouldn't want to make any unfortunate mistakes.

Luxury   *Amex/MC/V*

Piazza di Spagna area
Via Vittoria 65   **06 678 6536**
00187 Rome   Mon 3:30-7:30, Tues-Sat 10-7:30

Dancing Duck

If you ever dreamed of being one of the kids from *Fame*, you'll be in your element at Dancing Duck, named for the duck-like, splayed feet first position of ballerinas. There's a range of dancy wear by Dimensione Danza: sleeveless tees, vest tops, hooded sweatshirts, short shorts and cotton jersey pants, either full or three-quarter length. This year, shocking pink and green are the order of the day, with colours extending into the range of swimwear. You'll find all you need to look like you just stepped out of rehearsal (sweatbands and leg-warmers optional). The main store is on Via Belsiana, though a smaller outpost recently opened in the Piazza Colonna. You may end up buying more than you had bargained for here. Just try not to pirouette on your way out.   *dancingduck.it*

Moderate   *Amex/MC/V*

Piazza di Spagna area
Galleria Colonna (Alberto Sordi)   **06 699 25230**
Piazza Colonna   Mon-Fri 10-8, Sat 10-9, Sun 2-8
00187 Rome

Via Belsiana 96B/C   **06 679 4378**
00187 Rome   Mon 3:30-7:30, Tues-Sat 10-7:30

D&G

The Dolce & Gabbana magic works equally well in the Milan-based duo's second line which hits just the right note of casual hip. Loud colours leap out at you in this slightly confusingly mirrored store (stay alert or you'll walk into your own reflection), but hey, D&G never were the shy and retiring types. Their logo is omnipresent and you'll find it emblazoned on everything from sweatbands and watches to shoes to fuchsia-coloured beach bags. At the back of the store on the left is the D&G children's line: sweet jeans and dresses found next to cool gym shoes and hooded jackets. D&G's followers start young: the newborn line goes from 6 to 24 months, the 'baby' line from two to six-year-olds, and D&G junior up to 14. *dolcegabbana.it*

Expensive *Amex/MC/V*

Piazza di Spagna area

Piazza di Spagna 93 **06 693 80870**
00187 Rome Mon-Sat 10-7:30, Sun 11-7:30

☆ **Davide Cenci**

A haven for traditionalists since its foundation in 1926, this massive store takes up a whole city block (and has a queue much of the way round it during sales). Renovated in 2004, the store is an example of the restrained classic elegance that Cenci is famous for. If you're looking for the avant-garde you're in the wrong place; instead you'll find all you need for that European born-with-a-silver-spoon look: Ballantyne cashmere, coats by Burberry and Aquascutum, Church's shoes and, of course, Cenci's own classy suits, shirts and ties. Womenswear includes Tod's handbags, Etro silk dresses and Emilio Pucci bikinis, plus Cenci's own elegant designs. *davidecenci.com*

Expensive to luxury *Amex/MC/V*

Pantheon area

Via Campo Marzio 1-7 **06 699 0681**
00186 Rome Mon 4-8, Tues-Fri 9:30-1:30, 4-8
Sat 10-8

☆ **Degli Effetti**

Massimo Degli Effetti's fashion empire stretches across three stores on the same piazza within spitting distance of the Pantheon. A pioneer of the Roman fashion scene, he opened his first boutique in 1981 and soon found that a single shop couldn't hope to contain all the achingly hip lines he wanted to stock. These days, the seriously cool womenswear store sells hard-to-track-down lines like E2—exclusively on sale here—which takes vintage pieces from Chanel, Dior and Yves Saint Laurent and remodels them with lace appliqué. Other looks include Greg Parkinson's reworking of vintage fashion (including some splendid sparkly dresses), John Galliano's 'newspaper' bags (enlivened with neon straps) and Peggy Moffit's typeface-print dresses for Comme des Garçons (the perfect outfit for a lady of letters). Just across 'Piazza Degli Effetti' is the men's store with smart suits, trousers and shirts by Y3, Prada, et al. The 'Millennium' store across the square, for both men and women, is aimed at a younger clientele, and is therefore marginally more affordable. Don't miss the interior by design doyen Massimiliano Fuksas, a clever take on old-meets-new. *deglieffetti.com*

Expensive to luxury *Amex/MC/V*

Pantheon area

Piazza Capranica 75, 79 & 93 **06 679 1650**
00186 Rome Mon 11-2, 3-7:30
Tues-Sat 10-2, 3:30-7:30, Sun 3-7:30

☆ De Grillis

The Rome branch of Luisa Via Roma, Florence's boutique par excellence, is tucked behind the Emperor Trajan's markets (where Romans did their shopping almost 2,000 years ago) on a tiny blink-and-you-miss-it road off Piazza del Grillo. Behind anonymous doorbells in this charming maze of cobbled streets a stone's throw from the tourist honeypots lie apartments with spectacular terraces belonging to Messrs Bulgari, Prada etc. Locals drop into this this small store-cum-salon for a fruit juice and a chat. You'll spot them advising each other on who looks good in the latest pieces from Alessandro dell'Acqua, Jean Paul Gaultier, Chloé, Missoni and Antonio Marras, although you can hunt for pieces which won't break the bank, such as E/V4's lovely be-pearled silk skirts. The eclectic selection of shoes includes fabric sandals with jewelled and cameo detail by ex-Valentino stylist Angelica D, made for De Grillis from fabrics handpicked by manager Claudia Torella. If you can't stretch to Rene Caovilla, try the slightly more affordable Venetian label Elman. D&G's jewelled purselets complete the look. Feel free to check your e-mail on the computer, use the luxurious loo, and have a coffee while you make your mind up. Any colours or sizes not in stock can be sent down from Florence for next-morning arrival. *luisaviaroma.com*

Expensive to luxury *Amex/MC/V*

Via Nazionale area

Via Campo Carleo 25 (Piazza del Grillo) **06 678 7557**
00184 Rome Mon-Fri 11-8, Sat 11-3 (summer)
Mon 3:30-7:30, Tues-Sat 11-8 (winter)

Demoiselle

If you're in Rome before heading for a beach, here's the place to pick up a costume which will catch the eye of even the most seen-it-all bagnino. This somewhat dull-looking lingerie store hides a secret stash of some of the most stunning swimwear in the city. Roman-designed Delfina Swimwear's latest bikinis feature the palest of pinks, delicately sequinned; Pin-Up's two-pieces come in psychedelic red and yellow; and Emilio Pucci's costumes and bikinis have Sixties prints that carry over to matching hats and beach towels. The store also has a fabulous selection of swimwear from Missoni and La Perla.

Expensive to luxury *Amex/MC/V*

Piazza di Spagna area
Via Frattina 93   **06 679 3752**
00187 Rome   Mon-Sat 10-8

Diesel

Jeans of all sorts are the staple of this Italian urban street-style label, famous for its ironic ad campaigns. Latest looks include flares with lots of zips, short denim dresses and shoulder-revealing T-shirts all with the free (and definitely Italian) interpretation of Fifties American style that made them famous. This being an egalitarian label, there are also calico trousers and classic short-sleeved shirts for men. Roman ragazze also adore the cute accessories, like see-though plastic handbags, and the funky sneakers—ideal for performing streetwise break-dance numbers all day long. The Via del Corso store is the flagship, and far and away the best stocked. Otherwise check out the smaller boutique which opened in 2004 on Via del Babuino.   *diesel.com*

Moderate   *Amex/MC/V*

Piazza di Spagna area
Via del Corso 186   **06 678 3933**
00186 Rome   Mon-Sat 10:30-8, Sun 3:30-8

Via del Babuino 94   **06 693 80053**
00186 Rome   Mon 2-7:30, Tues-Sat 10:30-7:30
                                                   Sun 3:30-7:30

Via Cola di Rienzo area
Via Cola di Rienzo 245-249   **06 324 1895**
00192 Rome   Mon-Sat 10:30-8, Sun 3:30-8

Dior

Occupying three floors on the corner of the Via dei Condotti and the Piazza di Spagna, the Dior store claims pole position on the city's designer shopping streets. Inside, windows frame a dazzling view of the Spanish Steps, and sofas abound—stop and admire the view if you've worn yourself out trying things on. Seriously funky psyche-delic beach towels and bikinis will ensure that you'll catch the bagnino's eye, while a provocatively translucent silk dress will ensure you're the belle of the ball when the sun goes down. Accessories include saddle-shaped bags for that horsey look without the manure, and there is an occa-sional and small selection of children's clothes for fashion-istas in training.   *dior.com*

Luxury   *Amex/MC/V*

Piazza di Spagna area
Piazza di Spagna 73-75   **06 699 24489**
00187 Rome   Mon-Sat 10-8, Sun 2-8

DM

This charming neighbourhood boutique has been catering to Parioli's discerning clientele since 1986, and is as spa-cious and elegantly fresh as its stock. Not surprisingly, it carries a vast selection of Alberto Aspesi, including pinstriped, strappy and floaty summer dresses, ruched and strapless tops for the evening, and classic cotton tees and vests. In keeping with the store's one-stop philosophy, it also stocks a range of cleverly selected women's shoes—from heels with flowery insoles by Michele Bertelli to coloured leather heels and sandals from Les Tropeziennes and floral platform sandals from Cacharel. Bikinis are by Laura Urbinati and there are also wonderfully light summer dresses from Katharine Hamnett. Do drop in if you find yourself in Parioli. At the back of the shop there's a comfortable couch where you can rest your weary feet as you cast an eye over the stock; staff are helpful and knowlegeable.

Expensive to luxury *Amex/MC/V*

Parioli area

Via G.Antonelli 10/A **06 807 4350**
00197 Rome Mon-Sat 10-1, 4-7:30

Dolce & Gabbana

Since their explosion onto the fashion scene in 1985, Italian wonder boys Domenico & Stefano have reinvented the concept of seductive chic. Think slim severe black suits with silk push-up bras peaking from the décolleté. Or lean tailored coats with printed slip dresses underneath. Slide this stuff on and visions of pursuing paparazzi will immediately pass before your eyes. There are also accessories ranging from bangles to purses and wallets with the unmistakable D&G stamp. Men can go for the gangster-chic look with pinstriped suits, skinny jersey tops and tight ribbed sweaters. The Rome store is a constantly changing mirror of the duo's usual immodest style; last time we dropped by, velvet patchwork-covered baroque gilded thrones were the stars. *dolcegabbana.it*

Luxury *Amex/MC/V*

Piazza di Spagna area

Via dei Condotti 51-52 **06 699 24999**
00187 Rome Mon-Sat 10-7:30

Eddy Monetti

Après-skiing in a designer chalet? Strolling in an exclusive resort? This Rome classic, founded in 1887, has everything you need to avoid committing a high society fashion faux pas. The gentlemen's club-style interior of the men's store is the perfect setting for shirts in all colours and ties in every style you can imagine—from faux old-school stripes to witty motifs. There are belts for every occasion and classic shoes by John Lobb. For more casual moments you'll find Polo by Ralph Lauren and those stylish but never showy jackets by Fay in nylon or down. The women's store has a much lighter feel without an antiqued wood panel in sight. Labels include can't-go-wrong classics like Etro and Burberry. *eddymonetti.com*

Expensive *Amex/MC/V*

Piazza di Spagna area

Via Borgognona 35-36 (W)   **06 679 4389**
00187 Rome   Mon 3:30-7:30, Tues-Thurs 9:30-1:30
3:30-7:30, Fri-Sat 9:30-7:30

Via dei Condotti 63-63/A (M)   **06 678 3794**
00187 Rome   Mon-Sat 10-7:30

☆ Edo City

The Eternal City may not be the most obvious place to pick up a vintage Japanese kimono or haori (the jacket version of a kimono), but don't let this opportunity pass you by. Most of the pieces at Edo City are from the Sixties but you might be lucky and unearth something from an earlier decade. If you don't want to splash out on a kimono, you can opt for the next best thing: one of the bestselling lines of skirts made from old kimonos or even a hakama—an imitation of the Samurai skirts. Antique rice bowls and pots are also on sale, and there are regular exhibitions of Italian photographers and sculptors—so it won't be too much of a shock when you step outside and realise you haven't warped to Japan.

Moderate   MC/V

Campo de' Fiori area

Piazza del Paradiso 18   **06 681 92659**
00186 Rome   Mon 4-8, Tues-Sat 10:30-1:30, 4-8

☆ Eleonora

This flashy megastore comes complete with tanned body-guard types who greet you in serious black suits, and offers so much to look at you don't know where to start. The shop winds towards a glassed-over main hall with a vast central red chandelier—the essence of kitsch. In keeping with the camp mood, armchairs are leopardprint and the changing-rooms are padded with red velvet. Clothes are equally big on glitz: Ermanno Scervino takes ethnic style towards decadence with embroidered silk dresses and tops, Ungaro and Guerriero put their names to patterned silk frocks, and if you find a pair of blue jeans, perhaps by Eleonora's own label, they'll be sequinned and spangled. Other labels not especially renowned for their minimalist subtlety include John Galliano, Versace, Cavalli and Jean Paul Gaultier, and there are shoes by Les Tropeziennes, Dolce & Gabbana, Yves Saint Laurent and Sergio Rossi. If it's all too much, just retreat into the small bar-like area, and flick through the coffee-table books.   *eleonoraboutique.it*

Expensive to luxury   *Amex/MC/V*

Piazza di Spagna area

Via del Babuino 97   **06 679 3173**
00187 Rome   Mon 1-7:30, Tues-Sat 10-7:30

Emanuel Ungaro

A designer who obviously rejoices in women, Ungaro creates extravagant tools of feminine seduction. Colours are bright, occasionally verging on the psychedelic, and dress-es are joyfully sexy with lots of embroidery and dyed-lace appliqué. Accessories play with textures: woven straw and pale pink snakeskin combine in sandals and handbags, cre-ating the perfect accessories for balmy summer picnics with panache. At the time of writing the store on the fabulous Via Borgognona was being revamped.   *emanuelungaro.it*

Luxury   *Amex/MC/V*

Piazza di Spagna area

Via Borgognona 4/B-4/C   **06 699 23345**
00187 Rome   Mon-Sat 10-7

Emporio Armani

This long, neutral beige space on Via del Babuino is home to Giorgio's mid-priced classics, from soft cotton men's striped shirts to thick-knit silk ties. There's a range of suits, smart jackets and trousers in sober cuts and colours for both men and women. Aside from these, there are sporty looks in blue, red and white, though this year pink and turquoise duffel bags prove the exception to the rule. This is the kind of studiedly casual stuff that you'd expect to see on the decks of people posing on yachts in St Tropez—flip-flops included. The accessories include nifty umbrellas, watches, sunglasses, casual suede sneakers and the kind of leather sports bags favoured by soccer players in the Seventies.   *emporioarmani.com*

Moderate to expensive   *Amex/MC/V*

Piazza di Spagna area

Via del Babuino 140   **06 322 1581**
00187 Rome   Mon 3-7:30, Tues-Sat 10-7:30

Energie

The greatest challenge that most surf dudes will ever face in Rome is dodging the waves of pedestrians on Saturday afternoon on Via del Corso. But that doesn't stop the cream of Roman youth coming to stock up on the latest surfy looks at this hip store with its shabby, Sixties-style interior, pumping music and mouldering carpets. The main store is at 179 Via del Corso where the ground floor at is devoted to boys, with jeans of all shapes, sizes, shades of blue and levels of distress. If buying your jeans with that ready-worn look isn't enough, Energie also have their own range of bashed-up sneakers. Then there are short-sleeved shirts, Hawaiian shorts, flip-flops, hats and beach bags for an Italian version of surf style. For girls, there are sexy tops and teeny-weeny skirts from Energie's sister brand, Miss Sixty, on the mezzanine.   *energie.it*

Affordable to moderate   *Amex/MC/V*

Piazza di Spagna area

Via del Corso 486-487   **06 322 7046**
00186 Rome   Mon-Sat 9:30-8, Sun 10:30-8

Via del Corso 179   **06 678 1045**
00186 Rome   Daily 10-8

Via Cola di Rienzo area
Via Cola di Rienzo 143-147   **06 320 2493**
00192 Rome   Mon-Tues 10-8, Sun 4-8

Ethic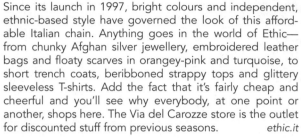

Since its launch in 1997, bright colours and independent, ethnic-based style have governed the look of this afford-able Italian chain. Anything goes in the world of Ethic—from chunky Afghan silver jewellery, embroidered leather bags and floaty scarves in orangey-pink and turquoise, to short trench coats, beribboned strappy tops and glittery sleeveless T-shirts. Add the fact that it's fairly cheap and cheerful and you'll see why everybody, at one point or another, shops here. The Via del Carozze store is the outlet for discounted stuff from previous seasons.   *ethic.it*

Affordable   *MC/V*

Campo dei Fiori
Piazza Cairoli 11-12   **06 683 01063**
00186 Rome   Sun-Mon 12-8, Tues-Sat 10-8

Pantheon area
Via del Pantheon 46-47   **06 688 03167**
00186 Rome   Mon 11:30-7:30, Tues-Sat 10-7:30
                                                Sun 12:30-7:30

Piazza di Spagna area
Via del Corso 85   **06 360 02191**
00186 Rome   Sun-Mon 12-8, Tues-Sat 9:30-8

Via delle Carrozze 20 (outlet)   **06 678 3352**
00187 Rome   Mon 3:30-7:30, Tues-Sat 10:30-7:30

Etro

This elegant, dark wood-panelled store (with a couple of handy and unusual red armchairs) provides a relaxing space to ponder Etro's sunny, Seventies-leaning styles. In recent collections, Mexican-inspired looks have dominated, with eye-warming rich striped dresses, skirts and jackets, bead-ed bags and brightly coloured glittery vest tops. Etro's sig-nature paisley print also appears in full-length and abbrevi-ated kaftan shift dresses. For men there's a fun collection of colourful pattered and striped shirts and trousers, plus sub-tly elegant twists on the classic pinstripe.   *etro.com*

Luxury   *Amex/MC/V*

Piazza di Spagna area
Via del Babuino 102   **06 678 8257**
00187 Rome   Mon 3-7, Tues-Sat 10-7

Expensive

Of course the whole point about this Roman chain is that it isn't jaw-droppingly costly. It is where fashion-conscious Roman teenagers get their fix of catwalk looks at prices which aren't nearly as knockdown as they once were. Witty and knowing enough to stay on the right side of tarty, there's loads of pink, jeans are very tight, and sequins abound. T-shirts with come-ons in (deliberately?) terrible English make a good souvenir. Mock snakeskin cowboy boots offer the Roman take on country style. The flagship store—which is easily the best stocked—is bang on the Piazza di Spagna. It's all a breath of fresh air after the hallowed portals of the Via dei Condotti.   *expensive-fashion.it*

Affordable to moderate   *Amex/MC/V*

Piazza di Spagna area

Piazza di Spagna 36   **800 311 678**
00187 Rome   Mon-Sat 10-8, Sun 11-8

Via del Corso 129 & 405   **(telephone as above)**
00186 Rome   Mon-Thurs 10-8, Fri-Sat 10-8:30
                                                      Sun 11-8:30

Via del Tritone 137   **06 488 5249**
00187 Rome   Mon-Thurs 10-8, Fri-Sat 10-8:30

☆ Fabindia

You probably didn't come to Rome to pick up traditional Indian clothes, but drop by Fabindia anyway for kaftans, Nehru jackets, saris, waistcoats, pashimas and kurtus (long shirts), in a variety of silks, cottons and wools. The company started in the Sixties, when American owner John Bissel stumbled upon the intricate work of Indian artisans while travelling in that country. He founded Fabindia in New Delhi with the aim of promoting the ancient patterns, techniques and colours used by these craftspeople. Most items are hand-coloured and the ancient method of wooden block printing is used to create the traditional patterns representative of the various regions of India from where the designs originated. At the back of the store there are household items like covers, tablemats and cloths and throws.   *fabindia.it*

Moderate   *Amex/MC/V*

Piazza Navona area

Via Banco di Santo Spirito 40   **06 688 91230**
00186 Rome   Mon 3-7:30, Tues-Sat 10-1:30, 3-7:30

☆ Fendi

Eighty years after Edoardo and Adele Fendi opened a small leather and fur store on Via del Plebiscito, the Roman mega-griffe celebrated the 2005 anniversary by launching the label's worldwide flagship store. At the junction of Via dei Condotti and Via del Corso the enormous 'Palazzo Fendi' was restyled at a cost of 25 million euros, and the store's launch was the occasion for owners LVMH to announce the continuing collaboration of Karl Lagerfeld with the label. The 19th-century Palazzo Boncompagni Ludovisi has been teamed with traditional Italian materials to spectacular effect by Peter Marino; undulating waves of travertine (the stone used to build the Colosseum) around the walls create a cool contrast to the slate floors. Take a break from pounding the streets in the cobbled internal courtyard overlooked by the palazzo's orignal moulded staircase, now painted gun-metal grey by Marino. Bags, bags, shoes, more bags and other accessories are on the ground floor. Up the splendid stairs is the ready-to-wear collection and, of course, the furs which made the Fendis so famous. The ex-flagship on Via Borgognona is now dedicated to the men's collection.   *fendi.it*

Luxury   *Amex/MC/V*

Piazza di Spagna area

Largo Goldoni 420   **06 696 661**
00187 Rome   Mon-Sat 10-7:30, Sun 10-7

Via Borgognona 36-37/A (M)   **06 696 661**
00187 Rome   Mon-Sat 10-7.30, Sun 10-2, 3-7

Foot Locker

If you're feeling the absence of sports footwear on your vacation, this branch of the Californian chain is the place to pick up your Roman pair. Rome's sports shoe mecca isn't nearly as big as superstores in other parts of the world, but as soon as school's out it's packed. Foot Locker prides itself on tailoring individual stores to the local market so sneaker-maniacs can spot differences between what's hip on Via del Corso and at home. Nike still reigns triumphant here, with the Air Max Plus far and away the biggest seller. Also very popular are Puma, Adidas (including the Olympic edition X-country exclusive to Foot Locker) and French line Le Coq Sportif.   *footlocker.com*

Affordable to moderate   *Amex/MC/V*

Piazza di Spagna area

Via del Corso 39-40   **06 360 02063**
00186 Rome   Mon-Sat 10-8, Sun 11-7:30

☆ Fornarina

This central Italian label has continued expanding its Roman empire; after opening the two-storey Via dei Condotti store in Rome's golden triangle in 2004, in 2005 they opened a branch on the Via Cola di Rienzo. Both stores have the trademark space-age Sixties-style interiors and are packed with attention-grabbing girly-girl looks from the wildly unforgiving mid-calf length jeans (sadly best worn by winsome teenagers) to seriously mini denim minis. Sequinned belts and shoes from the kind of trainers you'd never see in a marathon to teetering gold heels complete the look.   *fornarina.com*

Moderate to expensive   *Amex/MC/V*

Piazza di Spagna area

Via dei Condotti 36   **06 691 90708**
00187 Rome   Mon 12-8, Tues-Sat 9:30-8, Sun 11:30-8

Via Cola di Rienzo area

Via Cola di Rienzo 117   **06 323 6560**
00192 Rome   Mon 1-8, Tues-Sat 10-8, Sun 10-2, 4-8

Fratelli Rossetti

The Rome stores of northern Italian footwear company Rossetti are close by one another on two of the main shopping streets. The shop on Via del Babuino is a little bigger, but exactly the same lines are carried in both. Masculine wood panelling and dark wood floors show off the classic brogues and loafers for men and coloured heels for women. Some of the latest products have more modern twists—like the two-tone Bertie Wooster-style golfing shoes and the sneaker-influenced footwear in suede and coloured nylon. There are also leather jackets, briefcases and handbags and a small selection of children's shoes. The jewel in the Rossetti crown, however, is still the Flexa, a light-as-a-feather sports shoe with an extractable arch support and a technological rubber sole adopted by the Prada-sponsored Italian America's Cup crew. With that sort of an endorsement, you can bet it's good. *rossetti.it*

Expensive   *Amex/MC/V*

Piazza di Spagna area

Via Borgognona 5/A   **06 678 2676**
00187 Rome   Mon 3:30-7:30, Tues-Sat 10-7:30, Sun 11-7

Via del Babuino 59/A   **06 360 03957**
00187 Rome   (opening hours as above)

Fratelli Vigano

Selling English style to Roman gentlemen since 1870, this cosy store remains a family business—though they have been threatening to close for years. The eccentric proprietors are charmingly of another age, bemoaning the decline of the times when a man really knew how to furl an umbrella. Hats abound, with traditional panamas for summer and trilbies for winter. Other timeless classics include green loden coats, tweed from Scotland, raincoats from England, cotton shirts, cashmere pullovers and silk ties. It's best not to arrive too punctually at opening hours: they're seen more as a guideline than a rule.

Expensive   *Amex/MC/V*

Piazza di Spagna area

Via Minghetti Marco 8   **06 679 5147**
00187 Rome   Mon 5-7:30, Tues-Sat 10:30-1, 5-7:30

Furla

Bologna-based Furla started out as an accessibly priced bag line, but these days it makes pretty much anything, as long as it's crafted from leather. But the bags remain the star of the show—in bright fashion colours like eye-popping yellow and pink as well as more classic lines, particularly at the large Via dei Condotti store. Furla's footwear also asks to be taken pretty seriously. You'll find everything from ballet shoes and thong sandals to heels of all heights and colours—including black, pink and powder blue. The company's elegant, unfussy design philosophy also extends to wallets, watches, sunglasses and key-fobs. With prices within the reach of most pockets it's easy to see why Furla has such a following worldwide. Our only complaint is that the logo sometimes makes too prominent an appearance, particularly on the otherwise lovely flat sandals and on some of the bags.   *furla.com*

Moderate   *Amex/MC/V*

Piazza di Spagna area

Via dei Condotti 55-56	**06 679 1973**
00187 Rome	Mon-Sat 10-8, Sun 10:30-8
Piazza di Spagna 22	**06 692 00363**
00187 Rome	(opening hours as above)
Via Tomacelli 136	**06 687 8230**
00187 Rome	Mon-Sat 10-7:30
Via del Corso 481	**06 360 03619**
00186 Rome	Mon-Sat 10-8, Sun 10:30-8

Via Nazionale area

Via Nazionale 54-55	**06 487 0127**
00184 Rome	Mon-Sat 9:30-8

Via Cola di Rienzo area

Via Cola di Rienzo 226	**06 687 4505**
00192 Rome	Mon 10-2, 4-8, Tues-Sat 10-8

Gai Mattiolo

Located on an unkempt street just off the main Via Frattina drag, Roman designer Gai Mattiolo displays his wares in the (almost obligatory) gleaming white minimalist interior. The collection focuses on suits in crepe, with a distinctly feminine, individual twist. Most are in classic black and white, but the cut ensures they are anything but conservative. A white trouser suit, for instance, has a gold embroidered pinstripe. There are also suits in more adventurous colours like pink—with an asymmetrical skirt and a hewn heart-shaped crystal for the jacket's single button. Evening dresses are strappy, youthfully asymmetrical and colourful; bags are spangled with sequins.   *gaimattiolo.it*

Expensive to luxury   *Amex/MC/V*

Piazza di Spagna area

Via Mario de' Fiori 5	**06 699 40659**
00187 Rome	Mon 3-7, Tues-Sat 10-7

Galassia

The most serious of fashionistas will love Galassia, which has been defining the cutting edge in Rome since the early Eighties with its ever-changing collection from the avant garde of the avant garde. Eveningwear comes courtesy of Jean Paul Gaultier, and Belgian designer Ann Demeulemeester provides feminine post-apocalyptic hip—think diaphanous asymmetry. There are also edgy pieces from Issey Miyake, AF Vandervorst, The People of the Labyrinth and Vivienne Westwood.

Expensive to luxury   *Amex/MC/V*

Via Frattina 20-21   **06 679 7896**
00187 Rome   Mon 1-7:30, Tues-Sat 10-7:30

Galleria Colonna

Opened in December 2003, the Galleria Colonna (now officially renamed the Galleria Alberto Sordi after the late, great star of Italian cinema, but mostly known by its previous name) is as close as Rome gets to a shopping centre in the heart of the city. Here you'll find 20 shops and a bar under a coloured glass roof in a 19th-century arcade that has been modernised and saved from decades of dereliction. Stores not to miss include Jam, Zara, T'Store, Dancing Duck and Guess (see their separate entries).

Piazza di Spagna area

Piazza Colonna   **(see under individual stores)**
00187 Rome   Daily 10-10

☆ Gallo

Since 1927 Gallo have been making socks on the banks of Lake Garda, and very splendid socks (and tights) they are too. Men, women and children are catered for with every possible combination of colour and fabric—from horizontally striped knee-socks (spotted peeking out between Roman women's trousers and loafers in more than one smart location) to classic colours in cotton, wool and pure cashmere for the more conventionally inclined. This is also the place to pick up Friulani velvet slippers with soles made from recycled bicycle tyres—elegant enough for evenings out, yet comfortable enough to wear around the house. Other lines include thin-striped cotton bikinis, knitted-silk ties and lovely cotton baby shoes. A year ago, those striped knee-sock wearers heaved a collective sigh of relief when Gallo opened a store in smart Parioli.

Moderate   *Amex/MC/V*

Piazza di Spagna area

Via Vittoria 63   **06 360 02174**
00187 Rome   Mon 3:30-7:30, Tues-Sat 10-2, 3:30-7:30

Parioli area

Via Guidubaldo del Monte 5   **06 808 2339**
00197 Rome   Mon 3-7, Tues-Sat 10-2, 3-7

Gatto

Gatto have been making shoes in this most unlikely of spots (a recently refurbished apartment over a TV repair store off the Via XX Settembre) since 1912 when they became shoemakers to the then Italian Royal Family. Current incumbents Vincenzo Gatto and Gaetano Vastola are nearing retirement and say that the absence of young shoemakers means they'll soon be closing. But for now they are bursting with work and turning clients away. If you're lucky enough to be accepted onto their waiting list, you'll eventually find yourself with a pair of splendid classic shoes, entirely handmade in a variety of styles and the finest leathers. Shoes this beautiful don't come cheap and prices hover around the 2,000 euro mark. Then again, the sole alone takes two days to make.

Luxury   *Amex/MC/V*

Repubblica area

Via Antonio Salandra 34   **06 474 1450**
00187 Rome   (by appointment only)

Gente

More than one supermodel visiting the Eternal City has been spotted in Gente's somewhat sterile main branch on the über-cool Via del Babuino. It's no surprise when you learn that some of the hippest names in the fashion spectrum are represented here. The big attractions at the Via del Babuino store are Helmut Lang denims, Miu Miu girly tops and sandals and Marni's vintagey pieces, and Gente has also become the distributor for Narciso Rodriguez since his Rome branch closed last year. The men's section—stocking John Richmond and DSquared T-shirts—is on the second floor where there are also evening dresses and Jil Sander shoes. The Via Frattina store—a bold black and white mirrored affair—targets the younger end of the market with Diane von Furstenberg, DKNY, Ghost and Jamin Puech bags.

Expensive   *Amex/MC/V*

Piazza di Spagna area

Via del Babuino 80-82   **06 320 7671**
00187 Rome   Mon-Sat 10-7:30

Via Frattina 69   **06 678 9132**
00187 Rome   (opening hours as above)

Via Cola di Rienzo area

Via Cola di Rienzo 277-279   **06 321 1516**
00192 Rome   Mon 3:30-8, Tues-Sat 9:30-8

Geox

If you're traipsing around in 35° heat (95°F) for half the year, soggy socks can be a problem. Geox has solved this by producing 'the shoe that breathes'. Well, to be more precise, actual unaided respiration is a pipe dream at the moment but a special microporous membrane relies on the fact that perspiration drops are smaller than water drops and so the shoes can expel sweat without letting water in. You may have to sacrifice elegance for comfort, as the women's range consists of mostly round-toed flats with a small choice of low-heels. However, there is a good selection of smart gym-style shoes in mostly black and white as well as sandals in summer. Men have a slightly broader selection with lace-up city shoes, moccasins and trainers and there's an incredibly popular children's section in the back of both of the stores listed. Geox must be doing something right, because stores are cropping up all across town.   *geox.com*

Affordable   *Amex/MC/V*

Piazza di Spagna area
Via Frattina 3/A   **06 699 0480**
00187 Rome   Sun-Mon 4-8, Tues-Sat 10-8
Via Nazionale area
Via Nazionale 233   **06 481 4518**
00184 Rome   Mon-Sat 10-7:30

GF Ferré

At the entrance you are greeted with red shiny walls, and upstairs there's more drama with metal and mirrors. Once you've got over the dazzling stage set, you might want to turn your attention to the clothes. Ferré's origins as an architect come out in his attention to form, structure and balance and he concentrates on relaxed elegance rather than painstaking high fashion—just take a close look at one of his carefully structured, bestselling white shirts if you want to verify this. Downstairs, women will find suits, a sports range and a whole selection of accessories (as well as the shirts); upstairs, the menswear includes classically cut leather jackets, velcro-close gym shoes and anoraks, which Ferré has miraculously managed to make surprisingly funky.   *gianfrancoferre.com*

Luxury   *Amex/MC/V*

Piazza di Spagna area
Piazza di Spagna 70   **06 678 6797**
00187 Rome   Mon-Sat 10-7:30

Gianni Versace

Rome's Versace women's boutique is in the same opulent style as the men's store, replete with marble floors and neo-classical faux antiques—and fans certainly won't be disappointed. But unlike the toned-down men's collection, Donatella's women's range is high-sex, high-glamour, high-glitz. These are the kind of clothes that look best on super-models: you have to be pretty damn gorgeous to get away with vibrant pink evening dresses splashed with parrots and tropical fish and paired with handbags in neon yellow. But for lesser mortals there are one or two more restrained items—including surprisingly simple blouses and pants. You might think that clothes this brash necessitate service to match—but the assistants at both stores are utterly charming.   *versace.com*

Luxury   *Amex/MC/V*

Piazza di Spagna area
Via Bocca di Leone 26-27   **06 678 0521**
00187 Rome   Daily 10-7

Gianni Versace Uomo

This men's boutique looks like the lobby of a very smart hotel with faux antique furniture, gilded light fittings and mosaic floors. Downstairs, the clothing is surprisingly sombre and you could almost be deluded into thinking that Donatella has given up on the glitzy look: beautifully cut suits and shoes sit at the front of the shop, and elegantly bright ties add a spot of colour. Towards the back, there are Versace Sport's zip-up tops, T-shirts and sweaters in remarkably restrained colours. But once up the elegant staircase, you'll know you really are in Versace-land. Here, the world-famous prints are given free rein and colour abounds on embroidered tops and shirts printed in the style we've come to know and love. Sheer heaven for boys who want to have fashion fun. *versace.com*

Luxury *Amex/MC/V*

Piazza di Spagna area

Via Borgognona 24-25 **06 679 5037**
00187 Rome Mon-Sat 10-7:30, Sun 11-7

Giorgio Armani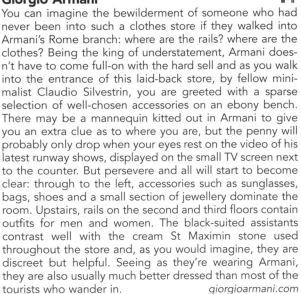

You can imagine the bewilderment of someone who had never been into such a clothes store if they walked into Armani's Rome branch: where are the rails? where are the clothes? Being the king of understatement, Armani doesn't have to come full-on with the hard sell and as you walk into the entrance of this laid-back store, by fellow minimalist Claudio Silvestrin, you are greeted with a sparse selection of well-chosen accessories on an ebony bench. There may be a mannequin kitted out in Armani to give you an extra clue as to where you are, but the penny will probably only drop when your eyes rest on the video of his latest runway shows, displayed on the small TV screen next to the counter. But persevere and all will start to become clear: through to the left, accessories such as sunglasses, bags, shoes and a small section of jewellery dominate the room. Upstairs, rails on the second and third floors contain outfits for men and women. The black-suited assistants contrast well with the cream St Maximin stone used throughout the store and, as you would imagine, they are discreet but helpful. Seeing as they're wearing Armani, they are also usually much better dressed than most of the tourists who wander in. *giorgioarmani.com*

Luxury *Amex/MC/V*

Piazza di Spagna area

Via dei Condotti 77 **06 699 1460**
00187 Rome Mon-Sat 10-7

☆ Giuseppe Messina

During the course of his 60-year career Giuseppe Messina has made shoes for everyone from the Queen of Denmark to Eileen Ford (a lovely woman, he says). You can go into his tiny workshop with an old shoe, a picture or just a vague idea and be wearing an original pair of handmade shoes a week or so later. Want a pair of sparkly ruby slippers like Dorothy? Six-inch winkle-pickers in calf leather? Giuseppe, his wife and son will see to it immediately: they're rare examples of real craftspeople who'll make you want to forget mass-produced shoes. Don't insult them by asking for mere repairs—quite rightly, you'll be chased away in disgust.

Moderate to expensive   *Amex/MC/V*
Piazza di Spagna area
Vicolo della Torretta 6   **06 687 2902**
00186 Rome   Mon-Sat 9:30-2, 3:30-8

Givenchy

Who can forget the gorgeously elegant and stick-thin Audrey Hepburn in top-to-toe Givenchy at the height of her fame? And even today, the myth of the effortlessly classy, fun-loving woman survives in ads featuring Liv Tyler for this legendary French fashion house. Given these precedents, the lack of style at the small, two-floor Rome store comes as something of a shock. Plonked on a corner of the relatively quiet Via Borgognona, the dark blue carpet and white walls and fittings seem uninspiring choices for a fashion brand of this stature. But come here anyway for classic black pantsuits and little black dresses with a twist—and, of course, the legendary pumpkin bag.   *givenchy.com*

Luxury   *Amex/MC/V*
Piazza di Spagna area
Via Borgognona 21   **06 678 4058**
00187 Rome   Mon-Sat 10-7

Gorietti

For a refined and unhassled shopping experience, Romans in the know head to the Margutta Arcade. Tucked in a quiet courtyard at the Piazza del Popolo end of the Via Margutta beloved of arty types for more than a century, it's a quiet and peaceful corner in an increasingly noisy and crowded city. One of the first stores that you'll come across is the yacht-like Gorietti, which started out as a cobbler early last century providing handmade shoes for both men and women. Nowadays, it also stocks high-quality footwear by a range of mostly Italian labels: Walter Violet's low-heeled slip-ons mix comfort and charm while Gianna Meliani's pastel suede mules hit just the right note of casual chic. Men have a choice of lace-ups and slip-ons from Gorietti's own brand in anything from crocodile to ostrich and kangaroo; some of their sturdy shoes employ the Norwegian double-stitching method. There's also a good range of handmade silk and cashmere ties—plain, striped and micro-patterned—as well as belts and Roberto del Carlo bags.   *gorietti.com*

Expensive   *Amex/MC/V*
Piazza di Spagna area
Margutta Arcade   **06 360 06110**
Via Margutta 3   Mon 3:30-7:30
00187 Rome   Tues-Sat 10:30-7:30
San Giovanni area
Piazza Ré di Roma 66   **06 703 00830**
00183 Rome   Mon 4-8, Tues-Sat 9:30-1, 4-8

Gucci

The single word—Gucci—stands out in enormous silver letters above the entrance to the Via dei Condotti store. And as you push back the door the presence of an imposing bouncer complete with ear-piece will remind you that this is where the serious shoppers head. The overwhelming displays of luxury goods make you want to float in a trance from the jewellery counter to the shelves and glass boxes stacked with belts, ties and scarves and those much-coveted bags. Afterwards, drift upstairs for luscious clothes (ladies to the right and gents to the left), classic shoes and amusing little niche products. Why not take home something for your newborn niece or nephew—or, failing that, for your pooch? Don't miss the fascinating little section containing Gucci dog collars, leads and bowls—some inscribed with the unmistakable Gucci 'G'. *gucci.com*

Luxury *Amex/MC/V*

Piazza di Spagna area

Via dei Condotti 8 **06 678 9340**
00187 Rome Sun 2-7, Mon-Sat 10-7

Gucci (accessories)

Gucci Accessories opened its doors in the former stables of Palazzo Torlonia in March 2003. The store may be stamped with the trademark grey/white Gucci decor with a generous sprinkling of mirrors and chrome, but what sets it apart from its sister stores—and from most stores in Rome—are the 19th-century frescoes of three beautiful religious scenes on the second floor. This may be the only Gucci boutique in the world where fans spend more time gazing at the ceiling than at the ties in finest silk and the cases and purses in calf leather which they dashed in here to buy. Downstairs, there are no such distractions and you can relax on the sofas while you contemplate the shoes, sandals and cases with the full concentration that shopping at Gucci requires. *gucci.com*

Luxury *Amex/MC/V*

Piazza di Spagna area

Via Borgognona 7/D **06 691 90661**
00187 Rome Mon 3-7, Tues-Sat 10-7

Gucci (jewellery)

When it opened three years ago, this was the first store in the world dedicated entirely to Gucci jewellery. The exterior may be small and discreet but the smoked-glass windows give you some idea of the dark den of opulence that lies beyond. Inside, various lines of jewellery remind you of Gucci's early associations with the horsy set. There's the Nail range which uses a horseshoe nail shape to create rings and bangles. Then there's the horse bit which you can wear around your neck, on your wrist or on your finger. If you just want a souvenir and have spent all your pocket money, there are five and ten gram white-gold coin pendants that you can buy for the kids back home at 200-400 euros. But most of the goods here are pretty serious—and have prices to match. *gucci.com*

Luxury *Amex/MC/V*

Piazza di Spagna area

Via dei Condotti 68/A **06 697 88266**
00187 Rome Sun-Mon 2-7, Tues-Sat 10-7

Guess/Guess by Marciano

Founded in the early Eighties by the French-born Marciano brothers, Guess mixes a love for the style of the American West with an unmistakably European cut. The classic Guess jeans line is at the two-storey Via del Corso store with a large range of jeans for both men and women upstairs; on the ground floor, you'll find little denim-print skirts with spangly belts, and wittily funky handbags. The Galleria Colonna store is the first dedicated Guess by Marciano store in Rome focusing on the more upmarket, trend-led Guess by Marciano label. Guess's targeting of local markets means that although the firm is based in California, a large proportion of the designs in this store won't be found outside il bel paese. This year it's tight glittery trousers for her—think full-on make-up for a night in a fashionably seedy casino—and a shiny purple suit for him. *guess.com*

Moderate *Amex/MC/V*

Piazza di Spagna area

Galleria Colonna (Alberto Sordi) **06 678 4333**
Piazza Colonna Daily 10-9 (Sat 10-10)
00187 Rome

Via del Corso 141-143 **06 678 8832**
00187 Rome Mon-Sat 10:30-7:30, Sun 11:30-7:30

Hermès

It's hard to forget the equine origins of this one-time sad-dler's workshop since horses and equine accessories are a recurrent theme in the decoration. But what else is on offer at this store? Well, tucked away in the cabinets that line the Roman outlet of the classy French label, there's a large selection of accessories ranging from 'I'm a 50s French film star incognito' printed silk headscarves to chunky porcelain ashtrays. There are also wallets, purses, bags (including the iconic Kelly bag), bracelets and ties for you to take a look at before going through to the smaller middle room which caters for men. Men's and women's clothing collections are made up of luscious cashmere coats and sweaters, luxuriant leather jackets, printed silk shirts and cashmere knits with metal buttons, all seemingly designed for life in a world where there are no regular homes, only chateaux. Naturally, their grounds will contain rows and rows of stables, packed with horses just longing for a morning gallop. *hermes.com*

Luxury *Amex/MC/V*

Piazza di Spagna area

Via dei Condotti 67 **06 679 1882**
00187 Rome Mon 3-7, Tues-Sat 10-7

Hogan

Bright red sofas and parquet floors provide the backdrop to Diego Della Valle's Hogan footwear line (Tod's little brother) which caters for men, women and children. The stars are the comfortably elegant bowling shoes and loafers, although there are also some heels and more formal designs. The hottest new styles include the Olimpia sneaker in leather and suede in a vast combination of colours for both men and women. There's also a range of leather handbags, again in a rainbow of colours. *todsgroup.com*

Expensive   *Amex/MC/V*

Piazza di Spagna area

Via Borgognona 45   **06 678 6828**
00187 Rome   Mon-Sat 10-7:30

Hugo Boss

There's nothing particularly Roman about this store from the German label; fans will be reassured to learn that they'll find the same classic Boss collections they can see the world over. Conventional guys can flip through the Black Label line, featuring both casual and dress, while sportier types should check out the Orange label—which has branched out into silver sneakers this year. Traditional suits and shirts abound, but there are also more playful seersucker jackets. The Boss range extends to undies and socks, aftershaves and scents, sunglasses and wallets. Here, it really is possible to kit a man out from head to toe. *hugoboss.com*

Moderate to expensive   *Amex/MC/V*

Piazza di Spagna area

Via Frattina 146-147   **06 678 6173**
00187 Rome   Mon 11-1, 2-7:30, Tues-Sat 10-7:30
                                              Sun 11-1, 2-7

Iceberg

The walls of this store are lined with pseudo Pop Art, reflecting the designs that led the Emilia-Romagna knitwear company to prominence in the Eighties. If you were in any doubt, fuchsia and shocking pink patterned silk palazzo pants let you know that this isn't the label for those looking to blend in at a tupperware party. Nowadays, bold is the key. Sandals and bags in neon pink 'crocodile' skin get you wondering what kind of post-apocalyptic crocodiles Iceberg are sourcing, and where they find them… Despite the frosty name the service is pleasingly friendly. *iceberg.com*

Luxury   *Amex/MC/V*

Piazza di Spagna area

Via del Babuino 87-88   **06 326 00221**
00187 Rome   Mon-Sat 10-7

Il Portone

This is where smart young men get their underwear, shirts and socks (always assuming Mamma hasn't already stocked up). At number 73, masculine shirts abound, in any colour, fabric, or collar type from buttoned-down to cut back to Nehru-style. Shirts can be embroidered with initials on request and you can also have them made-to-order for a reasonable price. At number 71, there's a sportier, more casual range of shirts, T-shirts, boxer shorts and pyjamas. There's also a concession to women who assist on these underwear-buying expeditions, with a small selection of T-shirts and sweaters. *ilportone.com*

Moderate Amex/MC/V

Piazza di Spagna area

Via delle Carozze 71 & 73 **06 679 3355 (M)**
00187 Rome **06 679 0265 (M/W)**
Mon 3:30-7:30, Tues-Sat 10-7:30

Indoroman

Gaia Franchetti has been purveying her ethno-chic wares at this location since 2002. Her husband's family is from Venice, where they became friends with Hemingway, and when the author saw the store for the first time he compared it to a Venetian fondaco, the ground floor of the palazzi where returning merchants displayed their oriental wares. Not many shops can boast a provenance like that—and it does-n't disappoint, even today. Its bazaar-like space houses a vast range of sarongs, skirts and trousers as well as quilts, tablecloths and other items for the home. Franchetti has them made up from the fabrics she brings back from her travels in India, combining them with Italian elements, both in the textiles and the inspiration. *indoroman.com*

Affordable to moderate Amex/MC/V

Piazza di Spagna area

Via Gregoriana 36 **06 691 90908**
00187 Rome Mon-Fri 10-7

Intimissimi

Come down here on a Saturday afternoon, and spot the hordes of Roman ragazze snapping up Intimissimi's young and sexy lingerie. An offshoot of the Calzedonia tights and socks stores, there are tiny branches everywhere so just dive into the nearest one. Recent looks have focused on demure lacy bits and pastel tones—particularly pinks and greens—but there are also some funkier, fresher designs. At these prices (around 20 euros for bras and eight for knick-ers) we're not talking La Perla, but the materials are surpris-ingly soft and avoid that scratchy I-just-picked-this-up-in-a-market feel. There's a smaller range for boys: classic T-shirts, singlets, boxers, briefs and pyjamas. Staff are young and helpful. *intimissimi.com*

Affordable Amex/MC/V

Piazza di Spagna area

Via del Corso 167 **06 699 24132**
00187 Rome Mon-Sat 9-8, Sun 11-8

Campo de' Fiori area

Via dei Giubbonari 42   **06 683 01784**
00186 Rome   (opening hours as above)

Via Nazionale area

Via Nazionale 189   **06 484 638**
00184 Rome   Mon-Sat 9:30-8, Sun 12-2, 3-8

Via Nazionale 227   **06 485 914**
00184 Rome   (opening hours as above)

Termini Station Concourse

Via Giolitti 9   **06 478 23171**
00185 Rome   Daily 8-10

Via Cola di Rienzo area

Via Cola di Rienzo 159-161   **06 324 3137**
00192 Rome   Mon 1-8, Tues-Sat 9:30-8
                                           Sun 11-1:30, 3:30-8

Iron G   👤

Rome's rich-kid clubbers come to this eclectic store with papa's cash to snap up outré outfits from some of fashion's edgiest labels. Distressed walls teamed with trashy chandeliers are the perfect setting for the dressy industrial look. Jeans are Levi's (but we're a long way from stone-washed 501s) and Shaft. Embroidered shift dresses, bags and sequined belts provide a little ethnic style courtesy of Antik Batik, while eastern-inspired sandals from Roman label Jorando complete the look (fans take note: this is one of the two stores in town stocking designer Francesca Jori's wares). For disco girls there are Fornarina customised denim minis and pointy heels from Kallisté, or fabulously kitsch jewelled leopardprint sandals for the very brave. Converse All-Stars and Playboy T-shirts are perfect for some elegant lounging the morning after. The store also stocks handmade jewellery from Afghanistan, Thailand and local Roman artisans.

Moderate   *Amex/MC/V*

Cola di Rienzo area

Via Cola di Rienzo 50   **06 321 6798**
00192 Rome   Mon-Sat 10:30-7:30

I Vippini   👤

Is your kiddie about to audition for a butter-wouldn't-melt-in-her-mouth part in one of those wholesome ads? Or do you have to attend an event where it's best to pretend that the Royal Wedding bridesmaid/page boy look is his or her usual style? As the name implies, this store with its candy-striped awnings is for kids who want (or, more likely, need) to look like mini-VIPs, and it's stuffed with traditional frocks, gorgeous little shoes and bonnets, smocked dresses and smart cords and shirts for boys. Like all self-respecting kids' stores in Vatican-dominated Rome, they also make frothy concoctions for baptisms and first communions. As well as the traditional styles, there are some sportier lines and little princesses can unwind in hooded tracksuits decorated with silver sequins. Lines run from 0-8 for boys, right up to 14 for more compliant girls.

Expensive   *Amex/MC/V*

Piazza di Spagna area

Via Fontanella di Borghese 65   **06 688 03754**
00187 Rome   Mon 3:30-7, Tues-Sat 9:30-1, 2 :30-7

Jam

This new, teenage fashion store may be owned by the La Rinascente group, but it's a million miles away from its stuffier older sister across the road. Packed with teen labels, from Ben Sherman, Duffer and Lonsdale to classic sports brands, Jam is every hip kid's dream. British shoppers may be reminded of Top Shop, but clothes at Jam don't come cheap. The customers are mostly rich teenagers and their indulgent mothers—plus twenty and thirty-somethings who can't quite believe that their adolescence is a thing of the past. The ground, mezzanine floors and basement are filled with girly looks, from skate-inspired sweats to teensy tops and skirts for dancing. There are also piles of accessories: chunky, plastic jewellery for the 13-year old in all of us, big belts and pretty bags. The top floor is mostly for boys, and includes everything you'll need to kit yourself out as a hip Roman teenager—from Eastpack backpacks to masculine sporty labels (North Sails, Murphy & Nye, Nike) galore. You'll even find a selection of designer helmets—for when Daddy gives in to your pleas for a motorino...

Moderate to expensive   *Amex/MC/V*

Piazza di Spagna area

Galleria Colonna (Alberto Sordi)   **06 678 4209**
Piazza Colonna   Mon-Sat 10-10, Sun 10-9
00187 Rome

☆ Josephine de Huertas

French designer and expert retailer Josephine de Huertas has made a name providing clothes for Roman It-girls, as well as for ads and films. Look carefully at the punters browsing the racks and you may spot the odd famous face. Vibrant colours and eye-catching patterns are de Huertas' thing. Fixed favourites include Joseph, Diane von Furstenberg and, predictably, an abundance of Paul Smith (everything from jeans to undies) as well as some emerging names. The original De Huertas boutique is the branch on Via di Parione, which she opened with fellow fashion student Mauro Crachi back in 1988. Here you'll find casual but chic daywear—including Mackintosh trench coats with heat-sealed seams, floaty flower-print blouses by Chloé, a whole range of Antik Batik (check out their kaftans) and Halison ballet pumps. Don't miss La Collana di Betta, a range of chunky jewellery in copper and agate handmade by an Italian architect living in Africa—the perfect way to finish off a simple little outfit with style.   *josephinedehuertas.com*

Expensive to luxury   *Amex/MC/V*

Piazza Navona area

Via del Governo Vecchio 68   **06 687 6586**
00186 Rome   Mon 3:30-7:30, Tues-Sat 10-2, 3-7:30

Via di Parione 19-20   **06 683 00156**
00186 Rome   Mon 4-8, Tues-Sat 10-2, 4-8

Just Cavalli Boutique   👤👤

Definitely not for minimalists, Florentine designer Roberto Cavalli appeals more to girls who would like Tarzan to take them clubbing somewhere loud. His loyal followers flock to the two-floor Piazza di Spagna store (womenswear is as you walk in, menswear is on the first floor) in search of spangly belts and gilded trainers. But the animal prints are the main draw; think super-kitsch leopardskin 'jewelled' sandals and, if you're feeling brave, team them with a sequined neon pink top and you'll be ready for anything. Jungle prints abound, although there are occasional moments of restraint; jungle-green three-quarter length skinny cords are for all those Janes who can't carry off a tiger-print mini.   *robertocavalli.net*

Moderate to expensive   *Amex/MC/V*

Piazza di Spagna area

Piazza di Spagna 82-83   **06 679 2294**
00187 Rome   Mon 1-7:30, Tues-Sat 10-7:30

Kristina Ti   👤

It's no wonder that up-town Italian girls as well as international jet-setters shop here (Catherine Deneuve is a fan). The daughter of a lingerie line owner, Torinese designer Cristina Tardito (Kristina Ti) started out with a range of bikinis in 1987 and has never looked back. The Rome store is large and airy with white walls, stone floors and vast windows and the clothes housed here have an equally light touch. The silk chiffon blouses are almost invisible they're so slight, while you could easily slip the dresses into your pocket (although we advise you to resist the urge). The marvellous creations in chiffon and tulle seem made for the flower fairies of the 21st century, and there's also a selection of barely-there sandals and boots.   *kristinati.it*

Expensive   *Amex/MC/V*

Piazza di Spagna area

Via Mario de' Fiori 40/C-41   **06 692 00170**
00187 Rome   Mon 3-7, Tues-Sat 10-7

Krizia   👤

This Milanese label by designer Mariuccia Mandelli may not have the cachet it once had, but it's still a safe bet for cleverly cut outfits that flatter your figure rather than making you rush off to enrol at the nearest gym. Styles are a mixture, moving from classic knitted cotton T-shirts and cardigans in navy blue to beautifully tailored suits mixed with beaded silk tops. The Piazza di Spagna store has two storeys, with a few tables upstairs where the friendly staff will help you concentrate on the task in hand by offering you a caffeine fix. If you can tear your eyes from the clothes, gaze out on the stunning view of the square below. *krizia.net*

Moderate   *Amex/MC/V*

Piazza di Spagna area

Piazza di Spagna 87   **06 679 3772**
00187 Rome   Mon 3-7, Tues-Sat 10-7

La Cicogna

This small-sized children's department store stocks upmarket labels for babies, children up to 14 and mothers-to-be. Downstairs there's a vast range of miniature designer looks from Armani Junior and Armani Baby, DKNY, Burberry, the Italian Miss Blumarine line, Napapijri, Mason's and Murphy & Nye for young yachters, plus tiny versions of Belstaff belted jackets. In the mid range, there are Replay's sweet jeans, dungarees and sweatshirts and itsy-bitsy Adidas trainers. Upstairs, there's a range of La Cicogna's own maternity wear and toys, cribs and prams. Signora Angela at the Via Frattina store is particularly helpful and speaks English.

Moderate to expensive   *Amex/MC/V*

Piazza di Spagna area

Via Frattina 135   **06 679 1912**
00187 Rome   Mon 3:30-7:30, Tues-Sat 10-7:30, Sun 11-7

Via Cola di Rienzo area

Via Cola di Rienzo 268   **06 689 6557**
00192 Rome   Mon 4:15-8, Tues-Sat 10-8

☆ Laltramoda

This Roman company is one of few in Italy that produces several reasonably priced runway-inspired collections a season—ensuring that its boutiques are always packed with fashionistas fighting over the freshest new looks. The first store opened in Rome 12 years ago, but there is now a sizeable chain of sister boutiques in Milan, Turin, Verona and beyond. Recent looks have included floaty little pastel skirts and almost transparent floral tops. It's also a good place to pick up basics—from beautiful knits in cotton, angora, silk or cashmere to shearling coats and city-slick leather suits. The best selections are at the Via Borgognona and Via Frattina stores. Since the most covetable pieces never stay on the racks for long, it's worth popping into both—so as not to miss that perfect leopardprint mini in just your size. *laltramoda.it*

Affordable to moderate   *Amex/MC/V*

Piazza di Spagna area

Via Frattina 113   **06 679 2987**
00187 Rome   Mon 3:30-7:30, Tues-Sat 10-7:30

Via Borgognona 42/B   **06 678 4444**
00187 Rome   (opening hours as above)

Via Cola di Rienzo area

Via Cola di Rienzo 54-56   **06 321 1622**
00192 Rome   Mon 3:30-8, Tues-Sat 9:30-8

☆ L'Anatra all'Arancia

Savvy Roman shoppers travel right across the city to get to this spacious wooden-floored boutique, nicely set off by a very glam chandelier. L'Anatra all'Arancia is named for that great classic of Seventies cordon bleu, duck à l'orange, and true to its name, it's all about pairing like with unlike to come up with the perfect match. Eighties baggy-thighed trousers, floaty summer dresses and geometrically cut double-breasted jackets jostle alongside pill-box hats. You'll also find interesting pieces by Marithé et François Girbaud and Louise Della, as well as Hervé Chapelier's elegant but practical bags and some of Camper's more eccentric numbers.

Moderate to expensive   Amex/MC/V

San Lorenzo area

Via Tiburtina 105-9	**06 445 6293**
00185 Rome	Mon-Sat 9:30-1, 4-8
Via Tiburtina 130	**06 4436 2144**
00185 Rome	Mon 4-8, Tues-Sat 9:30-1, 4-8

La Perla

As any stylish gal knows, it's no good slipping your best togs on over off-white and not particularly flattering underwear. That's why Italian women pay regular visits to 50-year-old Bolognese company, La Perla. They offer silk and lace decadence, but also keep an eye on the lower end of the market with more affordable lines, such as Malizia which includes Lycra and cotton basics. The newish Black Label isn't as expensive as the main Perla lines and is a little bit naughtier too. Then there's the flirty Glamour line geared towards the younger shopper. The Rome outpost also stocks chiffon dresses, while upstairs is a collection of swimwear. A soothing backdrop of cool marble, mirrors and chrome will convince you that even though you can't show off your purchases to everyone, you did the right thing by indulging yourself here.   *laperla.com*

Moderate to expensive   Amex/MC/V

Piazza di Spagna area

Via dei Condotti 78	**06 699 41934**
00187 Rome	Mon 3-7, Tues-Sat 10-7

La Rinascente

The smarter of Rome's (very) limited range of department stores, La Rinascente is Coin's posher city-centre cousin—but don't come here expecting innovation. Like every department store in the world, the ground floor is filled with cosmetics and perfumes from all the established major lines—it's a good place to pick up sun cream in the summer. Two floors are dedicated to menswear. There's casualwear (Dockers, Levi's and a small range of Diesel—slightly perplexing with Rome's flagship Diesel store next door) and formalwear, including a small selection of suits, shirts by Lacoste and Missoni's colourful ties for the boldest customers. The women's fashion floors are disappointing, though a few pieces from D&G's diffusion line '&' lift the gloom. The best bet is the lingerie, with sexy lines from D&G and lacy little bras from Calvin Klein. Both stores have a homewares store in the basement, and the Piazza Fiume store also has a large selection of sportswear on the top floor, plus childrenswear. *rinascente.it*

Affordable to moderate *Amex/MC/V*

Piazza di Spagna area

Piazza Colonna	**06 679 7691**
00186 Rome	Mon-Sat 9:30-10, Sun 10:30-8
Piazza Fiume	**06 884 1231**
00198 Rome	Mon-Sat 9:30-10, Sun 10:30-9

Laura Biagiotti

Dubbed the Queen of Cashmere, Laura Biagiotti has been a fixture on the Roman fashion scene for over 30 years—and her high-ceilinged store is as grand as you'd expect. A theatre at the beginning of the last century, the boutique retains a slightly stagey atmosphere—ideal for displaying Signora Biagiotti's captivating creations to a backdrop of classical music. Cashmere and silk, both plain and embroidered, and dolcetto, a mixture of the two, are the materials she prefers for her floaty dresses and tailored trousers. The accessory section includes scarves, bags, shoes and perfume. While you're at the cash desk, take a look at the two enormous paintings behind the sales assistant's head: they show Réné Gruau's depiction of the arrival and departure of the elegant Laura Biagiotti at a party; in these flashy-trashy times, her eternal sense of style comes as a welcome relief. *laurabiagiotti.it*

Expensive *Amex/MC/V*

Piazza di Spagna area

Via Borgognona 43-44	**06 679 1205**
00187 Rome	Mon 3:30-7:30
	Tues-Sat 9:30-1:30, 3:30-7:30

☆ Leam

If you thought Leam in the centre was good, just take a trip out to San Giovanni and try to stop your jaw dropping open in amazement. There's not one shop but three—all next to each other and covering 2,500 square metres. The most impressive is Leam Limited sandwiched between the first, more old-fashioned and traditional Leam (which only caters for men) and the company's three-floor mega-boutique. Leam Limited is a pseudo-industrial space with a stage in the middle, and it not only has the latest from Leam favourites Marni, Missoni, Alaïa Azzedine and Yamamoto but also limited-series lines and fabulous vintage pieces which sell like hot cakes. On top of that, it plays host to events and product launches, and if you prove to be a valued customer you might be able to wangle yourself an invitation to one of Leam's parties where the Roman glitterati come to rub shoulders and eye up the latest one-of-a-kind pieces in the boutique. The Leam on the left (the mega-boutique) could sate the hunger of the most obsessive fashionista. You'll find three floors of Gucci, Dior, Roberto Cavalli, Prada, YSL, Hogan, Tod's, Burberry, John Richmond and Fendi with a bar at the top where you can rest your aching feet when you just can't take it any more. *leam.com*

Luxury   *Amex/MC/V*

San Giovanni area

Via Appia Nuova 26-32/C   **06 772 07204**
00181 Rome   Mon-Sat 9:30-8

Leam

Roman men have been shopping at Leam for nigh on 50 years and you don't have to rack your brains to understand why. Not only is it located down one of the quieter shopping streets in the centre (thus avoiding the logo bag-wielding ankle-kickers on the main streets) but it also has everything under one roof. There's none of that traipsing from designer boutique to designer boutique to set up your new season's wardrobe—which puts a lot of men off the whole shopping scene for life. On two floors you'll find the latest cult items from Prada, D&G, Dior, Jil Sander, Yamamoto and Marni. D&G jeans casually hang from meat hooks; Prada thong-toed flip-flops remind you that you can even do nonchalant chic when you've just got out of the shower. The background ambient music, comfy sofas and laid-back but helpful assistants make the whole experience a pleasure rather than a chore.   *leam.com*

Luxury   *Amex/MC/V*

Piazza di Spagna area

Via Bocca di Leone 5   **06 678 7853**
00187 Rome   Mon 3:30-7:30, Tues-Sat 10-7:30

Le 3 C

In case you were wondering, the three Cs stand for Carla Cardillo (the owner) and Calzature—the Italian word for footwear. This small boutique with a big following has been in the same Roman family since 1937. Their Capri-style sandals come in all types of leather, but there are also French Pare Gabia handstitched espadrilles with rope soles, ballet shoes by E. Borselli, to be worn casually or for dance, and Tyrolean wool and deerskin house shoes. If you want to treat your feet, you could try a pair of Parini's ultra-soft and ultra-light handmade slippers—the Rolls Royce of the slipper world. Apart from brushes and products to clean shoes, Le 3 C also has bois de rose and leather accessory boxes which wouldn't be a bad present for a shoe fanatic friend.

Moderate   *Amex/MC/V*

Piazza di Spagna area

Via della Croce 40   **06 679 3813**
00187 Rome   Mon 3:30-7:30, Tues-Sat 10-1:30, 3:30-7:30

☆ Le Gallinelle

Le Gallinelle ('the little hens') is in a former chicken butcher's shop. Designer/proprietor Wilma Silvestri and her daughter

Giorgia offer a seriously stylish (and, for Rome, unusually alternative) mix of vintage and ethnic reworked with inventive flair. Eighties polka-dot silk is reincarnated as a Forties-style dress. Vintage souvenir silk scarves with details of cities (including Rome, of course) have been reborn as either short shorts or the kind of voluminous bags from which Mary Poppins might have produced her hat stand. Need something to set off your locks? Old silk flowers are given a new lease of life on hair bands.   *legallinelle.it*

Moderate   *Amex/MC/V*

Via Nazionale area

Via del Boschetto 76   **06 488 1017**
00184 Rome   Mon 3:30-8, Tues-Sat 10-1, 3:30-8

Lei 👤

Lei's minimalist white stores, refreshingly filled with bright colours, will put a smile on your face at any time of year. At both the larger Via Nazionale store and the Via dei Giubbonari boutique, you'll find Warhol-inspired prints on T-shirts and miniskirts, funky minidresses from Custo of Barcelona, and more serious stuff in the form of feminine silk floral dresses from the Belgian Chine collection. There are fresh linen dresses for summer from the Italian 120% Lino and elegantly feminine designs from Paris-based British designer Tara Jarmon. If you're looking for the funkier pieces from D&G's latest collection, head to the Via Nazionale branch: they're only stocked here. Alberto Biani's suits and shirts add a businesslike touch to both outposts of this fun store.

Moderate   *Amex/MC/V*

Campo de' Fiori area

Via dei Giubbonari 103   **06 687 5432**
00186 Rome   Mon 3:30-7:30, Tues-Sat 10-2, 3:30-8

Via Nazionale area

Via Nazionale 88   **06 482 1700**
00184 Rome   Mon 4-8, Tues-Sat 10-8

Le Ragazze Gold 👤

Babes with attitude come to this small boutique for hi-voltage party gear that'll get them noticed, no matter how big the room. The subdued lighting, which changes from baby blue to pale pink, and sparkly black marble floors provide the perfect setting for these sassy styles. Raunchy little items include a printed backless diamond-shaped handkerchief dress, with denim edging and a choker collar. Gypsy-style skirts and dresses are punctuated with skin-tight jeans of varying lengths and sexy low-cut tops. They also do a sportier line by an Italian brand appropriately named Sexy Woman.

Moderate   *Amex/MC/V*

Piazza di Spagna area

Via del Corso 500   **06 361 2364**
00187 Rome   Mon 3:30-8, Tues-Sat 9:30-8

☆ Loco

For almost a decade Loco has been providing Romans, fashion aficionados and celebrities with shoes that are weird, wonderful and sometimes just plain strange. The copper-and-wood store has a couple of handy Mies van der Rohe stools from which to admire Gianni Barbato's snakeskin boots for the urban cowboy in your life. Alima's playfully childish wood and cloth sandals will make you feel you're on the beach no matter where you are. Extraordinary jewelled gold and silver sandals from Alizeé will make you the belle of the ball (just as soon as you've practised walking in them). There are also trainers from Adidas, Puma and Gola to provide your feet with a break.   *loco.it*

Expensive   Amex/MC/V

Campo de' Fiori area

Via dei Baullari 22   **06 688 08216**
00186 Rome   Mon 3:30-8:30, Tues-Sat 10:30-8:30

☆ Loro Piana

Originally born 20 years ago to produce top-notch materials, Loro Piana moved into retail to ensure quality was maintained right along the production line. It subsequently became a world leader in the cashmere market. Pamper yourself with thick cashmere sweaters and shawls or waterproof cashmere jackets—they developed the first ever. On the left as you walk in the door you'll see a display case containing a book which tells you about the vicuña, a rare animal from the Andes whose wool provides the company with the most expensive cloth in the world. The clothes here are classically cut and don't bow to fashion, and the range extends to overcoats, padded jackets, silk and linen robes, plaid blankets, cashmere slippers, hats, gloves and bags. Men can enjoy their made-to-measure service: allow 30 days to receive the finished product. Not surprisingly, personal shoppers say that this is one of the most popular boutiques for luxury shopping in Rome.

Luxury   Amex/MC/V

Piazza di Spagna area

Via Borgognona 31   **06 699 24906**
00187 Rome   Mon-Sat 10-7

Louis Vuitton

It's hard to walk down a Roman street without someone trying to flog you a poor imitation of one of Louis Vuitton's iconic bags. But if only the real thing will do, head to the Via dei Condotti to pick out the latest looks in a refined ambience that resembles a chic apartment, with sofas, soft music and table lamps. Apart from the classic LV bags and luggage sets, you'll find more recent lines such as the Suhali, in kid with brass clasps, and Marc Jacobs' clothes and shoes. Long skirts in silk velvets and jackets in rich golds are punctuated with sharply contrasting blouses and dresses in turquoise silk. If you visit the San Lorenzo in Lucina branch, take time out for a coffee: the square outside is filled with hip pavement cafés...where better to flash your new bag?

Luxury   *Amex/MC/V*

Piazza di Spagna area

Via dei Condotti 15   **06 699 40000**
00186 Rome   Mon-Sat 9:30-7:30, Sun 11-7:30

Piazza San Lorenzo in Lucina 36   **06 688 09520**
00186 Rome   (opening hours as above)

Luisa Spagnoli

We all know that some 30% of the female population of the US is over size 50, but somehow the marketing geniuses seem to have forgotten them. At Luisa Spagnoli, sizes go up to an Italian 52 (American 22) and you can find evening-wear as well as business suits and practical daywear. There are also some classy raw-silk/linen pieces (though if you're not careful you may look as though you took your wardrobe advice from Cherie Blair). Sadly, however, we have to report that the staff in the Via Frattina store are among the rudest we've ever come across. You may prefer to hunt for larger sizes elsewhere.

Moderate to expensive   *Amex/MC/V*

Piazza di Spagna area

Via Frattina 84/B   **06 699 1706**
00187 Rome   Mon-Sat 10-8, Sun 11-2, 4-7

Via del Tritone 30   **06 699 22769**
00187 Rome   (opening hours as above)

Via Veneto 130   **06 420 11281**
00187 Rome   (opening hours as above)

Via Cola di Rienzo area

Via Cola di Rienzo 191   **06 360 03335**
00192 Rome   Mon-Sat 10-8

☆ Luna & L'altra

Biba Canella and her husband, Luigi D'Alessio, set up Luna & L'altra 23 years ago and still generously dispense fashion pearls of wisdom to eager clients. Issey Miyake with his technical genius is God in Biba's eyes (if you want to see someone brim with enthusiasm, mention his name to her). Apart from Miyake you'll find pieces by Gaultier, Dries Van Noten, delightful cashmere by Cruciani and intriguing jewellery engraved with extracts from Cyrano de Bergerac by Serge Thorval. Biba and her lovely assistant Elisabetta will give you sound advice on purchases. Check out the facade as you're leaving: this historical palazzo dates from 1600.   *lunaelaltra.com*

Expensive to luxury   *Amex/MC/V*

Piazza Navona area

Via del Governo Vecchio 105   **06 688 04995**
00186 Rome   Mon 3:30-7:30, Tues-Sat 10-2, 3:30-7:30

Mada

Unobtrusively hidden towards the Via del Corso end of Via della Croce (where there are as many food stores as boutiques), Mada is a little treasure-trove for shoe lovers. The three proprietresses are helpful, and definitely know their shoes; their devotees aged 18 to 80 come here looking for styles unavailable elsewhere. The watchword here is elegance and designers include Italian-made line Henry Béguelin, French label Accessoire and Spanish designer Pedro Rodriguez. There's also a selection of bags from Ferrara-based Felisi.

Expensive   *Amex/MC/V*

Piazza di Spagna area

Via della Croce 57   **06 679 8660**
00187 Rome   Mon 3:30-7:30, Tues-Fri 9:30-7:30
                                          Sat 10-2, 3-7:30

☆ Maga Morgana

Maga means sorceress in Italian, and owner/designer Luciana Iannace worked in theatre and cinema before setting up shop on Via del Governo Vecchio almost 30 years ago, so a touch of theatrical enchantment is only to be expected from these unusual little boutiques. At number 27 colourful bouquets of crepe paper sit in the windows, while inside knitted teddy bears and tailors' dummies swathed in wool perch above the racks; even the stairs to the store room are decorated with wool. Her designs are quirky and her ultra-feminine dresses are often decorated with whimsical ribbons, bows, flowers and cherries, while her enormous sweaters depict scenes that could be from Toytown. Iannace's twin sons deal with the running of the stores, but Signora Iannace can sometimes be found at number 98 which focuses on just the thing for that fairytale ball.

Moderate   *Amex/MC/V*

Piazza Navona area

Via del Governo Vecchio 27   **06 687 9995**
00186 Rome   Mon-Sat 10-7:30

Via del Governo Vecchio 98   **06 687 8095**
00186 Rome   Mon 3-7:30, Tues-Sat 10-7:30

☆ Malo

This classy shop is a temple to cashmere, with sweaters, socks and scarves so soft you feel you could bathe in them and shawls so light they could fly like kites. There's also a selection of non-cashmere stuff, ideal for a few days on a very smart yacht. Strike the right on-deck pose with bikinis, swimming trunks, beach towels, capacious beach bags and nifty towelling-heeled sandals—just in case the paparazzi get within shot. A leather CD case ensures your favourite tunes are carried in style, and vast-brimmed floppy straw hats keep off the sun. The store is as stylish as the clothes: it's fitted out in cool black stone and leather with just the occasional nod to hi-tech.   *malo.it*

Expensive   *Amex/MC/V*

Piazza di Spagna area

Via Borgognona 5
00187 Rome

06 679 1331
Mon-Sat 10-7:30

☆ **Mandarina Duck**

The Bolognese bag company has fans far and wide; hip young Japanese things in Rome make a beeline for the two-storey Via Due Macelli store (the biggest of the three) to stock up on witty ultra-functional techno-bags. Ranges of streamlined nylon and plastic luggage are just the thing for futuristic travel. Handbags and wallets range from classic leather to playfully colourful embroidered state-of-the-art synthetics. *mandarinaduck.com*

Moderate *Amex/MC/V*

Piazza di Spagna area

Via Due Macelli 59F/G
00187 Rome

06 678 6414
Mon 3:30-7:30, Tues-Sat 10-7:30

Via Cola di Rienzo area

Via Cola di Rienzo 270-272
00197 Rome

06 689 6491
Mon 3:30-7:30, Tues-Sat 10-2, 3:30-7:30

Largo Argentina area

Corso Vittorio Emanuele II 16
00186 Rome

06 678 9840
(opening hours as above)

Marco Polo

When Marco Paoletti first started going on shopping trips to India, his vendors nicknamed him Marco Polo. At first, he only brought clothes and jewellery back for his friends, but when he saw how they eagerly snapped everything up he decided to go into business. Clothes and jewellery come at you from every direction in this shop, which pays its dues to the decade of peace and love. As well as the predictable tie-dye T-shirts, floaty skirts and ethnic jewellery, there are patchwork velvet bags, thick wool scarves with pockets at both ends, dinky suede and leather money pouches and hand-embroidered Burmese silk scarves. The jewellery includes silver bangles, necklaces and beads as well as body piercing items for the more adventurous.

Affordable *Amex/MC/V*

Campo de' Fiori area

Via dei Chiavari 31
00186 Rome

06 687 7653
Mon-Sat 11-8

Mariella Burani

Mariella Burani is the creative director of the label that bears her name. It's part of the ever-expanding Mariella Burani Group, begun in 1960 by her husband Walter as a childrenswear company in the heartland of Italy's garment manufacturing belt near the northern city of Reggio Emilia. The brand has found its niche providing for ladies-who-lunch who like to stay ahead of the herd. Burani's clever pieces with a twist include eveningwear in sophisticated floral patterns finished with fabric flecked with metal. The minimalist white store on this lovely street in the heart of shopping land also stocks the group's Amuleti line for a younger clientele, with elegantly casual wide-knit jerseys, asymmetrical floral tops and lovely summer dresses. Then there's the Le Donne line for women with more generously cut figures, and a full range of accessories.   *mariellaburani.it*

Expensive   *Amex/MC/V*

Piazza di Spagna area

Via Bocca di Leone 28   **06 679 0630**
00187 Rome   Mon 3:30-7:30, Tues-Sat 10:30-7:30

Marina Rinaldi   🧍

You're a MaxMara fan but can't fit into all their clothes? Help is at hand in the guise of Marina Rinaldi, the plus-size branch of the elegant label we know and love. The Largo Goldoni store is the slightly more spacious of the two, with two simply furnished floors of goodies for curvier fashionistas. You'll find classic coats for winter, chic trousers, dresses and jackets and a good selection of eveningwear in the high-quality fabrics and finishing we have come to expect from the MaxMara group. Proof that you don't have to be Size 10 to look like you've stepped out of the pages of a fashion mag.

Moderate   *Amex/MC/V*

Piazza di Spagna area

Largo Goldoni 43   **06 692 00487**
00187 Rome   Mon-Sat 10-7, Sun 10-2, 3-7

Via Borgognona 6   **06 691 90753**
00187 Rome   (opening hours as above)

☆ Marisa Padovan   🧍

Signora Padovan has been providing Roman women with their beachwear for 35 years. Her elegant bikinis in vibrant reds, canary yellows and classic black and white come hot off the sewing machine in the workshop above her shop which is on a quiet street between Piazza di Spagna and Via del Corso. Showgirls, aristocrats and tourists alike lap up Marisa's demure white broderie anglaise bikinis and swimsuits. Her pleated bikinis in chilli-pepper red are particularly flattering for the more well-endowed shopper. Marisa's daughter Flavia has also got in on the act and designs a younger and less expensive range. The smallish store is a real Aladdin's cave with cupboards and drawers full of silk kimonos, brightly coloured sarongs, cashmere sweaters and swimwear of every type imaginable—from Lycra to embroidered to very elegant bikinis decorated with three cameos dangling from the cleavage.

Expensive   *Amex/MC/V*

Piazza di Spagna area

Via delle Carrozze 81-82   **06 679 3946**
00187 Rome   Mon 3-7, Tues-Sat 10-7

Marlboro Classics

You may think there's no point in heading to the boutique of this macho, all-American label while in Rome—but come here anyway to see how the Italians do fashion, cowboy style. Designed and manufactured by Marzotto, the venerable textile house who bought the licence from Philip Morris, the cargo pants, shirts, sweaters and jeans sold at this rustic-style store all have a rugged, masculine feel. Although most of these clothes would look perfectly at home in a corral, closer inspection reveals European finesse in the cut and finishing. Marlboro Classics coats and jackets are ideal for adventurous types who can't stay away from the great outdoors, and urban cowboys will also find it's worth dropping in for pseudo-country styles like a full-length leather outback coat priced at around 800 euros. There is a small range of womenswear—mostly jeans and shirts—for any budding cowgirls out there.

Moderate *Amex/MC/V*

Campo de' Fiori area

Via dei Giubbonari 61 **06 686 4062**
00186 Rome Mon 3:30-8, Tues-Sat 9:30-1:30, 3:30-8

Marni

Consuelo Castiglioni has been producing innovative Italian design since 1994 and the long-awaited Rome store opened in October 2004. Designed by hip London architectural studio Sybarite, who have stamped their mark on Marni's stores worldwide, curvy wood and steel interiors show off the feminine and colourful styles and natural textures of Castiglioni's elegant take on boho hippy chic. Leather thong sandals are adorned with what look like large chunky sugared almonds, hessian bags are embroidered with flowers, and petal-shaped steel stools illustrate the mix of organic and modern. There's also a small selection of menswear for the studiedly dishevelled, and some childrenswear, including summer dresses for flower fairies. *marni.com*

Expensive *Amex/MC/V*

Piazza di Spagna area

Via Bocca di Leone 8 **06 678 6320**
00187 Rome Mon-Sat 10-7.30

Max & Co

This roomy store, down the road from its big sister, hosts MaxMara's younger and more affordable line. It has something of an art gallery feel to it with its spaciousness and unobtrusive cream decor, although it's saved from dullness by the flirty red velvet curtains in the changing-rooms. Teenagers and twenty-somethings can let themselves loose on cute T-shirts and tops and floaty feminine dresses, or well-cut denim and leather jackets which can toughen up any look. An office line is also available in the form of fitted suits and shirts—all to be had without breaking the bank.

Moderate *Amex/MC/V*

Piazza di Spagna
Via dei Condotti 46-46/A   **06 678 7946**
00187 Rome   Mon-Sat 10-7:30, Sun 11-2, 3-7

MaxMara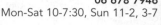

The sprawling MaxMara boutique stretches more or less halfway up Via dei Condotti and feels as if it will never end. But to help you avoid confusion and fatigue, it is very thoughtfully divided into sections, with much-needed sofas into which grateful clients frequently sink. The elegant label has become a lifeline for chic yet practical women who want clothes that fit, don't squeeze and are easy on the eye. The main line opts for traditional cuts and colours but there are other ranges, such as the younger and trendier Sportmax and the casual Weekend collection, to suit other moments in a busy woman's life. Somewhere in the midst of the MaxMara maze you'll stumble across Pianoforte, the eveningwear collection with its long and medium-length dresses in satins and silks that skim the body and make any woman look elegant, even if she has an extra lump or two. A small corner of the store is exclusively reserved for MaxMara hosiery: tights and stockings of every possible colour and design, and even brightly coloured jacquard socks.

Expensive   *Amex/MC/V*

Piazza di Spagna area
Via dei Condotti 19   **06 699 22104**
00187 Rome   Mon-Sat 10-7:30, Sun 11-7

Via Frattina 28   **06 679 3638**
00187 Rome   (opening hours as above)

Via Nazionale area
Via Nazionale 28-31   **06 488 5870**
00184 Rome   (opening hours as above)

Missoni

Once upon a time Ottavio, a tracksuit maker from Dalmatia, met Rosita, a bedding heiress from Varese. They fell in love and bought a few knitting machines (yes, a fairytale without spinning wheels). Soon afterwards they started producing for various companies and, amazingly, they've now been in the business for more than 50 years. Close your eyes as you enter Missoni's Piazza di Spagna store, lest the rip-roaring rainbow of colours and jagged patterns should make you feel dizzy. Daughter Angela has now taken over the design team and has brought zigzag patterns and interwoven silver threads out of the Sixties and into the third millennium. Accordingly, apart from the much-loved knits, Missoni now does sexy bikinis, casual wide-legged trousers, miniskirts, a huge range of ties for men and a selection of wedged, stiletto and flat shoes.   *missoni.com*

Luxury   *Amex/MC/V*

Piazza di Spagna area
Piazza di Spagna 78   **06 679 2555**
00187 Rome   Mon 3-7:30, Tues-Sat 10-7:30

Miss Sixty

If you want to be noticed and have a penchant for sequinned Oliver Twist hats, plastic kitten-heeled thong-toed sandals, ripped jeans, chained T-shirts and burnt orange fake-fur jackets, Miss Sixty is the place for you. A large range of fabrics and vibrant designs by this Abruzzo-based firm means you won't be confronted with your fashion clone at parties. Like the clothing, the Via del Corso branch has a Sixties-inspired aesthetic: the white faux-leather chairs beside glass-topped tables on optical-print rugs make you feel as though you've just walked onto an *Austin Powers* set. At the entrance to the Via del Corso store, a chrome wall with protruding bubble display cases shows the latest lines in shoes and bags—just so you know what's new since the last time you popped by. *misssixty.com*

Moderate   *Amex/MC/V*

Piazza di Spagna area

Via del Corso 510   **06 321 9374**
00186 Rome   Mon-Sat 10-8, Sun 3-8

Via Cola di Rienzo area

Via Cola di Rienzo 235   **06 320 0918**
00192 Rome   Daily 10:30-8

Modi di Campagna

Upper-crust Italians sometimes like to shrug off their Armani jackets and step into something a little more British. Tuscan store Modi di Campagna (Country Fashions) is tucked down a side street just off the Parliament Square and its entrance is usually obscured by a mass of parked mopeds. It has the feel of an olde-worlde elegant emporium with its oak display cases containing hunting horns, animal brooches, silver dog whistles and corks topped with silver birds of prey. The tiled floor and high-beamed ceiling (peeling and decorated with small flowers) are both from an age gone by. In the spacious back rooms you can browse through their range of Maremmani Spanish hunting boots, cord and tweed trousers and ties decorated with hunting themes. As you would expect there are waterproof Barbour jackets, cord jackets with leather elbow patches and Arfango bags. Oak tables display piles of cashmere, mohair and angora sweaters. Other brands include Grisalis, Filson, Husky, La Martina (Argentinian polo shirts) and Car Shoes. Women who hunt are catered for in much the same way as men—although if you're lucky you might find a fox fur-trimmed silk jacket to add a bit of glamour to the thrill of the chase.   *modidicampagna.it*

Expensive to luxury   *Amex/MC/V*

Piazza Navona area

Via dei Prefetti 42-44   **06 688 02631**
00186 Rome   Mon 3:30-7:30, Tues-Fri 10-1:30
                                     3:30-7:30, Sat 10-7:30

☆ **Molly Bloom** ♀

A favourite with fashion purists, this tiny store has shoes from Emma Hope, Stephen and a large selection of colourful Campers. Silk dresses and summery tops come from Atika and the small Italian label Rosso e Lavanda. Bolognese designer Lavinia Turra's elegant palazzo pants are just the thing for that lady-of-leisure look; Paris-based Ekjo from Japan has a nice mix of Europe and the Orient; and Accostages have some hip futuristic takes on the classic floaty summer dress. If you persuade them to let you go upstairs to their slightly disorganised stock room, you may find some real treasures.

Expensive to luxury   *Amex/MC/V*

Campo de' Fiori area

Via dei Giubbonari 27   **06 686 9362**
00186 Rome   Mon-Sat 10-8

Moschino ♂♀

As you walk into Moschino on Via Borgognona, an ice queen greets you. No, we don't mean a frosty sales assistant (staff are friendly and helpful, by the way) but a transparent lady seemingly sculpted from ice (but actually plastic). She's naked on top—but for a Moschino safety pin and hook-and-eye jacket—and wearing a ballgown skirt created from ice cubes on the bottom. She also has a crown on her head. Both upstairs and down, the tale of the Emperor's New Clothes is written on the wall in English and Italian. Go up the grand staircase in the centre of the store and marvel at the enormous chandeliers on the second floor. One is created by precariously hanging circle after circle of Cinderella-style glass slippers; the other uses over-sized light bulbs. You get the picture: Moschino gives us a mixture of fairytale with a dash of humour. On the ground floor, have fun with frocks splattered with daisy and heart prints and flower appliqués, or classy strapless little black dresses with tape measures for belts. Take a look at the Cheap & Chic line (chic, definitely, but cheap?) or the large display case of watches. Upstairs, get down to the more serious business of pinstriped suits and leather jackets with colourful Smartie-like buttons attached. You'll find a liberal sprinkling of press studs, hook-and-eyes and paper clips on quite a few of the things you look at.   *moschino.it*

Luxury   *Amex/MC/V*

Piazza di Spagna area

Via Borgognona 32/A   **06 678 1144**
00187 Rome   Mon 12-8, Tues-Sat 9:30-8, Sun 11-8

Moschino Jeans ♂♀♂

Surprisingly, considering its name, this store isn't full to bursting with denim. However, it is full of delightfully quirky Moschino at friendlier prices and with a more casual edge. As expected, the clothes are dynamically coloured and black is more or less banished. On the ground floor there's a good selection of Moschino perfumes and accessories—including watches, key-rings and sunglasses. The third floor, which has an enormous peace sign sculpted on the wall, is home to the kids department. It's a playful place in black, white and candy red. *moschino.it*

Expensive *Amex/MC/V*

Piazza di Spagna area

Via Belsiana 57 **06 692 00415**
00187 Rome Mon 12-8, Tues-Sat 9:30-8
Sun 11-7:30

Myriam B

Designer Myriam B set up in a tiny shop just off the market square of the lively San Lorenzo district in 2003. Like her neighbour, bag maker Claudio Sanò, she prides herself on her craftsmanship and the individuality of her products. She uses a variety of materials, some of which have been recycled from derelict factories such as lengths of machine chain, to create belts and other accessories. There is a selection of chunky jewellery which includes huge silver-plated copper pendants, earrings and large bracelets. She also creates bags—either tiny and beaded or enormous, organza and triangular—plus some items of clothing. *myriamb.com*

Affordable *Amex/MC/V*

San Lorenzo area

Via dei Volsci 75 **06 443 61305**
00185 Rome Mon 5-8, Tues-Sat 11-1, 5-8

☆ Nia

Erminia Ferrante, Nia to her pals, roped in a tailor to start producing her designs at home in the early Seventies—which explains her taste for the sartorial. Most pieces have a tailored feel, and include impeccable cashmere jackets by Neapolitan tailors Kiton and cashmere and silk coats by Antonio Fusco. Her taste also extends to the exotic—like the silk jackets from various parts of India. Nia's husband designed the shop along simple but elegant lines and there's a garden out back where customers are served with drinks on Saturdays in the summer.

Expensive to luxury *Amex/MC/V*

Piazza di Spagna area

Via Vittoria 48 **06 679 5198**
00187 Rome Mon 3-7, Tues-Fri 10-2, 3-7, Sat 10-7

☆ Nia & Co

This smaller shop just across the street from its big sister Nia concentrates on high-end casuals with a fresh twist. The store is run by Nia's son, Federico, and he offers sporty-chic in the form of Nike Trend sneakers, sweat pants and tops. Opt for Choose Juicy if you're looking for sportiness with a feminine and playful edge. His daywear includes Vanessa Bruno, Irma Bingham's checked trousers and those Alberto

Aspesi nylon windbreakers which are practically a uniform in Rome. He also stocks Un Jour un Sac bags and Hervé Chapelier's super-practical two-colour polyamide and nylon handbags which are so in demand that they need to be constantly re-ordered.

Moderate to expensive   *Amex/MC/V*

Via Vittoria 30-31   **06 322 7421**
00187 Rome   Mon 3-7, Tues-Fri 10-2, 3-7
                                  Sat 10-2, 2:30-7

Nicol Caramel

Milanese designer Nicoletta Neri launched herself on an unsuspecting maternity market in 1976 with the aim of providing prêt-à-porter for pregnant women. You're unlikely to find tent dresses in this small store; instead, she provides specific fitted sizes, which adopt elasticated panels and clever tailoring to accommodate your ever-growing bump. Her fabulous and endlessly stretchy wide-legged trousers can also be worn after the birth. The range not only features eveningwear, sportswear and fun casualwear—like the fringed denim three-quarter length trousers—but also includes pinstriped suits, skirts and waistcoats for those working well into their pregancy. In the back there are racks of trousers of varying lengths and styles, plus fitted jackets which you can mix and match.   *nicolcaramel.it*

Moderate   *Amex/MC/V*

Piazza di Spagna area

Via di Ripetta 261   **06 361 2059**
00187 Rome   Mon 3:30-7:30, Tues-Sat 9-1, 3:30-7:30

☆ Nuyorica

This striking red-white-and-black shop is the first port of call for shoe shoppers whenever there's a you're-no-one-if-you're-not-invited event in town. The selection, by owners Cristiano Giovangnoli and Emanuele Frumenti, is impeccable, and this is the only place in Rome where you're likely to find shoes by Marc Jacobs, Michel Vivien, and Rodolphe Menudier sitting side-by-side. It's no wonder that this temple to the shoe is a favourite with Italian celebs and the occasional visiting Hollywood star (including Cameron Diaz, well known for her footwear addiction). But you don't need to be a movie queen to wind up burning the plastic on merchandise including flat sandals from Lanvin for those *Ben Hur* days and spangly sequins or colourful summery block-heeled espadrilles from Marc Jacobs. And it's not all shoes. Cristiano and Emanuele are big fans of Chloé and Balenciaga and you can kit yourself out from dresses through swimwear to bags (last year's must haves from Chloé and Balenciaga, the Paddington and the Motorcycle, sold out fast).   *nuyorica.it*

Expensive   *Amex/MC/V*

Campo de' Fiori area

Piazza Pollarola 36-37   **06 688 91243**
00186 Rome   Mon 12-7:30 Tues-Sat 10:30-2, 3-7:30

Omero & Cecilia—Vestiti Vecchi

Omero and Cecilia got married, got a couple of dogs and set up a vintage shop. It sounds like a hippy Sixties song and much of the stock of this store is indeed inspired by the Flower Child era—although there is a great deal more to it than that. In the back there are rails of the ruggedly cool Dainese biker jackets and a satisfactorily large collection of Converse All-Stars. In the front you could stumble on anything from that vintage staple, the Burberry trench coat, to military and tweed jackets, Sixties Italian dresses, Seventies velvet coats and outrageous styles from the Eighties. Boot and shoe fetishists will be in heaven: Pucci, Sergio Rossi, Pollini, Valentino—all your wildest fantasies will be realised here.

Affordable   *MC/V*

Piazza Navona area

Via del Governo Vecchio 110   **06 683 3506**
00186 Rome   Mon-Sat 10-8

☆ Only Hearts

If you fancy yourself as a bit of a *Wuthering Heights* or DH Lawrence heroine you should go and frolic among the rails at innerwear-as-outerwear pioneers Only Hearts. Floaty skirts, trousers and sheer tops in molten pinks, creams, earthy greens and browns are decorated with lace, tiny rosebuds and delicate embroidered designs. Feminine all-in-ones, underwear and swimwear are also available. Designer Helena Stuart started out in Manhattan 25 years ago. She grew and grew until stars such as Cameron Diaz, Halle Berry and Madonna came flocking to her door for a touch of spiced-up Victorian romance. Non-US visitors take note: these are the only two branches outside the USA. While the Via Vittoria store is larger and busier, those who wish to browse might find it worth heading to the slightly out-of-the-way but quieter Piazza della Chiesa Nuova store opposite one of Rome's most dramatic churches. But you'll find personal and friendly service at both.   *onlyhearts.com*

Moderate to expensive   *Amex/MC/V*

Piazza di Spagna area

Via Vittoria 76/76A   **06 679 3446**
00187 Rome   Sun-Mon 12-8, Tues-Sat 10-8

Piazza Navona area

Piazza della Chiesa Nuova 21   **06 686 4647**
00186 Rome   (opening hours as above)

Onyx

Italian teenagers swarm here in their hordes to snap up flirty but ultimately innocent style; skimpy T-shirts are emblazoned with logos, and hipster jeans and denim minis are (of course) distressed. The stores reverberate to pounding music and banks of TV screens project swirls and psychedelic patterns. Shoes and accessories sit alongside trendy school bags and exercise books with the ubiquitous Onyx logo, a reminder that this place is off-limits for anyone out of school. If you need any help from the staff, be prepared to wait: most of them seem to think that their main purpose in life is to sit around and chat to their friends. Having to actually serve a client can come as a bit of a shock. *onyx.it*

Affordable   *Amex/MC/V*

Piazza di Spagna area

Via del Corso 132   **06 699 321**
00187 Rome   Mon-Sat 10-8

Cola di Rienzo area

Via Cola di Rienzo   **06 360 06073**
00192 Rome   (opening hours as above)

Pandemonium

Thinking of a spot of casual clubbing? This could be the place to pick up your gear. Teenagers and trend-obsessed thirty-somethings head into these Sixties and Seventies-style interiors for upscale street and clubwear from some of the edgier brands. Cast your eye over the transparent plastic shelving units for retro sportswear and funky feminine dresses, skirts and tops by Italian label Nolita. Jeans are by Bruce and Le Jean de Marithé at François Girbaud, T-shirts are by Rare and D&G (staples of Italian clubbers). Trainers are from Nike, and there are Birkenstocks for when your feet can take no more shopping or dancing.

Moderate   *Amex/MC/V*

Campo de' Fiori area

Via dei Giubbonari 104   **06 686 8061**
00186 Rome   Mon 4-8, Tues-Sat 10-8

Parioli area

Piazza Euclide 7-8   **06 807 7538**
00197 Rome   (opening hours as above)

Passion

Nip down a quiet street off Piazza di Spagna to this small store on a corner for clothes that are burning with passion. The two display windows always show something lacy, tight and with a plunging neckline that catches your eye as you walk past. Rails are packed (so packed that you can't really see anything unless you dive in there with both hands and drag something out to get a good look at it) with satin microdresses, sequin-covered long evening dresses, Paola Frani's flatteringly cut evening trousers, Helene Zoubedia's crepe and lace see-through dresses and pleated gym-style skirts which would look great on a 16-year-old Britney Spears lookalike. In addition there's Plein Sud, Geen Morgan (by Mila Schön's daughter), Amazone and shoes by Les Tropeziennes and Giuseppe Zanotti. Kinky knee and thigh-high leather boots are lined up against the wall for inspection in the winter. Chunky belts by Claudio Orciani with enormous metal buckles help you finish off any outfit with a flourish.

Moderate to expensive   *Amex/MC/V*

Piazza di Spagna area
Via delle Carrozze 39   **06 678 1527**
00187 Rome   Mon 3:30-7:30, Tues-Sat 10-1:30
                                                               3:30-7:30

Patrizia Pepe   🧍‍♀️

Patrizia Pepe offers you feminity with a twist. Chiffon slip
dresses and sexy microfibre tops are toughened up with
leather jackets and stilettos with wide ankle straps. Denim
minis are sequined and hot pants have orange stitching. An
olive tree adds a cool peaceful tone to this elegantly minimalist boutique just a stone's throw from the chaos of Piazza
di Spagna. Lines are constantly changing, so if you spot the
dress of your dreams snap it up.   *patriziapepe.com*

Moderate   *Amex/MC/V*

Piazza di Spagna area

Via Frattina 1   **06 678 4698**
00186 Rome   Mon-Sat 10-8, Sun 10:30-8

☆ People   🧍

Retro-chic chicks dig this cute little shop which pays homage to the glorious Sixties and Seventies. The leopardprint
fur-covered speakers, oval mirrors and multicoloured beaded curtain in the window are an ode to the Beatles' era.
Twenty-something Roman designers Germana Panunzi and
Sara Sorge use original fabrics from the Sixties and
Seventies to create optical-print miniskirts, tennis-style
dresses, bright hipsters and satin knee-length trousers.
They also do their own range of belts and necklaces and
there's a selection of large-lensed Jackie O and Starsky and
Hutch-style sunglasses.

Affordable   *MC/V*

Campo de' Fiori area

Piazza Teatro di Pompeo 4/A   **06 687 4040**
00186 Rome   Mon 3:30-8, Tues-Sat 10:30-2, 3:30-8

Petit Bateau   🧍‍♀️🧍

It might look like any other kids' shop, but savvy models and
even the occasional film star have been known to shop at
the Rome outpost of this French label which stocks clothing
for children from 0-8 and underwear and nightwear up to
16. As in most upmarket kids' stores in Rome, the look is
more classic and wholesome than trend-setting. Given the
French provenance, of course, there are blue-and-white
striped T-shirts as well as denim dungarees, shorts and plimsolls, and little sundresses and sandals for girls. It's a good
stop if you're looking for pint-pot beachwear: swimming
costumes, little bikinis, trunks and sunhats abound. There's a
range of T-shirts for mummies, too.   *petit-bateau.com*

Moderate to expensive   *Amex/MC/V*

Piazza di Spagna area

Via della Croce 45   **06 692 02154**
00187 Rome   Mon 1-7:30, Tues-Sat 10-7:30

Pantheon area

Via Campo Marzio 10/B   **06 679 2348**
00186 Rome   Mon 3:30-7:30, Tues-Sat 9:30-7:30

Via Cola di Rienzo area

Via Cola di Rienzo 311   **06 397 22928**
00192 Rome   Mon 3:30-7:30, Tues-Sat 9:30-7:30

Piccadilly   †

Run by the Bucci family since 1932, Piccadilly is yet another of those fabulously old-fashioned shops for children with which Rome is so well endowed. We're talking children's clothes (aged 0-10) of the highest quality. There are smocks with cache-coeur sweaters, blazers with velvet collars, tweed coats—in fact anything which would have looked good on little Prince Charles or Princess Anne circa 1955. Slightly off the beaten shoppers' track (ie at the top of the Spanish steps rather than the bottom) Piccadilly is worth a visit for its olde-worlde charm and discreet and personal service. Naturally, they also do made-to-measure baptism and first communion robes. Clients have included Anthony Quinn.

Moderate to expensive   *Amex/MC/V*

Piazza di Spagna area

Via Sistina 92   **06 679 3697**
00187 Rome   Mon-Sat 9:30-1, 3:30-7

Pinko   ♀

This northern Italian label has been putting catwalk style on the smarter end of the high street since the late Eighties, and it's always worth popping by to see if something suits your current fashion mood. The rapid turnover keeps everything seriously fresh, and the prices won't break the bank. Recent hits include sequined vest tops, a gold blouse for those occasions when you don't want to blend in, and patched clam-digger jeans. A staple of most collections are the elegantly distressed jeans which have been obligatory in every girl-about-town's wardrobe for as long as we can remember. If you're looking for something for a discerningly hip young lady back home pick up one of the shoulder bags embroidered 'Pinko Bag'—no Roman ragazza would be without hers.   *pinko.it*

Moderate   *Amex/MC/V*

Piazza di Spagna area

Via Due Macelli 92   **06 692 02091**
00187 Rome   Daily 10-7:30

Campo de' Fiori area

Via dei Giubbonari 76-77   **06 683 09446**
00186 Rome   Mon-Sat 10-8, Sun 12-8

Pantheon area

Via della Scrofa 24   **06 683 3136**
00186 Rome   (opening hours as above)

Via Cola di Rienzo area

Via Cola di Rienzo 121-125   **06 321 5256**
00192 Rome   Daily 10-8

Piquadro

This Bologna-based briefcase firm started in 1987, but in the last couple of years has begun a campaign to move to the head of the market. Smart briefcases and bags for portable computers are the main products: there are leather or leather/microfibre combinations in a variety of colours, from classic black and browns to the blue square range with sky-coloured edging to set off leather with the aged look. Travellers can also snap up stylish cabin bags, and those who need to get their lives in order will find pen cases, personal organisers and key-rings. The main boutique is on Via Frattina and there's a smaller (but very well stocked) store in the new Galleria Colonna, both decked out in the cutting-edge design that characterises Piquadro stores everywhere. *piquadro.com*

Moderate *Amex/MC/V*

Piazza di Spagna area

Galleria Colonna (Alberto Sordi)　　　**06 679 4346**
00187 Rome　　　　Mon 2-8, Tues-Sat 10-8, Sun 12-8

Via Frattina 125　　　　　　　　　　**06 679 2631**
00187 Rome　　　　　Mon 3:30-7:30, Tues-Sat 10-7:30

Planet Store

Flexi-bodied skater whiz-kids come here to get the look that goes with their territory—trying to ignore the fact that they'll be zapping past baroque palazzi and churches, rather than down an LA street. Baggy trousers and hooded sweatshirts by American roadwork clothing label Carhartt may not be particularly aerodynamic if you want to go flying through the air 10 feet above your skateboard. But they look pretty cool if you want to impress the chicks with your street cred. This minimalist grey store—the only concessions to colour are two enormous camouflage beanbags—also stocks Paul Frank and a whole range of skate accessories: boards, lighters, skull-and-crossbones water bottles, belts with Carhartt boldly written in studs, beach towels and parkas. To the right, there's the women's section which is usually less busy. Even if the skater scene isn't your thing, check out the tight Paul Frank T-shirts—among those increasingly hard-to-find models which aren't too short if you happen to be over 25.

Affordable to moderate *Amex/MC/V*

Campo de' Fiori area

Via dei Baullari 132　　　　　　　　**06 688 01396**
00186 Rome　　　　　　　Mon 4-8, Tues-Fri 10-1, 4-8
　　　　　　　　　　　　　　　　　Sat 10-1, 3:30-8

Via delle Convertite 21　　　　　　**06 699 24970**
00187 Rome　　　　　　　(opening hours as above)

Pollini

As you wander around Rome, you can't help noticing how many people look at your feet. It's incredible how, for many

Italians, badly fashioned footwear can ruin your whole outfit. Cesena-based Pollini can help you avoid impertinent glares from style-conscious Romans with their lines of amazingly well-crafted shoes. They only use top-notch leather, the seams are impeccable and you'll be wanting to put your feet up on many a table top just so you can show off their fine soles. And there's more. Their diamanté-encrusted strappy stilettos come with a matching bag. There's a line of fabric and leather shoulder bags, wallets and holdalls, all speckled with a simple 'P' logo—an original alternative to Vuitton. The firm has recently launched a limited clothes line featuring suede zip-up waistcoats, leather skirts and classic twill double-breasted jackets with matching trousers. The store is a U-shaped gallery with floor-to-ceiling mirrors and has two entrances on the same street. *pollini.com*

Expensive   *Amex/MC/V*

Piazza di Spagna area

Via Frattina 22-24   **06 679 8360**
00187 Rome   Mon 3:30-7:30, Tues-Sat 10-7:30

Prada ♀

Miuccia Prada reinvents contemporary cool season after season and is worshipped by everyone from stately signoras to chic chicks—who can forget the declarations of devotion to Ms Prada that Carrie used to dish out in *Sex and the City*? In what must be one of the best locations in the capital, Prada perches regally at the top of Via dei Condotti, with its second floor enjoying a spectacular view of the Spanish Steps (there's a huge oval bench in case you want to sit down and admire the scenery). Downstairs you'll find the unmistakable bags and sunglasses, while upstairs there's room after room of the ever-popular prints, ready-to-wear, cosmetics, stylish shoes and sublime chiffon lingerie. *prada.com*

Luxury   *Amex/MC/V*

Piazza di Spagna area

Via dei Condotti 92   **06 679 0897**
00187 Rome   Mon-Sat 10-7:30, Sun 10-7

Prada ♂

You'll find Prada Uomo next door to the ever-trendy Café Greco on Via dei Condotti—a good place to pump yourself full of coffee before venturing out onto the heaving street outside. However, you won't need a caffeine fix to visit Prada Uomo; for most shoppers, entering this store creates its own natural high. Inside this large subdued Prada-grey space you'll find everything from nylon travel bags to sharply cut shirts and predatory crocodile-skin shoes. Then, of course, there's the essential line of sober blue, beige and grey suits in a large room at the back, alongside the who-would-I-be-without-them sunglasses. You'll also find toys for the boys, like a tiny silver tea flask in a case, a fold-away set of mini dominoes and Prada-endorsed Shanghai sticks (all of which would make excellent gifts). A glance at the 12-piece portable spanner set brings on instant fantasies about a Prada-clad gent emerging from under a car bonnet covered from head to foot in sticky black oil.   *prada.com*

Luxury   *Amex/MC/V*

Piazza di Spagna area

Via dei Condotti 90   **06 679 0897**
00187 Rome   Mon 10-7:30, Sun 10-7

Prada Sport
As you'd expect, clothes at Rome's first Prada Sport boutique are so slickly styled that they don't look like anything you've ever worn to take part in sport. Techno fabrics, functional yet flattering cuts and the signature red tags are constant elements in these collections. From nylon down jackets with fur-trimmed hoods, to work pants, thick denim miniskirts, fleece tops and stretchy T-shirts, these garments are so cool that it would be a crime to wear them merely to work up a sweat. The store stretches across five rooms from the chic Via del Babuino to the celebrated artists' street of Via Margutta (immortalised in *Roman Holiday*). Like the service, the decor is low-key and discreet.   *prada.com*

Luxury   *Amex/MC/V*

Piazza di Spagna area

Via del Babuino 91   **06 360 04884**
00187 Rome   Mon-Sat 10-7:30, Sun 10-7

Prenatal
Although its trademark bright green sign might make you think Benetton, French chain Prenatal is worth a whirl if you're an expectant mother looking for maternity wear or have a child aged 0-11. The store winds from room to room, taking you on a journey past cute denim shorts, T-shirts depicting nursery rhymes, well-cut summer dresses, pyjamas, plastic nappy swimpants, underwear, thick padded jackets…and just about every other item of clothing your child might ever want or need. There is also a vast range of children's accessories: cribs, playpens, educative books, car seats, buggies and even mini-cams to keep an eye on sleeping newborns.   *prenatal.it*

Affordable   *Amex/MC/V*

Piazza di Spagna area

Via della Croce 50/A   **06 679 7181**
00187 Rome   Mon 11-7:30, Tues-Sat 10-7:30

Prototype
If you want a taste of street chic with all the right names, look no further. Located on the increasingly hip Via dei Giubbonari, Prototype attracts hordes of teens and twenty-somethings on the weekend. You can browse through rails full of Levi's and other jeans with elasticated lateral stripes. Or work your way along a table that's almost the length of the shop to pick out T-shirts and tops. Try on a baggy graf-

fiti'd E-Play turtleneck, or perhaps something more daring from the top end jeans line We Are Replay. Alternatively, go for a top-to-toe look from Fornarina, or one of their baby-pink fitted hooded zip tops if you want something practical but cute. There are also the perennial Converse All-Star sneakers as well as the latest Pumas. Guys get a slightly more subdued line with jeans, cargo pants and sweatshirts. The recently opened kids store next door has lovely little All-Stars, Diesel jeans and Nolita for girls, Rare for boys. From 3 months to 14 years.

Affordable to moderate   Amex/MC/V

Campo de' Fiori area

Via dei Giubbonari 50   **06 683 00330**
00186 Rome   Mon 3:30-8, Tues-Sat 10-8, Sun 4-8

Via dei Giubbonari 51   **06 689 2818**
00186 Rome   Mon 3:30-8, Tues-Sat 10-8, Sun 2-8

Pulp   ♀♀

Vintage fans will enjoy this treasure trove with an Italian slant in the hip Monti area. Recently revamped, pink and red Sixties-style swirls and lava lamps set the scene. Root through the racks of charity shop-style oddments to get to the real finds. The thrill of the chase builds as you check out Seventies flowery shirts, gypsy skirts, cord jackets and Eighties classics such as vast coloured hoop earrings (all of which have their fascination) before finally laying your hot little hands on that fabulous Fifties YSL purse.

Affordable   MC/V

Via Nazionale area

Via del Boschetto 140   **06 485 511**
00184 Rome   Mon 4-8, Tues-Sat 10-1, 4-8

Puma Concept Store   ♂♀♂

Whenever you decide to visit this red and white store, it's likely to be teeming with people. Puma sponsors Italy's national football team as well as Lazio, Rome's second team, which could be why the brand enjoys such a large following here. On the ground floor the adult range includes all manner of sportswear as well as the odd football. There's a small children's section upstairs, for 0-14. Assistants are suitably young and energetic, and will sprint off to fetch you pair after pair of shoes to try on as you relax on the faux leather recliners.   puma.com

Moderate   Amex/MC/V

Piazza di Spagna area

Via del Corso 404   **06 688 08205**
00186 Rome   Daily 10-8

☆ Pure   ♂

If your toddler's first words were 'Dolce & Gabbana' they'll just love it here. Walking into Pure is like entering some enormous children's funhouse. It's decorated with apple-green walls, bright orange faux leather padded tables, a see-through lift and floor-to-ceiling murals depicting trendy children having fun. The architects are Rome-based Lazzerini & Pickering—who also did the Fendi store. There's not that much downstairs but upstairs is like a maze. As they wander from room to room, label-conscious kids aged 0-16 can drool over collections by D&G, Roberto Cavalli, Tommy Hilfiger, Ralph Lauren and Pinko Pallino. When it all gets too much, they can settle down in front of one of the two PlayStations upstairs—while their parents go down to settle the (hefty) bill. *puresermoneta.it*

Expensive to luxury   *Amex/MC/V*

Piazza di Spagna area

Via Frattina 111   **06 679 4555**
00187 Rome   Mon 1-7:30, Tues-Sun 10-7:30

René Caovilla

If you missed his bigger store in Milan, drop by Caovilla's second Italian boutique on the ultra chic Via Borgognona. This is no ordinary shoe-shop but the jewel case we have come to expect from the top Venetian shoemaker. After learning his trade from his father, Caovilla was taken under the wing of Valentino Garavani. He soon went from strength to strength via Dior and Chanel before firmly establishing a family business—his wife is in charge of the accessories and his son and daughter deal with money and marketing. His extravagantly jewelled creations echo the gloriously exuberant spirit of Venetian carnival, and are shown off in a glorious mirrored setting complete with tapestries and palazzo furnishings all finished off with russet drapes and gilded display cases.

Luxury   *Amex/MC/V*

Piazza di Spagna area

Via Borgognona   **9/10 06 678 3879**
00187 Rome   Mon-Thurs 10-2, 3-7; Fri-Sat 10-7

Replay

Jeans of all shapes and sizes—ready-creased, ready-faded, some so distressed they're almost in tears—are the staple of this Italian group. There's also a great range of T-shirts, sweaters and jackets and (obligatory in this hipster era) a matching underwear line. As well as the classic Replay label there's the We're collection, launched in spring 2004, a trendier, clubbier set of clothes with some seriously cool T-shirts. Finish your outfit with cowboy boots and studded belts in the rodeo style that has proved so popular with the hip Tokyo crowd. The Salita De' Crescenzi store has the cute children's line.   *replay.it*

Affordable   *Amex/MC/V*

Pantheon area

Via della Rotonda 25   **06 683 3073**
00186 Rome   Mon 3:30-8, Tues-Sat 10-8

Salita De' Crescenzi 29   **06 686 4829**
00186 Rome   Mon 3:30-7:30, Tues-Sat 10-7:30

Piazza di Spagna area

Via Tomacelli 26 (W)   **06 682 10196**
00186 Rome   Mon 3-7:30, Tues-Sat 10-7:30

Via Tomacelli 96 (M)   **06 681 34901**
00186 Rome   (opening hours as above)

Roberto Cavalli

Just when we thought the Tarzan look was dead, Roberto Cavalli gave the world the jungle chic, which made women look like sexy beasts on heels. Exotic animal prints such as zebra and leopard are to be found on absolutely everything, from the miniskirts to the sofa they're sitting on. Other equally flashy looks include flowing gypsy skirts in loud colours and strappy sandals studded with multicoloured Swarovski crystals. But Cavalli is currently making an effort to turn the volume down a notch and has introduced some monochrome items, including glamorous evening dresses. Men get a look-in with (more) leopardprint slip-on shoes and deerskin cowboy-style jackets.   *robertocavalli.net*

Luxury   *Amex/MC/V*

Piazza di Spagna area

Via Borgognona 7/A   **06 693 80130**
00187 Rome   Mon 12:30-7:30, Tues-Sat 10-7:30

☆ Rubinacci

Mariano Rubinacci comes from a dynasty of Neapolitan tailors who made their name with jackets and shirts worn by kings cut with sleeves ample enough to move the arms freely—the 'Neapolitan jacket' was favoured by King Umberto and film director Vittorio de Sica. Suits, jackets, shirts and ties can be bought straight from the shop or made to order in the finest British fabrics. On the left as you walk in there's a vast selection of ties of every imaginable colour and pattern laid out in boxes. Go to the back and you'll see reams and reams of suit and shirt material just ready to be made up into a sharply cut outfit. Women can relax in Queen Anne chairs as they watch their men do a twirl in Signor Rubinacci's latest creation. *marianorubinacci.it*

Expensive   *Amex/MC/V*

Piazza di Spagna area

Via della Fontanella di Borghese 33   **06 688 92943**
00186 Rome   Mon 3:30-7:30, Tues-Sat 10-7:30

☆ SBU

Legend has it that 13th-generation Roman boys Cristiano and Patrizio Perfetti started out by taking suitcases full of their wares abroad to try and get people interested. Whatever they did, they must have done it right because today SBU (which stands unromantically for Strategic Business Unit) jeans grace the shelves of Harvey Nichols in London, Bergdorf Goodman in New York, Fred Segal in Los

Angeles and Isitan in Tokyo. And then there are the illustrious wearers of the jeans: Harrison Ford, Keanu Reeves, David Beckham, Britney Spears—need we go on? SBU buy their top-quality denim from Japan and finish the garments by hand in Italy. Their Rome shop, in a 15th-century palazzo, has the feel of a Wild West warehouse. Apart from shelves piled high with jeans, they also sell T-shirts—plain, printed and with the SBU logo—hooded sweat tops, fitted cashmere sweaters and unusual (for Rome) satin two-colour oriental blouson jackets decorated with embroidered tigers. Their bargain outlet, which is slightly away from the centre (try the 63 or 630 buses from Via del Tritone or the 86 and 92 from Termini) sells end-of-series and rejects at discounted prices.

Expensive   *Amex/MC/V*

Piazza Navona area

Via S. Pantaleo 68-69   **06 688 02547**
00186 Rome   Mon 3:30-7:30
                          Tues-Sat 10:30-1:30, 3:30-7:30

Salaria area

Via Chiana 73   **06 854 8575**
00198 Rome   Tues-Sat 10-12:45, 4-7:15

Salvatore Ferragamo

No nation in the world makes and wears shoes quite so well, scrutinises them on passers-by with quite such intensity or just plain adores them as much as the Italians do. In such a hothouse of shoe worship, is it surprising that small boys can grow up from humble beginnings in Naples and be propelled to Hollywood to become shoemaker to the stars? Legendary cobbler Salvatore Ferragamo was just such a boy, and from a small workshop created a worldwide empire whose clients included Marilyn Monroe, Audrey Hepburn and Greta Garbo. Ferragamo has two Rome outlets, just doors away from each other. The women's store includes the best-selling patent-leather Vara pumps with a grosgrain bow by Salvatore's daughter Fiamma, casual leather sneakers and ultra-feminine sandals. There is also a selection of ready-to-wear, featuring sombre cashmere coats, chiffon evening dresses and understated leather or quilted nylon jackets. Finally, these days the Ferragamo look also stretches to accessories, from a range of watches introduced in 2004 to sunglasses, scarves, and the bestselling Gancio Mediterraneo bag in white, lilac and beige. Upstairs, there are some unisex children's shoes and clothes, in conservative navy or bolder red.   *salvatoreferragamo.com*

Luxury   *Amex/MC/V*

Piazza di Spagna area

Via dei Condotti 73-74   **06 679 1565**
00187 Rome   Mon-Sat 10-7

Salvatore Ferragamo (men)

As you walk into this store, a grainy, eight-foot blow-up photograph provides a picture of a famous aristocratic Ferragamo male. It is Edward VIII, the King of England who behaved badly but dressed impeccably. Wallis Simpson, the divorcee for whom he abdicated the throne, also appears in the shot, and Ferragamo himself hovers in the background. In fact, various blow-up photos around this black and white store show you the parade of illustrious feet which have received the Ferragamo treatment. But in addition to the classic footwear styles, men can peruse the dazzling array of silk micro-patterned ties (one for every day of the year—or so it seems), stylish cufflinks and heavenly-soft baby-calf jackets. Watches are a fairly recent addition to the collection and there is also a selection of perfumes and sunglasses—and even silk teddy bears to match the ties. *salvatoreferragamo.com*

Luxury *Amex/MC/V*

Piazza di Spagna area

Via dei Condotti 66 **06 678 1130**
00187 Rome Mon 3-7, Tues-Sat 10-7

Santoni

From the heart of Italian shoe-making in the hills of the Marche, Andrea Santoni has won dedicated followers all over the world, and since October 2004 they have been flocking to the first dedicated Rome store. Grab one of the orange velvet chairs and browse the wares on display. Handmade classic men's styles are the big sellers. For the brave there are some more outlandish designs—think two-tone crocodile skin brogues with tassels—which apparently go down a storm at the Moscow store. There are also casual shoes for both men and women, including old-school suede sneakers and Car Shoe style studded leather moccasins.

Expensive *Amex/MC/V*

Piazza di Spagna area

Via Borgognona 4/A **06 678 4843**
00187 Rome Mon 3:30-7:30, Tues-Sat 10-7:30

☆ Scapa

An antique palazzo that once provided lodgings for Garibaldi is the only place in Italy where you'll find an outlet for the Anglo-Belgian brand Scapa. The Roman polo set (and those who pretend they're part of it) browse here below thick-beamed wooden ceilings with rows of small spotlights strung from wall to wall when they want to flirt with something casual but of quality. As well as tweed (in winter) and linen trousers in beige, khaki, blue, black and white (in summer), there are jackets with 10-button cuff details which will give the wearer a glorious hourglass figure. Other aristo treats include lightly embroidered summer dresses, luxuriously soft deerskin scarves and a whole host of accessories. If you're looking for a present for dad/son/husband/boyfriend, the display case at the cash desk has a good selection of ties, wallets and hip flasks. Children from 4-12 are catered for and, although the range isn't extensive, the cute dresses in pinks, lilacs and creams with sequinned flowers are well worth a browse.

Expensive   *Amex/MC/V*

Piazza di Spagna area

Via Vittoria 58-59   **06 678 9368**
00187 Rome   Mon 3:30-7:30, Tues-Sat 10:30-7:30

Schostal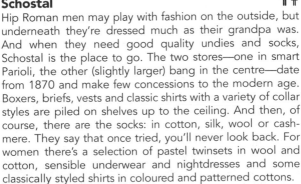

Hip Roman men may play with fashion on the outside, but underneath they're dressed much as their grandpa was. And when they need good quality undies and socks, Schostal is the place to go. The two stores—one in smart Parioli, the other (slightly larger) bang in the centre—date from 1870 and make few concessions to the modern age. Boxers, briefs, vests and classic shirts with a variety of collar styles are piled on shelves up to the ceiling. And then, of course, there are the socks: in cotton, silk, wool or cashmere. They say that once tried, you'll never look back. For women there's a selection of pastel twinsets in wool and cotton, sensible underwear and nightdresses and some classically styled shirts in coloured and patterned cottons.

Moderate   *Amex/MC/V*

Piazza di Spagna area

Via del Corso 158   **06 679 1240**
00186 Rome   Mon-Sat 9:30-7:30, Sun 10:30-7

Parioli area

Piazza Euclide 41-42   **06 808 0165**
00197 Rome   Mon 3:30-7:30, Tues-Sat 9:30-1, 3:30-7:30

Sem Vaccaro

This sunny yellow-and-orange store occupying a warren of mezzanines two steps from the Pantheon has everything the flashiest urban rodeo-girl could possibly want. The colours would have made John Wayne's eyes water: you'll find cowboy boots in electric blues and shocking pinks alongside mini and maxi skirts in denim and suede, fringed cowboy shirts and teeny-weeny pink lacy vests with beaded flowers and sequinned edging. Then, of course, there are jeans, done any way you please. Prices are not that high, so leave your pistol in its holster: you won't have to rob the saloon. There's a smaller store in the Galleria Colonna (and sister stores in Milan and the Costa Smeralda, for the yacht-based cowgirl).

Moderate   *Amex/MC/V*

Pantheon area

Via degli Orfani 91   **06 678 4226**
00186 Rome   Mon 3:30-7:30, Tues-Sat 10-7:30

Piazza di Spagna area

Galleria Colonna (Alberto Sordi)　　　　**06 691 90669**
Piazza Colonna　　　　　　　　　Mon-Sat 10-8 , Sun 10-9
00187 Rome

Sergio Rossi

Sitting pretty on one of the quieter corners of Piazza di Spagna, Sergio Rossi's store frequently creates a pedestrian traffic jam as people screech to a halt on the narrow pavement to take in the glory of his creations. Rossi has been designing shoes for 40 years and his footwear lends a subtle veneer of sexiness to ordinary feet without being overly bold or brassy. Whether you're looking for thong-toes, kitten-heel sandals with mosaic front panels, leg-hugging fabric knee-high boots or men's classics, you'll find them here. Make room in your closet...you may end up buying them all.　　　　　　　　　　　　　　　*sergiorossi.com*

Luxury　　　　　　　　　　　　　　　*Amex/MC/V*

Piazza di Spagna area

Piazza di Spagna 97-100　　　　　　**06 678 3245**
00187 Rome　　　　　　　　Sun-Mon 3-7, Tues-Sat 10-7

Sermoneta

When that howling icy wind hits Rome sometime in mid-December, you'd best take a trip to Sermoneta. They've got every type of glove design possible in materials from kid to pigskin to ostrich and in all the colours of the rainbow. Linings may be cashmere, silk, fur, rabbit, chinchilla or mink, among others. The Sermoneta boutique may be small, but they have made the most of the space in a recent makeover: the chrome and light wood store now has portholes cut into the wall on the upper floor in which they store the gloves which aren't displayed in glass cases. There's a constant stream of Japanese traipsing in and out and the friendly staff may astound you with their fluent Japanese, Chinese and Korean.　　　　　　*sermonetagloves.com*

Affordable　　　　　　　　　　　　　*Amex/MC/V*

Piazza di Spagna area

Piazza di Spagna 61　　　　　　　　**06 679 1960**
00187 Rome　　　　　　　　　　　Mon-Sat 9:30-8

Silvano Lattanzi

The man who made shoes for George Bush—and who is known to Japanese cognoscenti as the 'poet of shoes'—is relentlessly on the rise. Originally from near Ascoli Piceno in the shoe-producing Marche region, Lattanzi travels the world personally measuring the noblest of feet—particularly in Japan, the Middle East and the US. If your name doesn't yet appear in his little black book, do as Bill Clinton did on a recent trip to Rome and drop into the pale marble-floored store on the pretty Via Bocca di Leone. Here you can get measured up, or find ready-to-wear shoes artfully arranged on glass shelves. You'll also find the ever-expanding Lattanzi range of ties, shirts, pullovers and jackets in leather and fabric for both men and women. Depending on materials (from English calf to crocodile skin), made-to-measure shoes cost from 3,000 to 5,000 euros. If you miss him here, catch him at his newly opened store in Milan. *zintala.it*

Luxury *Amex/MC/V*

Piazza di Spagna area

Via Bocca di Leone 59	**06 678 6119**
Rome 00187	Mon 3:30-7:30, Tues-Sat 9:30-1 3:30-7:30

Sisley

Benetton's trendier sister has been having a hard time over the last few years, with stores closing left right and centre. Where once Sisley was on every high street, now just a handful of stores remain and the Tokyo babes who once swarmed the Via Frattina store are an ever smaller presence. But despite all this, Sisley stock stylish casual essentials that don't cost the earth and you'll catch young Romans flicking through the racks of black, white and navy trousers, tops and jackets, punctuated with primary colours, orange and lime. Get ready to fight over the best pieces—like beaded gold strappy sandals, ruched trousers, kinky plastic jackets and glittery tops. *sisley.com*

Affordable *Amex/MC/V*

Piazza di Spagna area

Via del Corso 413-5	**06 687 1008**
00186 Rome	Mon-Sat 10-8
Via Frattina 19/A	**06 699 41787**
00187 Rome	Mon-Sat 10-8

Stefanel

In these economically challenging times, Stefanel has become a staple for Italian women seeking inexpensive wardrobe basics with pleasant fabrics and reasonable design. The main Roman branch of this one-time knitwear company is on Via del Corso. Here you'll find pastel capri pants, neutral jackets, black pantsuits and the odd floral shirt, all forming a perfectly acceptable basis for a semi-professional/casual wardrobe. Accessories are also available—including floppy hats, shoes, bags and belts. *stefanel.it*

Affordable *Amex/MC/V*

Piazza di Spagna area

Via del Corso 122-125	**06 699 25783**
00186 Rome	Daily 10-8
Via Frattina 31-33	**06 679 2667**
00187 Rome	Mon-Sat 10-7:45, Sun 11-1:30, 3:30-7:30

Via Nazionale area

Via Nazionale 57-59	**06 478 26432**
00184 Rome	Mon-Sat 10-8

Via Cola di Rienzo 223   **06 321 1403**
00192 Rome   Mon-Sat 10-8, Sun 11-8

☆ **Sole by Soledad Twombly**

This intriguingly named Argentina-born designer turns out to be the daughter-in-law of the celebrated American artist Cy Twombly. She receives clients by appointment only at her atelier on the top floor of an apartment building close to the Spanish Steps, with a splendid view stretching over to St Peter's. Inside, floors are stripped and beams are painted white, offsetting her Sole collection of unique pieces. Jackets, dresses, skirts and trousers take their inspiration from the Orient with wide sleeves and luxuriant linings. Fabrics are strictly natural and include linen, silk, wool and cashmere. Twombly is like a chef who cooks whatever is fresh in the market that morning: if a piece of antique Persian fabric takes her fancy, she'll use it to conjure up some imaginative concoction. When we visited, she'd just found some particularly fine Argentinian wool, resulting in wonderful coloured scarves that begged to be wrapped up and taken home.   *soledadtwombly.com*

Expensive to luxury   *Amex/MC/V*

Piazza di Spagna area
Via Gregoriana 34   **06 699 24512**
Rome 00187   (by appointment only)

Sub dued

Ever-so-trendy but, true to their name, subdued. The basement Via Cola di Rienzo store is the flagship of this Rome-based label and the colours do tend to be subdued; think black and white sweat pants, zip-up tops, T-shirts and vest tops for sporty teens and twenty-somethings, though a few Bardot-style off-the-shoulder tops, bold stripes and bright colours liven up proceedings. Sub dued also sell jeans, underwear, coats and bikinis—all at teen-friendly prices. The Sub dued Kids store opened in September 2004, providing the jeans, summer dresses and stripey T-shirts for bambini. Staff are fresh-faced and friendly.   *subdued.com*

Affordable   *Amex/MC/V*

Piazza Navona area
Via di Parione 18   **06 687 1151**
00186 Rome   Mon 4-8, Tues-Sat 10-1, 4-8
Via Cola di Rienzo area
Via Cola di Rienzo 246   **06 683 00783**
00192 Rome   Mon 3-7:30, Tues-Sat 10-7:30

Sub dued Kids
Via Cola di Rienzo area
Via Lucrezio Caro 87-89   **06 321 7660**
00193 Rome   Mon 3:45-7:30, Tues-Sat 10-7:30

Parioli area
Viale Parioli 35   **06 807 3430**
00197 Rome   Mon 3:30-7:30, Tues-Sat 10-1, 3:30-7:30

Taba

Plumb in the middle of Campo de' Fiori, with its colourful fruit and flower market, is the even more colourful Taba store. (It also lies in the shadow of Giordano Bruno—a monk burned alive for his religious convictions, though the world inside this store couldn't be further away from such horrors). Here you'll get the staples for that Bali-babe look which are perfect for those scorching Roman summer days. Globe-trotting Argentinian owner Carlos Alberto Allevato scours Asia and South America for sequinned sandals, cotton snake-charmer trousers, tie-dyed tank tops, psychedelic sarongs, naturally dyed scarves and crotcheted dresses and skull caps. In addition there are thick Cleopatra-style bangles from Tibet, a vast array of earrings and chunky beads. Antique cartwheels and 1920s pewter lamps hang low over the merchandise, creating an intimate atmosphere in this tiny shop where the shelves and rails are always overflowing. Taba also has branches in Felice Circeo and on the popular island of Ponza.   *tabashop.com*

Affordable   *Amex/MC/V*

Campo de' Fiori area
Piazza Campo de' Fiori 13   **06 688 06478**
00187 Rome   Daily 10-1am

☆ TAD

A big hit with the Rome in-crowd, TAD is Rome's first (and only) concept store and has all you need to stay in the smart set. From the moment you enter it's all up for grabs; if you like the flowers or the mirrors, just ask and they're yours. Occasionally it hits a slightly provincial fashion-nerd note—and since Rome is so good at being Rome why should it strive to be anything else, we ask ourselves? Star features include those fabulous guys from Nuyorica who have picked a range of shoes and accessories including Pierre Hardy, Marc Jacobs and Chloé. High fashion comes courtesy of Balenciaga and A-V Hash adds a spot of Belgian avant-garderie. Men have to make do with a tiny collection of casual pieces from Zucca and Duarte. There's a selection of perfumes and cosmetics from Stephane Marais and scent from Comme des Garçons. Devotees apply the Tad touch to their home as well: the fairly run-of-the-mill ethnic-inspired collection has everything from bed linen to sushi plates. Dazed and confused by all this choice? Snap up a couple of international magazines and head to the in-house hairdressers to get your locks fixed while you have a think. After all that, you'll almost certainly be in need of a spot of Thai-Italian fusion sustenance at the studiedly stylish in-store bar/restaurant.   *taditaly.com*

Expensive   *Amex/MC/V*

Piazza di Spagna area
Via del Babuino 155/A
00187 Rome

06 3269 5131/3269 5122
Mon 12-8, Tues-Sun 10:30-8

Tebro

In a country which doesn't really have much truck with department stores, Tebro has been there for well-to-do Roman families seeking sheets, bathrobes and D&G undies for almost 140 years (okay, so perhaps they've haven't been stocking D&G for quite that long). The nine enormous display windows looking out onto Via dei Prefetti will give you a good idea of what this single-floor store has to offer. Apart from the above-mentioned items, there are towels, nightwear, shirts, socks, ties, quilts, bathmats and so on— all in every imaginable shade. Walk past the undies (by Roberto Cavalli as well as D&G) and down the red carpet into the back and you'll find a large range of women's underwear. The firm also makes made-to-measure sheets for cribs, children's beds and awkwardly shaped beds for yachts. *tebro.it*

Moderate to expensive   *Amex/MC/V*

Piazza Navona area
Via dei Prefetti 46-54
00186 Rome

06 687 3441
Mon 4-8, Tues-Sat 10:30-2, 4-8

Via Cola di Rienzo area
Piazzale Medaglie d'Oro 55
00136 Rome

06 354 20476
Mon 4-8, Tues-Sat 9:30-1, 4-8

Teichner

If time is of the essence, the 1,200-square-metre Teichner is the place to go. The San Giovanni metro stop is right outside the door, so there's no need to either walk or park, and the magnificent Basilica of San Giovanni in Laterano is just two minutes away—so you can fit in some sightseeing as well. The ground floor is a sea of jeans and casualwear with signs for Guess, Armani Jeans, Miss Sixty, Calvin Klein Jeans and DKNY Jeans emblazoned across the walls just to remind you who you're dealing with. You can get down to some serious shopping on the second, third and fourth floors with D&G, Roberto Cavalli, Ferré, Versace, Pirelli, MaxMara Weekend, Belstaff and Henry Cotton. Don't be confused by the two separate entrances which appear to be two separate shops. The entrance on the corner leads you straight into the fray of womenswear while the more discreet one slightly up Via Appia lets the guys slip straight into the men's department without having to wade through oceans of stuff that doesn't interest them first.

Expensive   *Amex/MC/V*

San Giovanni area
Via Appia Nuova 2
00183 Rome

06 700 0934
Mon-Sat 9:30-8, Sun 10-1:30, 4-8

☆ Thé Verde

Opened in the summer of 2004, the new Thé Verde carries on the ethos of the old shop on Via Vittoria, successfully mixing the traditional with the ethnic. Winter sees lush velvet jackets, flared skirts and warm trousers imported from Vietnam; summer lines featuring silks and linen are brought over from Morocco. In addition, there is minimalist pottery, beaded necklaces, big stuffed poufs, scarves and hats. The cherrywood store also has a food line which includes spices, dried fruit and jams, plus more than 100 types of tea (hence the name). But perhaps the main reason to come here is to enjoy the café, located in a covered courtyard down a quiet side street. Enjoy a light breakfast or lunch of the foods on sale, while contemplating which clothes to take home.

Moderate   *Amex/MC/V*

Piazza di Spagna area

Via Bocca di Leone 46   **06 699 23705**
00187 Rome   Tues-Sat 10-8

Timberland

Why bother checking out an American store while you're in Rome? Well, the cuts for men's and womenswear may vary from those sold in the US...slimmer for European figures. And it is a French company which makes clothes for Timberland—the French have always been brilliant at this. You should also cast your eyes over the beautifully soft suede bags and satchels: as with all the products, the quality's good and hard-wearing.   *timberland.com*

Moderate   *Amex/MC/V*

Piazza di Spagna area

Via del Corso 488   **06 322 7266**
00186 Rome   Mon-Sat 10-8, Sun 11-2, 3-8

Via delle Convertite 6-8   **06 699 24724**
00187 Rome   (opening hours as above)

Via Nazionale area

Via A. Depretis 100   **06 478 6401**
00184 Rome   Mon-Sat 10-8, Sun 11-8

Tod's

Entrepreneur Diego Della Valle entered the family shoe business in 1975 and soon found fame as the creator of Tod's, Fay and Hogan. Using nifty marketing he managed to put his trademark Tod's shoes with the little plastic 'pebbles' on the soles at the top of the wish list of some pretty impressive clients, including Princess Diana, Sharon Stone and Luca di Montezemolo. The recently opened Rome store is decorated in that Seventies David Hicks style with patterned parquet, walls covered in padded leather, dark brown display cases, chrome trimmings and white-vaulted ceilings. It's a pretty vast affair with room after room of shoes, accessories (wallets, key-rings, bags etc), the odd leather jacket for women and an abundance of assistants floating around and offering advice. *todsgroup.com*

Expensive *Amex/MC/V*

Piazza di Spagna area

Via della Fontanella di Borghese 56/A-57 **06 682 10066**
00187 Rome Mon-Sat 10-7:30, Sun 11-2, 3-7:30

Tricots

Sisters Flaminia and Fabrizia Baldelli set up this tiny white cube of a store in Parioli in the early Nineties when minimalism was at its height. With missionary zeal they set about converting the wayward natives of this flashy patch of Rome, whose insistence on gold-dripping ostentation was an affront to their strictly Zen aesthetics. Fifteen years later they're still here, and the store is often packed with converts to the cause. Featured designers (clothing and shoes) include high priests of avant-garde conceptualism such as Helmut Lang and Martin Margiela, though they've recently lightened up with more frivolous lines from Balenciaga and Zandra Rhodes. In spring 2004 they opened a men's boutique, a similarly white sliver of a store. Discerning Pariolini are now offered sporty lines by A.P.C. or serious pieces by Marc Jacobs and, of course, Helmut Lang.

Expensive *Amex/MC/V*

Parioli area

Via D.Chelini 15 (W) **06 808 5815**
00197 Rome Mon 4-8, Tues-Sat 9:30-1, 4-8

Via Luigi Luciani 39 (M) **06 360 06816**
00197 Rome Mon 4-8, Tues-Wed 9:30-1, 4-8
Thurs-Sat 9:30-8

Trussardi

Originating from Bergamo in the early part of the 20th century, Trussardi started out providing the Italian army with leather gloves. Revived by young creative director Beatrice Trussardi, it is now one of the royal princes of Italian leather products and the calfskin-padded walls of the Via dei Condotti branch don't let us forget it. High-quality skins such as deer, python and eel turn up in jackets, shoes and bags. Crespo, a mixture of cotton and PVC, is also used in a range of bags and luggage which are virtually impossible to scratch or ruin. The non-leather line of clothing has a casual but classic look: men can expect suits, finely cut shirts and sports jackets, while for women there are short but floaty evening dresses and tailored jackets and trousers. *trussardi.com*

Luxury *Amex/MC/V*

Piazza di Spagna area

Via dei Condotti 49-50 **06 679 2151**
00187 Rome Mon-Sat 10-7

T'Store

This is one of the multitude of offshoots of the Trussardi empire, which has been in almost constant expansion since its beginnings as a smart glove maker in 1911 and is still in the family under the guidance of Beatrice Trussardi. The lines under the Trussardi umbrella include Trussardi Bags, Jeans, Baby, Shoes, Eyes, Home, Scarves, Parfums and Sport, and that's just for starters. T'Store focuses on the more casual and affordable Jeans and Sport lines, leaving the hardcore catwalk stuff to the main Trussardi store on Via dei Condotti. Trussardi Jeans is the most constant and classic of the labels, and includes denim jackets, skirts and clean-cut striped cotton tees and vest tops for that clear-eyed, just-been-sailing look. Trussardi Sport is slightly funkier: think palazzo pants and clamdiggers with buckles. There's also a small selection of casual shoes for both sexes. The three-storey Via del Corso branch displays the men's collection down the blue-walled steel staircase; womenswear is upstairs in a spacious spotlit area with floor-to-ceiling mirrors and picture windows overlooking the street below. The new, smaller Galleria Colonna boutique, also on three floors, opened at the end of 2003. *trussardi.com*

Moderate to expensive *Amex/MC/V*

Piazza di Spagna area

Via del Corso 477-8 **06 322 6055**
00186 Rome   Mon 12-8, Tues-Sat 10-8, Sun 12:30-7:30

Galleria Colonna (Alberto Sordi) **06 699 24391**
Piazza Colonna   Mon-Fri 10-8, Sat 10-9, Sun 10-8
00186 Rome

Valentino Boutique

Having made his reputation decades ago with flawless cuts, simple and elegant shapes and luscious fabrics, Valentino Garavani hardly needs an introduction. The ground floor of his main Rome boutique plays host to a vast array of shoes as well as accessories such as perfumes, watches, sunglasses and cute patent clutch-bags with corna—the horn-shaped Italian good luck charm—attached to them. This season, jewelled butterfly appliqués are sprinkled liberally over both shoes and bags. A red carpet fit for an empress's abode covers the grand staircase that sweeps upstairs to the second floor. There you will find the prêt-à-porter collections, including the fairytale evening gowns which you probably saw at last year's Oscars, and the glamorous daywear collection. For a younger and sportier look, there is a selection from Valentino Roma. *valentino.it*

Luxury *Amex/MC/V*

Piazza di Spagna area

Via dei Condotti 13 **06 679 5862**
00187 Rome   Mon 3-7, Tues-Sat 10-7

Valentino Boutique

In tune with the more informal location, Valentino's second boutique is an airy gallery-like space which runs from Via del Babuino to Via Margutta. It is home to the master's Red collection, which is his younger and more affordable line aiming to turn a whole new generation onto the emperor of Roman fashion design. There is also the Roma collection which provides relatively affordable evening and daywear for elegant signoras. Wherever you look, the famous 'V' will catch your eye, whether on bags or sunglasses. In fact, the store has a whole range of Valentino accessories, from perfumes to shoes to eye-catching pieces of paste jewellery. Opposite the store there's the Canova Tadolini museum of 19th-century sculptures; a visit fits seamlessly with a spree at Valentino's. *valentino.it*

Expensive to luxury *Amex/MC/V*

Piazza di Spagna area

Via del Babuino 61 **06 360 01906**
00187 Rome Mon 3-7, Tues-Sat 10-7

☆ Valentino (men)

At the last count this was the only boutique in the entire world to be dedicated to the Rome-based designer's men's collections. Located just around the corner from the women's store in Via dei Condotti, Valentino Uomo is housed in what used to be the dépendance of the historic Palazzo Torlonia. The spacious store offers seas of suits from the hand-tailored Valentino Black line, plus a good selection from the relatively commercial Valentino White. Valentino Red is also available for those wanting a younger look. Oval and square-faced jewelled watches and leather bracelets will delight men who go with the philosophy that the smallest details count. Other accessories include briefcases and holdalls, while cufflinks—in delicate amethyst and jade—don't come any more elegant than this. *valentino.it*

Luxury *Amex/MC/V*

Piazza di Spagna area

Via Bocca di Leone 15 **06 678 3656**
00187 Rome Mon- 3-7, Tues-Sat 10-7

Valleverde

As Kevin Costner said in the Valleverde advertisement a few years ago: 'E bello camminare nella Valleverde'—it's beautiful walking in the green valley. True enough, if comfort rather than fashion is your guiding light. Women can expect mostly blunt-toed, low-heeled shoes—ideal for cobbles—in browns and blacks, though the odd tiger and leopard-print stiletto is available for the more predatory customer. The men's range is slightly more exciting, combining sharp Italian style with comfort. There is also a children's line, plus bags, vanity cases and holdalls. The tardis-like shop is opposite a house where James Joyce briefly stayed in 1906. Despite the company's reputation for service and fit, on their off-days staff may treat you as though you trod in something very nasty before you walked in. *valleverde.it*

Moderate   *Amex/MC/V*

Piazza di Spagna area

Via Frattina 109   **06 693 80364**
00187 Rome   Mon 12:30-8, Tues-Sat 9:30-8

Versace Jeans Couture

If you've always been convinced that you'll never be able to afford Versace, check out Versace Jeans Couture. A pair of the sex-meister's jeans in a range of colours will set you back less than you thought. As in most Versace stores, the company seems to have got its staff training policy right. Professional yet friendly personnel will conduct you around two marble-clad floors of men's and women's jeans, tops, leather jackets, sunglasses, perfume and catwalk shoes without putting the pressure on to buy. *versace.com*

Moderate   *Amex/MC/V*

Piazza di Spagna area

Via Frattina 116   **06 678 7681**
00187 Rome   Mon 3-7:30, Tues-Sat 10-7:30

☆ Verso Sud

You'll be hard pressed to find a decent boutique in the cobblestone artists' paradise of Trastevere, so when Udine-born Ornella de Falco opened Verso Sud in 1999 Trasteverian fashion junkies let out a collective sigh of relief. They rubbed their hands with glee at the intellectual looks à la Japanese but with a hip and feminine touch. Try pairing an Isabel Marant miniskirt with an angelic Alberta Ferretti chiffon blouse and sandals from Paul Smith. Clothes are showcased in two minimalist rooms with iron and glass details. Signora de Falco is usually on hand to offer friendly advice.

Moderate to expensive   *Amex/MC/V*

Trastevere

Via San Francesco a Ripa 168   **06 583 33668**
00153 Rome   Mon-Sat 10-2, 4-8

☆ Vestiti Usati Cinzia

If this gallery of vintage street style, with its racks neatly organised by decade, reminds you of the backstage of a theatre, there's a reason: owner Cinzia Fabbri once worked as a theatre costume designer. Located on the rambling arty street of Via del Governo Vecchio, the store is a favourite with Roman vintage aficionados who know that Cinzia only picks out the very best pieces. While jazz hums (or blares) in the background, you can flick through rails of Seventies embroidered shearling coats, Betty Barclay wool and fur jackets, Austrian leather jackets and Sixties striped knits. For your more casual moments, there are chunky Shetland sweaters and piles of Rockwood jeans (extra long—they have a sewing machine in the back room to take them up according to your height). Looking for something a bit more stylish? Keep your eyes peeled and you might pick up a vintage Valentino evening bag or a Vera Mont black velvet jewelled bolero jacket.

Affordable   *Amex/MC/V*

Piazza Navona area

Via del Governo Vecchio 45   **(no telephone)**
00186 Rome   Mon-Sat 10-8

Vicini

Just down the road from the stars' favourite Hotel de Russie (and the best martini in town), Vicini's boutique is handy for fans such as Britney Spears and Italian rock singer Irene Grande. You'll find stilettos, court heels and mules that hit just the right note of confident sophistication, and designer Giuseppe Zanotti's high-glitz styles go down a storm with the new Russians. Gold jewelled sandals will ensure your footwork is eye-catching, or head east for a spot of ethnic bling with Hindu icon print sandals complete with a 'jewel'-encrusted ring for your big toe. There's also a small collection of men's shoes.   *vicinishoes.com*

Expensive   *Amex/MC/V*

Piazza di Spagna area

Via del Babuino 136-137   **06 326 51925**
00187 Rome   Mon-Fri 10-7, Sat 10-2

Vicolo della Torretta Baby

A tiny boutique hidden from the chaos of Rome's main shopping streets, the Vicolo della Torretta Baby childrenswear store stocks mainly Dior (0-12) and Ralph Lauren (0-7). Along with Lauren polo shirts and trousers, you'll find cute Dior denim dresses with red epaulettes and denim jackets with Dior discreetly embroidered in navy on the back (just so everyone knows how much you spend on your kids). They also sell swimwear, sheets and shoes. A new range of Noblène bridesmaid and ceremonial dresses is also worth checking out if you have a very special occasion coming up.

Expensive to luxury   *Amex/MC/V*

Piazza di Spagna area

Vicolo della Torretta 17   **06 689 3224**
00186 Rome   Mon-Sat 10-7

☆ Vittoriana

The exclusive Margutta Arcade is home to a variety of stores selling handmade goods. On the second floor of the quiet courtyard complex you'll find Roman dressmaking legend Vittoriana who produces haute couture gowns for the city's smart set. She came out of nowhere in 1970 with the slave sandal boot and hasn't lost the ability to surprise. The boutique is a riot of organza, lace and colours: Vittoriana loves to experiment. Her blood-red jacket is scarred with tear-drop burns; other jackets are ripped within an inch of their lives. On the traditional side—though still slightly quirky—are sequinned evening dresses covered with a layer of chiffon so that the sequins are more or less hidden. Then there's a silver raincoat with a silk over-layer which may get wet but dries in a flash: it looks fabulous, of course. Vittoriana favours the use of embroidery, chiffon and lace and, refreshingly for an haute couture luxury label, refuses to use real fur. The store fills two adjacent spaces in the Margutta Arcade—one with a terrace where she sometimes holds cocktail parties for clients. There's also an atelier in the back where your purchases can be adjusted.

Expensive   *Amex/MC/V*

Piazza di Spagna area

Margutta Arcade	**06 321 8245**
Via Margutta 3	Mon 3:30-7:30
00187 Rome	Tues-Sat 10:30-7:30

Wolford

This Austrian brand is for women who have legs and know how to use them (in the immortal words of ZZ Top). There are tights, stockings and lingerie in every conceivable colour and style—from sheer black stockings with sexy rear seams and fun Playboy-bunny hold-ups, to second-skin bodies in microfibre and saucy embroidered-and-net balcony bras. The shop is small so you don't get the full impact of the Wolford range but you do get a very good selection of their undies and swimwear.   *wolford.com*

Expensive   *Amex/MC/V*

Piazza di Spagna area

Via Mario de' Fiori 67	**06 699 25531**
00187 Rome	Mon 11:30-7:30, Tues-Sat 10-7:30

Yves Saint Laurent Rive Gauche

The mood of this two-floor store down the quietish Via Bocca di Leone seems to hark back to a Sixties film when black and white was in, men always wore sharply cut suits and glaringly shiny shoes and the petite and perfect women never had a hair out of place. As heir to the inimitable Monsieur Yves, Tom Ford used all his powers of innovation; now that Stefano Pilati has taken over, you'll still find the classic trouser suits, tuxedo jackets, well-cut dresses and skirts—all with a new modern twist. Menswear is in the basement.   *ysl.com*

Luxury   *Amex/MC/V*

Piazza di Spagna area

Via Bocca di Leone 35	**06 679 5577**
00187 Rome	Mon-Sat 10-7

Yves Saint Laurent Rive Gauche (accessories)

You'll find this small, recently opened shop facing the Spanish steps right beneath Prada in what initially appears to be one of the most enviable positions in Rome. However, you may be disappointed once you get inside. From downstairs, you do get a view of the glorious landmark, but upstairs the low ceiling and even lower window means that you can only see the famous fountain in the middle of the square. However, this black and white French-inspired boutique contains the whole glorious range of YSL accessories—which is what you actually came here to see. You'll find Hobo bags, purses, cufflinks, skinny leather belts for men stamped with Yves Saint Laurent and suede moccasins. Huge crowds of tourists usually congregate on the corner outside, but sharpen your elbows and push through the throng. *ysl.com*

Luxury   *Amex/MC/V*

Piazza di Spagna area

Piazza di Spagna 77   **06 679 5577**
00187 Rome   Daily 10-7

Zara

Who needs the Villa Borghese gardens? When Zara finally opened this largish outpost in part of the Galleria Colonna shopping centre in December 2003, it became an instant attraction for Romans out for their Saturday afternoon passeggiata. Though the clothes (coats, suits, shirts, trousers and dresses, and accessories reflecting the latest runway looks) are no different from those in other branches of the Spanish chain around the world, the crowd here offers a unique lesson in style. Where else will you see women clad to the nines in Fendi fur with one of those giveaway dark blue paper bags tucked under her arm? Customers know that the materials may not be the best, but at these prices who cares? If your purchase is looking a bit shabby by next season, like that lady in the Fendi, you'll just head back for more. *zara.com*

Affordable   *Amex/MC/V*

Piazza di Spagna area

Galleria Colonna (Alberto Sordi)   **06 699 25401**
00187 Rome   Mon-Sat 10-10, Sun 10-9

For those who like outlet shopping and street markets...

Viale Parioli Market

The street market on the corner of Via Nino Oxilio and Viale Parioli (Mon-Sat 8-2) is always crowded with stalls of varying degrees of legitimacy. One of the best is undoubted the Carlini family stand with some stylish shoes from their factory in the shoe-producing Marche region, costing 40-50 euros at the very most. There are also stalls with tablecloths and uniforms for that Parioli staple, the maid. Then there are the less official vendors, displaying fake Tod's and Prada handbags perched on cars.

The Last Good Buy

Over the past couple of years, discount malls have been springing up like mushrooms all over Italy. Here are two of the most popular on the outskirts of Rome:

Fashion District

Forty kilometres from Rome at the Valmontone exit of the Rome-Naples motorway, this purpose-built bargain 'shopping village' is an ugly, pastel toy-town pastiche of every architectural style known to man. Sadly, on our last visit, the buildings were falling apart, the bathrooms were out of order and, tellingly, people weren't laden down with bags. The shops are dominated by looks and colours that talk more of abandoned trial designs than of last season's styles. The Malo store, for instance, is deeply disappointing: nothing could be further from the glorious cashmere fest of the Via Borgognona, although you might be luckier. Probably not worth making a special trip for, but if you're passing on your way south discounts are up to 70% and persistence will be rewarded with bargains. Replay, for men, women and children, is one of the better-stocked stores, and Gianfranco Ferré, Cacharel, Fornarina and Genoese sailwear label Slam are all worth a browse. *fashiondistrict.it*

Affordable to moderate   *Amex/MC/V (in most stores)*

Via della Pace, località Pascolaro   **06 959 9491**
00038 Valmontone   Mon-Fri 10-9, Sat-Sun 10-10

Castel Romano Outlet

Rome's first purpose-built factory outlet district, Castel Romano opened in October 2003 and is slightly more successful than its rival Fashion District so if you're looking to pick one or the other, come to Castel Romano. Located 20 kilometres south of Rome off the Via Pontina, the village contains 90 highly selected stores with discounted wares from D&G, Guess, Diesel (and Diesel Kids), Calvin Klein, Fratelli Rossetti, Etro, Versace and Petit Bateau—at up to 70% off. There's also Samsonite if the suitcases you brought with you are already full. *mcarthurglen.it*

Affordable to moderate   *Amex/MC/V (in most stores)*

Via Ponte di Piscina Cupa 64   **06 505 0050**
Castel Romano   Daily 10-10
00128 Rome

Rome Stores by District

Rome District Maps

Campo de' Fiori area

Flaminio

Largo Arentina

Pantheon area

Parioli

Piazza di Spagna area

Piazza Navona area

Repubblica

Salario

San Giovanni

San Lorenzo

Termini

Testaccio

Trastevere

Via Cola di Rienzo area

Via Nazionale area

Piazza Navona

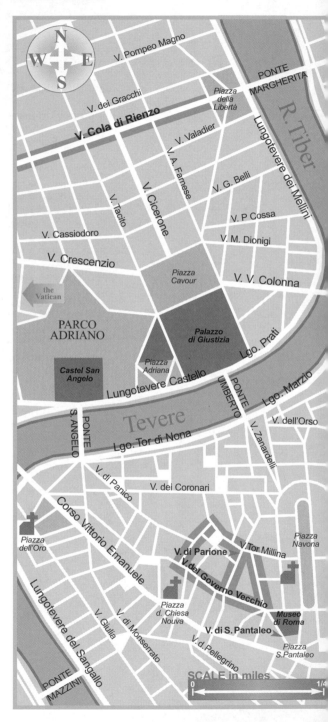

Piazza di Spagna

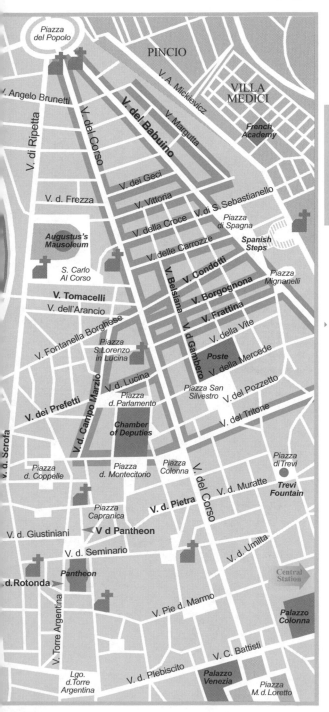

93

Rome—Via Nazionale

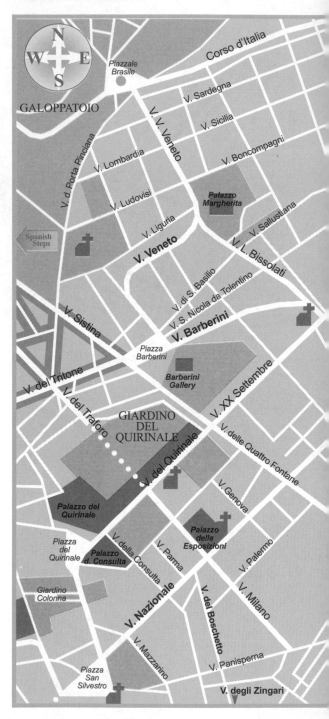

Rome—Campo de' Fiori

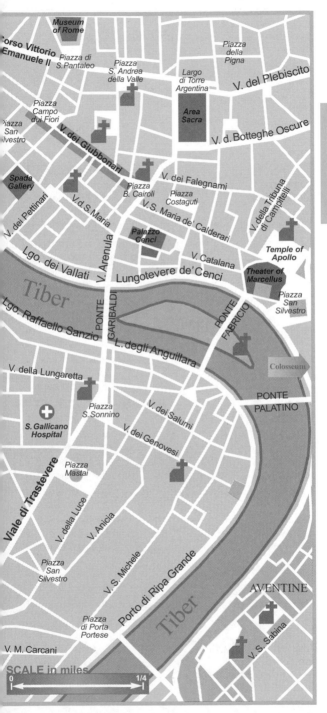

95

Campo de' Fiori area

See map page 95

Angelo di Nepi	Via dei Giubbonari 28
AVC by Adriana V. Campanile	Largo del Pallaro 1
Benetton	Corso Vittorio Emanuele II 77-79
Blunauta (outlet)	Largo del Pallaro 19/A
Borini	Via dei Pettinari 86-87
Cambalache	Via dei Chiavari 30
Edo City	Piazza del Paradiso 18
Ethic	Piazza Cairoli 11-12
Intimissimi	Via dei Giubbonari 42
Lei	Via dei Giubbonari 103
Loco	Via dei Baullari 22
Marco Polo	Via dei Chiavari 31
Marlboro	Via dei Giubbonari 61
Molly Bloom	Via dei Giubbonari 27
Nuyorica	Piazza Pollarola 36-37
Pandemonium	Via dei Giubbonari 104
People	Piazza Teatro di Pompeo 4/A
Pinko	Via dei Giubbonari 76-77
Planet	Via dei Baullari 132
Prototype	Via dei Giubbonari 50
Prototype Kids	Via dei Giubbonari 51
Taba	Piazza Campo de' Fiori 13

Flaminio

Arli Cashmere	Via Giorgio Vasari 10

Pantheon area

See map page 93

Benetton	Piazza Fontana di Trevi 91-94
Borsalino	Via Campo Marzio 72/A
Camiceria Albertelli	Via dei Prefetti 11
Davide Cenci	Via Campo Marzio 1-7
Degli Effetti	Piazza Capranica 75-79 & 93
Ethic	Via del Pantheon 46-47
Petit Bateau	Via Campo Marzio 10/B
Pinko	Via della Scrofa 24
Replay	Via della Rotonda 25
Replay (C)	Salita de' Crescenzi 29
Sem Vaccaro	Via dei Orfani 91

Largo Argentina

Alternative	Piazza Mattei 5
Mandarina Duck	Corso Vittorio Emanuele II 16

Parioli

AVC by Adriana V. Campanile	Viale Parioli 178
Bagheera	Via G.Antonelli 26
Bagheera Accessories	Piazza Euclide 30
BBC	Viale Parioli 122
Brugnoli	Viale Parioli 108

Carla G	Via Salaria 66
DM	Via G.Antonelli 10
Gallo	Via Guidubaldo del Monte 5
Pandemonium	Piazza Euclide 7-8
Schostal	Piazza Euclide 41-42
Sub dued	Viale Parioli 35
Tricots (W)	Via D.Chelini 15
Tricots (M)	Via Luigi Luciani 39
Viale	Parioli Market

Piazza di Spagna area

See map page 93

Abit Art	Via della Croce 46/47
Alberta Ferretti	Via dei Condotti 34
Alexander	Piazza di Spagna 49
Alviero Martini	Via Borgognona 4/G
Angelo di Nepi	Via Frattina 2
Angelo di Nepi	Via del Babuino 147
Armani Jeans	Via Tomacelli 137
Armani Jeans	Via del Babuino 70/A
AVC by Adriana V. Campanile	Piazza di Spagna 88
AVC by Adriana V. Campanile	Via Frattina 141
Bally	Via dei Condotti 38-40
Barbara Gregori	Via Vittoria 37/A-38
Barrilà	Via del Babuino 33
Battistoni	Via dei Condotti 60-61/A
Belsiana 19	Via Belsiana 94
Benetton	Via del Corso 423
Benetton	Piazza di Spagna 67-69
Blumarine	Via Bocca di Leone 24
Blunauta	Piazza di Spagna 35
Blunauta	Via dei Condotti 29
Bonpoint	Piazza San Lorenzo in Lucina 25
Borsalino	Piazza del Popolo 20
Borsalino	Piazza Fontana di Trevi 83
Bottega Veneta	Piazza San Lorenzo in Lucina 9
Braccialini	Via Mario de' Fiori 73
Brioni	Via Barberini 79-81
Brioni	Via dei Condotti 21/A
Brioni	Via Veneto 129
Brugnoli	Via del Babuino 57
Bruno Magli	Via dei Condotti 6-6/A
Bulgari	Via dei Condotti 10
Burberry Prorsum	Via dei Condotti 61
Calvin Klein	Via Borgognona 42b
Carla G.	Via del Gambero 24
Carla G.	Via del Babuino 121
Carpisa	Via Belsiana 59
Celine	Via dei Condotti 20/A
Centoventi	(Margutta Arcade) Via Margutta 3

Cesare Paciotti	Via Bocca di Leone 92
Chanel	Via del Babuino 98-101
Christian Dior	Piazza di Spagna 73-75
CK Jeans	Galleria Colonna, Piazza Colonna
Corner	Via Belsiana 97
Costume National	Via del Babuino 106
Custo	Via Tomacelli 101
Dal Co	Via Vittoria 65
Dancing Duck	Galleria Colonna, Piazza Colonna
Dancing Duck	Via Belsiana 96/B/C
D&G	Piazza di Spagna 93
Demoiselle	Via Frattina 93
Dolce & Gabbana	Via dei Condotti 51-52
Diesel	Via del Corso 186
Diesel	Via del Babuino 94
Eddy Monetti	Via Borgognona 35
Eddy Monetti	Via dei Condotti 63
Eleonora	Via del Babuino 97
Emanuel Ungaro	Via Borgognona 4/B-4/C
Emporio Armani	Via del Babuino 140
Energie	Via del Corso 179 & 486-487
Ethic	Via del Corso 85
Ethic	Via delle Carrozze 20
Etro	Via del Babuino 102
Expensive	Piazza di Spagna 36
Expensive	Via del Corso 129 & 405
Expensive	Via del Tritone 137
Fendi	Via Borgognona 36-37/A
Foot Locker	Via del Corso 39-40
Fornarina	Via dei Condotti 36
Fratelli Rossetti	Via Borgognona 5/A
Fratelli Rossetti	Via del Babuino 59/A
Fratelli Vigano	Via Minghetti Marco 8
Furla	Via dei Condotti 55-56
Furla	Piazza di Spagna 22
Furla	Via del Corso 481
Furla	Via Tomacelli 136
Gai Mattiolo	Via Mario de' Fiori 5
Galassia	Via Frattina 20-21
Galleria Colonna	Piazza Colonna
Gallo	Via Vittoria 63
Gente	Via del Babuino 80-82
Gente	Via Frattina 69
Geox	Via Frattina 3
GF Ferré	Piazza di Spagna 70
Gianni Versace	Via Bocca di Leone 26-27
Gianni Versace Uomo	Via Borgognona 24-25
Giorgio Armani	Via dei Condotti 77
Giuseppe Messina	Vicolo della Torretta 6

Givenchy	Via Borgognona 21
Gorietti	(Margutta Arcade) Via Margutta 3
Gucci	Via dei Condotti 8
Gucci	Via Borgognona 7/D
Gucci	Via dei Condotti 68
Guess by Marciano	Galleria Colonna, Piazza Colonna
Guess?	Via del Corso 141-143
Hermès	Via dei Condotti 67
Hogan	Via Borgognona 45
Hugo Boss	Via Frattina 146
Iceberg	Via del Babuino 87/88
Il Portone	Via delle Carrozze 71-73
Indoroman	Via Gregoriana 36
Intimissimi	Via del Corso 167
I Vippini	Via Fontanella di Borghese 65
Jam	Galleria Colonna, Piazza Colonna
Just Cavalli	Piazza di Spagna 82-83
Kristina Ti	Via Mario de' Fiori 40/C-41
Krizia	Piazza di Spagna 87
La Cicogna	Via Frattina 135
Laltramoda	Via Frattina 113
Laltramoda	Via Borgognona 42/B
La Perla	Via dei Condotti 78
La Rinascente	Piazza Colonna
Laura Biagiotti	Via Borgognona 43-44
Le 3 C	Via della Croce 40
Leam	Via Bocca di Leone 5
Le Ragazze Gold	Via del Corso 500
Loro Piana	Via Borgognona 31
Louis Vuitton	Piazza San Lorenzo in Lucina 36
Louis Vuitton	Via dei Condotti 15
Luisa Spagnoli	Via Frattina 84/B
Luisa Spagnoli	Via del Tritone 30
Luisa Spagnoli	Via Veneto 130
Mada	Via della Croce 57
Malo	Via Borgognona 5
Mandarina Duck	Via Due Macelli 59F/G
Mariella Burani	Via Bocca di Leone 28
Marina Rinaldi	Largo Goldoni 43
Marina Rinaldi	Via Borgognona 6
Marisa Padovan	Via delle Carozze 81-82
Marni	Via Bocca di Leone 8
Max & Co	Via dei Condotti 46-46/A
MaxMara	Via dei Condotti 19
MaxMara	Via Frattina 28
Missoni	Piazza di Spagna 78
Miss Sixty	Via del Corso 510
Modi di Campagna	Via dei Prefetti 42-44
Moschino	Via Borgognona 32/A

Moschino Jeans	Via Belsiana 57
Nia	Via Vittoria 48
Nia & Co	Via Vittoria 30-31
Nicol Caramel	Via di Ripetta 261
Only Hearts	Via Vittoria 76-76/A
Onyx Fashion Store	Via del Corso 132
Passion	Via delle Carrozze 39
Patrizia Pepe	Via Frattina 1
Petit Bateau	Via della Croce 45
Piccadilly	Via Sistina 92
Pinko	Via Due Macelli 92
Piquadro	Galleria Colonna, Piazza Colonna
Piquadro	Via Frattina 125
Planet Store	Via delle Convertite 21
Pollini	Via Frattina 22-24
Prada	Via dei Condotti 92
Prada Sport	Via del Babuino 91
Prada Uomo	Via dei Condotti 90
Prenatal	Via della Croce 50/A
Puma Store	Via del Corso 404
Pure	Via Frattina 111
Rene Caovilla	Via Borgognona 9/10
Replay (W)	Via Tomacelli 26
Replay (M)	Via Tomacelli 96
Roberto Cavalli	Via Borgognona 7/A
Rubinacci	Via della Fontanella di Borghese 33
Salvatore Ferragamo	Via dei Condotti 73-74
Salvatore Ferragamo Uomo	Via dei Condotti 66
Santoni	Via Borgognona 4
Scapa	Via Vittoria 58-59
Schostal	Via del Corso 158
Sem Vaccaro	Galleria Colonna, Piazza Colonna
Sergio Rossi	Piazza di Spagna 97-100
Sermoneta	Piazza di Spagna 61
Silvano Lattanzi	Via Bocca di Leone 59
Sisley	Via del Corso 413-5
Sisley	Via Frattina 19/A
Sole by Soledad Twombly	Via Gregoriana 34
Stefanel	Via del Corso 122-125
Stefanel	Via Frattina 31-33
TAD	Via del Babuino 155/A
Tebro	Piazza del Popolo 21
Thé Verde	Via Bocca di Leone 46
Timberland	Via del Corso 488
Timberland	Via delle Convertite 6-8
Tod's	Via della Fontanella di Borghese 56/A-57
Trussardi	Via dei Condotti 49-50
T'Store	Via del Corso 477
T'Store	Galleria Colonna, Piazza Colonna

Valentino	Via dei Condotti 13
Valentino Boutique	Via del Babuino 61
Valentino Uomo	Via Bocca di Leone 16
Valleverde	Via Frattina 109
Versace Jeans Couture	Via Frattina 116
Vicini	Via del Babuino 136-137
Vicolo della Torretta Baby	Vicolo della Torretta 17
Vittoriana	(Margutta Arcade) Via Margutta 3
Wolford	Via Mario de' Fiori 67
Yves Saint Laurent	Via Bocca di Leone 35
Yves Saint Laurent Rive Gauche	Piazza di Spagna 77
Zara	Galleria Colonna, Piazza Colonna

Rome Districts

Piazza Navona area   *See map page 93*

Abiti Usati	Via del Governo Vecchio 35
Arsenale	Via del Governo Vecchio 64
Fabindia	Via del Banco di Santo Spirito 40
Josephine de Huertas	Via del Governo Vecchio 68
Josephine de Huertas	Via di Parione 19-20
Luna & L'Altra	Via del Governo Vecchio 105
Maga Morgana	Via del Governo Vecchio 27
Maga Morgana	Via del Governo Vecchio 98
Omero & Cecilia	Via del Governo Vecchio 110
Only Hearts	Piazza della Chiesa Nuova 21
SBU	Via S.Pantaleo 68-69
Sub dued	Via di Parione 18
Tebro	Via dei Prefetti 46-54
Vestiti Usati Cinzia	Via del Governo Vecchio 45

Repubblica

Gatto	Via Antonio Salandra 34

Salario

La Rinascente	Piazza Fiume
SBU	Via Chiana 63-65

San Giovanni

Coin	Piazzale Appio 7
Gorietti	Piazza Re di Roma 66
Leam	Via Appia Nuova 26-32/C
Teichner	Via Appia Nuova 2

San Lorenzo

Claudio Sanò	Largo degli Osci 67/A
L'Anatra all'Arancia	Via Tiburtina 105-109 & 130
Myriam B	Via dei Volsci 75

Termini Station Concourse

Benetton	Termini Station Concourse Via Giolitti 9
Intimissimi	Termini Station Concourse Via Giolitti 9

Testaccio

Outlet: AVC by Adriana V. Campanile
Via Mastro Giorgio 66/68

Trastevere

Abit Art	Via della Scala 7
Verso Sud	Via San Francesco a Ripa 168

Via Cola di Rienzo area

See map page 92

Angelo di Nepi	Via Cola di Rienzo 267/A
Benetton	Via Cola di Rienzo 193-209
Blunauta	Via Cola di Rienzo 303-309
Carla G.	Via Cola di Rienzo 134
CK Jeans	Via Cola di Rienzo 151-153
Coin	Via Cola di Rienzo 173
Diesel	Via Cola di Rienzo 245-249
Energie	Via Cola di Rienzo 143-7
Fornarina	Via Cola di Rienzo 117
Furla	Via Cola di Rienzo 226
Gente	Via Cola di Rienzo 277-279
Intimissimi	Via Cola di Rienzo 159-161
Iron G	Via Cola di Rienzo 50
La Cicogna	Via Cola di Rienzo 268
Laltramoda	Via Cola di Rienzo 54-56
Luisa Spagnoli	Via Cola di Rienzo 191
Mandarina Duck	Via Cola di Rienzo 270-272
MaxMara	Via Cola di Rienzo 275
Miss Sixty	Via Cola di Rienzo 235
Onyx	Via Cola di Rienzo 225
Petit Bateau	Via Cola di Rienzo 311
Pinko	Via Cola di Rienzo 121-125
Stefanel	Via Cola di Rienzo 223
Sub dued	Via Cola di Rienzo 246
Sub dued Kids	Via Lucrezio Caro 87-89
Tebro	Piazzale Medaglie d'Oro 55

Via Nazionale area

See map page 94

244 Panisperna Via	Via Panisperna 244
Benetton	Via Nazionale 174
De Grillis	Via Campo Carleo 25 (Piazza del Grillo)
Furla	Via Nazionale 54-55
Geox	Via Nazionale 233
Intimissimi	Via Nazionale 189 & 227
Le Gallinelle	Via del Boschetto 76
Lei	Via Nazionale 88
MaxMara	Via Nazionale 28-31
Pulp	Via del Boschetto 140
Stefanel	Via Nazionale 57-59
Timberland	Via A. Depretis 100

Rome Stores by Category

Women's

Men's

Unisex

Children's

Women's Accessories

AVC by Adriana V.
  Campanile
Bally
Battistoni
BBC
Bottega Veneta
Bulgari
Calvin Klein
Carpisa
Claudio Sanò
Coin
Emporio Armani
Etro
Fendi
Furla
Gucci
Hermès
Hogan

La Rinascente
Louis Vuitton
Mandarina Duck
Mariella Burani
Marina Rinaldi
MaxMara
Moschino Jeans
Myriam B
Nia
Prada
Rene Caovilla
Salvatore Ferragamo
Sem Vaccaro
Sermoneta
Taba
TAD
Thé Verde
YSL Accessories

Women's Career

Blunauta
Carla G
Emporio Armani
Gai Mattiolo
Giorgio Armani

Luisa Spagnoli
Marina Rinaldi
MaxMara
Patrizia Pepe
Zara

Women's Cashmere/Knitwear

Alternative
Arli Cashmere
Battistoni
Celine
Davide Cenci
Eddy Monetti
Etro

Gallo
Kristina Ti
Krizia
Laura Biagiotti
Loro Piana
Malo
Prada

Women's Casual

Armani Jeans
Benetton
CK Jeans
Emporio Armani
Marlboro
Max & Co
Nia & Co
Pandemonium
Prada Sport

SBU
Sem Vaccaro
Sisley
Stefanel
Teichner
Timberland
T'Store
Zara

Women's Classic

Barbara Gregori
Battistoni
Brioni
Burberry Prorsum
Corner
Davide Cenci

DM
Eddy Monetti
Marina Rinaldi
Salvatore Ferragamo
Scapa

Women's Contemporary

244 Panisperna Via
Abit Art
Alexander
Alternative
Angelo di Nepi
Arsenale
Bagheera
Blumarine
Burberry Prorsum
Costume National
Custo
De Grillis
Fornarina
Gente
Gucci
Iceberg
Josephine de Huertas
Kristina Ti
Krizia
Laltramoda

L'Anatra all'Arancia
Le Gallinelle
Lei
Luna & L'Altra
Maga Morgana
Marni
Modi di Campagna
Molly Bloom
Moschino Jeans
Nia
Nuyorica
Patrizia Pepe
Prada
Sole by Soledad Twombly
TAD
Teichner
Tricots
Trussardi
Verso Sud
Vittoriana

Rome Categories

Women's Custom Tailoring

Battistoni

Women's Dance & Workout Apparel

Dancing Duck
Foot Locker

Women's Designer

244 Panisperna Via
Alberta Ferretti
Alternative
Blumarine
Calvin Klein
Celine
Chanel
Christian Dior
CK Jeans
Custo
Degli Effetti
Dolce & Gabbana
Eleonora
Emanuel Ungaro
Etro
Fendi
Gai Mattiolo
Galassia
Gente
GF Ferré
Gianni Versace
Giorgio Armani
Givenchy
Gucci
Hermès
Iceberg
L'Anatra all'Arancia
Laura Biagiotti
Leam
Louis Vuitton
Mariella Burani
Marni
Missoni
Moschino
Prada
Roberto Cavalli
Teichner
Valentino
Valentino Boutique
Versace Jeans Couture
Viktor & Rolf
Yves Saint Laurent

Women's Ethnic

Angelo di Nepi
Cambalache
Edo City
Ethic
Fabindia
Indoroman
Marco Polo
Taba
Thé Verde

Women's Eveningwear

Alberta Ferretti
Arsenale
Barbara Gregori
Blunauta
DM
Emanuel Ungaro
Gai Mattiolo
Giorgio Armani
Givenchy
La Perla
Maga Morgana
Mariella Burani
Valentino
Valentino Boutique
Vittoriana

Women's Furs

Christian Dior
Fendi

Women's Gloves

Sermoneta

Women's Handbags

Alviero Martini
AVC by Adriana V.
  Campanile
Bally
Bottega Veneta
Braccialini
Bulgari
Claudio Sanò
Dal Co
Eddy Monetti

Fendi
Furla
Gucci
Hermès
Louis Vuitton
Myriam B
Prada
Salvatore Ferragamo
Tod's
Trussardi

Women's Hats

Borsalino
Coin
La Rinascente

Women's Hosiery

Coin
Gallo

La Rinascente
Wolford

Women's Juniors

Diesel
Energie
Guess?
Jam
Miss Sixty

Onyx Fashion Store
Planet Store
Sub dued
Zara

Women's Leather

Brugnoli
Bruno Magli
Fendi
Gianfranco Ferré
Gucci
Hermès

Louis Vuitton
Prada
Sem Vaccaro
Silvano Lattanzi
Trussardi

Women's Lingerie

Coin
D&G
Intimissimi
Kristina Ti
La Perla

La Rinascente
Only Hearts
Prada
Tebro
Wolford

Maternity

Nicol Caramel
Prenatal

Women's Shoes

244 Panispena Via
Alternative
AVC by Adriana V.
  Campanile
Bagheera Accessori
Bally
Barrilà
Borini
Bottega Veneta
Brugnoli
Bruno Magli
Cesare Paciotti
Coin
Dal Co
De Grillis
Fratelli Rossetti
Furla
Gatto
Geox
Giuseppe Messina

Gorietti
Gucci
Hogan
Le 3 C
Loco
Mada
Nuyorica
Pollini
Prada
Puma Store
Rene Caovilla
Salvatore Ferragamo
Santoni
Sem Vaccaro
Sergio Rossi
Silvano Lattanzi
TAD
Tod's
Valleverde
Vicini

Women's Swimwear

Benetton
Coin
D&G
Demoiselle
DM
Gallo

Kristina Ti
La Perla
La Rinascente
Marisa Padovan
Tebro

Women's Vintage & Retro

Abiti Usati
Arsenale
Le Gallinelle
Omero & Cecilia—
  Vestiti Vecchi

People
Pulp
Vestiti Usati
  Cinzia

Women's Young & Trendy

244 Panispera Via
Alternative
D&G
Diesel
Energie
Expensive
Fornarina
Guess?
Jam
Just Cavalli
Le Ragazze Gold

Miss Sixty
Only Hearts
Onyx Fashion Store
Pandemonium
Pinko
Planet
Prototype
Replay
Sem Vaccaro
Sub dued
Zara

Men's Business Apparel

Battistoni
Belsiana 19
Brioni
Davide Cenci

Eddy Monetti
Salvatore Ferragamo
Valentino Uomo

Men's Casual

Belsiana 19
Benetton
CK Jeans
Corner
Fratelli Vigano
Marlboro
Modi di Campagna
Pandemonium

SBU
Sisley
Stefanel
Teichner
Timberland
T'Store
Vilebrequin
Zara`

Men's Cashmere/Knitwear

Arli Cashmere
Battistoni
Belsiana 19
Brioni
Davide Cenci
Gallo
Hermès

Loro Piana
Malo
Modi di Campagna
Prada Uomo
Rubinacci
Schostal

Men's Contemporary

Belsiana 19
Calvin Klein
Costume National
Degli Effetti
De Grillis
Emporio Armani
Etro
Gente

Gucci
Iceberg
Leam
Marni
Moschino Jeans
Prada Uomo
Teichner
Trussardi

Men's Custom Tailoring
Battistoni
Brioni
Rubinacci

Men's Designer
Calvin Klein
Christian Dior Homme
CK Jeans
Degli Effetti
Dolce & Gabbana
GF Ferré
Gianni Versace Uomo
Giorgio Armani
Gucci
Hermès
Hugo Boss
Iceberg
Leam
Marni
Moschino
Roberto Cavalli
Rubinacci
Teichner
Valentino Uomo
Versace Jeans Couture
Yves Saint Laurent

Men's Ethnic
Le Gallinelle
Marco Polo

Men's Furs
Fendi

Men's Gloves
Sermoneta

Men's Hats
Borsalino
Fratelli Vigano

Men's Juniors
Benetton
Diesel
Energie
Guess?
Jam
Onyx Fashion Store
Planet Store
Prototype

Men's Leather
Brugnoli
Bruno Magli
Fendi
Prada Uomo
Silvano Lattanzi
Trussardi

Men's Leather Goods

Alviero Martini
Bally
Bottega Veneta
Bruno Magli
Fendi
Fratelli Rossetti
Hermès
Louis Vuitton
Mandarina Duck
Piquadro
Prada Uomo
Salvatore Ferragamo
Trussardi

Men's Shirts

Belsiana 19
Camiceria Albertelli
Centoventi
Davide Cenci
Il Portone
Prada Uomo
Salvatore Ferragamo
Schostal
Tebro

Men's Shoes

Bally
Bottega Veneta
Brugnoli
Bruno Magli
Cesare Paciotti
Christian Dior Homme
Davide Cenci
De Grillis
Fendi
Fratelli Rossetti
Gatto
Geox
Gorietti
Hogan
Loco
Pollini
Prada Uomo
Puma Store
Salvatore Ferragamo
Santoni
Silvano Lattanzi
Tod's
Valleverde
Vicini

Men's Sportswear

Foot Locker
Fratelli Vigano
Modi di Campagna
Prada Sport

Men's Swimwear

Coin
Energie
Gallo
Il Portone
La Rinascente
Pandemonium
Tebro
Vilebrequin

Men's Ties

Centoventi
Davide Cenci
Fratelli Vigano
Gallo
Hermès

Il Portone
Rubinacci
Salvatore Ferragamo
Tebro

Men's Undergarments

Coin
D&G
Il Portone
Intimissimi

La Rinascente
Schostal
Tebro

Men's Vintage & Retro

Abiti Usati
Le Gallinelle
Omero & Cecilia—
  Vestiti Vecchi

Pulp
Vestiti Usati
  Cinzia

Men's Young & Trendy

D&G
Diesel
Energie
Guess?
Jam
Just Cavalli

Onyx Fashion Store
Pandemonium
Planet
Prototype
Replay
Zara

Unisex Accessories

Bally
Bottega Veneta
Coin

Gucci
La Rinascente
Piquadro

Unisex Athletic

Foot Locker
Puma Store

Tod's
Valleverde

Unisex Department Stores

Coin
La Rinascente

Unisex Ethnic

Cambalache
Marco Polo
Tebro

Unisex Jeans

Armani Jeans
Diesel
Just Cavalli
Pandemonium

Replay
SBU
T'Store

Unisex Outdoor Sports Equipment & Apparel

Foot Locker
Fratelli Vigano

Modi di Campagna
Prada Sport

Unisex Secondhand

Abiti Usati
Le Gallinelle
Omero & Cecilia-
  Vestiti Usati

Pulp
Vestiti Usati Cinzia

Children's Clothing

Arli Cashmere
Benetton
Bonpoint
Coin
Edo City
Gallo
Geox
I Vippini
La Cicogna
La Rinascente
Loro Piana

Marni
Moschino Jeans
Petit Bateau
Piccadilly
Prenatal
Prototype Kids
Replay
Scapa
Sub dued Kids
Tebro
Vicolo della Torretta Baby

Children's Designer

D&G
Gucci
Marni

Piccadilly
Pure

Children's Shoes

AVC by Adriana V.
  Campanile
Bonpoint
Bottega Veneta
Coin
Fratelli Rossetti
Hogan
I Vippini

La Cicogna
La Rinascente
Puma Concept Store
Pure
Timberland
Valleverde
Vicolo della Torretta Baby

Rome Restaurants

Rome In-Store Restaurant

Tad   06 326 95123
Via del Babuino 155/A
fusion Thai/Italian with glassed-in internal garden

Rome Restaurants

PIAZZA DI SPAGNA AREA

06   347 508 4733
Via del Leoncino 37
hip wine bar/pub hybrid with tempting oyster offer

Café Romano @ Hotel d'Inghilterra   06 699 81500
Via Borgognona 4/M
*pricey but good; shoppers won't find anywhere more conven-
ient than this*

Dal Bolognese   06 361 1426
Piazza del Popolo 1
*the best place in Rome for people-watching—if you can get a
table*

Dolci & Doni   06 699 25001
Via delle Carrozze 85/B
international snack bar

Fiaschetteria Beltramme   (no telephone)
Via della Croce 39
classic trattoria frequented by the artsy crowd

Gusto   06 322 6273
Piazza Augusto Imperatore 9
international, pizzeria; good for a quick buffet lunch

Il Margutta – Vegetariani dal 1979   06 326 50577
Via Margutta 118
help yourself from the vegetarian buffet

La Caffetteria   06 321 3344
Via Margutta 61/A
a huge theatrical place

L'Enoteca Antica   06 679 0896
Via della Croce 76/B
*wine bar with restaurant in the back at lunch-time; cold dishes
served all day*

Le Pain Quotidien   06 688 07727
Via Tomacelli 24-25
salads and sandwiches at rustic wooden tables

Matricianella   06 683 2100
Via del Leone 2/3/4
tasty Roman dishes and a great choice of wine

Naturist Club   06 679 2509
Via della Vite 14
vegetarian

Nino 06 679 5676
Via Borgognona 11
classic Tuscan; good, swift service

Osteria della Frezza 06 322 6273
Via della Frezza 16
the best cheese you've ever tasted

Rokko 06 488 1214
Via Rasella 138
Japanese

Settimio all'Arancio 06 687 6119
Via dell'Arancio 50
Italian

Shaki 06 679 1694
Via Mario de' Fiori 29/A
Designer wine-bar with food; grab an outdoor table if you can

Stravinskj Bar, Hotel de Russie
Via del Babuino
Fabulous garden with delicious views and the best martinis in town. The in spot for an aperitif.

Thé Verde 06 321 10174
Via Vittoria 23/Via Bocca del Leone 46
130 types of tea plus healthy snacks

PANTHEON AREA

Da Armando al Pantheon 06 688 03034
Salita de' Crescenzi 31
good-value, family-run trattoria, two steps from the Pantheon

Fortunato al Pantheon 06 679 2788
Via del Pantheon 55
traditional trattoria favored by journalists and politicians from parliament nearby

La Rosetta 06 686 1002
Via della Rosetta 9
fantastic fish; expensive

Maccheroni 06 683 07895
Piazza delle Coppelle 44
lively and frequented by a young hip crowd

CAMPO DE' FIORI AREA

Al Galletto 06 686 1714/686 5498
Piazza Farnese 102
Roman food best enjoyed at outdoor tables with views of Piazza Farnese

Al Sampietrino 06 688 02474
Piazza Campo de' Fiori 48
soups, salads

Crudo 06 683 8989
Via degli Specchi 6
food and wine-bar

Ditirambo
06 687 1626

Piazza della Cancelleria 74-75

reasonably priced, contemporary Italian in cozy surroundings; in summer, grab an outdoor table

Grappolo d'Oro Zampanò
06 689 7080

Piazza della Cancelleria 84

pizza in the evening; trattoria at lunch

L'Insalata Ricca
06 688 03656

Largo dei Chiavari 85-86

salad chain, fine for a quick, inexpensive light lunch

Monserrato
06 687 3386

Via Monserrato 96

moderately priced classic fish platters

New Jazz Café
06 682 10119

Via Giuseppe Zanardelli 12

delicious desserts

Osteria dell'Ingegno
06 678 0662

Piazza di Pietra 45

hip pasta and salad place favored by young professionals; great wines

Piazza Farnese
06 681 35104

Piazza Farnese 52

wine-bar with over 300 labels

Pierluigi
06 686 8717/686 1302

Piazza dei Ricci 144

classic Italian in pretty piazza beloved of tourists and suited politicians

PIAZZA NAVONA AREA

Antico Caffé della Pace
06 686 1216

Via della Pace 3-7

cozy coffee bar with timbered ceilings; views over Santa Maria della Pace from outdoor tables

Cul de Sac
06 688 01094

Piazza Pasquino 73

wine-bar with excellent cold cuts and salads; lunch until 4pm

Da Francesco
06 686 4009

Piazza del Fico 29

trattoria by day; pizzeria in the evening

L'Insalata Ricca
06 683 07881

Piazza Pasquino 72

salad chain, fine for a quick, inexpensive light lunch

Santa Lucia
06 688 02427

Largo Febo 12

VIPs, visitors and locals rub shoulders on the terrace; good food, variable service

VIA NAZIONALE AREA

Al Vino al Vino   06 485 803
Via dei Serpenti 19
tiny wine-bar with pasta, soup and cold cuts; great service

Doney   06 470 82805
Via Veneto 141
revamped historic café with buffet lunch

Fish   06 478 24962
Via dei Serpenti 16
pricey fish dishes in hip, hi-tech surroundings

Moma   06 420 11798
Via di San Basilio 42
Italian food in a colourful, minimalist setting

Valentini   06 488 0643
Via del Boschetto 37
Italian

PARIOLI

Al Ceppo   06 841 9696
Via Panama 2
*excellent, smart restaurant handy for the shops; not for those
who 'must dash'*

TRASTEVERE

Ivo   06 581 7082
Via San Francesco a Ripa 158
Cheap and cheerful pizzeria

Paris   06 581 5378
Piazza San Calisto 7/A
Excellent traditional Roman cuisine

Trattoria da Augusto   06 580 3798
Piazza de' Renzi 15
*rough-and-ready trattoria with paper-covered, wobbly tables
in pretty piazza. Service abominable*

SAN LORENZO

Arancia Blu   06 445 4105
Via dei Latini 57
*vegetarian in an elegant setting (dinner only, but lunch on
Sundays)*

Rome Services

Barbers

Haircuts (unisex)

Hair Salons

Beauty Treatments

Hair Removal

Manicures/Pedicures

Day Spas (unisex)

Massage Therapists

Make-up Artists

Fitness Studios

Yoga

Dry Cleaners

Mending & Alterations

Custom Embroidery

Custom Tailor

Shoe & Leather Repairs

Trimmings (ribbons, buttons etc)

Personal Shoppers

Drivers

Barbers

Antica Barberia Peppino　　　　　　　**06 679 8404**
Via della Vite 62　　　　　　　　　　　Tues-Sat 8:30-7

Barber Shop Mario　　　　　　　　　**06 687 9038**
Piazza del Teatro di Pompeo 44　　　　Tues-Sat 8:30-7

Fulciniti Antonio　　　　　　　　　**06 688 04258**
Via del Governo Vecchio 117　　　　　Tues-Sat 8:30-7

Valentino　　　　　　　　　　　　**06 688 01860**
Via dei Banchi Vecchi 8　　Tues-Sat 8:30-1:30, 3:30-7:30

Haircuts (unisex)

Aldo Coppola　　　　　　　　　　**06 692 00673**
Via Vittoria 78　　　　　Tues-Fri 9:30-7, Sat 9:30-6

Alternativa Hair Moda　　　　　　**06 686 9154**
Piazza della Cancelleria 70　　　　　Tues-Sat 9:30-7

Jean Louis David　　　　　　　　**06 681 36672**
Via Baullari 36　　　　　　　　　　Tues-Sat 9-7

Jean Louis David　　　　　　　　**06 688 03698**
Corso del Rinascimento 6　　　　　　(as above)

Jean Louis David　　　　　　　　**06 321 4751**
Via Cola di Rienzo 30-32　　　　　　Tues-Sat 10-7

Hair Salons

Alternativa Hair Moda　　　　　　**06 686 9154**
Piazza della Cancelleria 70　　　　　Tues-Sat 9:30-7

Compagnia della Bellezza　　　　**06 361 1003**
Via del Babuino 76　　　　　　　　Tues-Sat 9-6
compagniadellabellezza.it

I Cinque　　　　　　　　　　　**06 679 4331**
Via delle Carrozze 29　　　　　　Mon-Sat 9:30-7:30

I Sargassi　　　　　　　　　　**06 679 0637**
Via Frattina 48　　　　　　　　　Tues-Sat 9-6

Paride & Marco　　　　　　　　**06 686 4330**
Vicolo della Campana 2　　　　　　Tues-Sat 9-7

Roberto D'Antonio　　　　　　**06 679 3197**
Via di Pietra 90　　　　　　　　　Tues-Sat 9-7

Sergio Russo　　　　**06 678 1110/678 0457**
Piazza Mignanelli 25　　　　　　Tues-Sat 8:30-6

Sergio Valente　　　　**06 679 4515/679 1268**
Via dei Condotti 11　　　　　　Tues-Sat 9:30-6:30
sergiovalente.com

Viola　　　　　　　　　　　　**06 324 4500**
Via del Corso 36　　　　　　　　Tues-Sat 9-7

Beauty Treatments

Centro Benessere de Russie @ Hotel de Russie Spa
06 360 06028
Via del Babuino 9 — Daily 7-9

Compagnia della Bellezza — 06 361 1003
Via del Babuino 76 — Tues-Sat 9-6
compagniadellabellezza.it

I Sargassi — 06 679 0637
Via Frattina 48 — Tues-Sat 9-6

Oskarova — 06 841 5490
Via Savoia 20 — Mon-Fri 9:30-6

Sergio Valente — 06 679 4515/679 1268
Via dei Condotti 11 — Tues-Sat 9:30-6:30
sergiovalente.com

Viola — 06 324 4500
Via del Corso 36 — Tues-Sat 9-7

Hair Removal

Centro Benessere @ Hotel de Russie Spa — 06 360 06028
Via del Babuino 9 — Mon-Sun 7-9

Compagnia della Bellezza — 06 361 1003
Via del Babuino 76 — Tues-Sat 9-6
compagniadellabellezza.it

I Sargassi — 06 679 0637
Via Frattina 48 — Tues-Sat 9:30-6

Oskarova — 06 841 5490
Via Savoia 20 — Mon-Fri 9:30-6

Paride & Marco — 06 686 4330
Vicolo della Campana 2 — Tues-Sat 9-7

Sergio Valente — 06 679 4515/679 1268
Via dei Condotti 11 — Tues-Sat 9:30-6:30
sergiovalente.com

Manicures/Pedicures

Centro Benessere @ Hotel de Russie Spa — 06 360 06028
Via del Babuino 9 — Daily 7-9

Compagnia della Bellezza — 06 361 1003
Via del Babuino 76 — Tues-Sat 9-6
compagniadellabellezza.it

I Sargassi — 06 679 0637
Via Frattina 48 — Tues-Sat 9:30-6

Le Vespe — 06 420 12880
Via della Purificazione 13-14 — Tues-Sat 9:30-8:30

Paride & Marco — 06 686 4330
Vicolo della Campana 2 — Tues-Sat 9-7

Sergio Valente — 06 679 4515/679 1268
Via dei Condotti 11 — Tues-Sat 9:30-6:30
sergiovalente.com

Day Spas (unisex)

Aveda   **06 699 24257**
Rampa Mignanelli 9   Mon 3:30-7:30, Tues-Sat 10-8

Centro Benessere @ Hotel de Russie Spa   **06 360 06028**
Via del Babuino 9   Daily 7-9

Dabliù   **06 807 5577**
Viale Romania 22   Mon-Fri 7-10:30, Sat 9-8, Sun 10-2
dabliu.com

Hotel Hilton   **06 350 91**
Via Cadlolo 101   Mon-Fri 7-10, Sat-Sun 9-7
cavalierihilton.it

Massage Therapists

Centro Benessere @ Hotel de Russie Spa   **06 360 06028**
Via del Babuino 9   Daily 7-9

Mariuccia   **347 607 9705**
(by appointment)

Patrizia Ricagno (shiatsu massage)   **06 689 6054**
c/o Erboristeria degli Angeli   Mon-Sat 9-8
Piazza della Cancelleria 10

Make-up Artists

I Sargassi   **06 679 0637**
Via Frattina 48   Tues-Sat 9:30-6

Sergio Valente   **06 679 4515/679 1268**
Via dei Condotti 11   Tues-Sat 9:30-6:30
sergiovalente.com

Fitness Studios

Farnese Fitness   **06 687 6931**
Vicolo delle Grotte 35   Mon-Fri 9-10, Sat 11-6
                                  Sun (October-May) 10:30-1:30

Fight & Fitness (kick-boxing)   **06 806 87664**
Viale Parioli 162   Mon-Fri 10-10, Sat 10-8

The Health Club @ Hotel Excelsior   **06 470 82896**
Via Vittorio Veneto 125   Daily 7-10

Linea Fitness   **06 679 8356**
Via Bocca di Leone 60   Mon-Sat 8-9:30
lineafitness.net

Roman Sports Center   **06 320 1667/321 8096**
Via del Galoppatoio 33   Mon-Sat 8-10, Sun 9-3
romansportscenter.com

Spazio Danza Fitness   **06 688 05454**
Via Monte della Farina 14   Mon-Fri 9-10, Sat 9-8

Yoga

Associazione Kundalini Yoga   **06 573 00550**
Via G. Galvani 40   Mon-Sat 5-7:30

Daniele Rastelli c/o Ials   **06 323 6396**
Via Cesare Fracassini 60   Mon-Fri 9-11, Sat-Sun 9-8
ials.org

Margherita Peruzzo   **347 637 8303**
c/o Centro La Balena   classes Mon 1:30
Via dei Cappellari 127   Tues/Thurs 1:30 & 7:30
     (occasional Saturday workshops)

Dry Cleaners

(i) Haute Couture & Bridal

Tintoria La Flavia   **06 474 5544**
Via Flavia 85   Mon-Fri 9-3, 5-7:30

(ii) Leather & Suede

Tintoria al Parlamento   **06 687 3609**
Via dei Prefetti 15/A   Mon-Fri 8-1:30, 3:30-7, Sat 9-12:30

Tintoria La Torretta   **06 687 1325**
Piazza della Torretta 21   Mon-Fri 8:30-7:30, Sat 9:30-1

(iii) All-purpose

Tintoria Margutta   **06 323 6474**
Via Margutta 104   Mon-Fri 8:30-8, Sat 9-2

Tintoria al Parlamento   **06 687 3609**
Via dei Prefetti 15/A   (as before)

Tintoria La Torretta   **06 687 1325**
Piazza della Torretta 21   (as before)

Tintoria Rita   **06 687 9096**
Piazza Campo de' Fiori 38   Mon-Fri 8:30-8, Sat 8:30-2

Mending & Alterations

Orlo Jet   **06 687 3663**
Via Clementino 95/B   Mon-Fri 10-1, 3-7:30, Sat 10-3

Orlo Rapido   **06 353 43280**
Via della Balduina 130   Mon-Fri 9:30-7:30, Sat 9:30-2:30

Sartoria Cretara   **06 487 0657**
Via del Boschetto 75   Mon-Sat 10-2, 4.30-7

Sartoria Paola e Fabio   **06 683 07180**
Via dei Banchi Vecchi 19   Mon-Sat 8-1, 2-7

Speedy Orlo   **06 683 2086**
Vicolo dei Bovari 8   Mon-Fri 9:30-6

Custom Embroidery

Moltedo   **06 681 34223**
Via della Rotonda 37   Mon-Sat 9-8

Custom Tailor

Franco Cimenti   06 772 07288
Via Faleria 50   Mon-Sat 8-1, 3-8

Shoe & Leather Repairs

Calzolaio   (no telephone)
Via Monserrato 110

Giuseppe Di Iorio   (no telephone)
Via Arco della Ciambella 14

Leotta   06 481 9177
Via del Boschetto 20   Mon 3:30-7:30
          Tues-Fri 8:30-1, 3:30-7:30
          Sat 8:30-12

Mario   (no telephone)
Vicolo del Lupo 4

Sciuscià Chic (shoe shine only)   06 420 13733
Via Emilia 50   Mon-Fri 10-2, 3-7, Sat 10-2
sciusciachic.com

Trimmings (ribbons, buttons, etc)

Alfis   06 688 01970
Largo Ginnasi 6   Mon-Fri 9:30-6:30, Sat 9:30-1

Angelo Piperno   06 686 4394
Via S. Maria del Pianto 56   Mon-Sat 9-1, 4-8

Branciforte Filippo   06 686 5271
Piazza Paganica 12   Mon-Fri 9-7, Sat 9-1

Fermo Vallie al Tritone   06 488 2931
Via del Tritone 126-127   Mon-Sat 9:30-7:30

Liguori   06 678 3769
Via Belsiana 1   Mon 4-7:30, Tues-Sat 10-7:30

Passamanerie d'Epoca   (no telephone)
Via dei Cappellari 62

Personal Shopper

Elisa Rossi, Withstyle   06 481 9091
Via Monte Santo 2

Barbara Lessona   348 450 3655/06 855 1630
personalshoppersinitaly.com   06 4423 7225

Drivers

Anfici Limousine Service   06 630 918; 329 092 6700
Via Pio VIII 38   Daily 9-6

Taxis

06 3570

Where to Wear Florence 2006

Best Picks

Florence Best Picks

Here are our particular favourites (marked ☆ in
the Directory)

A Piedi Nudi nel Parco
Baroni
Borsalino
Bottega delle Antiche
  Terme
Bottega Veneta
Braccialini
Calvani
Casadei
Catwalk Collection
Celine
Dolce & Gabbana
Elio Ferraro Gallery/Store
Emilio Pucci
Ermenegildo Zegna
  Accessories
Etro
Gabs
Gerard
Gerard Loft
Gianfranco Lotti
Golubcik
Grevi
Gucci (jewellery)
Guya
Il Misio
Italobalestri

Loretta Caponi
Loro Piana
Louis Vuitton
Luisa Via Roma
Madova
Malloni
Mariella Burani
Mauro Volponi
MaxMara
Mazzini
Mila Schön
Nannini
Patrizia Pepe
Pinko
Poncif
Roberto Cavalli
Roberto Ugolini
Ruffo
Salvatore Ferragamo
Samples
Sergio Rossi
Spazio A
Stefano Bemer
Valentino
Vilebrequin
W.P. Store
Yves Saint Laurent

Florence Store Directory

Feeling guilty that your shopaholic urges have taken over, and you've replaced sightseeing with retail therapy? Don't despair, many of Florence's shopping spaces have been so beautifully restored that frescoes, Roman paving and vaulted ceilings litter the shops you will visit. Just think what you are saving on those entry tickets...all that extra cash to spend!

A word of warning, though. Newcomers to Italy's proudest cities may be amazed to discover that many stores close during the lunch hour, and in some cases the 'hour' is in practice two or two and a half hours. Don't despair, they will re-open! It's just that having invented one of the world's greatest cuisines, they see no reason why they shouldn't enjoy it. Our advice is to join them, and for each of the cities in this book we have provided a select list of restaurants, sidewalk cafés, salad bars, pizzerias etcetera, ideal for your shopping excursions.

We have also listed the opening hours for each store, though these may vary considerably; to avoid frustration, we recommend checking by telephone if in doubt. And finally, while Italian fashion and Italian clothing stores are among the most stylish in the world, you may be disappointed if you plan your shopping in August. The Italians have a special relationship with August (which is often fiendishly hot), and are happy to forsake retail in favour of the beach. If you too can't take the sweltering heat, follow the Florentines to Forte dei Marmi, only an hour and a half away. The private beaches there are well organized but not outstanding, but the shopping is a close match to what you get in Florence.

Allegri

The Via de' Tornabuoni store closed, but we are happy to say that everyone's favourite Italian rainwear brand is back with an elegant, slim-line little store close to Piazza degli Antinori. As ever, cutting a dash Allegri-style ensures innovative, impermeable fabrics in pieces that run from classic to contemporary. You're just as likely to find a conventional men's trench in a new generation super-light gabardine, as sharp jackets and raincoats in styles that are bang up to date. There are adorable women's raincoats in metallic fabrics that shimmer in scrunched-up pink, as well as pristine little zip-ups with white corrugated pleats. Let it rain, let it rain, let it rain! *allegri.it*

Expensive to luxury *Amex/MC/V*

Via de' Tornabuoni 72/R **055 213 737**
50123 Florence   Mon 3:30-7:30, Tues-Sat 10-1, 3:30-7:30

Anichini

Worried that the good old days when children only spoke when spoken to, girls only wore pink and all boys looked like Little Lord Fauntleroy have long gone? Not here. This is one of Florence's oldest family-run stores and it devotes itself entirely to handmade, beautifully crafted, traditional children's clothing. Sailor suits, smock dresses, bonnets, knitted booties—they are all here and Assunta Anichini, the proprietor, will even make items to order for that very special occasion. There is also a delightful collection of old-fashioned teddies to keep the little darlings occupied while you get carried away. Now all you need is the perambulator. *anichini.net*

Expensive *Amex/MC/V*

Via del Parione 59 **055 284 977**
50123 Florence   Mon 3:30-7:30, Tues-Sat 9-1, 3:30-7:30

☆ A Piedi Nudi nel Parco

'Barefoot in the Park' is the English translation of this idiosyncratic clothing and accessories boutique, just off the usual tourist track. The energetic owner Stella Falautano is a big fan of the unusual but practical, and stocks Italian ready-to-wear labels with that little edge. Her colour preferences are muted but she revels in quirky details. Current favourites are Rose & Sassi from Tuscany with intriguing jackets made from panels of silk and cotton attached with poppers, and Roman label Morfosis whose simple black linen pleated skirts have darts adorned with multicoloured zips. Most striking of all are linen dresses, skirts and trousers by Malloni, with details like slipped waistbands or layered hems. Unusual accessories complete the mix with a strong line from Unica Collezione: their gorgeous twill scarves which convert into shoulder bags and bikinis will stop the traffic if you dare to wear them in the street. If you don't find Stella here, look out for her presiding over her new baby, the Malloni store on Via Calimala.

Moderate *Amex/MC/V*

Borgo degli Albizi 46/R
50122 Florence

055 234 0768
Mon 3-8, Tues-Sat 10-8

Athletes World

Athletes World is aimed more at cool kids in search of hot trainers, sportswear and street style than at serious sports enthusiasts looking for professional kit (go to Il Rifugio Sport if that's what you need). One whole wall is given over to a comprehensive run-through of the latest line-up of trendy trainers from Adidas, Nike, Converse and Puma. It comes as no surprise, then, to learn that the chain actually belongs to the international shoe empire, Bata, which has a strong fashion orientation. The rest of the store is an infectious mix of streetwear for men and women (or perhaps we should say boys and girls) by German label Time Zone, some cute tees with cartoony doggy heads by Custard House, as well as the usual range of tracksuits, vests, sweats and parkas by Adidas, Nike and co. True athletes need not darken the doorstep. *bata.it*

Affordable   *Amex/MC/V*

Via de' Cerretani 26-28/R
50123 Florence

055 288 094
Daily 9:30-7:30 (Sun 11-7:30)

Bagamunda

Not in the mood for serious fashion? Head to Bagamunda to check out the latest wacky bag and shoe line by Florentine Paola del Lungo. (The designer also does more heavyweight accessories—see under Paola del Lungo). The philosophy here is light-hearted but commercial, as reflected in the decor which features a mega screen over the door and loads of funky purple. The wisecracking bags and shoes look great on first impact, though, like bad jokes, their rather obvious irony may soon wear off. Still, they do raise an immediate laugh and make the perfect icebreaker at parties. This season, del Lungo is playing with pop art and has splashed Warhol-type Campbell's Soup and Brillo-pad logos over stilettos and slim shoulder bags—the effect is surprisingly clean and striking. On a different tack, there are also nappa bucket bags that look like voluptuous corsets laced up over brimming bosoms. *bagamunda.it/genius2000.it*

Affordable   *Amex/MC/V*

Via de' Cerretani 72/R
50123 Florence

055 280 642
Daily 9-7:30 (Sun 11:30-7:30)

☆ Baroni

Baroni is part of the noble Florentine tradition of embroidered, hand-finished linens for the dining table, bathroom and bedroom. Fortunately for your kids, it also makes handmade clothes in natural fabrics like silk, cotton, wool and linen for children up to 5. Founded in 1912 by three sisters, this family-run company has its own workshop in Florence and ships all over the world. Even if you've never threaded a needle on your life, take time to study just one exquisitely embroidered tablecloth: you will soon fall under its spell. Children's clothes are irresistible, with delicious little white smocked dresses and seersucker dungarees to bend your heart. The Tornabuoni shop offers the core of Baroni's classic range. Head to the Porta Rossa store for childrenswear in more accessible, modern styles like Petit Bateau and OshKosh. baroni-firenze.com

Expensive   *Amex/MC/V*

Via de' Tornabuoni 9/R   **055 210 562**
50123 Florence   Mon 3:30-7:30, Tues-Sat 10-7:30

Via Porta Rossa 56/R   **055 280 953**
50121 Florence   (opening hours as above)

Via Senese 25/R   **055 233 5147**
50124 Florence   Mon-Fri 9-1, 3:30-7:30, Sat 9-1

Benetton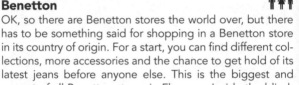

OK, so there are Benetton stores the world over, but there has to be something said for shopping in a Benetton store in its country of origin. For a start, you can find different collections, more accessories and the chance to get hold of its latest jeans before anyone else. This is the biggest and newest of all Benetton stores in Florence. Inside the blinding white interior you'll find an extensive collection of kids', teenagers', men's and women's clothing and accessories. Just remember to keep your shades on. benetton.com

Affordable   *Amex/MC/V*

Via Borgo San Lorenzo 17/R   **055 264 5643**
50100 Florence   Mon 3:30-7:30, Tues-Sat 10-7:30
                                          Sun 10:30-7:30

Benetton 0-12

Italian mammas head to Benetton 0-12 in search of trendy togs for kids aged 0-12 at excellent prices. The store is much larger than it appears from the street and sprawls over two spacious floors with each area clearly marked according to age group. Downstairs, you'll find terrycloth romper suits, bibs, booties and useful baby accessories, plus a small corner dedicated to mammas-to-be with casual trousers, skirts, shirts and tees made from extra-comfortable fabrics. The clothes won't last for ever, but who cares? Baby will have grown out of them quite soon.

Affordable   *Amex/MC/V*

Via de' Cerretani 60-62   **055 214 639**
50123 Florence   Mon 3:30-7:30, Tues-Sat 10-7:30
                                    (winter, Sun 11-7:30)

Bonora

Here's a little secret that you might like to know: classic Tuscan shoemaker Bonora part-owns the Milan-based Car Shoe brand with Prada. Indeed, Bonora has been even known to sell the identical Car Shoes that you'll find up the street in Prada, for 70 euros less…keep that under your hat! Bonora also offers candy-coloured Car Shoe moccasins and pumps with dinky little shoulder bags to match. That's on the ready-made side of the house, but the true appeal lies in the classic, made-to-measure footwear. The handmade men's brogues and lace-ups are monumental—130 phases of manual work go into every shoe. All you have to do is sit down on the cosy, quilted seats and pick a leather while your feet are being measured. It is no surprise that it can take up to six months for these shoes to be completed. They will be worth the wait.

Luxury   *Amex/MC/V*
Via del Parione 11-13-15/R   **055 283 280**
50123 Florence   Mon 3-7, Tues-Sat 10:30-1, 1:30-7

☆ Borsalino

Via Porta Rossa, just opposite a beautiful colonnaded open-air marketplace, is where the Borsalino story began back in 1857. Even though Borsalino is rapidly expanding into a global chain, do not expect to be wowed by the very average decor of the shop. Borsalino's success is not based on its cutting-edge branding but on the quality of the handcrafted products. One wall of this small shop is completely taken over by the most popular model, which switches from the panama (to shade sensitive skins in blazing summer) to the winter warmer, the classic rabbit felt hat. If you wish to be more fashionable, try the waterproof Travel range; and if you are looking for something extra special there are stripey peak caps in three pastel colours (as worn by Madonna and Guy). Another irresistible classic is the 1940s-style button cap which could have walked straight off *The Cotton Club* film set. You can also find shirts, ties and a small range of leather accessories. For something more feminine, go up the scuffed stairs to the second floor and you will find a display of hats perfect for weddings. Their styles are made to play the supporting role, and are not meant to take centre stage in a wedding outfit ensemble.   *borsalino.com*

Expensive   *Amex/MC/V*
Via Porta Rossa 40/R   **055 218 275**
50123 Florence   Mon-Sat 9:30-7:30
Via della Vigna Nuova 60/R   **055 295 431**
50123 Florence   Mon 3:30-7:30, Tues-Sat 10-7:30

☆ Bottega delle Antiche Terme

The Bottega delle Antiche Terme sits on one of the tiniest but most charming squares in Florence, the Piazza del Limbo, oddly named after the nowhereland bordering on Hell. In fact, you won't get any closer to heaven than this delightful store where Simone Abbarchi makes made-to-measure shirts in a busy atelier that was once an ancient spa. With over 500 fabrics to choose from in silk, cotton and linen, and 20 different collar designs, it's no wonder customers who shop here don't want too many people to know about it. But try as they may, word travels and those lucky enough to hear about Abbarchi are quick to place their orders for one-off pieces which no one else will have. Abbarchi makes trousers too...just try not to tell anyone.

Luxury   *Amex/MC/V*
Borgo Santissimi Apostoli 16/R   **055 210 552**
50123 Florence   Mon 3-7:30, Tues-Sat 10:30-1, 3-7:30

☆ Bottega Veneta

Bottega Veneta's Florence store is hidden away at the top of Via de' Tornabuoni opposite Ferragamo in the historic Palazzo Gianfigliazzi. The small frontage hides a fabulous high-ceilinged room behind. First, though, you have to brave a merciless corridor of mirrors. If you make it to the other side, you'll find yourself in a wonderland full of the bags on every fashion editor's must-have list. It is easy to see why. The signature plaited leather is butter-soft and woven into a bewitching range of classic and quirky styles. Take a look at the shoes as well. Snub-nosed kitten-heel courts with Bottega's familiar butterfly motif discreetly punched into them are adorable, whilst simple plaited slingbacks are superlatively elegant. As befits this dream store, the staff are relaxed and welcoming.   *bottegaveneta.com*

Luxury   *Amex/MC/V*
Via de' Tornabuoni 7/R   **055 284 735**
50123 Florence   Mon-Fri 10-7, Sat 10-7:30

BP Studio

These Italian knitwear specialists certainly spin a mean weave. Brilliant polka-dot twinsets, delicate cobweb scarves and cute little tulle popsocks are among the winners at their bright, slim-line store which kicks off Via della Vigna Nuova. There are also sweaters, tops and shawls made from the very best wool, cashmere, linen and cotton. The architects-turned-fashion-designers behind the label take their inspiration from faraway lands: India, Nepal and Morocco are just a few of the places which influence their choice of exotic colours and styles. They also offer pieces by labels like Paul Smith and Custo.

Expensive   *Amex/MC/V*
Via della Vigna Nuova 15/R   **055 213 243**
50123 Florence   Mon 3-7, Tues-Sat 10-2, 3-7

☆ Braccialini

Give Braccialini the benefit of the doubt. If you are a minimalist or monochromatic type, chances are that its riotous window of handbags bursting with spring flowers, colourful graffiti, or even thatched roofs and cottage gardens may send you running. But stick your nose into the bright little shop anyway. Once you really study the bags you have to marvel at the wealth of detail that goes into stitching swirling buds and leaves all over them. The younger Tua line even includes dinky little holdalls with multicoloured flowers that popper on and off. What's more, Braccialini is a local company with a serious pedigree. Based in Pontassieve just outside Florence, it is now part-owned by the Mariella Burani group and also produces bags for Patrick Cox and Vivienne Westwood. Nobody is going to use a Braccialini bag for business meetings, but it will cheer up the cloudiest day or inject humour into the soberest little black outfit. And you know what they say about those who insist on 'all work and no play'. *braccialini.it*

Expensive	*Amex/MC/V*
Via della Vigna Nuova 30/R	**055 288 442**
50123 Florence	Mon 3-7, Tues-Sat 10-7

Brioni

Brioni now has only one store in Florence, hidden away on Via de' Rondinelli. There is a hushed air as you are ushered into the spacious rooms, but the company's history deserves respect. It goes back to the post-war period when the likes of Clark Cable, Gary Cooper and Kirk Douglas used to hotfoot it to Rome to stock up on classic Brioni style. Nowadays, Pierce Brosnan picks out immaculate made-to-measure suits and casual wear here. He'll have to wait two months for a suit, not least because the wool has to breathe and adjust after it has been pressed 184 times during preparation. If you are in a rush, though, the ready-to-wear collection maintains the timeless style (as well as saving you a euro or two). Menswear definitely dominates but there are also some elegant (if pricey) womenswear pieces, including some wonderful pashminas. *brioni.it*

Luxury	*Amex/MC/V*
Via de' Rondinelli 7/R	**055 210 646**
50123 Florence	Mon-Sat 10-7

Bruno Magli

Bruno Magli has been passing through some choppy financial waters recently, but all remains serene at the Florence store. The sumptuous brown and rich orange interior envelops you in a state of pure luxury and it is impossible to resist the expertly crafted leather shoes and accessories displayed like jewels in glass cases. The women's collection of butter-soft leather jackets, shoes and handbags can be found towards the front of the shop, while the men can indulge themselves in jackets, shoes, ties and bags towards the rear. If your budget is more little league than major league, don't despair because there are a number of smaller items to be had, packaged just as beautifully. Even the shop assistants are in awe. *brunomagli.com*

Expensive *Amex/MC/V*
Via Roma 26-28/R **055 239 9497**
50123 Florence Mon-Sat 10-7

Cabo

Don't go anywhere near this shop if you are feeling fragile. If the colours and patterns don't send you over the edge, the strident swirly-whirly marble flooring definitely will. If, on the other hand, you're desperate for a little Missoni magic in Florence, this is your best bet. Cabo boasts a huge collection of the label's luxurious knitwear with its famously attention-grabbing swirls and stripes, and delights in those items that push the knitwear boundary just that little bit further. Currently the collection spans from sweeping cardigans to suits and further still to bikinis and dressing-gowns. The limelight-shy may want to check out some of the toned-down looks created by Angela Missoni.

Expensive *Amex/MC/V*
Via Porta Rossa 77-79/R **055 215 774**
50121 Florence Mon-Sat 10-7:30

☆ Calvani

For shoes that are ideal for stepping off the beaten track, head to Maurizia Calvani's unorthodox store. Take your time to browse its serpentine corridor of windows: you'll gradually be drawn into her unique vision of shoes as convention-shattering artworks, more worthy of a museum plinth than a fashionista's foot. Alongside more familiar names like Dirk Bikkenberg, Dries Van Noten and Camper, Calvani stocks footwear by new talents whom she has hunted down around Italy. Recent additions to the constantly evolving line-up include Ash's dinky kitten-heeled courts in high-lighter-pen fluorescent green, pink and orange and Premiata's ruched leather peep-toe pumps. Relax, though: there is nothing precious about this shop. The staff are laid-back and Maurizia's golden labrador, Linda, is usually on hand to welcome shoppers.

Moderate *Amex/MC/V*
Via degli Speziali 7/R **055 265 4043**
50123 Florence Mon 2:30-7:30, Tues-Sat 10-7:30
Sun 3:30-7:30

Calzoleria Bologna

Calzoleria Bologna's main store is slap bang in front of the cathedral's dramatic, octagonal baptistery, but it doesn't seem too cowed by such an august setting. There is something of the market stall about this open-fronted shop. It acts as a beacon to Florentine youth who buzz around the windows commenting on the boisterous mix of flash and sexy shoes. For the girls, there are dimity little pumps with myriad lines of horizontal stitching and zany, multicoloured fan-bows on the front, or Vivien Lee stilettos in sweetie-box colours. For the boys there are distressed-croc pointed loafers from Next Tech, but also more conventional hand-stitched moccasins from American label Harris. Finally, there are cool Paciotti 4US sneakers for everyone.

Moderate   *Amex/MC/V*

Piazza S. Giovanni 13-15/R   **055 290 545**
50129 Florence   Mon 2:30-7:30, Tues-Sat 9:30-7:30
Sun 3-7:30

Via S. Antonino 9-11/R   **055 283 145**
50123 Florence   Mon 2-8, Tues-Sat 9:30-8

Via de' Cerretani 50/R   **055 238 1849**
50123 Florence   Sun-Mon 2:30-7:30, Tues-Sat 9:30-7:30

Camper

If you are not familiar with Camper, this line-up of ethnic, mostly flat unisex shoes displayed on a simple green plat-form may look a tad earnest. Step inside, though, and you soon discover the Majorcan company's sense of humour. The simple green platform is actually Astroturf with a clever mirrored hole carved into it so that you can eye up your feet while you're trying on. Pairs made of two odd shoes (the Twin series) are bestsellers—we had to laugh at white stitched spermatozoa squiggling mischievously from one red shoe to another. Be sure to inspect the soles—there may be a quirky design hiding there too. Bright young staff complete the light-hearted mix.   *camper.com*

Moderate   *Amex/MC/V*

Via Por Santa Maria 47/R   **055 267 0342**
50120 Florence   Mon-Sat 10-7:30, Sun 11-2, 2:30-7:30

☆ Casadei

Casadei is up there with Sergio Rossi for sharp, sexy footwear destined for the Hollywood set. The Via de' Tornabuoni store was the Emilia-Romagna-based brand's first ever free-standing store, and it still feels more like a local shoe shop than part of a global chain—with the warm staff welcome you'd expect. Browse the deep-set windows before stepping inside. You'll soon be marvelling at exquis-itely made shoes in materials that you never thought you'd see gracing anyone's feet. The latest looks include knee boots in rich velour, summer ankle boots in open weave camouflage-printed nets, and sandals made from deck-chair canvas. Men may be tempted by the snappy crocodile boots…but if you're looking for a basic brown lace-up, head elsewhere.   *casadei.com*

Luxury   *Amex/MC/V*

Via de' Tornabuoni 33/R   **055 287 240**
50123 Florence   Mon 3-7, Tues-Fri 10-1:30
2:30-7, Sat 10-7

☆ Catwalk Collection ♀

This new store from London-based Catwalk Collection spe-cialises in bustiers and corset dresses that maximise your assets and make you feel all woman. In fact, curves this womanly can surely give Dolce & Gabbana a run for their money. There are provocative black-and-red combinations that may be just too risqué for some. But look out, too, for delicious softer colours that are more country wench, and that delight and entice with delicate lacing, beading and rose buds. Still, make no mistake, designer Lionel Parks' vision is deliberately OTT, and it comes as no surprise to learn that Catwalk Collection has dressed women with heavy-duty stage presences from Shirley Bassey to Lil Kim and busty desert island icon Jordan. The question is: are you hussy enough? *catwalk-collection.co.uk*

Expensive *Amex/MC/V*

Borgo Ognissanti 69/R **055 260 8978**
50123 Florence Mon-Sat 10-2, 3-8, Sun 4-8

☆ Celine ♀

Michael Kors, who took charge of this label a few years ago, gave Celine a breath of fresh air and the label was sudden-ly centre stage. He has now left and a new designer was about to be announced as we went to press, but the underlying New York Park Avenue power look is defintely still on the table. Celine is the latest big name to open on Tornabuoni. The space is sleek, with an all-white decor with dark wood trim on a floor covered with crisp sea-grass mat-ting. You can see the perfect cut of the clothes even as they drape over the hangers. They are timeless, wearable things not targeted to a certain age or look; they are aimed at the fashion conscious rather than the fashion victim. Stylish celebrities who love this easy look include Angelica Huston, Lauren Hutton, Claire Danes, Gwyneth Paltrow and Rene Russo, who wore Celine beautifully in *The Thomas Crown Affair* remake. You will also find plenty of logo-splattered bags, and if you are looking for something a little different grab a pair of flip-flops for the beach in three fluorescent colours. *celine.com*

Expensive *Amex/MC/V*

Via de' Tornabuoni 24-26-28/R **055 264 5521**
50123 Florence Mon-Sat 10:30-7:30

Celyn b. ♀

Bologna-based Celyn b. started out in 1998 and now has a chain of stores throughout provincial Italy. The striking Florence boutique opened in 2003, with its tall, glass-walled white space scythed in two by a massive floor-to-ceiling black column of uncertain purpose. Is it a design feature, or is it actually holding up the building? It looks fab, but the staff have a hard time maintaining their cool as they bob either side trying to keep tabs on you. In fact, Celyn b. is altogether rather unpredictable. It all looks so high-end, yet the clothes turn out to be inexpensive and heavy on the bimbo quotient with loads of fringing, lacing and peek-a-boo lace on the bottom of bouclé micromin-is. Women over 25 with a lump or two in excess, enter at your peril. *celynb.it*

Affordable *Amex/MC/V*

Via Tosinghi 18/R **055 285 823**
50100 Florence Mon 3:30-7:30, Tues-Sat 10-7:30
(last Sunday of the month 3:30-7:30)

Cesare Paciotti

Like so many retail spaces in this city, the Cesare Paciotti store is little more than a slim alleyway with just enough room for the shoes and bags to line the walls. No prob-lem, these are shoes that will grab the limelight wherever they find themselves. Paciotti's style is seriously sexy. For men he pays particular attention to the choice of leathers to produce sharp, ostentatious results. Look out for python, kangaroo (particularly for lightweight summer shoes) and rooster-foot (hardwearing but, logically enough, only comes in small strips which have to be joined together). Women's styles have less adventurous leathers but equally wild designs with acid colours, vertig-inous spikes and bondage straps. After all this aggression, it comes as a pleasant surprise to find the welcome is mild and easy-going. *cesare-paciotti.com*

Expensive *Amex/MC/V*

Via della Vigna Nuova 14/R **055 215 471**
50123 Florence Mon 3-7, Tues-Sat 10-7

Champion

The Florence store of American sportswear label Champion could have warped here from a shopping mall anywhere in the States, or anywhere in the world for that matter. You are not going to get a Florentine experience in here—unless you are prepared to take the tight store dimensions into consideration. Expect a whole range of casual styles for just hanging out in or for getting down to a serious workout. Hooded sweat tops, T-shirts, track-suits, footwear and socks are all splashed with the Champion logo. Prices are distinctly reasonable. Downstairs there is a children's department, well stocked with mini trainers, T-shirts, swimsuits and vests for bud-ding young Olympians. *champion.it*

Affordable *Amex/MC/V*

Via Por Santa Maria 52-54/A **055 280 120**
50100 Florence Daily 10-7:30 (Sun 10:30-1:30, 2:30-7:30)

Christian Dior

It may not be large, but the narrow Christian Dior store still manages to stir frissons of fashion excitement as you enter. Sleek mirrored walls frame larger-than-life screen images of the latest runway collection to get you in the mood. Shimmy past the saddlebags and shoes to get to the serious ready-to-wear collections in the middle of the store. For autumn/winter 2005-2006 OTT is OUT! John Galliano's latest collection is less outrageous and even more wearable. Aside from the black and white stripey mohair dresses, the daywear focus is on combat which comes in crocodile, khaki, satin and shearling. For the evening there are little baby doll numbers and lots of puffed and ruched velvets. Travel down to the end of the store and you will come across the micro jewel and kids departments. Over at the *haute joaillerie* you can gawp at Victoire Castellane's fabulous creations. Here you can go from the smallest ring ever made to giant gems which can set you back over 13,000 euros. Don't despair at the smallness of the store: the walls and cabinets are full of invisible compartments, and the ever helpful assistants are at your service to whip out whatever whimsical item you may be feeling the need of…say a Dior baby bottle?   *dior.com*

Luxury   *Amex/MC/V*

Via de' Tornabuoni 57-59   **055 266 9101**
50123 Florence   Daily 10-7 (Sun 2-7)

Coccinelle

Need to inject fresh life into your entire wardrobe without starting from scratch? Invest in a handbag! Coccinelle is one of three brands (along with Furla and Florentine contender Nannini) that offer outstanding quality and design in handbags, shoes and accessories—from travel bags to make-up cases and purses, at reasonable prices. Be prepared for a tidal wave of colour in leather, canvas, crocodile and suede. Never fear, there are usually safer classic colours hidden away in the drawers below. But why not indulge? The latest looks include St Tropez bags of softest ochre suede punched with a simple line of silver holes through which you thread your own choice of brightly-coloured scarf to create the straps. When you're out and about, you'll spot Coccinelle bags with metallic edgings, suede fringes, and costume jewellery applications swinging from some of the most stylish shoulders in town.   *coccinelle.it*

Moderate   *Amex/MC/V*

Via Por Santa Maria 49/R   **055 239 8782**
50122 Florence   Daily 10-7:30 (Sun 11-7:30)

Coin

Florence's Coin is a breezy little outpost of the Veneto-based department store chain, housed in a 16th-century palazzo. It doesn't satisfy on all fronts, but let's begin with its strong points. The MAC make-up corner is definitely worth a visit; the hats, bags, scarves and hosiery on the ground floor are bright, innovative and usually reasonably priced; the homewares in the basement often include great Italian-designed Indian textiles; and the menswear department (towards the back on the ground floor) is well stocked with Trussardi Sport, Timberland and Marina Yachting. Not so strong are the clothing choices for women, with too much repetitive Esprit, some cheap-looking department store labels and a disappointingly thin smattering of Trussardi Sport and D&G. Hidden away on the top floor is a stationery department and childrenswear. Still, the overall mood is upbeat and fresh. Give it a whirl.　　*coin.it*

Affordable to moderate　　　　　　　　　*Amex/MC/V*

Via dei Calzaiuoli 56　　　　　　　　**055 280 531**
50122 Florence　　　　　　　　Daily 10-8 (Sun 11-8)

Desmo

By the time you've strolled down Via della Vigna Nuova to get to Desmo, you will have realised that you're in a little corner of handbag heaven. There's something for every taste and budget, and up there at the very apex of luxury, along with Gianfranco Lotti, you'll find Desmo. Like Lotti, this is a Florence-based family company, but whilst Lotti uses restrained, modern lines, Desmo careers off into wilder, more eclectic territory. The minimalist store is in simple burnt Siena tones with a linear central catwalk, a perfect foil or the company's complex bags. This season, there are delicate netted shoppers with frothy organza linings, and funky Zanzibar bags in orange-tinted patent python, with scrunched borders and ornate cowboy buckles. The prices are not for those who need to examine the tag—but with only two other stores in Italy you can pretty much guarantee that you won't see your bag swinging off too many other shoulders as you wander back down the street.　　　　　　　　　　　*desmo.it*

Luxury　　　　　　　　　　　　　*Amex/MC/V*

Piazza Rucellai 10/R　　　　　　　　**055 292 395**
50123 Florence　　Mon 3-7:30, Tues-Sat 10-1:30, 2:30-7:30

Diesel

As the younger generation of jeans wearers discovered a long time ago, this maverick denim brand, under Italian designer Renzo Russo, is for anyone who wouldn't be seen dead in a pair of 501s. Florence's Diesel store may not be one of the brand's official flagships, but it's certainly not lacking in choice. With an overwhelming range of engineered jeans on the ground floor, and the complete womenswear and accessories collection on the first, the store has a spacious feel and a seriously hip groove. Whether you're looking for funky stone-washed hues or just plain blues, neat hems or mile-high turn-ups, you're bound to find something to suit.   *diesel.com*

Moderate   *Amex/MC/V*

Via dei Lamberti 13/R   **055 239 9963**
50123 Florence   Sun-Mon 2-7:30, Tues-Sat 10:30-7:30

☆ Dolce & Gabbana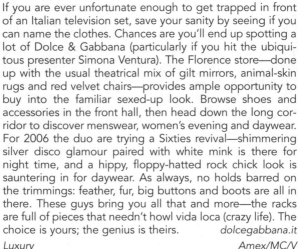

If you are ever unfortunate enough to get trapped in front of an Italian television set, save your sanity by seeing if you can name the clothes. Chances are you'll end up spotting a lot of Dolce & Gabbana (particularly if you hit the ubiquitous presenter Simona Ventura). The Florence store—done up with the usual theatrical mix of gilt mirrors, animal-skin rugs and red velvet chairs—provides ample opportunity to buy into the familiar sexed-up look. Browse shoes and accessories in the front hall, then head down the long corridor to discover menswear, women's evening and daywear. For 2006 the duo are trying a Sixties revival—shimmering silver disco glamour paired with white mink is there for night time, and a hippy, floppy-hatted rock chick look is sauntering in for daywear. As always, no holds barred on the trimmings: feather, fur, big buttons and boots are all in there. These guys bring you all that and more—the racks are full of pieces that needn't howl vida loca (crazy life). The choice is yours; the genius is theirs.   *dolcegabbana.it*

Luxury   *Amex/MC/V*

Via della Vigna Nuova 27/R   **055 281 003**
50123 Florence   Mon 3-7, Tues-Sat 10-7

Du Pareil Au Même

Sunny French childrenswear chain Du Pareil Au Meme now has a foothold in Florence with this busy little store on bustling Via Panzani. Frazzled Florentine mothers crowd in to fight over affordable pieces for babies and children up to the age of 11. Space is tight and racks and shelves are bulging with brightly coloured tees, dresses and jeans with DPAM's signature animal and flower drawings printed, appliquéd and embroidered everywhere. The mood is light-hearted and at these prices it is difficult to resist picking up something, even if just as a gift.   *dpam.fr*

Affordable   *Amex/MC/V*

Via Panzani 36/38R   **055 265 8315**
50123 Florence   Mon 1-7:30, Tues-Sat 10-7:30

☆ Elio Ferraro Gallery/Store

Sicilian-born Elio Ferraro was right to call his vintage boutique a gallery. Walking in here is like stepping inside the glass displays at the Victoria & Albert Museum; you can actually touch original pieces by YSL, Dior, Chanel and many other designers from the Thirties on. No wonder creative teams from Calvin Klein, Pucci and Coach have visited in search of inspiration. There is something almost moving about trying on a silk daydress by 'old Gucci' as if you were buying it for the first time—unfortunately the price will be strictly up-to-date, so don't expect to stumble on a bargain. Ferraro trawls Japan, New York and Paris for clothing and accessories for both men and women, while also finding time to design some one-off pieces himself. His nostalgia extends back half a century to furniture by the likes of Sotsass, Panton and Jacobson. With plans for a New York opening, though, Ferraro is definitely not stuck in the past.   *elioferraro.com*

Expensive   *Amex/MC/V*
Via del Parione 47/R   **055 290 425**
50123 Florence   Mon 3-8, Tues-Sat 9:30-8

☆ Emilio Pucci Boutique

The Marchese Emilio Pucci was born in Tuscany, and in the Fifties one of the original inspirations for his unique swirling prints were the colourful flags of Siena's contrade (city districts) at Palio time. Nowadays Christian Lacroix is in charge of design and spins those prints in hot new Mediterranean combinations that are guaranteed to warm up even the most miserable of summers. Sultry, dark-skinned girls look great in these vibrant prints but if you have a pale English rose complexion you'll probably fade to grey in them. But check out the stunning white space-pod store anyway just for the sheer sunshiny fun of it. There are also gorgeous beach bags, sandals and accessories that anyone can wear.   *emiliopucci.com*

Luxury   *Amex/MC/V*
Via de' Tornabuoni 20-22/R   **055 265 8082**
50123 Florence   Mon-Sat 10-7

Emporio Armani

Fittingly, Emporio Armani stands in the monumental, austere Piazza Strozzi whose clean, simple lines make the perfect antechamber for Giorgio's designs. Armani's innovative diffusion line offers sportier, younger styles (at slightly more affordable prices) than the main label, but exhibits the same high-quality fabrics, careful tailoring and aversion to frippery. The vast collection includes eyewear, perfume, men's and women's apparel and a full range of unassuming accessories. Count on finding some seriously streamlined jackets, trouser suits, evening dresses and jackets cut as only Giorgio knows how. But it's not all restrained sobriety: like the merry-go-round that occasionally disturbs the serious serenity of Piazza Strozzi, Giorgio is quite capable of throwing in splashes of colour that effortlessly inject just the right amount of fizz.   *emporioarmani.com*

Expensive   *Amex/MC/V*
Piazza Strozzi 16/R   **055 284 315**
50123 Florence   Mon 3-7, Tues-Fri 10-7
                                            Sat 10:30-7:30

E-Play

The Florentine E-Play store has a bleak, hard-edged feel with underfloor lighting creeping through the cracks and steel netting writhing above your head…a steaming sidewalk manhole cover and the scene would be complete. Expect Replay's streetwise sibling to propose rebellious, sexy dressing with the clear aim of shocking the parents: think tiny shredded white linen minis and black-and-white check capri pants with go-faster stripes and corset lacing. And boys and girls can hang on street corners in the We're jeans line, which mixes vintage with a tougher vibe. *e-play.it*

Moderate *Amex/MC/V*

Via de' Tosinghi 14/R **055 293 440**
50123 Florence Mon 3-7:30, Tues-Sat 10-7:30

Ermanno Scervino

Florentine designer Ermanno Scervino may not be up there with other city-born brands like Pucci, Gucci and Roberto Cavalli—just yet—but his international reputation is building nicely and Uma Thurman figures among his clientele. It's worth checking out this large, comfortable flagship to get the low-down, though only the brave will risk their bank manager's wrath by making a purchase. Scervino mixes exquisite fabrics and leathers with a taste for textures plus the occasional dash of whimsy, but nothing comes cheap. A demure daytime corset in sober grey, spotted with adorable cotton tufts, for instance, costs 995 euros. Trawl the ground floor for superb suede and leather pieces, then head downstairs for menswear—including some great scrunched, embroidered shirts. Save upstairs for last, where you'll find Scervino's gossamer-shredded, ethereal evening dresses. *ermannoscervino.it*

Luxury *Amex/MC/V*

Piazza degli Antinori 10/R **055 260 8714**
50123 Florence Mon 3-7:30, Tues-Sat 10-7:30
(last Sunday of the month, 3-7:30)

Ermenegildo Zegna

Zegna is approaching its centenary and has deservedly become the gold standard for the finest suiting fabrics and menswear. The perfectionism that is invested into developing ever lighter, more wearable weaves cannot be overstated. For the past few years, the company has run the Vellus Aureum (Golden Fleece) Trophy to find the finest wool on the planet and then weave it into just 100 made-to-measure suits. For mere mortals, Zegna's superfine 15milmil15, a merino wool and silk blend, is quite sufficient to create an immaculate suit …and send your bank manager into a spin. Gentlemen can also browse Zegna's classic Couture collection or the more modern Sartorial range for readymade suits that can be altered in four weeks. Alternatively the Z Zegna range, favoured by the three boys from *Friends* and modelled by Adrien Brody, has a trendier vibe, and the Zegna Sport line offers casual weekend styles.　　*zegna.it*

Expensive to luxury　　　　　　　　　　*Amex/MC/V*

Piazza Rucellai 4-7/R　　　　　　　　**055 283 011**
50123 Florence　　　　　　　　　　Mon-Sat 10-7:30

Via de' Tornabuoni 3/R　　　　　　　**055 264 254**
50123 Florence　　　　Mon 3-7, Tues-Sat 10-1, 2:30-7:30

☆ Ermenegildo Zegna (accessories)

Slicing the corner off Bottega Veneta is the newest of the Zegna offspring, the accessories store. This place naturally focuses on their scarf/tie/shawl and luggage/bags/belt ranges, but the clincher is the complete shoe range. It's a men's only collection, offering all the office classics together with the new generation of smart trainers which could even pass as casual shoes. Furthermore, it is only here that you can benefit from their competitive made-to-measure shoe service, which offers clients a handmade shoe (about 670 euros) after one fitting and a six-week wait. *zegna.com*

Expensive　　　　　　　　　　　　　*Amex/MC/V*

Via de' Tornabuoni 3/R　　　　　　　**055 283 011**
50123 Florence　　　　　　　Mon-Sat 10-1, 2:30-7:30

Escada

Escada girls have never been wallflowers. On entering this store, brace yourself for impact with high-wattage dressing that always packs a visual punch. You might be knocked sideways by the sharp knitwear in acid clashes, or the flicky little cocktail dresses that are just too sharp to lose their cool. If all this seems too full-throttle for you, the decor of this Germany-based brand offers respite, with its exquisite turn-of-the-century art nouveau wood panelling and ceiling mouldings from a quieter, bygone age. Penetrate beyond and you'll find that downstairs there are slinky couture dresses for Hollywood premieres and sharp navy, red and white jeans and tops in the Sport range for snappy weekends on the yacht. Word has it that Florence has also been selected to trial the Escada children's line.　　*escada.com*

Expensive　　　　　　　　　　　　　*Amex/MC/V*

Via degli Strozzi 32/R　　　　　　　**055 290 404**
50123 Florence　　　　　　　Mon 3-7, Tues-Sat 10-7

Ethic

Ethic looks like it must be the one-off brainchild of some local designer or architect. You enter down a long corridor, with glimpses of an intriguing alternative world at the far end. Venturing on, you find yourself in a bright, tented space that feels like a temporary art installation, with original paintings on the walls and an eclectic display of clothing, compact discs, ethnic home furnishings and arty magazines. The reasonably priced clothes are a mix of streetwear and Prada-inspired dressy pieces. It may take you a while to realise that Ethic is actually a cleverly marketed lifestyle formula—launched in Rome in 1997 and already successfully rolling out through Italy. Gradually, though, small clues like the overly casual staff, ubiquitous Ethic labels and piles of glossy catalogues on the cash desk give the game away. *ethic.it*

Affordable *Amex/MC/V*

Borgo degli Abizi 37/R **055 234 4413**
50122 Florence Sun-Mon 3-8, Tues-Sat 10-8

☆ **Etro**

There's a startling contrast between sober, monumental Palazzo Rucellai and the exuberant Etro store it houses. What would Giovanni Rucellai (1403-81, one of the Florentine Renaissance's most respected intellectuals) have made of the full-scale riot of colour in his home? The question is unavoidable as your eye is drawn from the delicate frescoes on the ceiling to the mayhem of brilliant, clashing colours below. Every garment, scarf or handbag seems to dance to its own rhythm in blithe disrespect of its neighbour. This year a Frida Kahlo palette dominates. Scorching fuchsia skirts are frilled with hula-hoops of emerald braid. There are deckchair-striped jackets trimmed with dimity flowered ribbon. In the men's department, parrots and humming-birds squawk on brilliantly coloured shirts. It all adds up to pleasant pandemonium. *etro.it*

Luxury *Amex/MC/V*

Via della Vigna Nuova 50/R **055 267 0086**
50123 Florence Mon 3-7, Tues-Sat 10-7

Expensive

Expensive? Not. Which explains why young fashion victims seasonally raid this flashy Rome-based chain packed with runway looks shamelessly reproduced. Get your sunglasses out for the assault of synthetic colours under neon lights and prepare for pumping tunes that either get you in the spending groove or send you running. The fabrics may be somewhat lacking in quality but prices are budget. Expect dressy jeans, skirts and tees that are figure-hugging and disposable. You can also pick up classics—like black, stretch trousers with a surprisingly good fit—if you hit the right day. Staff are used to a steady flow of foreign language students and there are handwritten signs around the store in English. It all feels alarmingly like Oxford Street. *expensive-fashion.it*

Affordable *Amex/MC/V*

Via dei Calzaiuoli 78/R **055 265 4608**
50122 Florence Daily 10-8 (Sun 11-8)

Fausto Santini

Fausto Santini's Florence branch may be smaller and dingier than his flagship stores in Milan and his home city of Rome, but it has an added attraction that only Rome can rival. As well as shoes and handbags from the current range, it works as a discount outlet selling Santini's shoes from past and present collections at around 50% less than usual. His unique designs, for both men and women, with their soft round toes and ultra-flat heels, are more like sculpted objects than shoes. His colour wheel is equally delicate, ranging from powdery blue to slate-grey and plum. The staff can be a little off—it depends on the day. *faustosantini.it*

Affordable   *Amex/MC/V*

Via dei Calzaiuoli 95/R   **055 239 8536**
50122 Florence   Mon 3:30-7, Tues-Sat 11-2, 2:30-7:30
(June-July, Sun 12-7)

Fendi

You can enter Fendi in two ways. The obvious one is from the street, but why not take the Alice-in-Wonderland route and fall down a discreet side corridor when you are in Louis Vuitton? That way you get the full benefit of the shock of the new which is so very Fendi. After Vuitton's warm cherry-wood tones, Fendi's stark black and steel interior belongs to a tougher (braver?) new world. Women's and men's luxurious ready-to-wear hang enticingly along the back walls, but it's the bags at the front of the store that are the biggest draw. The staff are used to coping with dazed and confused customers and are always ready to help. Take a guided tour of the latest models favoured by the likes of J.Lo, Cameron Diaz and Sharon Stone and decide which way your future lies. *fendi.it*

Luxury   *Amex/MC/V*

Via degli Strozzi 21/R   **055 212 305**
50123 Florence   Mon-Sat 9:30-7:30, Sun 2-7

Flavio Castellani

Expect Castellani's svelte white store on Via Calimala to be monothematic, with a black/white focus. Some of his clothes might be questioned by the taste masters, but linger a little longer and you will see why we rate him. Castellani is really successful in his research of synthetic fabrics, and in these racks are items that are both crease-free and soft in a way our much-loved naturals will never be. There are cascading backless tops, ruched halter necks, and stretchy fitted jackets and trousers which can be recklessly squashed into a suitcase. Once released, these clothes just instantly mould themselves around your body. *flaviocastellani.it*

Moderate   *Amex/MC/V*

Via Calimala 19/R   **055 265 8073**
50123 Florence   Mon 3-7:30, Tues-Sat 10-7:30

Foot Locker

Even in January, when it's drizzling and the tourists are still months away, Foot Locker will be heaving with Florentine youth and the few visiting Americans. One of the staff will no doubt be hanging off the front step in the familiar black-and-white uniform gassing with a friend in the street outside. All's right with the world. Quite simply, as the sneaker culture continues to boom, this US sportswear and athletic shoe specialist is a must for all sneaker heads. At the Via de' Calzaiuoli store you'll find the big names such as Nike, Puma, Adidas and Converse. The shoes, together with some of the coolest urban and specialist Italian sportswear from the likes of Fila, Lotto and Umbro, are displayed in one rather cramped and dreary ground-floor space. But the fans seem happy and are currently hotfooting it there for Foot Locker exclusives like Nike Tuned Series 1 and Adidas X Country. *footlocker.com*

Affordable   *Amex/MC/V*

Via Borgo San Lorenzo 19/R   **055 291 400**
50121 Florence   Mon-Sat 10-7:30
                                          Sun 11:30-1:30, 3:30-7:30

Via de' Calzaiuoli 27-35/R   **055 214 030**
50100 Florence   (opening hours as above)

Francesco Biasia
If you're looking for a reasonably priced handbag and haven't found it at Furla, Coccinelle or Nannini, then this slip of a store gives you one last chance. The interior is sleek, expensive-looking and linear, yet serves up surprisingly affordable leather handbags, wallets, belts and make-up cases. This season, Vicenza-based Biasia revels in playing with detail and some of the bags are possibly playing just a little too hard. Take the Portogallo, which combines black stitching on white leather with a gathered, ruched effect, all held together by complex straps with four buckles. Phew! Quite heavy on the eye. Still, the distressed leather Bulgaria collection in red with big white stitching has a slouchy, funky feel to it. And there's always the Ciclamino bag in distressed white, beige or black leather, a modern classic. *biasia.com*

Moderate   *Amex/MC/V*

Via della Vigna Nuova 16/R   **055 282 961**
50123 Florence   Mon 3:30-7:30, Tues-Sat 10-7:30

Fratelli Rossetti
The large, wood-panelled Fratelli Rossetti shop, with its strategic location on Piazza della Repubblica, is difficult to ignore. This is one of those stores that deals exclusively in pure Made-in-Italy style. If you are onboard for the expenditure, you too can buy a little piece of consummate Italian good taste. The house style extends from classic lace-ups for men, to cute little summer sandals or winter ankle boots for women, to lightweight Flexa Sailing Pro sneakers for everybody. Every shoe is immaculately finished and the quality of the materials is beyond reproach. Throw in a desirable line of leather and suede jackets and see if you manage to resist stepping inside. *rossetti.it*

Expensive   *Amex/MC/V*

Piazza della Repubblica 43-45   **055 216 656**
50123 Florence   Mon-Sat 10-7:30, Sun 11-7

Frette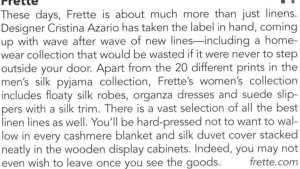

These days, Frette is about much more than just linens. Designer Cristina Azario has taken the label in hand, coming up with wave after wave of new lines—including a home-wear collection that would be wasted if it were never to step outside your door. Apart from the 20 different prints in the men's silk pyjama collection, Frette's women's collection includes floaty silk robes, organza dresses and suede slip-pers with a silk trim. There is a vast selection of all the best linen lines as well. You'll be hard-pressed not to want to wal-low in every cashmere blanket and silk duvet cover stacked neatly in the wooden display cabinets. Indeed, you may not even wish to leave once you see the goods.   *frette.com*

Expensive to luxury   *Amex/MC/V*

Via Cavour 2/R   **055 211 369**
50126 Florence   Mon 3-7, Tues-Sat 10-7

Furla

Fizzing with fashion colours, Furla's two shops in Florence are always buzzing with customers. These handbags, shoes and accessories are particular favourites with British women. Perhaps it's because they seem less accessible when seen in Bond Street and Harvey Nicks; or perhaps it's the happy mix of light-hearted details (like the internal lights in some of the more memorable handbags, which their owners now swear they cannot live without). Most like-ly, though, it's simply the chance to pick up a great Italian handbag or a pair of shoes (a category the company is cur-rently expanding) at a sensible price. Furla is also worth vis-iting for classy little gift ideas—like cool, geometrical silver jewellery or adorable ice-cream-cone purses.   *furla.com*

Moderate   *Amex/MC/V*

Via dei Calzaiuoli 47/R   **055 238 2883**
50123 Florence   Daily 9:30-7:30 (Sun 10:30-7:30)

Via della Vigna Nuova 28/R   **055 282 779**
50123 Florence   Daily 10-7:30 (Sun 11:30-7:30)

☆ Gabs

If you have a sharp eye for a bright handbag you may already have spotted Gabs bags in store windows around Florence. This new label, the brainchild of thirtysomething Franco Gabrielli, has already established a foothold in Japan. It's easy to understand why the colourful bags with the motto 'Don't worry...be Gabs' have such appeal. Take the red, white and blue holdalls with dinky notepads in poppered suede covers attached by a leather cord. Or the sunflower-yellow shoulder bags with gorgeous chunky straps in plaited rope. Go to the Via San Egidio store for the full range...it has a great Mediterranean feel. But if you're not up for the hike, look out for Gabs bags and other funky labels at Emanuela and Makiko's new bag store at Via Parione 35/R (055 239 9770, Mon-Sat 10-7). *gabs.it*

Affordable   *Amex/MC/V*

Via S. Egidio 9/R   **055 200 1013**
50122 Florence   Mon 2:30-7, Tues-Sat 10-1:30, 2:30-7

Geox

Geox is a quiet Italian success story. The company from Treviso has the surely unique mission of 'converting people into consumers of breathing products'. Its shoes are now found in thousands of stores throughout Italy as well as in London's South Molton Street and, since 2004, on Madison Avenue in New York—as well as on vast numbers of the feet that have just walked past you as you trotted to this store. The secret lies in the soles. In the mid-Nineties, wine expert Mario Moretti Polegato made a canny career move and patented a perforated sole which ventilates but remains impermeable. On the underside of techie-looking sneakers, this looks pretty cool (in every sense of the word)—think of an affordable version of Hogan. On women's court shoes and ballerinas, and men's lace-ups and moccasins, it can sometimes look clumpy, but the price is right and the comfort undeniable—one reason why Italian mothers love to buy them for their kids. The dazzling white Florence store opened in 2002 and offers most of the Geox range, displayed on rather alarming metal-sprung arms. There are also a few clothing items which—yes, you've guessed it— breathe. *geox.com*

Affordable   *Amex/MC/V*

Via dei Panzani 5/R   **055 283 606**
50123 Florence   Mon 3:30-7:30, Tues-Sat 10-7:30
                                                      Sun 2:30-7:30

Geraldine Tayar

Geraldine Tayar (her family is Maltese in origin) has had her tiny un-named shop and workshop near Piazza Pitti for five years. She started by producing accessories but then branched out into clothing (predominantly dresses) for women and children. Tayar keeps her fabrics crisp and unfussy. Her signature handbags are made from fresh cotton with contrasting colours and designs for the shoulder straps: the most striking are white with elegant Japanese kimono'd figures winding up the shoulder. She also offers a bright selection of happy-clash silk shawls in brilliant colours: the combination of this season's fuchsia with acid green is right on target. Her collection of shift dresses and skirts is not groundbreaking, but she'll make them to measure in double-quick time and each piece is fresh and unique.

Moderate   *Amex/MC/V*

Sdrucciolo de' Pitti 6/R   **055 290 405**
50125 Florence   Mon-Sat 9-1, 3-7

☆ Gerard

The Pecchiolis are considered *the* fashion family by many in Florence's inner circle, and quite right too. Whereas Guya goes for no-frills avant-garde, and Raspini is more conventionally oriented to the big names, Gerard's style is radical boudoir-chic. The pink-padded silk walls, black and white marble flooring and pounding music will immediately set your fashion pulse racing. There are little satin dresses from See by Chloé, Luna Bi knitwear and tees, svelte jersey dresses by Vivia and cocktail outfits by Balenciaga. Hip Bologna-based label Flu's Ear and Stella Forest are also in attendance. Hop upstairs for jeans and menswear from Helmut Lang, Levi's and Parosh, then flop onto the fabulous vintage sofa by Louis Vuitton. If all this is just too racy for you, try visiting Gerard's more chilled-out little brother at Gerard Loft.

Expensive to luxury   Amex/MC/V
Via Vacchereccia 18-20/R   **055 215 942**
50123 Florence   Mon 2:30-7:30, Tues-Sat 10-7:30

☆ Gerard Loft

The Loft is the younger, streetwise end of the Pecchioli family's retail empire. A light, airy space with bare boards, iron bedsteads and experimental art installations occasionally hanging from the ceiling, this is as edgy as Florence gets, yet there's something for all the family here. Kids can expect miniature versions of Vintage 55 sweats and tees, and cute limited-edition Adidas sneakers. Women get to pick from Marc Jacobs shoes in Forties round-nosed styles as well as funky favourites like Flu's Ear by hip young designer Fulvia Marengo from Bologna, Parosh and Custo. Men can browse extra-distressed denim from Japanese jeans brand Edwin, Vintage 55, sneakers by Swear and Gerard's own label. The atmosphere is laid-back, so take your time.   gerardloft.com

Expensive   Amex/MC/V
Via de' Pecori 34-40/R   **055 282 491**
50123 Florence   Mon 2:30-7:30, Tues-Sat 10-7:30

☆ Gianfranco Lotti

Florentine designer Gianfranco Lotti's only store is a temple to the handbag. The air is hushed, the walls are burnished with gold leaf and the minimalist spiky decorations are just so. (The Mantegna fresco is a fake, in case you hadn't noticed—joke handbags have been painted in.) The softly spoken staff give reverent explanations of the technical challenges in constructing each piece and pull out white gloves when they display a 6,000-euro croc bag. The look is generally conservative—there are some handbags with arched handles and hinged clasps that wouldn't look out-of-place on the queen's arm—but ultimately true class wins out. Envelope bags in the softest plaited napa leather will make you swoon as they melt at your touch. A new line in women's shoes offers some perfect kitten-heeled courts, and the men's backpacks and briefcases are immaculate. Leatherwork at its very best.   *lotti.it*

Luxury   *Amex/MC/V*

Via della Vigna Nuova 45/R   **055 211 301**
50123 Florence   Mon 3-7, Tues-Sat 10-7

Gilardini

Gilardini is one of those long-lived Florentine shops that sits, Canute-like, against the rising fashion tide on frenzied Via Cerretani. The shop fittings are proof of its longevity; they were probably last renovated sometime in the Eighties. Still, there is a reassuring solidity here that encourages you to stop and browse and to hope that this is one shop that doesn't get washed away by the accelerating swell of uniformity. Beyond the brassy entrance hall there is a wealth of shoes to choose from, with something for every budget, from cheap and cheerful Unisa to exquisite modern classics from Bruno Magli or hand-finished brogues and leather moccasins by Santoni. Service is measured and polite, so take your time. For the moment they are not going anywhere.

Affordable to expensive   *Amex/MC/V*

Via de' Cerretani 8   **055 212 412**
50123 Florence   Sun-Mon 3:30-7:30, Tues-Sat 9:30-7:30

Via de' Cerretani 20   **055 214 297**
50123 Florence   (opening hours as above)

Giorgio Armani

When you feel an Indiana Jones moment coming on, head for Florence's very own Temple of Doom, the Giorgio Armani store. Just joking, but its huge sandstone block walls and secret corridors—by minimalist Claudio Silvestrin, responsible for the new image of Armani stores worldwide—are very reminiscent of ancient Egypt. In the atrium (after you've negotiated a contemplative pool of water) you'll find accessories. Sunglasses are displayed under heavy glass boxes which the staff have to heave off in a Harrison Ford-like sweat whenever a customer wants a closer look. After that, access to the rest of the store is something of a mystery. Keep your cool, though. Head for the back wall, turn left and miraculously you will find yourself in a corridor of rooms with all Armani's gorgeous treasures laid out before you. Casualwear is towards the front, eveningwear at the back. Upstairs, under slightly more Florentine wooden ceiling beams, is the men's department. It's all so easy when you're in the know.   *giorgioarmani.com*

Luxury   *Amex/MC/V*

Via de' Tornabuoni 48/R   **055 219 041**
50123 Florence   Mon-Fri 10-7, Sat 10:30-7:30

Giotti

This large, silent store is housed in the 14th-century Palazzo Lenzi, owned by the French Institute. It's all rather serious, with no muzak or frivolous details to distract, but the beauty of the objects on display is no laughing matter. The store is divided in two: the front half is dedicated to Bottega Veneta's range of canvas and leather travel cases and bags, while in the large open room behind you'll find slick, unfussy men's and women's leatherwear under the Giotti label, made in the Giotti family's Florentine workshops. The quality and workmanship are superb. There are trousers, skirts and covetable jackets and three-quarter length coats that reverse from butter-soft leather to satiny suede. Colours are delicious too, with unusual reds and greens. They'll also make up to order. *giotti.com*

Luxury   *Amex/MC/V*
Piazza Ognissanti 3-4/R   **055 294 265**
50123 Florence   Mon-Sat 9-1, 2-7

Golden Point

Golden Point is one of those useful little chains that often gets you out of a tight corner—it's a lifesaver if you need a speedy supply of tights, underwear, socks or swimwear in anything from classic colours to rainbow combinations. You'll find it plum in the centre of town, on a busy corner between the Via de' Calzaiuoli and the Piazza della Repubblica. If you have forgotten your swimsuit, you could do worse than fill the gap with Movie, one of their classic white, Ursula Andress-style bikinis, or a Fair costume with slinky silver side-buckles. There's a lively range of children's clothes and a compact corner dedicated to men's socks and underwear. Most of the goodies are packed into tiny, plastic envelopes—which thankfully the staff don't object to your unwrapping. If you believe that all good things come in small packages, this store will be right up your street. *goldenpointonline.com*

Affordable   *Amex/MC/V*
Via de' Calzaiuoli 51   **055 277 6224**
50123 Florence   Daily 9-7:30 (Sun 10-7:30)

☆ Golubcik

Federica Leonardi and Emiliano Gori's tiny shop-cum-workshop is hidden away down the side of the church of Santo Spirito in a nondescript street of lock-up garages. Here you are a world away from the polished glitz of Via de' Tornabuoni but raw creative talent is available in abundance. Leonardi and Gori's offbeat creations will surprise and delight you with their obvious technical skill, but their prices will never shock. Take the ingenious little tunics made out of thick strips of plaited linen, or an apparently demure pinafore with harlequin loops of brown linen falling from the waist, lined in eye-catching lime-green, that swing and swirl as you move. Pick anything off the rack, and Leonardi and Gori will make it up to measure using the sewing machines at the back of their store. This is a business at the very earliest stages whose future is yet to be defined. Catch them now, before their talents take this couple to greater heights.

Affordable   *No credit cards*

Via de' Coverelli 27/R   **335 686 1494 (Emiliano Gori)**
50125 Florence   **339 825 8919 (Federica Leonardi)**
Tues-Sat 10-1, 3-7:30   (open some Sundays when there is
                                    the market in Piazza Santo Spirito)

☆ Grevi

Once upon a time, in the town of Signa on the east side of Florence, they used to make finely woven Florentine straw into immaculate hats. Think of Helena Bonham Carter in *Room with a View* demurely lowering her gaze beneath a slim straw brim. Materials and styles have diversified since then, but the hat-making tradition continues. This year the Grevi family of Signa have finally opened a store in the centre of Florence. Their affordable ribbon-braid hats in offbeat, informal colours for women are especially tempting, but there are also Sicilian-style flatcaps or coppolas for men, crocheted skulls for babies and adorable little straws for children. Forget your best friend's wedding, these are hats you'll want to wear all day long.   *grevi.com*

Moderate   *Amex/MC/V*

Via della Spada 11-13/R   **055 264 139**
50100 Florence   Mon-Sat 10-7:30

Gucci (accessories)

Who can doubt the certainties of the Gucci universe? Like the main store on Via de' Tornabuoni, the decor at this three-floor boutique has the brand's signature look by William Sofield: super-cool taupe and steel delivered everywhere in cubist chunks, from the stairway to the lighting blocks, from the handrails to the display cases. The site is slightly cramped but you'll forgive it anything as you ascend to a grandstand view of the Duomo from upstairs. On offer is a full range of handbags and luggage (top floor), jewellery (mezzanine) and small leatherwear (ground). That's the serious stuff. Then of course there are all the other accessories (ice-cube Gucci Gs, anyone?) to reassure you that the Gucci way really is the only way.   *gucci.com*

Expensive to luxury   *Amex/MC/V*

Via Roma 32/R   **055 759 221**
50123 Florence   Daily 10-7 (Sun 2-7)

☆ Gucci (jewellery)

The new Gucci jewellery nestles, dark and mysterious, alongside the main store on Via de' Tornabuoni. This is not the place for an affordable injection of Gucci glitz. This is the real McCoy. They buzz you in. They invite you to take a seat. Diamond bracelets begin at 6,000 euros—you are entering the upper stratosphere. There are only two or three pieces like those on show in the world, and anyway there are only two other dedicated Gucci jewellery stores in existence—in Rome and Beverley Hills (though corners do exist within larger stores in the major metropolises). Women's jewellery and watches predominate, with interlocking Gucci Gs strongly in evidence, particularly on the tough, urban-looking Icon collection. But there are also pieces of bewitching simplicity which do not publicise their parentage. All this is pretty awe-inspiring. Relax, though, the welcome is warm and surprisingly unprecious. *gucci.com*

Luxury *Amex/MC/V*

Via de' Tornabuoni 81/R **055 7592 3111**
50123 Florence Mon-Sat 10-7

Gucci (ready-to-wear)

As befits a fashion colossus, Gucci sits astride Florence's two chicest streets, the Via de' Tornabuoni and the Via della Vigna Nuova. The store has has a much-needed overhaul, and the once bland and labyrinthine rooms have been replaced by William Sofield's distinctive mix of taupe, steel, ebony and natural pebble tones. And not before time—after all, where more appropriate to pay homage to Gucci than in Florence? Guccio Gucci opened the Florentine house's first store just down the street in 1921, and Gucci today still draws on Tuscan expertise for its range of jaw-droppingly beautiful leatherwear and handbags. Even the departure of Tom Ford and the uncertain times ahead will not change that. *gucci.com*

Luxury *Amex/MC/V*

Via de' Tornabuoni 73/R **055 264 011**
50123 Florence Daily 10-7 (Sun 2-7)

Guess?

Guess's rangy store packs the familiar punch of this sassy California-based denim giant. There's a small area dedicated to menswear on the ground floor, otherwise it's all about girls having fun. Start out with the spacious jeans department at the back and then head downstairs for more dressy, glittery styles. The accessories deserve a particular mention, with groovy repeating Gs on shoes, neat little canvas hats and handbags (it's a Guess G of course; don't be tempted to confuse it with anyone else's!). *guess.com*

Affordable *Amex/MC/V*

Via degli Speziali 9-11/R **055 213 035**
50123 Florence Sun-Mon 3-7:30, Tues-Sat 10-7:30

☆ Guya

Guya (along with Gerard and Raspini) forms the first point in Florence's golden triangle of high fashion stores at the corner of Via Por Santa Maria and Via Vacchereccia. (The slightly larger sister store on Via Calimala stocks diffusion lines and menswear.) At the Via Por Santa Maria boutique, you will find more than enough Vivienne Westwood, Hussein Chalayan, Comme des Garçons and Bernard Willhelm to set your fashion antennae on full alert. Marithé & Francois Girbaud are strongly featured with pretty, mismatched floral dresses as well as foreshortened combats in microfibre. There are also complex pleated shirts from Cappucci and desirable cotton knits by Boboutic. The display style in both stores is simple rather than showy, and there are no fancy shop fittings or gushy assistants. It's all about the clothes, shoes and accessories ...well, what else is there?

Expensive to luxury   *Amex/MC/V*

Via Por Santa Maria 76/R   **055 282 764**
50123 Florence   Mon 2:30-7:30, Tues-Sat 10:30-7:30

Via Calimala 29/R   **055 219 163**
50123 Florence   (opening hours as above)

Hermès

This was once an elegantly fresco'd pharmacy. The setting is undoubtedly striking, and the atmosphere is hallowed. They open the door to you personally and a member of staff is quickly attached to your elbow. And yet, despite the arrays of elegant French products displayed in dark wooden cabinets, there is something of the emporium about it all. How many stores can offer you a saddle, a silk scarf, a bracelet, a dog-collar or a complete set of silver cutlery in such a compact space? It is all in the best possible taste, of course, and the prices are distinctly luxury, but the shift from handbags to jewellery to porcelain can (excuse us!) jar. Still, once over that, there is no denying the seductively simple design lines that characterise most pieces of Hermès clothing, jewellery and footwear. Jean Paul Gaultier, the relatively new womenswear designer, has brought some razzmatazz to recent collections but only in the smallest details, as in France there is nothing more sacred than this legendary brand. This place remains a safe bet for picking up luxury gifts for people you don't know very well.   *hermes.com*

Luxury   *Amex/MC/V*

Piazza degli Antinori 6   **055 238 1004**
50123 Florence   Mon 3-7, Tues-Sat 10-7

H.Neuber

Neuber is a Florentine institution. It has dressed generations of well-heeled Florentines in classic British style (only better) since 1886, and you can still see its initials etched into the glass at the original address in Via degli Strozzi where Escada now hangs out. Today you have to be a true Florentine (or possess this guide) to find the intimate Neuber store hidden away in a tiny mall off Via de'

Tornabuoni. A measured sense of calm rules. This is the kind of store where there are counters and the stock is brought out for you to survey. For men there are classic shirts, ties and knitwear by Braemar, Fedeli, Oliver & Brown and Façonnable, and leather jackets by Schiatti. For women there is Aquascutum, a good selection of Burberry's more timeless pieces, plus a huge selection of fine Italian knitwear by Maria di Ripabianca and Innocenti and cashmere by Ciocca. Don't be intimidated…the service is gentle and personal in true old-world style.

Expensive   *Amex/MC/V*

Galleria Tornabuoni /Via de' Tornabuoni 17   055 215 763
50123 Florence   Mon 3:30-7:30
                                              Tues-Sat 9:30-1, 3:30-7:30

Hogan

When Hogan opened on Via de' Tornabuoni in 2002, Florentines wore long faces and made gloomy comments about times-a-changing. The shoe store's crime was to take over the historic site of the Profumeria Inglese, home of the very best in soaps, perfumes and face creams since 1843. But the Profumeria can now be found in Piazza dell'Olio, and Hogan has almost religiously maintained the original wooden display cases and elegant stucco'd ceilings. The sporty sneakers, lace-ups, sandals and accessories sit meekly here, looking somewhat on their best behaviour in such formal surroundings. Let's be clear: these are casual, laid-back shoes more accustomed to being seen on the feet of film stars at play than in glass cases. Still, the overall effect is to add gravitas to the brand, and it certainly is an extremely handsome store.   *todsgroup.com*

Expensive   *Amex/MC/V*

Via de' Tornabuoni 97/R   055 274 1013
50123 Florence   Mon-Sat 10-7

Hugo Boss

Florence's display case for the German line sits in a spectacular position on the Piazza della Repubblica, but to date it presents only the current men's lines. Look for sophisticated tailoring and styled pieces from the brand's Black Label, sportier weekend looks from the Orange Label, and the red-label Hugo line for trendier, high fashion dressing that wants to be noticed. All that is missing are the women's lines…are you listening, Mr Boss?   *hugoboss.com*

Moderate   *Amex/MC/V*

Piazza della Repubblica 46/R   055 239 9176
50123 Florence   Mon 3:30-7:30, Tues-Sat 10-7:30
                          (last Sunday of the month, 3:30-7:30)

Il Bisonte

Il Bisonte is yet another Florentine leather goods success story. It began in 1970 when Wanny and Nadia DiFilippo established a workshop producing hard-wearing handbags, luggage and accessories. Il Bisonte means 'bison', and the image is exactly right. These are not the delicate little pieces of exquisitely soft napa that you will find at Gianfranco Lotti or Desmo. Instead, Il Bisonte promises sturdy, timeless objects in durable vacchetta leather which mellows with use and takes on rich lived-in tones. The store, with its heavy oak tables and display cases, reinforces this sense of durability without frippery. If you are looking for a no-nonsense backpack, briefcase or cowboy belt to sling round your waist, head here. We got a pretty no-frills reception too, but perhaps it was just a bad day.　　*ilbisonte.com*

Moderate	*Amex/MC/V*
Via del Parione 31/R	**055 215 722**
50123 Florence	Mon-Sat 9:30-7

Il Giglio

If you have a magpie eye for spotting bargains on market stalls, this store is for you. It requires a bit of a walk and when you get there it looks like a jumble sale—but with discounts hovering at around 60% for last season's looks, who cares? The higgledy-piggledy store is stacked with job-lots of labels you love like Dolce & Gabbana, Katharine Hamnett, Costume National, Allegri and Paciotti, as well as ones that have sunk without trace (and you can see why). What you find on any particular visit is a matter of luck, but get talking to Rolando and he'll quickly start showing you his best buys. The shoe department to the right of the door is more like an assault course of half-opened dusty boxes, but if you persist you can find pairs at 150 euros that once cost 600. Don't be afraid to bargain…Rolando is always up for a quick sale.

Affordable to moderate	*Amex/MC/V*
Borgo Ognissanti 64	**055 217 596**
50123 Florence	Mon-Sat 9:30-1:30, 3:30-7:30

☆ Il Misio

If time and money do not hinder you in the pursuit of the perfect shoe, this delicately perfumed micro atelier is the place for you. It takes an instant to see that these are intricate masterpieces of craftsmanship. Their creator, Hidetaka Furaya, began his career in fashion in Japan, but soon changed to shoes and moved to Italy to study and work. He wanted to be involved in something more technical, and was drawn to the complexity of shoemaking. After looking at his logbook and his endless diagrams and measurements, one begins to get the point. Did you know that your foot size changes as you make a step? And that is just the beginning. Your 'last' (the exact mould of your foot) involves two fittings and a two-month wait. Once that is out of the way, there is one more fitting and a further three to four months to go; it is all down to Hidetaka, working alone in his little back room. It costs, of course, maybe 2,500 euros…

Luxury   *Amex/MC/V*

Via de' Federighi 6/R   **055 212 295**
50123 Florence   Mon-Sat 9-1, 3:30-7:30

Il Rifugio Sport

Off skiing? Need new football boots? Looking for training weights? Il Rifugio Sport in Piazza Ottaviani is our best address in central Florence for satisfying the serious sporting enthusiast. Don't be fooled by the modest frontage—as with so many stores in Florence a secret subterranean world lies behind, bursting with stock and enthusiastic staff. All the big names are here…Nike, Adidas, Puma, New Balance and Arena. Meanwhile, at the second address, in Via dei Fossi (which is actually next door, but in that quirky Florentine way the street suddenly changes name), you'll find activewear with a different spin. Here the sporting emphasis is purely theoretical and we have moved to a clubhouse atmosphere. On offer are casualwear brands like Fred Perry, Franklin & Marshall and Napapijri—great for cool slouching, but no one would seriously expect you to wear them to break into a sweat.   *rifugiosport.it*

Affordable to moderate   *Amex/MC/V*

Piazza Ottaviani 3   **055 294 736**
50123 Florence   Mon 3:30-7:30, Tues-Sat 9:30-7:30
                                                            Sun 3-7

Via dei Fossi 67/R   **055 238 1326**
50123 Florence   Mon 3-7:30, Tues-Sat 9:30-1, 3-7:30

Intimissimi

Mass-market chain Intimissimi delights in combining colours and prints that you might be shy to wear on the outside but work perfectly hidden away. The Via de' Calzaiuoli store can sometimes look the worse for wear after the hordes have been through, but you'll soon be joining the hunt for that sexy black-and-navy lace bra or tomboy white-netted vest with orange go-faster stripes. You won't want to keep them forever, but they don't break the bank and are great little pieces of harmless fun. Intimissimi also sell classic monotone pieces, infinitely useful stretchy tees and surprisingly demure cotton nightwear. The boys get a look in too, with a range of cotton underwear in colours just as lively.   *intimissimi.it*

Affordable   *Amex/MC/V*

Via de' Calzaiuoli 99   **055 230 2609**
50122 Florence   Mon 10-8, Tues-Sat 9:30-8, Sun 12-8

Via de' Cerretani 17   **055 260 8806**
50123 Florence   Mon-Sat 9-9, Sun 10-9

☆ **Italobalestri**

Italobalestri is a Florentine company with a 40-year history of producing stylish, sexy shoes that cut a certain dash. The look (for women) is feminine with a touch of showy detail, be it embroidery or a flash of diamanté. Heels are usually high and lines are sleek rather than snub. All this is particularly attractive in the quiet context of an ex-optician's shop with the original 1870s wood fittings, fresco'd wall panels and attractive chandelier. Don't miss the tiny wooden drawers for spectacles along the wall behind the till. Balestri only produces women's shoes, but a selection of men's brands including Tremp, the Pisa-produced line of moccasins with a twist, fills the gap.   *italobalestri.com*

Moderate   *Amex/MC/V*

Piazza Santa Maria Maggiore 7/R   **055 211 230**
50100 Florence   Mon 3-7:30, Tues-Sun 9:30-1, 3-7:30

Lacoste

You could easily walk past Lacoste—after all, you've see those French polo shirts with snappy little crocodiles a million times before. But step inside and you may stumble across a few surprises. Certainly, this compact store is packed to the brim with the famous sports shirts in the full colour wheel of shades. But there is also a cute line of airtex summer dresses for women in polka dots, plus a new stretch tee which is flatteringly shaped, cool white cotton sweaters in honeycomb weave and some Juicy Couture look-alike velour tracksuits. For the men there are quality staples like casual check shirts, jeans and trainers. Go to the back of the shop for dinky versions of everything for the kids.   *lacoste.com*

Moderate   *Amex/MC/V*

Via della Vigna Nuova 33/R   **055 216 693**
50123 Florence   Mon 3:30-7:30, Tues-Sat 9:30-7:30

La Perla

As any seasoned traveller to the European continent knows, the French and Italians really do lingerie. Every city has delicious little stores offering enticing morsels of lace, silk and satin with just enough invisible engineering to make a girl feel like a million dollars. Take a peak at the sexiest and most expensive Black Label line to see exactly how far the imagination can go, and there are a few pieces from Allessandro Dell'Acqua's beautiful La Perla ready-to-wear collection to slip on top. Luxury and La Perla go hand in hand. The company is famous for its detailing, delicate fabrics and intricate lace bras but you can also find diffusion ranges for people who want something sweeter and more demure and everyday; the Studio and Malizia lines fit the bill and are less expensive (40-50 euros). La Perla also make swimming costumes that look more for spectacular poolside lounging than for actually getting in the water. *laperla.com*

Luxury *Amex/MC/V*

Via della Vigna Nuova 17-19/R **055 217 070**
50123 Florence Mon 3-7:30, Tues-Fri 10-2, 3-7:30
Sat 10-7:30

La Rinascente

La Rinascente is an institution in Italy as its longest surviving department store chain. The Florence branch stands in a key position on Piazza della Repubblica but fails to stir up much excitement. Up until recently, the main reasons for visiting were La Perla Studio (the only undies worth buying in the lingerie department), Alessi home gadgets on the fourth floor and La Prairie's cellular anti-ageing creams and make-up on the ground floor. But the big news is that it's now worth taking a ride to the top floor where the home-wares department has acquired a fabulous glass roof, and an open-air café with elegant white umbrellas and an unrepeatable view of the Duomo has been created. The food is nothing to write home about, but it is decidedly pleasant sitting up here on a sunny day. Arrive early for lunch because there is always a queue. *rinascente.it*

Affordable to moderate *Amex/MC/V*

Piazza della Repubblica 1 **055 219 113**
50123 Florence Mon-Sat 9-9, Sun 10:30-8

Les Copains

Don't be fooled by the French name: these luxurious knits in simple, relaxed lines, are 100% Italian—the Trend Les Copains line, for instance, is designed by Antonio Marras from Sardinia. However, you won't find anything too revolutionary hanging from the racks. Work your way through this long, deep shop to discover undemanding silk, cashmere and linen that speak of easy Italian casual-chic. It's worth persisting right to the back, because colour mixes and mood shift noticeably as you move from room to room. You may find silk-linen shimmery knits in the entrance hall, followed by a room of more youthful, red, white and blue jeans, trenches and tees. Those who want to track down that uniquely Italian look of effortless, relaxed style can't do better than this.

Expensive *Amex/MC/V*

Piazza degli Antinori 2-3/R **055 292 985**
50123 Florence Mon 3-7, Tues-Sat 10-7

Le Silla

Are you due to appear on Italian TV? Have you browsed Sergio Rossi, then gone a little wilder at Casadei, but still not found that elusive show-stopping pair of shoes? Then it's time to head for Le Silla. Enio Silla's wham-bam-thank-you-Ma'am shoes are pure spectacle and yes, we are talking brash. Downstairs, with the neon pop-art screen, you begin to get the idea. This season there are patent pink stilettos with diamanté-encrusted hearts and spiky sandals with Carmen Miranda-style fruit teetering on the nose. Steady your nerves and head upstairs to discover more. You will not be disappointed. *lesilla.com*

Expensive   *Amex/MC/V*

Via Roma 23/R   **055 265 8969**
50123 Florence   Mon 3-7:30, Tues-Sat 10-7:30

L'Essentiel

Florence-based designer Micha Layl likes to keep things simple. In fact, L'Essentiel stocks clothes that are so simple that at times you wonder whether you are looking at a calico toile rather than the finished garment. A summer dress in lightest pale tangerine cotton has a line of basic poppers down the front and raw-edged shoulder holes. Black tulle skirts are lined with contrasting lilac cotton and splashed with streaks of rubber. Every piece is made by hand in Layl's small Florentine workshop and shop owner Lara has often had a hand in dyeing some of the pieces herself. No one garment is quite the same as another, but despite this you'd be hard pushed to find anything priced over 50 euros and most pieces come in at around 30-40.

Affordable   *Amex/MC/V*

Via del Corso 10/R   **055 294 713**
50122 Florence   Mon 3:30-7:30
                                Tues-Sat 10-1.30, 3:30-7:30

Liu Jo

The contrast between Liu Jo's clothes and their Florentine setting could not be greater. This striking shop—part of the Modena-based chain that you find in city centres throughout Italy—has been carved out of a Renaissance palazzo on the corner of Via Calimala. Original features—including a Latin inscription, the Medici crest and spectacular internal arches—have been brought into the 21st century with historic-ironic additions, like a magnificent chandelier of barbed wire. The clothes are pure disposable, high-adrenalin teenage: think tiny little T-shirt sundresses, studded jeans and Seventies-inspired jersey tops. It won't break the bank, and you bought it in splendid surroundings. *liujo.it*

Moderate   *Amex/MC/V*

Via Calimala 14/R   **055 216 164**
50123 Florence   Mon 3:30-7:30, Tues-Sat 10-7:30
                                (last Sunday of the month, 11-7)

Liverano & Liverano

Liverano & Liverano is where male members of Florence's noble set head when they need a new suit. This family-run tailor has seen its fair share of styles since it was established by Luigi Liverano back in 1950. These days, however, most customers ask Luigi and his brother Antonio for two-piece ensembles, jackets and narrow trousers, made from the finest wools that Ermenegildo Zegna, Loro Piana and Marzotto have to offer. There's also a good selection of English wools and tweeds. The historic atelier has a work room at the back where master tailors stitch away after closing hours, and you can be sure that the shirts, suits and accessories are all made according to old-school tailoring traditions. The staff are rather gruff, but just tell yourself it's all part of its charm.

Luxury   *Amex/MC/V*

Via dei Fossi 43/R   **055 239 6436**
50123 Florence   Mon 3:30-7:30, Tues-Sat 9-1, 3:30-7:30

☆ **Loretta Caponi**

Loretta Caponi is one Florentine masterpiece your other guidebooks may overlook. How easily you might walk by this modest frontage on Piazza degli Antinori. Don't. Push through the bell-tinkling doorway and enter a corridor of rooms furnished with paintings and antique mirrors and resembling a private house. Soon you'll find yourself in an enormous salon with fresco'd ceilings and intimate lighting. You'll see antique dressers neatly stacked with embroidered linens, and wall closets filled with nightgowns in sweet florals and slinky satins, underwear and children's clothes. On the right, busy ateliers are hard at work. This is the Palazzo Altobrandini where gentle Loretta Caponi personally welcomes customers who come from all over the world to order her made-to-measure handmade goods. Believe us: Caponi is one shop in Florence that you can almost justify skipping the Uffizi to see. (Note that although there are two addresses, they both refer to the same store).

Luxury   *Amex/MC/V*

Piazza degli Antinori 4/R   **055 213 668**
50123 Florence   Mon 3:30-7:30, Tues-Sat 9-1, 3:30-7:30
Via delle Belle Donne 28/R   **055 211 074**
50123 Florence   (opening hours as above)

☆ **Loro Piana**

Enter and you will realise at once that this store is much bigger than it appears from the street windows. Endless rooms burrow into the building and contain all the Loro Piana countryclub-style ranges. In the last vaulted cellar right at the end is the service for made-to-measure suits. There's an exhaustive selection of fabrics, in a multitude of weights, mixes, and thread counts to suit your needs. One fitting and one month later, you too can take your very own suited masterpiece home. Those on the hunt for the ultimate shawl have a hard time choosing between rivals Agnona and Loro Piana, both based near Vercelli in Piedmont. Each promises to fold you in a tender cashmere embrace. Each offers gorgeous colour palettes—from pastels to spices—that will reduce you to abject indecision. The difference comes more with the clothing choices. Loro Piana offers risk-averse knits and sports styles. As the world's largest manufacturer of cashmere products, Loro Piana has nothing to prove. It's tempting to rest in one of their cashmere-covered sofas, slip on their cashmere slippers, pull out a cashmere blanket and take a luxurious power nap. And as well as the luxurious goods, you'll get a professional but warm welcome from the staff, which goes some way to softening the blow when you part with 600 euros for a shawl.

Luxury   *Amex/MC/V*
Via della Vigna Nuova 37/R   **055 239 8688**
50123 Florence   Mon-Sat 10-7

☆ Louis Vuitton

We have visited more than 200 stores in Florence for *Where to Wear*, but Louis Vuitton wins our prize as the store with most star quality. The silent gentlemen who open the door to you and stand immobile on the upper floor give the impression that Naomi Campbell is probably even now in the fitting rooms trying on one of Marc Jacobs' bewitching little Marilyn-style cocktail dresses. The store just oozes big spending. Downstairs you'll find menswear and the ubiquitous handbags and wallets. On the stairs, you come face to face with a life-size screening of the latest season's catwalk show. Upstairs, under a series of attractive arches, are the shoes and clothes that will make you swoon. The silent minders watch you throughout, but seem benign. Perhaps they are there to carry you out when the beauty of it all becomes too overwhelming.   *vuitton.com*

Luxury   *Amex/MC/V*
Piazza degli Strozzi 1   **055 266 981**
50123 Florence   Mon-Sat 9:30-7:30, Sun 2-7

☆ Luisa Via Roma

Luisa Via Roma is the kind of shop that the infamous AbFab team would have simply adored. You know the form: the window displays are given over to experimental artists; periodically everything in Via Roma has to screech to a halt because some visiting celebrity is attending a Juicy Couture party here; tourists who browse without intent are treated to chilly indifference by the staff. Still, you can't deny the appeal. Heavyweight names like Chloé, Gucci, YSL and Dolce & Gabbana fill the cool white space. An endlessly evolving roster of other designers like Yohji Yamamoto's sporty Y3 line, Undercover, DSquared and John Richmond adds to the buzz. Luisa's shoe island is impossible to circumnavigate without snatching a few treasures by Venetian master Rene Caovilla, and at the back of the store the latest arrival is a beauty bar dedicated to Aussie hair and skin-care products Aesop. Come on in and pay homage. Just be careful not to exit looking like you, too, should have been on AbFab.   *luisaviaroma.com*

Expensive to luxury   *Amex/MC/V*

Via Roma 19-21/R   **055 217 826**
50123 Florence   Mon-Sat 10-7:30, Sun 11-7

☆ Madova

Madova is the sort of shop that you travel to Florence especially to visit. Family-run, it has been making hand-finished leather gloves since 1919. The walls of this box-like store are heaving with neatly packed secrets that you will only discover if you surrender yourself to the friendly, English-speaking staff. Give in! Just place your elbow on the counter with your hand in the air and allow them to slide on a glorious cashmere, wool or silk-lined glove. The palette of colours is startling. Enjoy jaunty gloves with contrasting colours for the finger insets, or feel the flutter of fashion temptation when you discover this year's hottest shades with cashmere lining and contrasting stitching. They'll make to order as well, and if you stock up on presents for the family but are not sure about the sizes, they'll change all unworn items by post. There's also a mail order service.   *madova.com*

Moderate   *Amex/MC/V*

Via Guicciardini 1/R   **055 239 6526**
50125 Florence   Mon-Sat 9:30-7:30

☆ Malloni

Stella Falautano of A Piedi Nudi Nel Parco now has a foothold in the centre of town with this small store dedicated to her favourite label, Malloni. Founded just four years ago in Ascoli Piceno in the Marche region, Malloni mixes natural fabrics in muted, organic tones with idiosyncratic design details that make for an offbeat, creative feel. Nothing is too loud or faddy. Like the clothes, the store captures the earthy, organic feel of the Australian outback or the African plains. Heavy linens and cottons are favourite fabrics, and this season a gutsy black-and-white batik design features strongly. Calf-length skirts have not one but two waistbands, with the second slipping lopsided for a carefree, tearaway image. They look great on tall girls, slung round with Malloni's own chunky leather belts and teamed with their flat canvas sandals.

Moderate   *Amex/MC/V*

Via Calimala 7/R   **055 288 708**
50123 Florence   Mon 3:30-7:30, Tues-Sat 10-7:30

Mandarina Duck

The Duck is having a face-lift. The teensy Via de' Cerretani store is already sporting a fresher new look with yellow livery and windows frosted with gigantic Mandarina Duck logos, and the larger Via Por Santa Maria store is to follow suit soon. It all makes for a suitably upbeat backdrop to Mandarina Duck's range of high-tech, high-design curvilinear handbags, backpacks and luggage in hard-wearing synthetics and plastics. Everything feels as if it should be used for carrying your protein pills to Mars and back on a NASA mission. The label really excels when it comes to combining functionality with techno design. Dinky little handbags, on the other hand, which try to marry echoes of the Fifties with cutting-edge 21st century, have to work harder to convince. Also on offer are glasses and watches. *mandarinaduck.com*

Affordable   *Amex/MC/V*

Via de' Cerretani 64-66   **055 219 210**
50122 Florence   Mon-Sat 9:30-7:30

Via Por Santa Maria 23-25/R   **055 210 380**
50123 Florence   Mon-Sat 9:30-7:30, Sun 11-2, 3-7

Mannina

Mannina is a modest little shoe store that has been sitting on the busy thoroughfare that takes you from Ponte Vecchio to Piazza Pitti since the Fifties. Quietly and unpretentiously it offers the kind of personal service and production of which Florentines justifiably feel proud. You'll probably find Signora Mannina tending the shop, with her Sicilian-born husband, Calogero, and a small team of artisans making the shoes in the workshop out back. Ask about made-to-measure, too, if you are interested—they take about a month to produce. In the little wood-panelled store you'll find a surprisingly inviting and well-priced range of court shoes and sandals for women, plus lace-ups for men. Their moccasins are notoriously comfortable. Colours change radically every season, so once you have found a style you like you can pick up a new shade each time you visit.

Moderate   *Amex/MC/V*

Via de' Guicciardini 16/R   **055 282 895**
50125 Florence   Mon-Sat 9:30-7:30, Sun 10:30-1, 2-6:30

☆ Mariella Burani

Mariella Burani opened its first Florence store only two years ago, and by amazing sleight of hand the decor successfully mixes the urban minimalism so beloved of Italian designers with *Out of Africa*. Gleaming aluminium ducts frame the ceiling and the sand-blasted walls, while the changing-rooms are delicate tents of mosquito netting and the store is dotted with white-cushioned wicker chairs straight from the veranda of a big-game lodge. This season's tough, gypsy-chic collection is happily encamped here. The look is all lace and chiffon, oversized low-slung belts and trailing layers. But Burani is no dreamer. The label has a habit of adapting black-and-white photographs to create edgy, strong prints. Better still, they cut clothes for real women. Also on offer are the two more affordable diffusion lines, Amuleti (younger) and Notizie. *mariellaburani.it*

Expensive *Amex/MC/V*

Via della Vigna Nuova 32/R **055 213 014**
50123 Florence Mon 3-7, Tues-Sat 10-7

Massimo Rebecchi

Last year Tuscan designer Massimo Rebecchi rationalised his two Florence locations into one: you'll now find the menswear at the back of the brilliant white store and the womenswear at the front. But there's still ample room to appreciate Rebecchi's vision of sharp, vibrant dressing for a youthful, fun-loving crowd. Snappy skirts in shocking fuchsia silk hang alongside denim pedal-pushers with just the requisite amount of distressing. There are sinuous aquamarine silk dresses for showing off that hard-won tan at the cocktail hour after a long day on the beach. Men will find streamlined suits, jackets and shoes.

Expensive *Amex/MC/V*

Via della Vigna Nuova 26 **055 268 053**
50123 Florence Mon 3-7:30, Tues-Fri 10-1:30
3-7:30, Sat 10-7:30

Matucci

Matucci's stores are in your face. They dazzle with white lights, low-cost shop fittings and lots of big names. Go to the Via del Corso 44-46 shop for a glitzy, girly explosion from Miss Sixty, Kookaï, DKNY and Diesel. The excitement builds when you discover that the larger store at 71-73 has a new womenswear department on the top floor offering classy lines like D&G, Armani Jeans and Versace. Hold your horses, though. The common denominator is fast and furious, disposable fashion. You are more likely to find a dinky pair of D&G flip-flops for 25 euros than have a heart-stopping epiphany with a pair of designer jeans. But you never know, and it costs nothing to take a look.

Affordable to moderate *Amex/MC/V*

Via del Corso 44-46/R (W) **055 212 018**
50142 Florence Mon 3:30-7:30, Tues-Sat 10-7:30

Via del Corso 71-73/R **055 239 6420**
50142 Florence (opening hours as above)

Via Martelli 20/R (W) **055 283 712**
50129 Florence Mon 3:30-7:30, Tues-Sat 9:30-7:30

☆ Mauro Volponi

Mauro Volponi is the kind of independent footwear store that defies categorisation and is all the better for it. The only point of consistency in the company's eclectic selection is the unrelenting pursuit of quality: you won't find any slick, modern merchandising tricks here. An incongruous stampede of women's cowboy boots greets you upstairs in a room decorated with oak paneling, Persian carpets and classic flower arrangements. But, hey, just look at the crafts-manship. The tequila-sunrise shaded snakeskin boots are awesome. Or what about those orange croc boots with gold lining for 2,000 euros? If these don't hit the spot, look in the corner for handmade lace-ups for women by Roman shoe maestro Silvano Lattanzi which evoke immediate respect for their almost puritanical severity. Downstairs you'll find their immaculate male counterparts plus other handmade shoes by Enzo Bonafé. Volponi also offers non-handmade shoes at slightly less gut-wrenching prices. Drop by…the choice is unorthodox, but surely unique.

Expensive to luxury   *Amex/MC/V*

Via Orsanmichele 12/R   **055 211 900**
50123 Florence   Mon 3:30-7:30, Tues-Sat 9:30-7:30

Max & Co

If you've always admired MaxMara's class but found it ever-so-slightly staid, head to its younger and more affordable, sibling, Max & Co. Skirts may be shorter and T-shirts tinier than at its older sister, but the quality is still good. The big-ger brand's trademark elegance hasn't been skimped on either: flick through the racks for natty suits with classic pin-stripes or Prince of Wales checks but with that detail—a wider leg, a lower waistline—that ensures a younger vibe. This is a large store by Florentine standards, spread over two generous floors. The staff hasten to greet you but then seem content to let you browse. If you're shopping with a long-suffering partner, park him at the door where there's a comfortable armchair and daily newspapers (including the *Herald Tribune*). Then take all the time you need.

Moderate   *Amex/MC/V*

Via dei Calzaiuoli 89/R   **055 288 656**
50122 Florence   Mon 3:30-7:30, Tues-Sat 10:30-7:30
                                                          Sun 11-7

☆ MaxMara

Florentines wrung their hands in despair when the historic bookstore Seeber was forced out of its Via de' Tornabuoni address by skyrocketing rents; the news that clothes were to replace books seemed to add insult to injury. Today the MaxMara emporium is fabulous and nobody can complain that it has not respected its setting. This heavenly store is surely one of the best looking in Florence—and the newly-discovered frescoes, reverently restored behind the ground-floor cash register, are a testament to the owner's serious intent. This grand space hosts the company's six lines: Maxmara—classic contemporary, killer coats and simple suits; Sportsmax—Sienna Miller-style hippy chic, for the young and trendy; Sportsmax Code—jeans and sporty clothes; Weekend Maxmara—daywear, less expensive basics; 'S' MaxMara—stylish casualwear often mixed with silk; and finally Pianoforte—elegant everyday wear. There is also a space dedicated to the 'anticipo', which is a preview of the following season. Don't forget to save the best till last and take the stairs on the back left-hand wall to admire the fresco'd ceilings on the first floor with gorgeous evening gowns nestling beneath. All in all, a great shopping experience. The Via de' Pecori store is spacious too, and both branches are characterised by immediate and attentive service.

Moderate to expensive   *Amex/MC/V*

Via de' Tornabuoni 66-70/R   **055 214 133**
50123 Florence   Mon-Sat 10-7:30, Sun 11-7

Via de' Pecori 23/R   **055 287 761**
50123 Florence   Mon-Sat 10-7:30

☆ Mazzini—Shop in Progress

You may have to do a double-take in front of the new Mazzini boutique to work out where the door is because the whole store looks like a stage set. Last time we checked, the imaginary interior of a Fifth Avenue boutique was sketched on the plain walls and the only dashes of colour came from the handbags on display. It's called 'Shop in Progress' because the sketched interior will change periodically. The Tuscany-produced bags have a cheerful fashion vibe, with clean design lines and reasonable prices. They range from ponyskin shoulder bags with simple silver rings to delightfully fresh, pink-striped canvas shoppers. If your luck is in you may also find some one of their striking shawls at give-away prices.

Affordable   *Amex/MC/V*

Via della Vigna Nuova 58/R   **055 295 215**
50100 Florence   Mon 3-7:30, Tues-Sat 10-1:30, 3-7:30

☆ Mila Schön

Though this airy, vaulted-ceiling boutique sits in plum position across the piazza from Ferragamo, it is still easy to miss. Mila Schön may be a household name in Italy, holding its own historically along with the rest of the Tornabuoni line-up, but today it's hard to compete with all those big global brands. Schön started her career back in the Fifties, a contemporary of Balenciaga and Dior. She played a similar role, offering tailored elegance to the *haute bourgeoisie*. Today Balenciaga and Dior with their flamboyant designs represent something very different from what they originally set out to offer, but Schön has continued to create items for the same sort of reserved, elegant client. Her clothes encapsulate the effortless style of which Italians are known masters.

Her pieces are uncomplicated and understated, suited for special events; there is pattern, colour and ruffles but all in a measured degree. *milaschon.com*

Expensive *Amex/MC/V*

Piazza Santa Trinità 1/R **055 265 4451**
50123 Florence Mon-Sat 10-1, 3-7

Miss Sixty

Vroom! You've time-warped into a mid-Sixties world of oval plastic furniture, optical prints and pile carpets. Miss Sixty doesn't stint on the props—the small store rather staggers under all the decor, which makes it feel even smaller than it really is. In fact, there are two rooms on the ground floor and semi-hidden steps on the right leading to equally cramped spaces upstairs. But once you stop to look, Miss Sixty's fab collection more than holds its own. Expect to find the signature low-as-they-go jeans with studded, appliqué and sequin details, as well as dresses and denims zigzagged by glittery fuchsia lightning flashes. We were also amazed to spy an outrageous pair of jeans that rise right to the waistline. Buy them if you dare. *misssixty.com*

Moderate *Amex/MC/V*

Via Roma 20/R **055 239 9549**
50123 Florence Mon-Sat 10-8, Sun 11-7:30

Miu Miu

Miuccia Prada's experimental Miu Miu collection is always on the cutting edge of fashion. This store is a huge open space on Via Roma opposite that other Florentine fashion lodestone, Luisa Via Roma. The floor-to-ceiling glass frontage dwarfs everything. Despite Miuccia's relish of mock vintage detailing and bright colours, the collection manages to look as spartan as the interior as it clinkety-clinks on metal hangers around the walls. Shoes, accessories, men's and womenswear are all comfortably accommodated here with enough space left over to turn a couple of cartwheels as you discover a flurry of knee-length looks, all charmingly kooky, not overtly sexy but with an unmistakable allure. *miumiu.com*

Expensive *Amex/MC/V*

Via Roma 8/R **055 260 8931**
50123 Florence Daily 10-7:30 (Sun 10-7)

Moda Sartoriale

Brother Piero and Franco Cisternino have been putting chalk to cloth for as long as they can remember. There are plenty of tailors in Florence, but this is where insiders like to shop. The brothers modestly dispense the finest in men's suits, outerwear and shirts to a distinguished clientele including politicians, diplomats and the occasional more exuberant dresser like Sting (who has an estate and vineyard in the Valdarno). They will take one initial measuring and then require a subsequent fitting before delivering immaculate pieces of tailoring to you anywhere in the world.

Luxury   *Amex/MC/V*

Via del Purgatorio 22/R   **055 280 118**
50123 Florence   Mon 10:30-7:30, Tues-Sat 9:30-7:30

Montgomery

Watch out, girls: despite the somewhat masculine appearance and name, Montgomery is for you too. Step inside and be charmed by a welcome from owners Massimo Facchini and Patrizio Bonciolini and their staff—which is less about pushy selling than a passion for clothes. The vibe is designer street-style, with a particular penchant for British names. Alongside Fake Genius and Fake London you'll find newcomers Griffin, Religion and gothic Buddies Pink. But pride of place goes to Japanese designer Michiko Koshino's line of sweat shirts with intricate embroidered Chinese dragons and humorous long grey vests with Y-front seaming. There are limited-edition Levi's, too—look out for the new 100%s with distinctive pockets running continuously from back to front.

Moderate   *Amex/MC/V*

Via Pellicceria 22/R   **055 216 283**
50123 Florence   Mon 3:30-7:30, Tues-Sat 9:30-1, 3-7:30

Murphy & Nye

Don't let anyone say you wasted time shopping in Florence when you should have been imbibing 'culture'. Murphy & Nye may be an American brand, but at its Florentine outpost you can do both. Located in the glorious Casa della Lana, the old Wool Merchants Guild, the store is the happiest marriage possible between Retail and Renaissance. The store's interior says it all, combining a vaulted ceiling, fresco'd walls, a medieval arch (leading into the first-floor women's department) and a shiny silver, boat-shaped sales counter. If you can tear your gaze from these venerable surroundings, stock up on Murphy & Nye's nautically-inspired men's and women's casualwear which always keeps a weather eye on fashion colours and trends. Expect denims, tees and jackets in Gore-tex, as well as canvas boat shoes in funky colours. Serious sailors will be drawn to the specialised Crew line which includes boat shoes designed for the New Zealand America's Cup team. Sadly, parents of pint-size, would-be yachters should note that the boutique no longer stocks the company's cute JR (junior) line.   *murphynye.com*

Moderate   *Amex/MC/V*

Via Calimala 16-18/R   **055 265 8035**
50123 Florence   Daily 10-8 (Sun 11-8)

☆ **Nannini**

Nannini is a Florentine family company with a strong local tradition. If you have stumbled across their bright, upbeat handbags, shoes and accessories in the small Via dei Calzaiuoli shop, it's worth marching the extra metres to the flagship store in Via Porta Rossa where the full range is available. Prices are sensible and the season's hot colours are never missing. So, in warmer weather, splash on a slick shoulder bag in white canvas with postmodern kiwi and violet swirls. Alternatively, in more practical mode, ask about the range of briefcases and laptop bags, with feminine detailing that steers them delightfully away from sobriety. *nannini.it*

Moderate *Amex/MC/V*

Via Porta Rossa 64/R **055 213 888**
50121 Florence Mon 3:30-7:30, Tues-Sat 10-7:30

Via dei Calzaiuoli 82/R **055 238 2763**
50122 Florence (opening hours as above)

Nara Camicie

Italian chain Nara Camicie has been operating since 1981 and has over 100 outlets in Italy specialising in shirts for men and women. The size of the shop is inhibiting—it's shoebox small—but the concept is simple: men's shirts are displayed on one side and women's down the other. Pick out a style that you like and you will be whisked away to the back of the store to try it on. The range is big, from blander classic styles to more daring zipped, patterned and ruffled numbers. This year there are some great women's dress shirts with micro-pleating down the front, as well as rough silk fuchsia evening shirts with sharp collars designed to be worn up to your ears. Not everything is right on target—there are some dodgy synthetics and embroidery that would look better on a market stall—but Nara occasionally delivers affordable wardrobe resuscitation. *naracamicie.com*

Affordable *Amex/MC/V*

Via Porta Rossa 25 **055 264 5721**
50121 Florence Mon 2-7:30, Tues-Sat 10-7:30
Sun 3:30-7:30

Nero Giardini

Nero Giardini's Florence store, opened in 2004, is only his second own-brand opening after Milan. The producer from the footwear specialist Marche region has finally come out of the shadows to market his own label of casual shoes and handbags. The most striking feature about this modest little black-and-silver store on the road up the Ponte Vecchio are the prices, many refreshingly under the 100-euro mark. Styles are mainly laid-back leather lace-ups, sneakers, thong sandals and sabots, with a sprinkling of more formal models. Colours are natural tans, beiges, browns and blacks. These are the kind of the shoes you buy in three minutes, never think about again, and yet wear into the ground. *nerogiardini.it*

Affordable *Amex/MC/V*

Ponte Vecchio 64/R **055 274 0549**
50125 Florence Mon 2-7, Tues-Sat 10-7

Paola del Lungo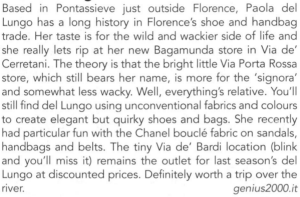

Based in Pontassieve just outside Florence, Paola del Lungo has a long history in Florence's shoe and handbag trade. Her taste is for the wild and wackier side of life and she really lets rip at her new Bagamunda store in Via de' Cerretani. The theory is that the bright little Via Porta Rossa store, which still bears her name, is more for the 'signora' and somewhat less wacky. Well, everything's relative. You'll still find del Lungo using unconventional fabrics and colours to create elegant but quirky shoes and bags. She recently had particular fun with the Chanel bouclé fabric on sandals, handbags and belts. The tiny Via de' Bardi location (blink and you'll miss it) remains the outlet for last season's del Lungo at discounted prices. Definitely worth a trip over the river. *genius2000.it*

Affordable to moderate *Amex/MC/V*

Via Porta Rossa 7/R **055 284 881**
50121 Florence Daily 9-7:30 (Sun 11:30-7:30)
Via de' Bardi 69/R **055 212 356**
50125 Florence Mon-Sat 9-1, 3-7:30
Via de' Cerretani 72/R (Bagamunda) **055 280 642**
50123 Florence Daily 9-7:30 (Sun 11:30-7:30)

Paolo Tonali

Varese-based Paolo Tonali has stores throughout Italy on some of the most strategic shopping strips. In the last year he has traded up in Florence from a compact site on Via Roma to a more spacious store on Via della Vigna Nuova. The move has been welcomed by smart thirty and forty-somethings who have been stocking up on desirable knits, shirts and workwear here for seasons. Tonali won't shock you, but he may just wow you with the perfect white poplin shirt, hound's-tooth skirt or chunky cashmere sweater. The price may make you gulp for such seemingly unremarkable pieces but, as Tonali regulars know, these are clothes that you will wear and wear. All in all, it's an efficient mix. Be prepared for seriously professional staff who know their stock inside out. *paolotonali.it*

Expensive *Amex/MC/V*

Via della Vigna Nuova 18-20/R **055 213 583**
50123 Florence Mon 3-7, Tues-Sat 10-7

Parody

For a streetwise antidote to all the high fashion next door on Via de' Tornabuoni, pop into Cristina Lunarde's corner store on Via della Spada. Flash shop fittings are not the order of the day here. You could be on Portobello Road in London rather than within spitting distance of the zebra-striped, jewel-encrusted Roberto Cavalli store. There is a strong Gallic presence, with French 'jeanologists' Marithé + François Girbaud presenting their ever-evolving experiment in deconstructing and redesigning denim. Then there is kitsch Parisian label Paco Chicano—much favoured by the likes of Vanessa Paradis and Sophie Marceau—with a strong line in highly coloured tees. For something a little more conventional, look out for perfect stretch cotton tops by Petit Bateau. Just to maintain the entente cordiale, British names like Paul Smith and Katharine Hamnett complete Lunarde's eclectic mix.

Moderate	*Amex/MC/V*
Via della Spada 18-20/R	**055 214 583**
50123 Florence	Mon-Sat 10-7:30

☆ Patrizia Pepe

Patrizia Pepe's store just wants you to look at it. There's star quality in the air here and we once witnessed a crush of Florentines round its windows admiring a girl inside trying on a drop-dead-gorgeous red dress. Certainly, the space is expensively lofty—and the clothes, in slinky silk, gauzy chiffon and tousled linen, are right on the mark. But look again…those price tags are far too accessible. This is middle-market, not high design. The product life cycles are short and sweet, and you can be sure that Patrizia Bambi and Claudio Orrea, the canny Florentine design team behind Pepe, are already surfing for the next big thing. So ride the wave, with slashed, transparent chiffon halters, bare-shouldered denim sundresses and funky white canvas trenches for summer. Oh, and cast a glance outside too—from upstairs there's a fabulous view of the Duomo. *patriziapepe.com*

Moderate	*Amex/MC/V*
Piazza S. Giovanni 12/R	**055 264 5056**
50129 Florence	Mon 3:30-7:30, Tues-Sat 10-7:30

Peruzzi

Let's be clear, Peruzzi is not a pleasant shopping experience. It is a labyrinth of interconnecting rooms that is brash, brazen and bewildering. The lights dazzle you, the shop assistants either ignore or harass you, and the layout is inexplicable. But if big-name brands are what you are after, look no further. Burberry, Gucci, Zegna, Dunhill, Coccinelle, Nannini, Celine, Etro, Dior, Bruno Magli, Moschino, YSL…they are all here (although sometimes in rather muted form with their less scintillating styles). As well as the obligatory shoes, handbags, wallets and belts, you will find sunglasses and even a cosmetics and perfume counter. The philosophy appears to be: if you can get it in, sell it. Unsurprisingly, this does not lead to an enjoyable afternoon, but you might come away with a little gem—just try and forget where you bought it. *peruzzispa.com*

Moderate to expensive   *Amex/MC/V*

Via Anguillara 5-23/R   **055 238 2670**
50122 Florence   Daily 9-7

Piero Guidi

Piero Guidi, from Urbino in the Marche region, takes the honours as one of the few leatherwear stores on Via della Vigna Nuova which is not Tuscan-based. His design formula takes a pinch of functional, adds a dash of classic and then whips in his own personal, original touch. Take for example his Intreccio collection of conventionally styled bags woven from brightly coloured strips of leather, or his Magic Circus range of classic shoulder bags with tan trimming made zany by a troupe of acrobats, clowns and performing animals tumbling over a white background. If this makes Guidi sound too offbeat, check out the rail of thoroughly functional leather and synthetic biker-style jackets nestling at the back of the store. *pieroguidi.com*

Expensive   *Amex/MC/V*

Via della Vigna Nuova 46-48/R   **055 264 5503**
50123 Florence   Mon 3:30-7, Tues-Sat 9:30-1, 3:30-7

☆ Pinko

Pinko is an Italian high street staple, riding along with Liu Jo, Laltramoda and Patrizia Pepe. They all carry the same sexy and trendy clothes, often sprinkled with sequins, in a price range that won't melt your credit card at the checkout. Pinko is made up of a team of designers, so there a lot going on at the same time. The company adds glamour by getting 'celebrities' to help out. Recently it was the Pink Panther, and now the Black Panther herself is taking over. Naomi Campbell has not only adorned their slinky campaign, but is also a creative director on a new line called Pinko Black. A new store is set to open in Via Roma, just across the piazza from the existing shop.

Moderate   *Amex/MC/V*

Via de' Cerretani 2/R   **055 294 323**
50123 Florence   Mon 3:30-7:30, Tues-Sat 10-7:30

Pollini

Pollini's main Florence store on Via Calimala is a fishbowl. Even when it's closed you can browse the entire bright, L-shaped space from the outside, right down to the clothing and leatherwear collection (a recent addition from this footwear producer) in the far back corner. But this is not as ridiculous an exercise as it might seem. With so much space given up to windows, you will only see half the stock from inside. Still, the brand itself probably needs no introduction. Now owned by Alberta Ferretti's Aeffe group, it promises top-quality, elegant footwear, clothing and accessories which call for attention, yet never grab it. The more moderately priced Pollini Studio line brings this philosophy within reach of smaller budgets. Head for the tiny Via Por Santa Maria store for accessories only. *pollini.com*

Expensive   *Amex/MC/V*

Via Calimala 12/R   **055 214 738**
50123 Florence   Mon 2-7, Tues-Sat 10-7

Via Por Santa Maria 42   **055 288 672**
50123 Florence   Mon 2-7, Tues-Sat 10-1, 2-7

☆ Poncif

Recently refurbished, Poncif is an open airy space offering a selection of alternative labels—including two produced by Sandra Ferro, the Turin-based designer behind the store. The clothes are fluid and deconstructed, with occasional injections of strong tailoring. Ferro's eponymous Poncif label leads the way with wide-legged trousers in herringbone tweed that successfully manage to combine free, flowing movement with a snug fit in all the right places. Quite an achievement. In the last year Ferro has added the quirky Wabi-Sabi line, in which she turns over her finished garments to artists to paint on as they choose. One-of-a-kind pieces—like a fabulous brown overcoat with flashes of orange—are rightly displayed with the reverence due an oil painting. The store also stocks transparent mesh tops by Mariona Gen from Barcelona, easy skirts and tees by Italian Pier Antonio Gaspari and Sarah Pacini's draped and layered knits.

Moderate   *Amex/MC/V*

Borgo degli Albizi 35/R   **055 263 8739**
50122 Florence   Mon 10-1, 3:30-7:30
                         Tues-Fri 10-1:30, 3:30-7:30, Sat 10-1:30

Prada (men)

Bored partners in search of the masculine version of a Prada fix won't have to walk too far from the women's boutique. The men's store—also done up in the brand's famous toothpaste-green livery—is just a couple of doors away. Miuccia Prada splashes many of the same elements she uses in womenswear into the men's collection. Those offbeat colour schemes, plush fabrics and unusual cuts form its basis; with silk shirts and buffed leather shoes amongst the bestsellers. But there's nothing Miuccia does better than a sharp, close-fitting black suit—go ahead, try one on. This store is also great for travel bags and small leather goods such as wallets and belts to complete your oh-so-stylish Prada look. *prada.com*

Luxury *Amex/MC/V*

Via de' Tornabuoni 67/R **055 283 439**
50123 Florence Mon-Sat 10-7:30

Prada (women)

Entering Prada is like diving into mysterious green waters. The soft grey-green walls subtly distinguish this store from any other on the street. It gradually draws you into its depths. Plunge down the skinny front hall, past the accessories, towards the glorious shoe treasures at the back. From delicate as well as clumpy little strappy sandals to soft, slouchy car shoes and wedges, you are not disappointed. Beyond, to the right, lie more green rooms full of all the Prada favourites. Prada is sticking with the Fifties-style vintage success story that it has been following for the past few years. The conservative, buttoned-up, perfectly tailored suits belie an undercurrent of repressed sexuality. Black is the predominant colour for winter 2006, and the fussiness of pattern and colour are out. If you start to lose your bearings raise your eyes to admire the elegant 15th-century frescoes dancing overhead. And if all that shopping has left you in need of a little freshening-up, linger in the neat little cosmetics corner just by the exit before you head out. *prada.com*

Luxury *Amex/MC/V*

Via de' Tornabuoni 53/R **055 267 471**
50123 Florence Mon-Sat 10-7:30

Prenatal

Prenatal takes bringing up baby very seriously. The mass-market Brianza-based chain has almost 190 stores in Italy and another 100 in Spain. Their sizeable Florence branch reflects the group's ethos. Children's clothing (0-11 years), all branded Prenatal, is appealing, bright and sensibly priced. A well-stocked equipment section offers a comprehensive choice of prams, cots and pushchairs. Upstairs, the businesslike range of affordable maternity wear includes more formal styles as well as jeans and every pregnant woman's fashion nightmare, the dreaded dungarees. Alongside, snuggled up under the arched ceiling, is the newborn department. But Prenatal's service does not stop here. The store offers counselling and free publications for new parents as well as access to regularly updated local listings for pregnant mums and guides to choosing a nursery school in the area. You can also access this information on the comprehensive website. *prenatal.it*

Affordable *Amex/MC/V*

Via Brunelleschi 22/R **055 213 006**
50123 Florence Sun-Mon 3:30-7:30, Tues-Sat 10-7:30

Quelle Tre

On dreary Via de' Pucci this bright little shop, run by the three Scardigli sisters, is an unexpected ray of sunshine. The sisters come from a long family tradition of tailors and dressmakers, so it is no surprise that for 15 years they have been expertly producing their colourful range of women's and childrenswear. They favour tough day-to-day fabrics like corduroy and denim in sunny colours for a happy, slightly hippy feel. Their immaculate padded waistcoats in bright contrasting corduroy, or simple denim tunics with sharp red detailing, would make functional but spirit-lifting additions to any harassed mother's daily wardrobe. They offer a made-to-measure service, too, and even have an outpost in faraway New York. *quelletre.it*

Moderate *Amex/MC/V*

Via de' Pucci 43/R **055 293 284**
50122 Florence Mon 3-7, Tues-Sat 11-2, 3-7

Raspini

Raspini has been a Florentine by-word for high-quality footwear since 1948 and they still make their own-brand shoes in up-to-the-minute styles. Nowadays, though, the three Raspini stores in Florence are just as well known for their selection of top designer clothing. Look out for Armani, DKNY, Blumarine and oceans of Prada. The Via Por Santa Maria boutique is the sleekest store. The other two have a comfortable worn feel, with Via Martelli offering younger, more casual styles and Via Roma sporting a complete green floor of Prada. The layout is always the same—shoes get pride of place on the ground floor with clothes up ever-narrower staircases above. The newest addition to the Raspini family is the Vintage store in Via Calimaruzza in the centre of town where you will find top label clothes, shoes and bags from last year discounted by up to 60%. It's certainly worth checking out before you book your cab to the Prada outlet 45 minutes out of town. *raspini.com*

Expensive to luxury *Amex/MC/V*

Via Por Santa Maria 70-72/R **055 215 796**
50122 Florence Mon 3-7, Tues-Sat 10-7

Via Martelli 5-7/R **055 239 8336**
50129 Florence (opening hours as above)

Via Calimaruzza 17/R **055 213901**
50123 Florence (opening hours as above)

Replay

Replay appears to be taking Diesel head-on—so let the battle of the logos commence. At the Florence stores, jeans hang from meat hooks in a variety of different cuts, from funky hipsters to shredded denim leg-huggers. Tiny tees, distressed and graffiti'd for the girls, and combat shirts, logo'd and crumpled for the boys, keep the vibe streetwise and edgy. You may find an oriental touch, with satin bomber jackets and bright cotton shirts embroidered with

Chinese dragons—more menacing Triads than winsome *Last Emperor*. To complete this mood of urban neurosis meets *Blade Runner*, the two Florence stores hang mega mutant insects from the ceiling—if that doesn't shock you, nothing will. *replay.it*

Affordable   *Amex/MC/V*

Via de' Pecori 7-9/R   **055 293 041**
50123 Florence   Mon 3-7:30, Tues-Sat 10-7:30
Sun 2:30-7:30

Via Por Santa Maria 27/R   **055 287 950**
50123 Florence   Sun-Mon 3-7:30, Tues-Sat 10-7:30

Roberto Biagini

If you're planning to attend a really la-di-da wedding (your own perhaps?) and have time for at least one fitting, head to Biagini to get kitted out the old-fashioned way. This shop might look a bit fusty from the outside, but once inside you'll forget about aesthetics when faced with some of the finest menswear this side of the Arno. Biagini caters to a gentleman's stylish requirements—pure cotton shirts, three-button overcoats and classic Italian suits, all made to measure from the pick of Italian and British fabrics. And in addition to the choice of staples and the exquisite artisan cut which goes into each piece, Biagini's beautiful handmade leather shoes are among the finest in town.

Luxury   *Amex/MC/V*

Via Roma 2-3/R   **055 294 253**
50123 Florence   Daily 10-7:30 (Sun 10-1, 3:30-7:30)

☆ Roberto Cavalli

Roberto Cavalli is the biggest name to emerge from the Florentine fashion scene over the past decade. A favourite with glitz-loving celebrities, Cavalli was born in Florence in 1940, and still lives here in a luxurious farmhouse just outside town. He's often spotted hanging out in his Florence store, a relatively new addition to his empire, which squeezed the historic Café Giacosa out of its Tornabuoni premises three years ago. A rock-chic version of the café survives next door and is a smart spot for a cappuccino before you get down to some serious shopping. Afterwards, you can walk straight through into Cavalli's Tex-Mex outpost with its cactuses and sandblasted walls and browse his fabulous jewel-encrusted jeans, animal-print silk shirts and plunging scarlet evening dresses. Alongside the café, the men's department dazzles with silk tracksuits and wantonly garish shirts surely designed with fave client Lenny Kravitz in mind. (p.s. If the prices here are out of range, Cavalli has an outlet selling last season's looks on the fringes of town: Via Volturno 3/3, tel: 055 317 754. Well worth the cab fare.) *robertocavalli.it*

Luxury   *Amex/MC/V*

Via de' Tornabuoni 83/R   **055 239 6226**
50123 Florence   Sun-Mon 3-7:30, Tues-Sat 10-7:30

☆ Roberto Ugolini

Robert Ugolini is part of a new breed of Florentine crafts-people who are determined that their city's artisan heritage will continue into the 21st century and beyond. The walls of Ugolini's workshop are covered in black and white photos of the city and of its craftsmen sewing leather hides and hammering pins into men's handcrafted shoes. Antique wall brackets are lined with wooden lasts of feet past and present. In front of them, Roberto and his two-man team fashion shoes on a huge table, using a mind-boggling array of instruments that demonstrate the amazing complexity of this craft. Part of Florence's savvy thirty-something generation, they know exactly what's hot on the footwear scene and will update classic styles, including brogues and classic lace-ups, using the traditions which have been passed down to them.   *roberto-ugolini.com*

Luxury   *Amex/MC/V*

Via Michelozzi 17/R   **055 216 246**
50125 Florence   Mon 3:30-8, Tues-Sat 9:30-1:30, 3:30-8

Rosa Regale

Are you at the point where all this Italian good taste is beginning to get you down? Rosa Regale will bring you back down to earth with a joyful bump. Sneak down her discreet alleyway for a hit of pure madness. Designer Gianna Mattei is fixated on roses and rosebuds, frou-frou and flounces. She makes them into voluptuous velvet cushions and sofas. She turns them into frilly taffeta evening dresses which she adapts to become crazy chair covers. She invents frothy, lace-trimmed Ascot hats which she converts into frivolous lamp-shades. Fortunately, she also designs clothes that you can actually wear. Her small womenswear collection contains wacky crocheted ponchos and one-off jackets in gold filigree brocade. Colour (mainly red) predominates. Fun prevails. Even if it's not for you, it will make you laugh.   *rosaregale.it*

Moderate   *Amex/MC/V*

Via Tosinghi Volta dei Mazzucconi 3   **055 267 0613**
50123 Florence   Mon 3:30-7:30
                              Tues-Sat 10-1:30, 2:30-7:30

☆ Ruffo

Top leatherwear producer Ruffo is lying in wait for you. The minimalist glass frontage of this new store slinks, elegant and almost nameless, along a nondescript street near the Duomo. Walk on by. If you go inside you'll be ensnared by desirable pieces. There are drawstring pyjama trousers in softest suede, white leather jackets with delicious drapes, and even funky suede blouses with gently scooped necklines. Upstairs you'll find equally beautiful pieces for men. Here leather is no longer rigid and static, it's soft and sinuous. You'll find nappa carta, paper-light

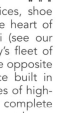

and delicately scrunched, and nappa seta, the softest, most expensive leather to be found. No wonder Gucci, Prada and Jill Sander are supplied by these guys. There's no way out. Even if the fit is not quite right they'll simply take your measurements and make a piece up for you in around a week. They're local, after all. Don't say we didn't warn you. *ruffo.it*

Luxury *Amex/MC/V*

Via de' Pecori 10/R **055 265 8422**
50100 Florence Mon 3-7, Tues-Sat 10-7

☆ Salvatore Ferragamo

Ferragamo is rigorously Florentine and its offices, shoe museum and main store are still housed in the heart of town in the monumental Palazzo Spini-Ferroni (see our Services section for more on the fashion family's fleet of hotels and restaurants). It is worth crossing to the opposite pavement just to admire this incredible palace built in 1289. It is no less impressive inside, with a series of high-ceilinged, fresco'd rooms accommodating the complete Ferragamo collection. A quietly aristocratic mood pervades but is not unduly oppressive—you are welcome to browse without being pressed. Of course, the shoes are the highlight and are to be found in the central rooms. Drift round to the right to find womenswear in three spacious rooms, before heading on to menswear with one room dedicated to a fabulous display of Ferragamo's ties. Turn left to find a small selection of luxury childrenswear and, beyond, the famous silk headscarves. At sales time, you may find a door is opened beside the taxi rank on Piazza Santa Trinità to a subterranean discount zone. Ferragamo is nothing if not discreet. *ferragamo.com*

Expensive to luxury *Amex/MC/V*

Via de' Tornabuoni 4-14/R **055 292 123**
50123 Florence Mon-Sat 10-7:30

☆ Samples

Thirty-something Swiss-French designer Sarah Buchi is a bundle of enthusiasm and energy. If you are lucky enough to find her in her store, prepare to be caught up in a tidal wave of words and new ideas. Samples is testament to this. Here she has created a contemporary lifestyle store far removed from Florence's usual Renaissance-nostalgia; instead, a select list of designers and artists display limited-edition pieces of crystal, ceramics and furniture. Buchi's own chunky, functional shoulder bags are at the centre of it all. Sit down with her in the atelier at the back of the store and finger samples of leather and suede as she explains her designs. She'll modify them to your needs and ship to you. Particular winners are Giulio, a two-in-one portfolio/computer case, and Alfonsina, a sharp shopper.

Expensive *Amex/MC/V*

Via de' Bardi 23/R **055 247 8872**
50125 Florence Tues-Sat 10-1, 2-7

San Lorenzo Market

Located between the Medici-Riccardi palace, the basilica of San Lorenzo and the Medici chapel, the sprawling San Lorenzo market is an obligatory stop for those in search of a cheap and cheerful thrill. Stalls are cram-packed with clothes and accessories and the quality is surprisingly high. Of particular note are the soft leather jackets, fine-spun silk scarves and excellent knock-off handbags. Currently, colourful Louis Vuitton look-alikes seem to be cropping up everywhere; they're so well made that no one will spot the difference. You'll also find some seasonal clothing as well as the usual ethnic tat and Florentine memorabilia. Go early to avoid the crowds and don't be afraid to negotiate, particularly if you are paying cash.

Affordable   *some stalls accept Amex/MC/V*

Piazza del Mercato Centrale
and around San Lorenzo   Mon-Sat 9-6

Sarah Pacini

On brash, commercial Via del Corso, Sarah Pacini's store stands out as an oasis of serenity. Like so many shops in Florence, the store is barely more than a single line of clothes running from front to back, but the atmosphere is stylish in subdued, organic tones with great lighting and a welcoming sense of calm. This Belgian-Irish brand, which is produced in Italy, goes for monochromatic knits, linens and silks that drape and swathe. The colour palette runs from black to earthy brown, aubergine and navy to khaki. You may need help to decipher the wealth of choice in each shade, but once your eye gets accustomed, you discover the intriguing games that the label plays with easy knits that wrap and swirl to create a long, lean look that hides a multitude of sins. Maternitywear isn't officially Pacini's thing, but anyone in search of the perfect bump-hiding frock would do well to start here.   *sarah-pacini.com*

Moderate   *Amex/MC/V*

Via del Corso 43/R   **055 268 461**
50122 Florence   Mon 3:30-7:30, Tues-Sat 10-7:30

☆ Sergio Rossi

If you gravitate to Sergio Rossi, understatement probably isn't your style. These are seriously sexy shoes for people without hang-ups about how they look. Sky-high spikes and sassy colours predominate. But step right in: it's such fun, and you might even find the odd piece that won't send your grandmother into a dead faint. True, the rock-star style footwear—like metallic pink stilettos with a knee-high shin-guard of rose rhinestones—is the first thing to grab your eye. But right behind, you'll find simple sandals, perhaps with a single rhinestone loop, for an altogether quieter effect. Similarly, for men there are loud-mouthed mod loafers in red and white kidskin, as well as peaceable brogues and ankle boots. The new handbag collection is worth watching, too: the stylish, asymmetrical Solaro bag could even turn your granny into a die-hard Sergio Rossi fan.   *sergiorossi.com*

Luxury   *Amex/MC/V*

Via Roma 15/R   **055 294 873**
50123 Florence   Mon 3-7, Tues-Sat 10-1, 2-7

Sisley

Like Stefanel, this mass-market chain (part of the Benetton empire) is a safe stop-off for wardrobe essentials and affordable interpretations of whatever may be this season's big idea. Of the two Florence stores, the Via de' Cerretani branch packs a cooler vibe, with more space to allow you to browse for sports and casualwear, plus more formal and elegant styles. Both stores are well frequented by Japanese girls buying into the raunchy Parisian image made so memorable in those ads.   *sisley.com*

Moderate   *Amex/MC/V*

Via de' Cerretani 57/R   **055 210 683**
50123 Florence   Mon-Sat 9:30-7:30, Sun 3:30-7:30
                              (closed Sundays June-August)

Via Roma 16/R   **055 286 669**
50123 Florence   Daily 10-8 (Sun 12-8)

Space

This slim store—in a glass-covered former alleyway remodelled by architect Paolo Vasi—has a definite fashion groove with names like Costume National, Dries Van Noten, Paul Smith and Helmut Lang lining the racks. This year, Marc Jacobs for women is billed as an imminent addition to the mix. The shop smells great, too. French perfumes from the super-exclusive Different Company are now to be found here, including, most appropriately, the aristocratic Bois D'Iris, the result of a painstaking eight-year process of distillation using the Florentine Iris Pallida flower.

Expensive   *Amex/MC/V*

Via de' Tornabuoni 17/R   **055 216 943**
50123 Florence   Mon 3-7:30, Tues-Sat 10-7:30

☆ Spazio A

Run your finger down the stellar list of stablemates here—from elegant Alberta Ferretti to wisecracking Moschino, from idiosyncratic Jean Paul Gaultier to sculptural Narciso Rodriguez—and you'll see that Spazio A plays host to some very different styles. In fact they are all part of Ferretti's Aeffe Group, and the Florence shop is the first in a new string of multibrand stores. The concept is for a neutral space in ivory tones in which everyone can shine. So expect to find diversity, such as an ironically dowdy Moschino cardigan, complete with mini knitting booklet and needles, sitting within metres of a diaphanous mulberry silk chiffon evening dress from Alberta Ferretti. Don't miss the elegant window displays either, with videos of the collections projected onto vertical water cascades. Fabulous.   *aeffe.com*

Expensive *Amex/MC/V*
Via Porta Rossa 107/R **055 212 995**
50123 Florence Mon 3-7, Tues-Sat 10-7

Stefanel

Stefanel, the middle-market casualwear chain from Ponte di Piave near Treviso, has quickened its fashion pulse in recent years. You can still find wardrobe staples here such as T-shirts, denims, leathers and knits, but expect to see more fast-moving, single-run lines. Deliveries are now fortnightly, so stock moves on faster than you can whip out your credit card. Sadly, the candy-striped knitted camisoles and canvas Jackie O dresses with zip pockets that we spotted on our visit will be long gone by the time you get there—but no doubt there'll be something equally desirable hanging in their place. For the small menswear department, head to the back of the Via dei Calzaiuoli shop. The store in Via de' Cerretani offers the younger, more economical, Stef-in-Time line: ideal for students and Florentine teenagers dashing to catch a train at nearby Santa Maria Novella station. *stefanel.it*

Affordable *Amex/MC/V*
Via de' Calzaiuoli 44/R **055 212 418**
50122 Florence Mon-Sat 10-8, Sun 11-1, 3-7:30
Via de' Cerretani 46-48/R **055 215 526**
50123 Florence (opening hours as above)

☆ Stefano Bemer

Like Roberto Ugolini, Stefano Bemer is one of the younger generation of craftspeople who believe that Florentine's artisan tradition should not be allowed to die. This self-taught shoemaker started out in the Tuscan town of Greve in 1983, and opened his smart, lilac-sponged Florence store and workshop five years later. Today, he and his seven assistants turn out just 210 pairs of men's shoes a year. Not surprisingly, the waiting list is long. Each pair is entirely handmade, from the hand-stitched uppers to the soles; even the waxed, flat-cotton laces are woven on an antique machine. Bemer's best-known styles include classic oxfords and brogues, and closed shoes with side-buckles on the upper strap. The twist comes in the materials, which clients select from a vast range of hand-picked leathers. Hippopotamus, sharkskin or elephant, anyone? *stefanobemer.com*

Luxury *Amex/MC/V*
Borgo San Frediano 143/R **055 222 558**
50124 Florence Mon-Sat 9-1, 3-7:30

Sutor Mantellassi

Discreet, quietly moneyed types know where to go for their shoes and leatherwear—they head for the small Sutor Mantellassi store nestling under the arches of Piazza della Repubblica alongside the bookshop Edison. The

Mantellassi family has been making superb shoes by hand for 80 years (sutor means cobbler in Latin), and there has been a conscious choice not to compromise quality by expanding internationally. And where's the rush, if you already have the King of Spain and Inès de la Fressange on your client list? Gentlemen's shoes tend to be classic brogues and lace-ups. For women there are timeless court shoes and stiletto styles, as well as gorgeous creamy white suede cowboy boots that inspire instant love but stain even as you contemplate them. The comfortable wood-panelled store also offers a selection of highly desirable leather jackets, handbags and briefcases. *sutormantellassi.com*

Luxury   *Amex/MC/V*

Piazza della Repubblica 25/R   **055 287 275**
50123 Florence   Mon 3:30-7:30, Tues-Sat 10-1:30, 3-7:30

Tanino Crisci

Rest assured, frivolous fashion seasons may come and go but the mahogany-panelled Tanino Crisci store will never change. The company has been under the watchful eye of the same family for four generations and looks set to continue for another four. Head here for timeless men's and women's handmade shoes, handbags, wallets and belts in styles that may be too sedate for fashion junkies, but will have classic dressers going quietly wild. The mood is old money, from the crisp silk twill ladies' scarves to the ivory-handled men's umbrellas. Look harder, though, and you'll find a fresh citrus twist in flat yellow summer sandals that could have been worn by Jackie Kennedy in the Camelot years. *taninocrisci.com*

Expensive   *Amex/MC/V*

Via de' Tornabuoni 43/45R   **055 214 692**
50123 Florence   Mon 3-7, Tues-Sat 10-7

Temporary Store

The name may give the impression that this is an outfit run by fly-by-nights but, as so often on this street, a Florentine family with a long history in the leather trade lies behind this one-off, cheap-and-cheerful handbag store. In this case the Chiarini family offer light-hearted, light-on-the-bank-balance leather goods that you won't mind ditching at the end of the season. The corrugated cardboard displays underline that nobody is making any pretence about the products standing the test of time. Instead, you'll find loads of wacky-coloured bags and accessories to give your wardrobe a temporary lift. The store carries two lines: the slightly more expensive Gianni Chiarini and the less costly Guidit. Look out for multicoloured plastic shopping bags at 30 euros—ideal if you've already filled all those extra bags you brought. *giannichiarini.it*

Affordable   *Amex/MC/V*

Via della Vigna Nuova 52/R   **055 265 4306**
50123 Florence   Mon 3-7:30, Tues-Sat 10-7:30

Tod's

Tod's reassures. This is a cool, airy space with dark-suited staff and a comprehensive shoe and handbag selection that greets you at the door with this season's new trends and colours and then, if nothing quite grabs your eye, reliably serves up all your old favourites in the room alongside. It's difficult not to find something that appeals here. There are dainty seasonal sandals and matching clutch bags, or the familiar, more robust moccasins, sneakers and driving shoes. New on show is the curled Dega line, whose taut elasticated sides make the shoes look like they are about to spring off the shelf. Due to the success of the sporty Owens line, a second-generation line named Running has been developed. This is all part of Tod's continuing research into the elegant sports shoe market, a fast-growing sector as we begin to realise that it's time for our feet to have a holiday too. *todsgroup.com*

Expensive to luxury   *Amex/MC/V*

Via de' Tornabuoni 103/R   **055 219 423**
50123 Florence   Daily 10-7 (Sun 2-7)

Trussardi

If your shopping budget is nearing its limit you may be terrified of walking into Trussardi but believe us, there is something here for everyone, and in every price range. Setting out at the Tornabuoni end you'll find top-priced ready-to-wear in luxurious nappa leather and silk chiffon, just as you would expect. But start on a journey towards the far end of the shop, working your way through the various Trussardi lines from Jeans to Sports to Junior, and prices begin to dip. By the time you reach the middle section in what was once a flag-stoned stable yard you'll find batik-printed handkerchief dresses just right for your next beach holiday at accessible prices. On the far side, you emerge into the children's and babies' department with cute little pink baby dresses for a thoroughly acceptable 35 euros. *trussardi.com*

Moderate to luxury   *Amex/MC/V*

Via de' Tornabuoni 34/R   **055 219 903**
50123 Florence   Mon 3-7, Tues-Sat 10-7

Universo Sport

Tuscan sportswear chain Universo Sport has four stores in the greater Florence area and others in Arezzo, Livorno, Siena (opening soon) and Milan. Head through the electric-blue atrium on the ground floor to find shoes, branded sportswear and equipment. It is all well enough stocked but we recommend Il Rifugio Sport for serious athletes. The casualwear, reached by taking the escalators upstairs, is the real reason for your visit. Discover Prada Sport, Moncler, Guru, and Carhartt. There's even a funky Swiss jeans brand Alprausch (yes, Swiss, and with the endearing little tagline Swiss street life). Everything is available in male, female and children's versions and, for once in Florence, there's enough space to swing a cat. *universosport.it*

Moderate   *Amex/MC/V*
Piazza Duomo 6-8/R   **055 284 412**
50122 Florence   Mon 10:30-7:30, Tues-Sat 9:30-7:30
                        Sun 10:30-1:30, 2:30-7:30

☆ Valentino

In the last year Valentino has abandoned its compact Via della Vigna Nuova store for a new, two-floor space on Via de' Tosinghi which runs off Via Roma. Although it doesn't quite have the red-carpet night-time feel of its predecessor, the new store wins out on spaciousness and choice. Visit the ground floor so that you can gasp out loud over fairy-tale evening dresses and accessories. It seems an honour to be in the presence of these creations, even without a Hollywood diva wearing them. Afterwards, prove that you are not just another star-struck tourist by heading upstairs to check out the more affordable Valentino Roma collection. These are everyday clothes that are expensive but not prohibitive. Crisp white linen shirts and nautical striped knitwear are among the welcome surprises. The staff are helpful and down-to-earth.   *valentino.it*

Expensive to luxury   *Amex/MC/V*
Via de' Tosinghi 52/R   **055 293 142**
50123 Florence   Mon 3-7, Tues-Sat 10-2, 3-7

Versus

The atmosphere in this cavernous shop is a reflection of recent bad times, as troubles have beset the house of Versace since Gianni's murder. A flock of shop assistants linger aimlessly, and the surrounding look is dated; time has been frozen in the Eighties, the Versace heyday. The bright colours that recall those happier times are mostly gone from the ground and lower floors where the accessories and menswear are shown. But on the top floor you'll find the women's collection which thankfully is still strong on red carpet slinky sexiness, and here at least the happy colours have survived.   *versace.com*

Luxury   *Amex/MC/V*
Via de' Tornabuoni 13/R   **055 239 6167**
50123 Florence   Mon-Sat 10-7

Versus

You might want to hold off on the tiramisu before paying a visit to Versus. As you would expect from the youngest child in the house of Versace, the energy is full-on. The main problem is that you have to have model proportions or be stick-thin to get into some of these clothes. Perhaps we were unlucky, but most sizes on our visit seemed to be extra small. Still, the selection of jeans and tees is worth checking out because there are more than just spray-on styles. You'll also find neat suits and dresses that are not aggressively rock-chic—all at accessible prices. The women's collection in this black and white boutique, splattered with the ubiquitous Medusa heads, is on the ground floor; men's is upstairs.   *versace.com*

Moderate   *Amex/MC/V*
Via della Vigna Nuova 38/R   **055 217 619**
50123 Florence   Mon 3:30-7:30, Tues-Sat 10-7:30

Via Maggio Officina Denim Store

Via Maggio is best known for the echoing halls of its imposing antiques sellers where collectors pour over furniture and paintings from bygone ages. The Denim Store cocks a snook at all that. It's a favourite with Florence's hip student population and you can't help but be won over by the youthful optimism here. This little shop offers vintage and one-off clothing and accessories, and the pricing is decidedly friendly. Recent bestsellers include a line of Royal Mail knitwear and anoraks (yes, from the dear old British Post Office—not some funky new label that had slipped your attention). The owners, MTV stylist Tommaso del Vecchio and Aldo Zengiaro, seek out streetwear and vintage pieces in Italy, France and Britain. Their eye is drawn to the sporty and casual, like unworn Seventies Levi's stretch shirts or Rudolf Dessler rugby shirts. They also stock unusual accessories such as Florentine label Stondo's clutch bags with finger holes, but overall there's quite an anglophile flavour. The boys have even invented a brand called Andy Richardson to market vintage polo shirts.   *andyrichardson.me.uk*

Affordable   *Amex/MC/V*
Via Maggio 7/R   **055 267 0017**
50125 Florence   Mon 3:30-7:30, Tues-Sat 10-7:30

☆ Vilebrequin

Planning to make for one of Tuscany's pine-shaded beaches, just as soon as you've had your fill of Florence's retail charms? If so, head for this tiny shop, an outpost of stylish swimwear label St Tropez. Even in the gloomiest weather, the shipshape interior seems to be drenched in year-round sun and weathered by gentle maritime breezes: you can almost hear the soft swish of azure surf breaking onto white sand even without a conch shell in your hand. The place is packed to the gunnels with multicoloured swimming trunks. Pasta-overindulgers needn't despair: there's nothing tight or figure-hugging here, just a riot of shorts in brightly coloured prints which you know you will wear for years. Those who really want to splash out should ask about the VIP range of limited-edition trunks with sterling silver-tipped drawstrings and numbered labels. At closing time, staff spin round a notice that declares 'gone tanning'.   *vilebrequin.com*

Moderate to expensive   *Amex/MC/V*
Via Roma 12   **055 291 008**
50123 Florence   Mon 3-7, Tues-Sat 10-7

VIP Store

Hip young Florentines with a taste for street style but limited access to Daddy's credit card head here for clothes, shoes and accessories. In this comfortable, unpretentious space they can browse a mix of international labels and lesser-known local ones. The first room is dedicated to menswear, with pride of place going to an extensive selection of JPG jeans and super-distressed denim from British label Andrew Mackenzie. The larger room alongside is just for the girls, with shoes by Stephane Kélian's younger line Moskito, Moschino Cheap & Chic and elegant slingbacks by Les Tropeziennes. The clothes run from Voyage-reminiscent floaty dresses by Florentine line IngressoVM18 (translation: No Entry to Under 18s), to JPG and cheap-and-cheerful Bologna jeans label Gaudi. *vipstore.it*

Moderate *Amex/MC/V*

Borgo Ognissanti 15-17/R **055 219 611**
50123 Florence Mon 4-8, Tues-Sat 10-8

Wolford

Wolford keeps good company. Like Valentino, the Austrian hosiery and lingerie brand swapped its Via della Vigna Nuova store for more spacious premises on Via de' Tosinghi. The company's teensy products are the ultimate in 'capsule' wardrobe dressing, hence the walls neatly lined with tights-packet-size photographs which you browse rather like a catalogue. There is nothing to touch. Sleek vests, polo-necked tops and slimming teddies are all neatly packaged in cellophane envelopes. Then, of course, there are wonderful bras, bikinis and a few figure-hugging dresses and skirts. To locate products and prices you place yourself entirely in the hands of the friendly staff (there are none on show). Best to visit before lunch when body-slimming lingerie still sounds plausible. *wolford.com*

Expensive *Amex/MC/V*

Via de' Tosinghi 46/R **055 239 6546**
50123 Florence Mon 3:30-7:30, Tues-Sat 10-7:30

☆ W.P.Store

An antique canoe hangs from the roof, a fake swordfish dangles from the wall, and there are even neatly framed fishing flies. They all create the right backdrop for this very American store, whose clothes and contents could fit well into a cabin in a rugged wilderness. The beautifully decorated space is filled with clothing lines that have been around for even longer than the antiques hanging on the walls. Long-term success stories like Barbour, Hang Ten, Woolrich or the Aussie boot brand Blundstone fill the racks. It is foolproof retro-college Americana-feel clothing, but if you dig deeper there are some surprises, like a pink quilted Barbour. Most of the styles in the kids' section also come in adult sizes, so you can make Me and Mini Me.

Moderate *Amex/MC/V*

Via de' Federighi 3-5/R **055 277 6399**
50123 Florence Mon-Sat 9:30-1, 3:30-7:30

☆ Yves Saint Laurent

It's an absolute pleasure to walk into the deep-pile carpeted Yves Saint Laurent shop. The simple elegance of the grey/black store is the perfect backdrop for this enduring style powerhouse. On the ground floor are the accessories, the success stories which came along with Tom Ford like the big-fringed slouchy bags with chained antler handles. Stefano Pilati is now in charge but he has been careful to credit the original designers throughout the store. For his first collection, Pilati stayed close to the rule book, offering little of himself, but for winter 2006 he is beginning to be braver: collars that rise up to just beneath the ears, and skirts puffed into an egg shape, are looks which do play tribute to the original master, but for eveningwear Pilati experiments a little on his own, bringing in a beautifully romantic Byzantine feel.   *ysl.com*

Luxury   *Amex/MC/V*

Via de' Tornabuoni 29   **055 284 040**
50123 Florence   Mon-Sat 10-7

The Last Good Buy

In case you hadn't already noticed, Tuscany is the production point of much of the best in Italian fashion. So it's not surprising that the region is packed with factory outlets where you can buy desirable items at a fraction of their original price. Often the outlets are in the middle of nowhere, so you'll need to organise transport and have a clear idea of where you are going. The good news is that the biggest outlet hub (including the Mall, D&G, Fendi and Celine) can now be reached by a range of shuttle buses and taxi services, which you can track down via the internet or your hotel. A word of warning: outlet shopping tends to be time-consuming, so allow yourself at least half a day.

Dolce & Gabbana Industria S.P.A

It may seem a little strange to be browsing Dolce & Gabbana's slick urban dressing in a warehouse in the Tuscan countryside but believe us, once you see the prices you'll soon get over it. Here you'll find leftovers and end of lines all under one 300 square metre roof. If you're lucky you'll also find seconds or (the real gold-dust) one-off samples but if not, make do with last season's looks from the main and diffusion lines with discounts running at a tempting 30-50%. You'll find sparkly eveningwear, tailored suits, colourful tees and casualwear plus some great shoes. The main hiccup may be sizing—most of the clothing is teensy. For women, sizes concentrate around 40/42, for men around 48.   *outlet-firenze.com*

Moderate to expensive   *Amex/MC/V*

Località Santa Maria Maddalena 49   **055 833 1300**
50066 Pian dell'Isola, Rignano sull'Arno   Mon-Sat 9-7
                                                            Sun 3-7

Fendi

The Fendi outlet is near both Celine/Loewe and Dolce & Gabbana, and dedicated discount-hunters rush from one to the other trying to grab the best bargains before anyone else. At Fendi there is not only clothing but (gasp!) also the handbags, including the world-famous baguettes, with price tags you can just about afford. There are occasional samples as well as left-over lines, including some pieces from the current season, but don't get your hopes up too high. Discounts tend to hover well under 50%, so prices are still relatively hefty, though if you're used to shopping on Via Montenapoleone they feel like a snip. *outlet-firenze.com*

Expensive *Amex/MC/V*

Via Europa 8 **055 865 7030**
50066 Leccio Reggello Mon-Sat 10-7, Sun 3-7

I Pellettieri d'Italia

Prada was one of the first houses to realise the potential of outlet shopping, and there's a well-beaten path to its door laid down by coachloads of Japanese tourists who are joined by hordes of Tuscan locals on weekends. On bad days you may find yourself waiting in a queue outside with a numbered ticket before you can enter—don't think the coaches haven't learnt about getting there early to miss the crowds. Inside you will find clothing by Prada and Miu Miu plus a good selection of shoes and handbags, usually from previous seasons. There are occasional knock-down prices on small wallets and purses, so you can pick up great little designer-label stocking-fillers to impress your unsuspecting friends. *prada.it*

Moderate to expensive *Amex/MC/V*

Località Levanella 69 **055 919 01**
52025 Montevarchi Mon-Sat 9:30-7, Sun 2-7

The Mall

Of course Gucci knows how to do everything bigger and better, and the Mall is the proof. A couple of years back, this was a modest store on a country road offering just Gucci—now it's a shopping complex with a parade of smart designer stores, a spacious café and parking facilities gradually spreading over the surrounding green fields. The line-up includes Bottega Veneta, Armani, Loro Piana, Ungaro, La Perla, YSL, Ferragamo, Valentino and Sergio Rossi. In 2004 (set slightly apart in what was the original Gucci store) came Tod's and Hogan with some great shoes at around 110 euros. The presentation and service throughout is top-notch but, if you are not used to shopping for these labels, the prices may still seem steep (even if the luscious discounts occasionally tip the 60% mark). Check out the jeans section in Armani for the cheapest deals. *outlet-firenze.com*

Moderate to expensive *Amex/MC/V*

Via Europa 8 **055 865 7775**
50060 Leccio Reggello Mon-Sat 10-7, Sun 3-7

Florence Stores by District

Florence Map

Central Shopping Zone

Duomo area

North of Duomo

South of Duomo

Piazza Ognissanti area

Ponte Vecchio area

South of the Arno

Santa Croce area

Via de' Tornabuoni area

Via della Vigna Nuova area

Florence

195

Central Shopping Zone *See map pages 194–195*

Athletes World	Via de' Cerretani 26-28/R
Bagamunda	Via de' Cerretani 72/R
Baroni	Via Porta Rossa 56/R
Benetton 0-12	Via de' Cerretani 60-62/R
Brioni	Via de' Rondinelli 7/R
Bruno Magli	Via Roma 26-28/R
Cabo	Via Porta Rossa 77-79/R
Calvani	Via degli Speziali 7/R
Calzoleria Bologna	Via de' Cerretani 50/R
Celyn b.	Via de' Tosinghi 18/R
Coin	Via de' Calzaiuoli 56/R
Diesel	Via de' Lamberti 13/R
Du Pareil Au Même	Via dei Panzani 36-38/R
E-Play	Via de' Tosinghi 14/R
Expensive	Via de' Calzaiuoli 78/R
Fratelli Rossetti	Piazza della Repubblica 43-45
Geox	Via dei Panzani 5/R
Gerard Loft	Via de' Pecori 34-40/R
Gilardini	Via de' Cerretani 8
Golden Point	Via de' Calzaiuoli 51
Gucci (accessories)	Via Roma 32/R
Guess?	Via degli Speziali 9-11/R
Guya	Via Calimala 29/R
Hugo Boss	Piazza della Repubblica 46/R
Intimissimi	Via de' Calzaiuoli 99
Intimissimi	Via de' Cerretani 17
Italobalestri	Piazza di Santa Maria Maggiore 7/R
La Rinascente	Piazza della Repubblica 1
Le Silla	Via Roma 23/R
Liu Jo	Via Calimala 14/R
Luisa Via Roma	Via Roma 19-21/R
Malloni	Via Calimala 7/R
Mandarina Duck	Via de' Cerretani 64-66
Mauro Volponi	Via Orsammichele 12/R
Max & Co	Via de' Calzaiuoli 89/R
MaxMara	Via de' Pecori 23/R
Miss Sixty	Via Roma 20/R
Miu Miu	Via Roma 8/R
Montgomery	Via Pellicceria 22/R
Murphy & Nye	Via Calimala 16-18/R
Nannini	Via Porta Rossa 64/R
Nannini	Via de' Calzaiuoli 82/R
Nara Camicie	Via Porta Rossa 25
Paola del Lungo	Via Porta Rossa 7/R
Pollini	Via Calimala 12/R
Prenatal	Via de' Brunelleschi 22/R
Replay	Via de' Pecori 7-9/R
Roberto Biagini	Via Roma 2-3/R

Rosa Regale	Via de' Tosinghi Volta dei Mazzucconi 3
Sergio Rossi	Via Roma 15/R
Sisley	Via de' Cerretani 57/R
Sisley	Via Roma 16/R
Spazio A	Via Porta Rossa 107/R
Stefanel	Via de' Calzaiuoli 44/R
Stefanel	Via de' Cerretani 46-48/R
Sutor Mantellassi	Piazza della Repubblica 25/R
Valentino	Via de' Tosinghi 52/R
Vilebrequin	Via Roma 12
Wolford	Via de' Tosinghi 46/R

Duomo area

See map pages 194–195

Calzoleria Bologna	Piazza San Giovanni 13-15/R
Patrizia Pepe	Piazza San Giovanni 12/R
Pinko	Via de' Cerretani 2/R
Ruffo	Via de' Pecori 10/R
Universo Sport	Piazza del Duomo 6-8/R

North of Duomo

Benetton	Borgo San Lorenzo 17/R
Calzoleria Bologna	Via S. Antonino 9-11/R
Foot Locker	Borgo San Lorenzo 19/R
Frette	Via Cavour 2/R
Quelle Tre	Via de' Pucci 43/R
Raspini	Via dei Martelli 5-7/R

South of Duomo

A Piedi Nudi Nel Parco	Borgo degli Albizi 46/R
Ethic	Borgo degli Albizi 37/R
Gabs	Via S. Egidio 9/R
L'Essentiel	Via del Corso 10/R
Matucci	Via del Corso 44-46/R & 71-73/R
Poncif	Borgo degli Albizi 35/R
Sarah Pacini	Via del Corso 43/R

Piazza Ognissanti area

See map page 194

Catwalk Collection	Borgo Ognissanti 69/R
Giotti	Piazza Ognissanti 3-4/R
Il Giglio	Borgo Ognissanti 64
Il Rifugio Sport	Piazza Ottaviani 3
Il Rifugio Sport	Via de' Fossi 67/R
Liverano & Liverano	Via de' Fossi 43/R
VIP Store	Borgo Ognissanti 15-17/R

Ponte Vecchio area

See map page 194

Bottega delle Antiche Terme	
	Borgo Santissimi Apostoli 16/R
Borsalino	Via Porta Rossa 40/R
Camper	Via Por Santa Maria 47/R

Florence Districts

Champion	Via Por Santa Maria 52-54/A
Coccinelle	Via Por Santa Maria 49/R
Gerard	Via Vaccherecia 18-20/R
Guya	Via Por Santa Maria 76/R
Mandarina Duck	Via Por Santa Maria 23-25/R
Nero Giardini	Ponte Vecchio 64/R
Pollini	Via Por Santa Maria 42
Raspini	Via Por Santa Maria 70-72/R
Raspini Vintage	Via Calimaruzza 17/R
Replay	Via Por Santa Maria 27/R

South of the Arno
See map pages 194–195

Geraldine Tayar	Sdrucciolo de' Pitti 6/R
Golubcik	Via de' Coverelli 27/R
Madova	Via de' Guicciardini 1/R
Mannina	Via de' Guicciardini 16/R
Paola del Lungo	Via de' Bardi 69/R
Roberto Ugolini	Via de' Michelozzi 17/R
Samples	Via de' Bardi 23/R
Stefano Bemer	Borgo San Frediano 143/R
Via Maggio Officina Denim Store	Via Maggio 7/R

Santa Croce area

Peruzzi	Via dell'Anguillara 5-23/R

Via de' Tornabuoni area
See map page 194

Allegri	Via de' Tornabuoni 72/R
Baroni	Via de' Tornabuoni 9/R
Bottega Veneta	Via de' Tornabuoni 7/R
Brioni	Via de' Rondinelli 7/R
Casadei	Via de' Tornabuoni 33/R
Celine	Via de' Tornabuoni 24-26-28/R
Christian Dior	Via de' Tornabuoni 57-59/R
Emilio Pucci	Via de' Tornabuoni 20-22/R
Emporio Armani	Piazza degli Strozzi 16/R
Ermanno Scervino	Piazza degli Antinori 10/R
Ermenegildo Zegna	Via de' Tornabuoni 3/R
Escada	Via degli Strozzi 32/R
Fendi	Via degli Strozzi 21/R
Giorgio Armani	Via de' Tornabuoni 48/R
Gucci	Via de' Tornabuoni 73/R
Gucci Jewellery	Via de' Tornabuoni 81/R
Hermès	Piazza degli Antinori 6
H.Neuber	Via de' Tornabuoni 17
Hogan	Via de' Tornabuoni 97/R
Les Copains	Piazza degli Antinori 2-3/R
Loretta Caponi	Piazza degli Antinori 4/R
Louis Vuitton	Piazza degli Strozzi 1
MaxMara	Via de' Tornabuoni 66-70/R

Mila Schön	Piazza S. Trinità 1/R
Parody	Via della Spada 18-20/R
Prada (women)	Via de' Tornabuoni 53/R
Prada (men)	Via de' Tornabuoni 67/R
Roberto Cavalli	Via de' Tornabuoni 83/R
Salvatore Ferragamo	Via de' Tornabuoni 14-4/R
Space	Via de' Tornabuoni 17/R
Tanino Crisci	Via de' Tornabuoni 43-45/R
Tod's	Via de' Tornabuoni 103/R
Trussardi	Via de' Tornabuoni 34/R
Versace	Via de' Tornabuoni 13/R
Yves Saint Laurent	Via de' Tornabuoni 29

Via della Vigna Nuova area   *See map page 194*

Anichini	Via Parione 59
Bonora	Via Parione 11-15/R
Borsalino	Via della Vigna Nuova 60/R
BP Studio	Via della Vigna Nuova 15/R
Braccialini	Via della Vigna Nuova 30/R
Cesare Paciotti	Via della Vigna Nuova 14/R
Desmo	Piazza de' Rucellai 10/R
Dolce & Gabbana	Via della Vigna Nuova 27/R
Elio Ferraro	Via Parione 47/R
Ermenegildo Zegna	Piazza de' Rucellai 4-7/R
Etro	Via della Vigna Nuova 50/R
Francesco Biasia	Via della Vigna Nuova 16/R
Furla	Via della Vigna Nuova 28/R
Gianfranco Lotti	Via della Vigna Nuova 45/R
Grevi	Via della Spada 11-13/R
Il Bisonte	Via Parione 31/R
Il Misio	Via de' Federighi 6/R
Lacoste	Via della Vigna Nuova 33/R
La Perla	Via della Vigna Nuova 17-19/R
Loro Piana	Via della Vigna Nuova 37/R
Mariella Burani	Via della Vigna Nuova 32/R
Massimo Rebecchi	Via della Vigna Nuova 26
Mazzini – Shop in Progress	Via della Vigna Nuova 58/R
Moda Sartoriale	Via del Purgatorio 22/R
Paolo Tonali	Via della Vigna Nuova 18-20/R
Piero Guidi	Via della Vigna Nuova 46-48/R
Temporary Store	Via della Vigna Nuova 52/R
Versus	Via della Vigna Nuova 38/R
W.P.Store	Via de' Federighi 3-5/R

Florence Districts

Florence Stores by Category

Women's

Men's

Children's

Women's Accessories

A Piedi Nudi Nel Parco
Bagamunda
Benetton
Bonora
Borsalino
Bottega Veneta
Braccialini
Calzoleria Bologna
Celine
Christian Dior
Coccinelle
Coin
Desmo
Elio Ferraro
Ermanno Scervino
Ermenegildo Zegna
Escada
Fendi
Francesco Biasia
Furla
Gabs
Geox
Geraldine Tayar
Gerard
Gerard Loft
Gianfranco Lotti
Giotti
Grevi
Gucci
Guya
Hermès
Il Bisonte
Il Giglio
La Rinascente
Loro Piana
Louis Vuitton
Mandarina Duck
Mazzini—Shop in Progress
Nannini
Patrizia Pepe
Peruzzi
Quelle Tre
Raspini
Rosa Regale
Salvatore Ferragamo
Samples
Sisley
Stefanel
Tanino Crisci
Temporary Store
Via Maggio Officina
VIP Store

Women's Activewear

Athletes World
Benetton
Champion
Coin
Expensive
Foot Locker
Geox
Golden Point
Il Rifugio Sport
Lacoste
La Rinascente
Murphy & Nye
Universo Sport
W.P.Store

Bridal

Ermanno Scervino
Valentino

Women's Cashmere/Knitwear

Benetton
BP Studio
Cabo
Escada
Fendi

Guya
H.Neuber
Les Copains
Loro Piana
Paolo Tonali

Women's Casual

Benetton
Celyn b
Coin
Diesel
E-Play
Ethic
Expensive
Gerard Loft
Guess?
La Rinascente
L'Essentiel
Liu Jo
Matucci
Max & Co
MaxMara

Miss Sixty
Montgomery
Parody
Patrizia Pepe
Pinko
Quelle Tre
Raspini
Replay
Sisley
Stefanel
Universo Sport
Via Maggio Officina
 Denim Store
VIP Store
W.P.Store

Women's Classic

Allegri
Borsalino
Celine
Castellani
Coin
Ermenegildo Zegna
Escada
Etro
Giorgio Armani
Hermès
H.Neuber
La Rinascente
Loro Piana

Luisa Via Roma
MaxMara
Mila Schön
Nara Camicie
Paolo Tonali
Ruffo
Salvatore Ferragamo
Sarah Pacini
Trussardi
Valentino
Versace
Yves Saint Laurent

Women's Contemporary

Allegri
A Piedi Nudi Nel Parco
BP Studio
Diesel
Gerard
Golubcik
Guess?
Guya
L'Essentiel
Luisa Via Roma
Malloni
Mariella Burani
Massimo Rebecchi
Matucci
Max & Co
Parody
Patrizia Pepe
Pinko
Poncif
Raspini
Raspini Vintage
Rosa Regale
Ruffo
Space
Spazio A
Via Maggio Officina
  Denim Store
VIP Store

Women's Department Store & High Street Chains

Athletes World
Benetton
Camper
Celyn b
Champion
Coin
Diesel
Ethic
Expensive
Foot Locker
Furla
Golden Point
Intimissimi
La Rinascente
Liu Jo
Nara Camicie
Pinko
Replay
Sisley
Stefanel
Universo Sport

Women's Formalwear, Eveningwear & Special Occasions

Casadei
Catwalk Collection
Christian Dior
Dolce & Gabbana
Ermanno Scervino
Escada
Etro
Fendi
Geraldine Tayar
Gerard
Giorgio Armani
Grevi
Gucci
Luisa Via Roma
Mariella Burani
Mila Schön
Quelle Tre
Raspini
Raspini Vintage
Salvatore Ferragamo
Spazio A
Trussardi
Valentino
Versace
Yves Saint Laurent

Women's Designer

Allegri
Bottega Veneta
Bruno Magli
Cabo
Catwalk Collection
Celine
Christian Dior
Dolce & Gabbana
Emilio Pucci
Emporio Armani
Ermanno Scervino
Escada
Etro
Fendi
Gerard
Giorgio Armani
Gucci
H.Neuber
Hermès
Les Copains
Louis Vuitton

Luisa Via Roma
Mariella Burani
Massimo Rebecchi
MaxMara
Mila Schön
Miu Miu
Paolo Tonali
Piero Guidi
Prada
Raspini
Raspini Vintage
Roberto Cavalli
Ruffo
Salvatore Ferragamo
Sergio Rossi
Space
Spazio A
Trussardi
Valentino
Versus
Yves Saint Laurent

Women's Handbags

A Piedi Nudi Nel Parco
Bagamunda
Bottega Veneta
Braccialini
Bruno Magli
Celine
Christian Dior
Coccinelle
Coin
Desmo
Elio Ferraro
Ermanno Scervino
Ermenegildo Zegna
Escada
Etro
Fausto Santini
Fendi
Francesco Biasia
Furla
Gabs
Geraldine Tayar

Gerard
Gianfranco Lotti
Giotti
Gucci
Guya
Hermès
Il Bisonte
Le Silla
Louis Vuitton
Mandarina Duck
Mazzini – Shop in Progress
Nannini
Peruzzi
Piero Guidi
Prada
Salvatore Ferragamo
Samples
Tanino Crisci
Temporary Store
Valentino
Yves Saint Laurent

Women's Hats (and gloves*)

Borsalino
Coin

Grevi
*Madova

Women's Leather Goods

Bagamunda
Bonora
Borsalino
Bottega Veneta
Braccialini
Bruno Magli
Calzoleria Bologna
Celine
Christian Dior
Coccinelle
Coin
Desmo
Etro
Fendi
Francesco Biasia
Furla
Gabs
Geox
Gianfranco Lotti
Giorgio Armani
Giotti
Gucci
Hermès

Il Bisonte
Louis Vuitton
Madova
Mannina
Mauro Volponi
Mazzini – Shop in Progress
Nannini
Nero Giardini
Peruzzi
Piero Guidi
Prada
Raspini
Raspini Vintage
Ruffo
Salvatore Ferragamo
Samples
Sutor Mantellassi
Tanino Crisci
Temporary Store
Trussardi
Yves Saint Laurent
VIP Store

Women's Lingerie & Nightwear

Baroni
Coin
Frette
Golden Point
Intimissimi

La Perla
La Rinascente
Loretta Caponi
Wolford

Maternity

Baroni
Benetton 0-12

Coin
Prenatal

Women's Shoes

Bagamunda
Bottega Veneta
Bruno Magli
Calvani
Calzoleria Bologna
Camper
Casadei
Celine
Cesare Paciotti
Christian Dior
Coin
Desmo
Ermanno Scervino
Escada
Fausto Santini
Fendi
Foot Locker
Francesco Biasia
Fratelli Rossetti
Geox
Gerard
Gerard Loft
Gianfranco Lotti
Gilardini
Gucci
Guya
Hermès
Hogan
Il Giglio
Italobalestri
Le Silla
Luisa Via Roma
Mannina
Mauro Volponi
Miu Miu
Nannini
Nero Giardini
Paola del Lungo
Peruzzi
Piero Guidi
Pollini
Prada
Raspini
Raspini Vintage
Salvatore Ferragamo
Sergio Rossi
Sutor Mantellassi
Tanino Crisci
Tod's
Valentino
VIP Store

Women's Trend & Streetwear

Athletes World
Benetton
Champion
Coin
Diesel
E-Play
Ethic
Expensive
Foot Locker
Geox
Gerard Loft
Guess?
Il Rifugio Sport
Lacoste
Liu Jo
Matucci
Miss Sixty
Montgomery
Murphy & Nye
Parody
Pinko
Replay
Sisley
Stefanel
Universo Sport
VIP Store
W.P.Store

Women's Vintage

Elio Ferraro
Gerard Loft
Via Maggio Officina Denim
   Store

Men's Accessories

Athletes World
Benetton
Bonora
Borsalino
Brioni
Bruno Magli
Coin
Diesel
Dolce & Gabbana
Elio Ferraro
Ermenegildo Zegna
Etro
Fendi
Fratelli Rossetti
Gerard
Gerard Loft
Gianfranco Lotti
Giorgio Armani
Giotti
Gucci
Guya
Hermès
H.Neuber
Hugo Boss

Il Bisonte
Il Giglio
Liverano & Liverano
Loro Piana
Louis Vuitton
Mandarina Duck
Matucci
Miu Miu
Montgomery
Murphy & Nye
Peruzzi
Piero Guidi
Prada
Roberto Biagini
Roberto Ugolini
Salvatore Ferragamo
Sisley
Stefanel
Sutor Mantellassi
Tanino Crisci
Trussardi
Versace
Vilebrequin
Yves Saint Laurent

Men's Activewear

Athletes World
Benetton
Champion
Coin
Foot Locker
Geox
Golden Point
Il Rifugio Sport
Lacoste

La Rinascente
Murphy & Nye
Replay
Universo Sport
Via Maggio Officina
Denim Store
Vilebrequin
VIP Store
W.P.Store

Men's Cashmere/Knitwear

Dolce & Gabbana
Fendi
Gerard
Giorgio Armani
Guya
H.Neuber
Hugo Boss

Les Copains
Loro Piana
Luisa Via Roma
Prada
Roberto Biagini
Stefanel

Men's Casual

Allegri
Athletes World
Benetton
Coin
Diesel
Elio Ferraro
E-Play
Geox
Gerard Loft
Il Rifugio Sport
Montgomery
Murphy & Nye
Parody
Raspini
Replay
Roberto Biagini
Sisley
Space
Stefanel
Universo Sport
Via Maggio Officina Denim
    Store
VIP Store
W.P.Store

Men's Classic

Allegri
Borsalino
Bottega delle Antiche
    Terme
Brioni
Ermenegildo Zegna
Fendi
Gerard
Giorgio Armani
Gucci
H.Neuber
Hugo Boss
Liverano & Liverano
Loro Piana
Luisa Via Roma
Massimo Rebecchi
Moda Sartoriale
Prada
Roberto Biagini
Salvatore Ferragamo
Trussardi
Yves Saint Laurent

Men's Contemporary

Allegri
Coin
Dolce & Gabbana
Emporio Armani
E-Play
Ermenegildo Zegna
Ethic
Geox
Gerard
Gerard Loft
Giorgio Armani
Guya
Hugo Boss
Luisa Via Roma
Murphy & Nye
Parody
Raspini
Raspini Vintage
Replay
Sisley
Space
Stefanel
Universo Sport
VIP Store
W.P.Store

Men's Department Store & High Street Chains

Athletes World	Il Rifugio Sport
Benetton	La Rinascente
Coin	Sisley
E-Play	Stefanel
Golden Point	Universo Sport

Men's Designer

Allegri	Loro Piana
Brioni	Luisa Via Roma
Bruno Magli	Miu Miu
Diesel	Prada
Dolce & Gabbana	Raspini
Emporio Armani	Raspini Vintage
Ermanno Scervino	Ruffo
Ermenegildo Zegna	Salvatore Ferragamo
Etro	Space
Fendi	Tod's
Gerard	Trussardi
Giorgio Armani	Universo Sport
Gucci	Versace
Hermès	Versus
Hugo Boss	Yves Saint Laurent

Men's Formalwear & Special Occasions

Bottega delle Antiche Terme	Loro Piana
Brioni	Luisa Via Roma
Dolce & Gabbana	Massimo Rebecchi
Ermenegildo Zegna	Moda Sartoriale
Etro	Prada
Fendi	Raspini
Giorgio Armani	Roberto Biagini
Gucci	Salvatore Ferragamo
Hermès	Trussardi
Hugo Boss	Versace
Liverano & Liverano	Versus
	Yves Saint Laurent

Men's Hats (and gloves*)

Borsalino	Giotti
Coin	*Madova

Men's Leather Goods

Bonora
Borsalino
Bruno Magli
Calzoleria Bologna
Coin
Ermenegildo Zegna
Etro
Fendi
Fratelli Rossetti
Geox
Gianfranco Lotti
Giotti
Gucci
Hermès
H.Neuber
Hogan
Hugo Boss
Il Bisonte

Louis Vuitton
Madova
Mandarina Duck
Peruzzi
Piero Guidi
Pollini
Prada
Raspini
Roberto Biagini
Salvatore Ferragamo
Samples
Space
Sutor Mantellassi
Tanino Crisci
Trussardi
Versace
Versus
Yves Saint Laurent

Men's Shirts

Borsalino
Bottega delle Antiche
  Terme
Brioni
Coin
Dolce & Gabbana
Emporio Armani
Ermanno Scervino
Ermenegildo Zegna
Etro
Fendi
Gerard
Gerard Loft
Giorgio Armani
Gucci
Guya

H.Neuber
Hugo Boss
La Rinascente
Liverano & Liverano
Luisa Via Roma
Massimo Rebecchi
Moda Sartoriale
Nara Camicie
Prada
Raspini
Roberto Biagini
Salvatore Ferragamo
Space
Trussardi
Versace
W.P.Store

Men's Shoes

Athletes World
Bonora
Brioni
Bruno Magli
Calvani
Calzoleria Bologna
Camper
Casadei
Cesare Paciotti
Champion
Coin
Dolce & Gabbana
Emporio Armani
Ermenegildo Zegna
Etro
Fausto Santini
Fendi
Foot Locker
Fratelli Rossetti
Geox
Gianfranco Lotti
Gilardini
Giorgio Armani
Gucci
Hogan

Il Giglio
Il Misio
Il Rifugio Sport
Italobalestri
Luisa Via Roma
Mauro Volponi
Montgomery
Nero Giardini
Paola del Lungo
Peruzzi
Piero Guidi
Pollini
Prada
Raspini
Roberto Biagini
Roberto Ugolini
Salvatore Ferragamo
Stefano Bemer
Sutor Mantellassi
Tanino Crisci
Tod's
Trussardi
Universo Sport
W.P.Store

Men's Tailors

Bottega delle Antiche
  Terme
Liverano & Liverano

Loro Piana
Moda Sartoriale

Men's Trend & Streetwear

Athletes World
Benetton
Diesel
E-Play
Foot Locker
Gerard
Gerard Loft
Hugo Boss
Lacoste
Montgomery

Murphy & Nye
Replay
Sisley
Stefanel
Universo Sport
Via Maggio Officina Denim
  Store
VIP Store
W.P.Store

Men's Vintage

Elio Ferraro
Gerard Loft

Via Maggio Officina Denim
  Store

Children's Clothes

Anichini
Athletes World
Baroni
Benetton 0-12
Champion
Christian Dior
Coin
Du Pareil Au Même
Geraldine Tayar
Geox
Golden Point
Grevi
Hogan
Il Rifugio Sport

Lacoste
La Rinascente
Luisa Vis Roma
Murphy & Nye
Peruzzi
Prenatal
Quelle Tre
Replay
Sisley
Stefanel
Trussardi
Universo Sport
Vilebrequin
W.P.Store

Children's Shoes

Calzoleria Bologna
Foot Locker
Salvatore Ferragamo

Florence Restaurants

Florence In-Store Restaurants/Bars

Caffè Giacosa   **055 277 6328**
Via della Spada 10/R (corner Via de' Tornabuoni)
(near Roberto Cavalli)
one of the city's best known cafés; you may
spot the designer himself hanging out here

La Rinascente   **055 219 113**
Piazza della Repubblica 1
average café fare on roof terrace with
spectacular view of the Duomo

Florence Restaurants

DUOMO/CENTRAL SHOPPING AREA

Astor Caffè   **055 239 9000**
Piazza Duomo 20/R
cocktails with complimentary mini plates of pasta

Bar San Firenze   **055 211 426**
Piazza di San Firenze 1/R
coffee bar with lots of ice cream

Caffè Concerto Paszkowski   **055 210 236**
Piazza della Repubblica 31-35   *paszkowski.it*
good quality lunchtime plates of pasta
overlooking Piazza della Repubblica

Caffè Gilli   **055 213 896**
Piazza della Repubblica 39/R   *gilli.it*
traditional old-time Florentine café

Caffè Rivoire   **055 214 412**
Via Vaccherecio 4/R (Piazza della Signoria)
hot chocolate and delicious club sandwiches (closed Monday)

Cantinetta Antinori   **055 292 234**
Piazza Antinori 3
world-renowned winemaker's bar and restaurant

Cantinetta dei Verrazzano   **055 268 590**
Via dei Tavolini 18-20/R
enoteca with delicious focaccia

Chiaroscuro   **055 214 247**
Via del Corso 36/R
fantastic coffee and salads

Colle Bereto   **055 283 156**
Piazza Strozzi 5/R
serious sunglasses-clad shoppers' bar

Coquinarius   **055 230 2153**
Via delle Oche 15/R
unrushed lunchtime salads for the girls

Da Mario   055 218 550
Via Rosina 2/R (Piazza Mercato Centrale)
family-run trattoria, a favourite with locals

Eito   055 210 940
Via dei Neri 72/R
sushi bar (closed Monday)

L'Incontro @ Hotel Savoy   055 27351
Piazza della Repubblica 7
stop by for a glamorous lunch or drinks on the terrace

Nerbone   055 219 949
Mercato Centrale, San Lorenzo
traditional Tuscan with extensive wine list

Paoli   055 216 215
Via dei Tavolini 12/R
old-worldly traditional Tuscan

Ristorante Oliviero   055 212 421
Via delle Terme 51/R
(open for dinner; lunch by arrangement only)
pumpkin ravioli to die for

VIA DE' TORNABUONI/VIA DELLA VIGNA NUOVA AREA

Beccofino   055 290 076
Piazza degli Scarlatti 1/R
inventive Tuscan in a contemporary setting

Il Latini   055 210 916
Via Palchetti 6/R
atmospheric Tuscan

Rose's   055 287 090
Via del Parione 26/R
fashionable sushi bar

Tredici Gobbi   055 284 015
Via del Porcellana 9/R
traditional Tuscan

PONTE VECCHIO/LUNGARNO ACCIAIUOLI (RIVERSIDE)

Capocaccia   055 210 751
Via Lungarno Corsini 12-14/R
the place to be seen at the cocktail hour

The Fusion Bar (Gallery Hotel Art)   055 27263
Vicolo dell'Oro 5
for tasty snacks
The name Fusion is no accident. This is a uniquely Florentine
fusion of fashion and hotels. The Gallery Hotel Art is owned by
the Ferragamo group, which also owns Lungarno Suites at
Lungarno Acciaiuoli 4 and the ultra-hip, pink-and-white
Continentale Hotel opposite the Fusion Bar at Vicolo dell'Oro
6/R. For information, call 055 2726 8000 or visit lungarnoho-
tels.com)

PIAZZA OGNISSANTI AREA

Harry's Bar   055 239 6700
Lungarno Vespucci 22/R
needs no introduction. It's for the stars,
of course, but why shouldn't that include you?

SANTA CROCE AREA

Baldovino   055 241 773/7220
Via San Giuseppe 22/R
enoteca and lively restaurant

Boccadama   055 243 640
Piazza Santa Croce 25-26/R
fabulous seasonal menu; great wines

Cibreo   055 234 1100
Via Andrea del Verrocchio 8/R
a clear favourite of Americans in Florence

Finisterrae   055 263 8675
Via de' Pepi 3-5/R
Mediterranean meets Middle Eastern;
excellent cocktails and pre-meal snacks

La Baraonda   055 234 1171
Via Ghibellina 67
basic trattoria (pasta, risotto etc)

Osteria dei Benci   055 2344 923
Via dei Benci 13/R
hip Tuscan with a twist

Osteria del Caffè Italiano   055 289 368
Via Isola delle Stinche 11-13/R
best puddings on the planet

SOUTH OF THE ARNO

Il Borgo San Jacopo   055 272 61
Borgo San Jacopo 62/R
modern Italian cuisine with views over the river

Cammillo   055 212 427
Borgo San Jacopo 57/R
high-quality, pricey Tuscan in simple but
sophisticated ambience (closed Wednesday)

Hemingway Bar   055 284 781
Piazza di Piattellina 9/R
for the best hot chocolate in town;
also great Sunday brunch

La Dolce Vita   055 284 595
Piazza del Carmine 6/R
cocktail hang-out for 20-somethings
and 40-something divorcees

Le Volpi e l'Uva   055 239 8132
Piazza de' Rossi 1
enoteca with wines from boutique
estates and amazing cold platters

Olio e Convivium   055 265 8198
Via Santo Spirito 4
exceptional deli and café—dine in or take out

Osteria del Cinghiale Bianco   055 215 706
Borgo San Jacopo 43
*genuine rustic, wooden tables,
and wild boar is the specialty (closed Wednesday)*

Ristorante Ricchi   055 215 864
Piazza Santo Spirito 8/R
seafood with a southern slant

Teatro del Sale   055 200 1492
Via dei Macci 111/R
*the private club that has taken Florence
by storm—join for evening entertainment
and eating all day*

Trattoria Angiolino   055 239 8976
Via S.Spirito 36/R
*for the best bistecca fiorentina
(T-bone) with fagioli (beans)*

Trattoria del Carmine   055 218 601
Piazza del Carmine 18/R
Typically Tuscan

Florence Services

Hairdressers (unisex)

Barbers

Beauty Treatment Centres & Solariums

Hair Removal

Manicures/Pedicures

Massage Therapists

Dance & Fitness Studios

Yoga

Dry Cleaners

Mending & Alterations

Custom Tailor

Shoe & Leather Repairs

Handbag & Luggage Repairs

Trimmings (fabrics, lace, embroidery etc)

Key Cutters

Drivers

Taxis

Hairdressers (unisex)

Aldo Coppola   **055 239 9402**
Via del Parione 62/R   Mon 2-7, Tues-Fri 8:30-7, Sat 9-7

BH Salone   **055 264 5561**
Via Borgo Ognissanti 12/R   Mon 10-3, Tues 2-7
                                            Wed 10-7, Thurs-Fri 10-10
                                                          Sat 10-3

Carlo Bay Hair Diffusion   **055 681 1876**
Via Marsuppini 18   Mon-Sat 9-7
carlobay.it

Gabrio Staff   **055 214 668**
Via de' Tornabuoni 5   Tues-Sat 9:30-7
gabriostaff.it

Gianni & Andrea   **055 239 6525**
Via dei Pescioni 7/R   Tues-Sat 9-7

I Parrucchieri di Firenze (Pistolesi Group)   **055 216 007**
Borgo Santi Apostoli 50/R   Tues-Sat 9-6

Jean Louis David   **055 216 760**
Lungarno Corsini 50/R   Tues-Sat 9-7

Mario di Via della Vigna   **055 294 813**
Via della Vigna Nuova 22/R   Tues-Thurs 9-6, Fri-Sat 9-7
mariodiviadellavigna.it

Barbers

Luigi   **(no telephone)**
Via Calimaruzza 12   Tues-Sat 9-7:30

Pratesi   **055 247 9814**
Borgo Pinti 47/R   Tues-Thurs 9-1, 3:30-7:30
                                                          Fri-Sat 9

Mario di Via della Vigna   **055 294 813**
Via della Vigna Nuova 22/R   Tues-Thurs 9-6, Fri-Sat 9-7
mariodiviadellavigna.it

Beauty Treatment Centres & Solariums

Aldo Coppola   **055 239 9402**
Via del Parione 62/R   Mon 2-7, Tues-Fri 8:30-7, Sat 9-1

Beauty Centre Vanita   **055 290 809**
Via Porta Rossa 55/R   Tues-Sat 9:30-7:30
levanitaprofumerie.it

Benessere   **055 217 003**
Via Monalda 1   Mon-Fri 9-7:30, Sat 9-1 (summer)
                                                 Sat 9-6 (winter)

Fonbliu Urban Spa   **055 233 5385**
Piazzale di Porta Romana 10/R   Mon 3-9, Tues-Fri 8-9
fonbliu.com   Sat 8-6

International Studio   **055 281 838/293 393**
Via Porta Rossa 82/R   Mon 1-8, Tues-Sat 10-8

Hair Removal

Benessere   **055 217 003**
Via Monalda 1   Mon-Fri 9-7:30, Sat 9-4 (summer)
        9-7:30 (winter)

Contrasto Hair   **055 239 8553**
Via della Mosca 8/R   Tues-Fri 9-7, Sat 8:30-6:3

Giuliana e Fernanda   **055 219 227**
Via de Benci 5/R   Tues-Fri 9-7, Sat 9-6

International Studio   **055 281 838/293 393**
Via Porta Rossa 82/R   Mon 1-8, Tues-Sat 10-8

Oasi Firenze   **055 234 6696**
Via degli Alfani 53/R   Mon-Sat 9:30-8
oasifirenze.com   (winter, Sun 3:30-7:30)

Manicures/Pedicures

Beauty Centre Vanita   **055 290 809**
Via Porta Rossa 55/R   Tues-Sat 9:30-7:30
levanitaprofumerie.it

Benessere   **055 217 003**
Via Monalda 1   Mon-Fri 9-7:30, Sat 9-1 (summer)
        Sat 9-6 (winter)

Freni   **055 239 6647**
Via Calimala 1   Mon 3-6:30, Tues-Fri 9-6:30, Sat 9-1

Giuliana e Fernanda   **055 219 227**
Via de Benci 5/R   Tues-Fri 9-7, Sat 9-6

International Studio   **055 281 838/293 393**
Via Porta Rossa 82/R   Mon 1-8, Tues-Sat 10-8

Mario di Via della Vigna   **055 294 813**
Via della Vigna Nuova 22/R   Tues-Thurs 9-6, Fri-Sat 9-7
mariodiviadellavigna.it

Parrucchiere Gianna   **055 238 1694**
Borgo Santissimi Apostoli 25   Tues-Sat 9-7

Massage Therapists

Beauty Centre Vanita   **055 290 809**
Via Porta Rossa 55/R   Tues-Sat 9:30-7:30
levanitaprofumerie.it

Diane Bailey   **335 684 7266**
Via Romana 34   (by appointment only)
chiropractor & osteopath

Enrico e Luca Toccafondi @ Blue Fitness   **055 238 2138**
Via il Prato 40   Mon-Fri 10-9 (by appointment only)

Hito Estetica	**055 284 424**
Via de' Ginori 21	Mon-Sat 9-7:30
International Studio	**055 281 838/293 393**
Via Porta Rossa 82/R	Mon 1-8, Tues-Sat 10-8
Tropos Club	**055 678 381**
Via Orcagna 20/A	Mon-Fri 8-9:30, Sat 8-7
troposclub.it	

Dance and Fitness Studios

Associazione Danza Scuola Toscana	**055 351 530**
Via Claudio Monteverdi 3/A	Mon-Fri 9-10
danzatoscana.it	
Blue Fitness	**055 238 137**
Via il Prato 40	Mon-Sat 10-9 (by appointment only)
Florence Dance Centre	**055 289 276**
Borgo della Stella 23/R	Mon-Fri 9-1, 3-8
florencedance.org	
Fonbliu Urban Spa	**055 233 5385**
Piazzale di Porta Romana 10/R	Mon-Fri 8:30-9
fonbliu.com	Sat 8:30-6
Maxballet Academy	**055 331 816**
Via Landini 9	Mon-Fri 9:30-11
maxballet.it	
Sports Clinic Centre	**055 676 141**
Via Scipione Ammirato 102/A	Mon-Fri 8-8, Sat 9-1
sportscliniccenter.com	
physiotherapy, sports medicine, pilates	
Studio A	**055 292 887**
Via de' Ginori 19	Mon-Fri 10-9, Sat 10:30-1
Tropos Club	**055 678 381**
Via Orcagna 20/A	Mon-Fri 8-9:30, Sat 8-7
troposclub.it	

Yoga

Blue Fitness	**055 238 137**
Via il Prato 40	Mon-Sat 10-9 (by appointment only)
Centro Yoga	**055 234 2703**
Via de' Bardi 5	Mon-Fri (class times vary)
Studio A	**055 292 887**
Via de' Ginori 19	Mon-Fri 10-9, Sat 10:30-1

Dry Cleaners

Elensec	**055 483 415**
Via S. Gallo 52/R	Mon-Fri 8:30-1, 3:30-7:30
	Sat 9-12:30

Fiorentina (suede, leather & fur) **055 450 493**
Via E. Spinucci 8-10/R Mon, Thurs 9-7:30
Tues-Wed, Fri 9-1, 3:30-7:30

Lavanderia Lorenzi **055 224 536**
Via dei Serragli 71/R Mon-Fri 8-1, 2:30-7:30

Lavanderia O.M. **055 248 0167**
Via Ghibellina 32/R Mon-Fri 8:30-1, 3-7

Lavanderia Patrizia (rapid home delivery) **055 571 622**
Via A. Volta 183/C Mon-Fri 8:15-1, 4-7:30
Sat 8:30-12:30

Tintoria Serena **055 218 183**
Via della Scala 30-32/R Mon-Sat 8:30-8
general dry cleaning, also bridal, eveningwear & leather

Zagros **055 214 879**
Via delle Belle Donne 17/R Mon-Fri 9:30-1, 3-8
Sat 9:30-1

Mending & Alterations

Ago e filo **055 711 917**
Via Pisana 193/R Mon-Fri 9-1, 3:30-7:30

Arte del Rammendo **055 238 2363**
Via Camillo Benso di Cavour 32/R Mon 3:30-7:30
invisible mending Tues-Fri 9-1, 3:30-7:30, Sat 9-1

Punto Marina **055 283 883**
Via dello Studio 7/R Mon 3:30-7:30
Tues-Sat 8:30-12:30, 3:30-7:30

Rammendi e riparazioni Nisetta **055 679 606**
Via Capo di Mondo 28/R Mon-Fri 9-1, 3:30-7:30

Custom Tailor

Milord **055 280 739**
Piazza Strozzi 12-13/R Mon-Sat 9:30-7:30

Shoe & Leather Repairs

Guido **(no telephone)**
Via Santa Monaca 9 Mon-Fri 7-1, 3-6

Il Ciabattino **338 390 5792**
Via del Moro 88/R Mon-Fri 8-1, 2-7, Sat 8-1

Il Veloce Ciabattino di Vincenzo Arezzo **(no telephone)**
Via delle Terme 8 Mon-Fri 8:30-12:45, 3-7

Handbag & Luggage Repairs

Brovelli **055 213 840**
Borgo S. Frediano 11/R Mon-Fri 7-1, 3-8, Sat 7-1, 3-7:30

Trimmings (fabrics, lace, embroidery etc)

Lisa Corti Home Textile Emporium   **055 264 5600**
Via de' Bardi 58   Mon-Sat 10-1, 3:30-7:30
lisacorti.com

Lisa Corti Home Textile Emporium   **055 200 1200**
Via S. Niccolo 95-97/R   Mon-Sat 10-1, 3:30-7:30
lisacorti.com

Key Cutters

Masini   **055 212 560**
Via del Sole 19-21/R   Mon-Fri 9-1, 3:30-7:30, Sat 9-1

Presto Service   **(no telephone)**
Via Faenza 77   Mon 3:30-7:30,
Tues-Sat 9-12:30, 3:30-7:30

Drivers

Excelsior   **055 321 15397; 055 321 6947**
Via Lulli 76   337 685 959 (emergencies)
(available 24 hours)

Auto Centrale (Luca Grazi)   **055 973 8815; 338 372 3504**
(available 24 hours)
Via Dante Alighieri 13/F Terranova Bracciolini (Arezzo)
pick-ups for designer outlets and shopping tours

Taxis

055 4242

055 4798

055 4499

055 4390

Where to Wear Milan 2006

Best Picks

Milan Best Picks

10 Corso Como
10 Corso Como (outlet)
Anna Fabiano
Antonia
Antonioli
Armani (Via Manzoni 31)
Baldinini
Banner
Basement
Biffi
Brioni
Carla Sai Bene
Casa Del Bianco
Cavalli e Nastri
Coccinelle
Co-co
Cut
Daad Dantone
Decathlon
Diesel
Docks Dora
Dolce & Gabbana (men)
Domo Adami
Francescatrezzi
Franco Jacassi
Frip
Gentucca Bini
Gianfranco Ferré
Gianni Campagna
Gibo
Giò Moretti
Guess?
Henry Cuir
Il Salvagente

Jil Sander
Jimmy Choo
Joost
Just Cavalli
Laboratorio Italiano
La Vetrina di Beryl
Le Solferine
Les Tropeziennes
Louis Vuitton
Mariella Burani
Marni
Miss Ghinting
Narciso Rodriguez
No Season
Outlet Matia's
Paul Smith
Prada (Galleria Vittorio
  Emanuele)
Pupi Solari
Purple
René Caovilla
Sadogy
Sebastian
Silvano Lattanzi
SportsMax
Tim Camino
Valentino
Vanilla
Viktor & Rolf
Vierre
Vintage 55
Vivienne Westwood
Zap

Milan Store Directory

Newcomers to Italy's proudest cities may be amazed to discover that many stores close during the lunch hour, and in some cases the 'hour' is in practice two or two and a half hours. Don't despair, they will re-open! It's just that having invented one of the world's greatest cuisines, they see no reason why they shouldn't enjoy it. Our advice is to join them, and for each of the cities in this book we have provided a select list of restaurants, sidewalk cafés, salad bars, pizzerias etcetera, ideal for your shopping excursions.

We have also listed the opening hours for each store, though these may vary considerably; to avoid frustration, we recommend checking by telephone if in doubt. And finally, while Italian fashion and Italian clothing stores are among the most stylish in the world, you may be disappointed if you plan your shopping in August. The Italians have a special relationship with August (which is often fiendishly hot), and are happy to forsake retail in favour of the beach.

And one further word of warning. In Fashion and Design weeks Milan is turned upside down. For keen shoppers the 'up' is that shopping hours are extended, and many shops even open on Sunday to mark the occasion. The 'down' is that everything will be overbooked so forward planning is essential.

☆ 10 Corso Como

Global nomads passing through Milan seek out three attractions: the spiky, gothic Duomo, Leonardo's Last Supper—and 10 Corso Como. Established in 1991 by former *Vogue Italia* editor and lifestyle guru Carla Sozzani, when you enter the whimsically decorated boutique/book and music store/art gallery you step into a superior aesthetic. There's everything from candles to cook books, but the emphasis is on fashion and accessories. Here are Sozzani's personal favourites from all the top international collections, whether mainstream (Gucci, Prada) or more offbeat like Yamamoto, Balenciaga and Zandra Rhodes. The courtyard café is one of the hippest meeting spots in town, while the photography gallery offers some of the city's most avant-garde exhibitions. In 2003 Sozzani also opened a luxury B&B with three rooms overlooking the interior courtyard. Each is furnished with artworks by her partner, the American artist Kris Ruhs, and vintage Fifties to Seventies furniture by the likes of Arne Jacobsen. But don't be fooled into thinking that this B&B comes cheap—a couple of nights combined with a shopping spree here could cost as much as a weekend in a luxury hotel.   *10corsocomo.com*

Luxury   *Amex/MC/V*

Corso Como 10   **02 290 02674**
20154 Milan   Mon 3:30-7:30, Tues, Fri-Sun 10:30-7:30
Wed-Thurs 10:30-9

☆ 10 Corso Como (outlet)

If there's one store that's worth straying far from the beaten fashion path to see, it's the outlet store of Carla Sozzani's legendary emporium, 10 Corso Como. Situated in a small street near Garibaldi station, the entrance to the store is in a cobbled courtyard laid out with tables and chairs. Inside, you'll find rails of discounted designer clothes organised in price ranges and starting at 35 euros. Climb the stairs for all the labels you'd expect to find in the main store—at discounts of 50-70%. All the racks up here are arranged by designer, so it's easy to track down your favourite names. After rummaging through the womenswear, look out for discounted shoes, accessories and menswear. We're talking last season, of course, but at these prices who cares?

Moderate   *MC/V*

Via Tazzoli 3   **02 290 02674**
20154 Milan   Wed-Fri 1-7, Sat-Sun 11-7

Acqua di Parma

This little boutique on Via Gesù is the perfect place to pick up gifts on a Milanese shopping trip. Inside, you find a calm oasis of soothing smells, with perfumed candles glowing and two floors of heavenly beauty products beckoning. From soaps and massage oils to shaving foam and talcum powder, everything exudes the subtle fresh scent for which this company is known all over the world. Recent additions to the lengthy product list include a 180ml limited-edition gift pack of elegant Colonia perfume, and a new range of scented candles called Flower Cocktail. If the stunning aromas of Sicilian citrus fruits, verbena, lavender and the rare Bulgarian rose don't seduce you, perhaps you'll be tempted by the cashmere dressing-gowns, gorgeous soft towels and caramel leather travelling bags and slippers. In typically Milanese style all purchases are exquisitely wrapped, with Parma's yellow paper and thick black ribbons bearing the crest of the Duke of Parma. Beauty doesn't come much smarter than this. *acquadiparma.it*

Expensive   *Amex/MC/V*

Via Gesù 3   **02 760 23307**
20121 Milan   Mon 3-7, Tues-Sat 10-7

Agatha Ruiz de la Prada

Located in the upcoming Via Maroncelli, this new showcase for the vibrant designer opened in November 2003. A celebrity in her native Spain, Ruiz de la Prada shocked guests at Prince Felipe's 2004 wedding by turning up in a heart-splattered red and yellow minidress, and indeed most of her creations wouldn't look out of place on an Almodovar set. The spacious, totally white, almost clinical interior of this boutique sets off the wild colours of her clothes. Lime-green and pink miniskirts and trousers clash with bright orange and yellow cotton dresses with naive floral prints. Turquoise linen jackets hang from chrome rails next to geometric-jacquard knitwear combining all the colours in the collection. You'll also find bright flat, casual footwear in soft leather and a small collection of children's clothes. *agatharuizdelaprada.com*

Moderate to expensive   *Amex/MC/V*

Via Maroncelli 5   **02 290 14456**
20154 Milan   Mon 3:30-7:30, Tues-Sat 10:30-7:30

Agnona

No elegant woman's wardrobe is complete without a piece from Agnona's luxurious and timeless collection of ready-to-wear, knitwear, accessories and homewares. Founded in 1953 by Francesco Ilorini, Agnona spins super-luxurious clothes from the finest cashmere, alpaca, vicuña, camelhair, mohair and wool. Today, as part of the Zegna group, Agnona demands lip-biting decisions: will it be the double-faced cashmere jacket in cranberry and grey, the two-in-one coat with water-resistant and wrinkle-free outer and cashmere lining, or the alpaca wool drape coat with a salt and pepper fox fur collar? The luminous shop, designed by Andrea Zegna and Silvio Caputo, incorporates glass, volcanic stone, brass and cypress—though it's somewhat cramped for such a venerable brand. A new CEO has been brought in to hook younger clients with Agnona's impeccably styled and comfortable garments. *agnona.com*

Luxury   *Amex/MC/V*

Via della Spiga 3	**02 763 16530**
20121 Milan	Mon-Sat 10-1, 2-7

Alan Journo

It's almost impossible to leave this Milan-based designer's funky Via della Spiga store without at least one new bag swinging from your arm. There are big ones, small ones, round ones, square ones, Toblerone-shaped ones, leather ones and fabric ones—all bright and loud and splattered with sequins, feathers and glitter. Whether you're looking for a kitschy occasional bag with 'RICH' emblazoned across them, or a sophisticated clutch for your best friend's wedding, you're guaranteed to find it here. One of the delights of this store is the way that Journo unselfishly mixes accessories by other like-minded designers with his own creations. Follow the stairs, with their curly metal banisters, down to the basement and you will pass handbags from the Queen of Shock Vivienne Westwood and wig-like feathery numbers by Philip Treacy. Downstairs, you'll find crisp Journo-designed black and white suits, skirts, bustiers, trousers and jackets highlighted with bright red or blue piped seams—all of which look great with Westwood and Treacy's eccentric creations. *alanjourno.com*

Expensive   *Amex/MC/V*

Via della Spiga 36	**02 760 01309**
20121 Milan	Mon 3-7, Tues-Sat 10:30-2, 3-7

Alberta Ferretti

Don't be put off by the barely-there window display and the hotel reception-like entrance: the joys of this store are in the back. Ferretti's hallmarks—delicate chiffon fabrics with ruffles, pleating, smocking and decorative details—are ever present. So is her favourite colour palette of ice-blue and brown, fuchsia and grass green. Jackets, skirts and trousers in a sophisticated, feminine style complete the range of delights. Look out for bold prints on Fifties-style dresses, all presented with a small range of accessories. *albertaferretti.com*

Luxury   *Amex/MC/V*

Via Montenapoleone 21	**02 760 03095**
20121 Milan	Mon-Sat 10-7

Alberto Guardiani

If you are looking for high-quality Italian-made footwear with a twist, join Milan's best-shod twenty to forty-somethings and head to this store. Key looks by the Marche-based designer include two-tone sneaker-shoe hybrids, pointy stiletto mules for women and fashionable classics for men. But there are also more outré styles—like the men's driving shoes made from eelskin, or thong sandals in bright turquoise or lime. You'll find the most central branch at the end of a short gallery off Via Montenapoleone but, for a funkier vibe, dive into the newer outpost on Corso di Porta Ticinese where original 15th-century fixtures (wood-beamed ceiling, nail-studded door) are spiced up with Sixties-inspired rugs and tuffets (poufs) in orange and hot pink. There's also an original artwork inspired by those bright orange perforated fences you see around building sites in Italy—which sums up the edgy attitude Guardiani gives to his designs. *albertoguardiani.it*

Expensive *Amex/MC/V*

Via Montenapoleone 9 **02 760 21697**
20121 Milan Mon 3-7, Tues-Sat 10-1:30, 2:30-7

Corso di Porta Ticinese 67 **02 832 41650**
20123 Milan Mon 3-7:30, Tues-Sat 10:30-1, 3-7:30

Alexander McQueen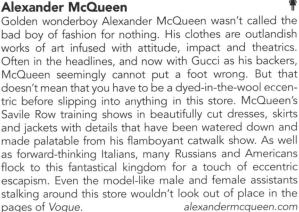

Golden wonderboy Alexander McQueen wasn't called the bad boy of fashion for nothing. His clothes are outlandish works of art infused with attitude, impact and theatrics. Often in the headlines, and now with Gucci as his backers, McQueen seemingly cannot put a foot wrong. But that doesn't mean that you have to be a dyed-in-the-wool eccentric before slipping into anything in this store. McQueen's Savile Row training shows in beautifully cut dresses, skirts and jackets with details that have been watered down and made palatable from his flamboyant catwalk show. As well as forward-thinking Italians, many Russians and Americans flock to this fantastical kingdom for a touch of eccentric escapism. Even the model-like male and female assistants stalking around this store wouldn't look out of place in the pages of *Vogue*. *alexandermcqueen.com*

Expensive to luxury *Amex/MC/V*

Via Verri 8 **02 760 03374**
20121 Milan Mon-Sat 10-7

Alfonso Garlando

Ever just had to have that dress, but couldn't find the shoes to match? Alfonso's on the corner of Via Madonina/Piazza del Carmine is your answer. This little gem carries a discreet range of shoes in a weirdly wonderful variety of colours, and if you get really stuck on colour they are even ready to make up any of their shoes just for you at a small extra cost (though they need a month for this). Another lifesaver is their wide selection of bridal shoes. The style emphasis is on sensible classics which can verge on the matronly side, but directly opposite in his other store Garlando displays his sexier and more expensive stuff—the heels are higher and the shoes carry much more frou-frou.

Moderate *Amex/MC/V*

Via Madonina 1 **02 874 679**
20121 Milan Mon 12:30-7:30,Tues-Sat 10-7:30
Sun 11-1:30, 2:30-7

Alibi

Alibi is one of those places where stylish 30-plus women on a budget go to put together their wardrobe at the start of each season. Opened in November 2003, the boutique has built up a reputation for offering great design at prices most can afford. From bright Pucci-inspired tailored jackets to chic pieces by Sotto Marino and floral crêpe chiffon dresses by Acciaio, the clothes here cater to many tastes. There's also a selection of lush accessories to tempt you to part with just a little more of your hard-earned cash.

Moderate   *Amex/MC/V*
Via Broletto 43 (corner Via Cusani)   **02 874 452**
20121 Milan   Mon 2-7, Tues-Sat 10-7

Alviero Martini

Italian designer Alviero Martini takes the notion of going global to fashion extremes. At his two-floor Milan boutique just about everything—from suits to shoes to leather goods and even motorcycle helmets—is decorated with maps, whether of the antique geographical type or inspired by the brightly coloured modern classroom globe. The collection also includes sunglasses, ties and recently launched perfumes in map-splattered packages for both women and men. If all this continent spotting makes your head spin, there's a ready-to-wear range with bold black and white prints and a motoring pit-stop theme to bring you back down to earth.   *alvieromartini.it.*

Expensive   *Amex/MC/V*
Via Montenapoleone 26   **02 760 08002**
20121 Milan   Mon 3-7, Tues-Sat 10-7

Angelo Fusco

Follow the red carpet down the narrow passage lined with flowers and past the wall of an ancient church to this small store selling men's silk ties and cashmere/silk scarves for women. The ties are as razor-sharp as you'd expect from Angelo Fusco—a practising plastic surgeon who designs these classic accessories on the side. Each has seven precise folds, handstitching along a single seam and a wax-sealed presentation box. Both ties and scarves are available in a rainbow of colours, from classic bordeaux, navy and grey to salmon-pink, aqua blue, apricot and lime-green. Fusco's signature design is a tiny chestnut motif: his latest ties pick them out in shining gold thread.

Moderate to expensive   *Amex/MC/V*
Via Montenapoleone 25   **02 763 18933**
20121 Milan   Mon 3-7, Tues-Sat 11-1:30, 3:30-7

☆ Anna Fabiano

Anna Fabiano met Milanese designer Elio Fiorucci when she was 13, and was inspired to start making clothes. She has never looked back, and her tiny boutique—one of the longest standing on upcoming Corso di Porta Ticinese—is a showcase for her hand-finished, one-of-a-kind clothes. Anna and her staff are so enthusiastic and friendly it's impossible not to be caught up in her mission to dress the world. Every piece has something different, be it a pocket on a pair of trousers or an unusual lining print. Recent hits have included swinging on-the-knee skirts in red, navy or white, with a triangular insert in a patchwork of colourful fabrics, and Fifties-style suits with handpainted cartoon-like designs. Though skinny types naturally look fabulous in them, the clothes have the added bonus of looking great on less that perfect figures, so it's a good place to head when you're in need of a stunning outfit at a time when you've gained a pound or two. With prices at reasonable levels, you can't afford to miss this store.

Moderate *Amex/MC/V*

Corso di Porta Ticinese 40 **02 581 12348**
20123 Milan   Mon 3:30-7:30, Tues-Fri 10:30-2, 3-7:30
Sat 10:30-7:30

Anna Molinari Blumarine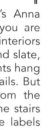

Get ready! The ornate door handle on Milan's Anna Molinari/Blumarine boutique is a warning that you are about to enter one of the most interesting shop interiors in the city. Inside, floors are made from copper and slate, lights are in bright red spaghetti wire, and garments hang from complicated metal and wooden sculptural rails. But don't let the whimsical interior distract you from the clothes. Follow the twisted iron walkway down the stairs and you'll find the Anna Molinari and Blumarine labels hanging side by side. The ultra-feminine Blumarine collection includes antique-look lace bodices, delicately embroidered knitwear with exquisite tiny buttons, lightweight soft tailored linen suits and sexy black lace eveningwear. Don't miss the aquarium-inspired prints (floaty, romantic fabrics swimming with tropical fish), or the tangy, lemon-print dresses (more Sorrento than Milan) for everyday wear. *blufin.it*

Expensive *Amex/MC/V*

Via della Spiga 42 **02 795 081**
20121 Milan   Mon 3-7, Tues-Fri 10-1:30, 2:30-7
Sat 10-1, 3-7

Anteprima

Until recently, this brand has been renowned for its understated chic. But in 2002 a new accessories store opened next to the larger clothing store, adding an explosion of colour, beads, sequins and glitter on bags and shoes to spice up the label's muted clothes. These conceptual accessories, under the label Plastik, often look like little pieces of artwork, with odd shapes, unique cut-outs and innovative constructions. In total contrast, the industrial, minimalist store with Anteprima's clothes by Japanese designer Izumi Ogino hasn't changed much. Ogino keeps both her palette and cuts for Anteprima's womenswear line super-clean, using chocolate brown, the palest pale delicate pink and ice blue on her simple sheath dresses, pleat-

235

ed skirts and straight pants. Dresses and tops are fluid, never indecently tight. A favourite of women looking to stand out, but quietly.   *anteprima.it*

Moderate to expensive   *Amex/MC/V*

Corso Como 9   **02 655 2373**
20154 Milan   Mon-Sat 10-7

Corso Como 9 (Plastik)   **02 654 211**
20154 Milan   (opening hours as above)

☆ Antonia

Owned by pint-sized girl-about-town Antonia Giacinti, this fashion-forward boutique is a mecca for Milan's most stylish women, who come here to check out the latest arrivals from the hottest names on the international fashion scene. Antonia brings on board the usual suspects—Dolce & Gabbana, Missoni, Valentino, Chloé, Gucci, Ungaro—but whittles the selection down to a masterly and supremely original edit which will have you wondering why you don't own every piece on the shelves. Alongside Balenciaga trousers, Borbonese dresses, Stella McCartney suits, Missothen and Alessandro Dell'Acqua, you'll come across new finds like the cool Haute label (by Vincenzo de Cotiis, who also designed the Straf hotel, opened in 2004 in Milan). If the clothes aren't enough for you, tucked away in a corner is the Place des Lices toiletries range. Next door, Antonia Accessori supplies an international offering of the season's best stilettos, hottest pumps and must-have bags by names like YSL, Gucci and Rene Caovilla. Even the window displays are worthy of an art gallery—no surprise from this junior princess of fashion.

Expensive to luxury   *Amex/MC/V*

Via Ponte Vetero 1   **02 869 98340**
20121 Milan   Mon 3-7, Tues-Sat 10-2, 3-7

Antonio Fusco

Aimed at thirty-something professionals, this collection for both men and women combines deluxe fabrics (all Italian, of course) with low-key styling and the occasional design flourish. A smiling photograph of Sr Fusco greets you at the cash desk downstairs in this spacious store, where you'll also find select items from the current collection. The full collections are upstairs, where Fusco's roots in Neapolitan tailoring become instantly apparent. Take your time to spot the subtle details in tailored suits, shirts and ties for men, and separates, suits, daydresses and eveningwear with Swarovski crystals for women. (p.s. As Milan's smartest bargain hunters know, Antonio Fusco also has a discount outlet on the road out towards IKEA, near Chicco. Via ex-Cascina Lavagna 5, 20094 Corsico, Milan. Tel: 02 447 1966.)   *antoniofusco.it*

Luxury   *Amex/MC/V*

Via Sant'Andrea 11   **02 760 02957**
20121 Milan   Mon-Sat 10-7

Milan Directory

☆ **Antonioli**

Once a cinema, this space was recently transformed into an edgy boutique, complete with black walls, a steel skateboard-style ramp and clothes hanging from massive chains. Its dark vibe epitomises underground chic and so does its location—the store is nearly impossible to find in Milan's canal district. But finders will be keepers at this treasure-chest packed full of original works by London label Preen, Rick Owens, Ann Demeulemeester, Dries Van Noten, Alexander McQueen, Dsquared, Ring, Helmut Lang, Raf Simone, Antonio Marras, Jan & Carlos and Tim Van Steenbergen. The only big brand to make it past owner Claudio Antonioli's iron wall is a highly edited selection of Dolce & Gabbana. Accessories like J.A.S handbags, Martin Margiela chains and Japanese teddy-bear gadgets add a quirky twist to the serious fashion mood. *antoniolishop.com*

Luxury   *MC/V*

Via Pasquale Paoli 1   **02 365 66494**
20143 Milan   Mon 3-7:30, Tues-Sat 11-7:30

Armani Collezioni

If you've already visited the massive Armani megastore in Via Manzoni, you may wonder why bother coming here. But if you want to check out the white-labelled Armani Collezioni diffusion line, this is the place to do it: it's not on sale at the megastore. The line features tailored clothing, sportswear, eveningwear, outerwear and accessories for both men and women—all with Giorgio's unmistakable cuts and subtle colours, but at slightly lower prices than the main line. This well-lit, long, narrow store showcases a vast selection from the latest collections—from plum-coloured jackets over smart white trousers for women, to elegant suits for men in grey, black or white. If you're shopping with a partner of the other sex, a useful corridor links the spacious men's and women's stores. *giorgioarmani.com*

Expensive   *Amex/MC/V*

Via Montenapoleone 2   **02 763 90068**
20121 Milan   Mon-Sat 10:30-7:30

Armani Jeans

Giorgio Armani is one of the first of Italy's big brand names (together with Diesel) to hook into the up-and-coming coolness of the offbeat Porta Ticinese, which is now the Milanese barometer for individual, original style. Armani's spacious store spans two floors, and about 50% of what you see is made of denim. It is young, casual wear, and about as risqué as Armani will ever get (i.e. not very). At the back of the ground floor is a café which serves snacks during the day, preps up for cocktails at 6pm, and serves brunch on Sundays.

Moderate   *Amex/MC/V*

Corso di Porta Ticinese 60	**02 832 41924**
20123 Milan	Mon 4-8, Tues-Sat 11-8

Armani Junior

Tucked away in a courtyard just off the main thoroughfare, Armani grooms the next generation of fashion followers aged 1-14. You'll find mini versions of the famous deconstructed jackets, cool cotton shirts and trousers, beautiful satin party trousers, leather jackets and T-shirts...with that all-important Armani logo. The kids will grow out of this clobber rather than wear it out, so you're investing in family heirlooms.   *giorgioarmani.com*

Expensive   *Amex/MC/V*

Via Montenapoleone 10 (internal)	**02 783 196**
20121 Milan	Mon 3-7, Tues-Sat 10-7

☆ Armani/Manzoni 31

Where else would Giorgio Armani open his largest store if not Milan, the city where he made his name? Born in Piacenza, 20 minutes down the railway tracks, 'King George' started out as a window dresser for La Rinascente before climbing the slippery ladder to the top of the fashion kingdom. Opened in 2000 as a 25th anniversary present to himself, this three-floor megastore is a fitting tribute to his achievements, displaying just about everything he's ever designed—from Oscar-worthy evening frocks and chocolates to silver coffee pots. In fact, this clean-lined temple—by the American minimalist architect Michael Gabellini—is more of a mini shopping centre than a department store. The main Armani label (ground floor), Emporio Armani and the affordable Armani Jeans line (first floor) each get their own separate boutique. On the first floor, there's a store dedicated to the Armani Casa household collection, plus a book shop where you can browse the fashion/design books and mags and pick up a gift to impress a friend (they come in Armani fabric bags). There's more opportunity for gift buying back on the ground floor, where you might want to order a bouquet of exquisitely arranged flowers from the Armani florist, or a box of exquisitely designed Armani chocs (they taste as good as they look). In the basement, dominated by Sony, you can savour a couple of pralines as you relax on an Armani sofa and enjoy a film in the Sony home theatre. To complete the experience, pop into the Armani café on the ground floor for a snack, or go directly upstairs and have a more formal lunch in the elegant restaurant. For the 360° Armani lifestyle trip you can come back in the evening for an aperitivo at Nobu (happy hour 7:30-9). Expect to pay that bit extra for the privilege of sipping in Armani-land, though the free sushi buffet makes it well worth while. And if you can still keep going, Armani's nightclub Privé under Nobu opens at 11:30, and from there you can almost dance to dawn. Still need something to tell your friends back home?

Giorgio himself often passes by to check that everything in his kingdom is hunky-dory. *giorgioarmani.com*

Moderate to luxury *Amex/MC/V*

Via Manzoni 31 **02 723 18600**
20121 Milan Mon-Sat 10:30-7:30

Ars Rosa

If the frenetic fashion rhythms of the boutiques among Via Montenapoleone are beginning to get you down, take respite inside this small, old-fashioned store—more like an intimate dressing-room than anything so vulgar as a shop. Most of the garments are tucked away in wooden wardrobes around the room which is dominated, instead, by a high Murano glass chandelier. You'll have to ask the devoted assistants to pull out the luxurious custom-made lingerie and bathrobes, made in Italy from silk and cashmere and embellished with touches of embroidery and lace. Christening gowns and other special occasion babywear can also be found here, along with beautiful household linen. If by some miracle, nothing catches your eye, you can always have something made-to-measure.

Expensive to luxury *Amex/MC/V*

Via Montenapoleone 8 **02 760 23822**
20121 Milan Mon 2:30-7, Tues-Sat 9-12:30, 2:30-7

Atelier Aimée

Located at the far end of an arcade hung with ornate lanterns, this unique boutique makes you feel like you've lost your way and wandered backstage at La Scala. A huge glass chandelier illuminates fairytale wedding gowns that can be custom-made or bought ready-to-wear. The enchanted feel continues in caffé latte coloured silks, beaded bodices with layers of skirts that blossom gently like calla lilies and ballerina gowns in ivory trimmed with rich ruby flowers, all with delicate jewelled sandals to match. Every year brings 300 new designs to choose from, so you won't have to worry about looking last-season. Mothers of the bride can keep up with their daughters by choosing smart wedding party attire—including perfectly tailored Italian suits. *aimee.it*

Expensive to luxury *Amex/MC/V*

Via Montenapoleone 29 **02 799 300**
20121 Milan Mon 3-7, Tues-Sat 10-1, 2-7

A.Testoni

As you enter this store (one of only three in Italy) the whiff of quality leather Italian shoes will make your purchasing pulse begin to quicken. Despite a change of management and a new image, this formerly family-run company from Bologna continues to produce classic, handcrafted shoes from the finest Italian skins, now displayed in a sophisticated wood and Indian slate interior. Office and casual shoes for men as well as more luxurious styles are complemented with simply styled travel bags, briefcases, belts, a small range of men's and women's jackets and woven silk ties. There is also a range of classic women's shoes. If you are struggling to carry all your purchases down from the first-floor showroom, you'll be relieved to discover the in-store lift. *testoniusa.com*

Expensive   *Amex/MC/V*

Via Montenapoleone 19   **02 760 03697**
20121 Milan   Mon 3-7, Tues-Sat 10-7

Bagutta

This teensy shop with branches in the city centre and in the Brera area is where the Milanese head when they're looking for a moderately priced, decent shirt. They're the kind of shirts that help create that easy, bourgeois-chic look which is second nature to the Milanese and a source of envy to the rest of the world. If you'd like some of that crisp cool-ness for yourself, head here for well-pressed linen shirts with woven stripes, checks or slub weaves, just-so collars and perfect fits. You'll also find collarless shirts with looser cuts and brighter colours, which make perfect cover-ups on the beach. Most of the goods hang on metal kitchen hooks, and there's also a central display unit that doubles as a seat. To complete the look, try Bagutta's cotton knits, casual linen trousers and shorts.

Moderate   *Amex/MC/V*

Via San Pietro all'Orto 26   **02 782 315**
20121 Milan   Mon 3-7, Tues-Sat 10-7

Via Fiori Chiari 7   **02 890 13498**
20121 Milan   Tues-Sat 10-7:30

☆ Baldinini

If you like your shoes to shout 'I'm Italian, look at me!', this is the place for you. Sexy, stylish pointy stilettos in bright colours and unusual materials with co-ordinating bags for women are displayed along side high-quality loafers, lace-ups, and sneakers for men and women. There are very rea-sonably priced briefcases, men's and women's jackets and other classic leather accessories all made in the company's factories at San Mauro Pascoli, in the Emilia-Romagna region (one of Italy's top shoe-producing areas). The shop assistants are ever helpful. *baldinini.it*

Moderate to expensive   *Amex/MC/V*

Via Montenapoleone 15   **02 760 22002**
20121 Milan   Mon 3-7, Tues-Sat 10-7

Piazza Meda 3 (M)   **02 783 481**
20121 Milan   (opening hours as above)

Bally

The days when Bally made the sort of shoes that even your grandmother wouldn't walk down the street in have long gone. The Swiss label's familiar classic but dull shapes have been replaced by a flourish of funky new shoes, accessories and rtw collections for both men and women—as a quick scout around this well-placed store will confirm. On the ground floor the latest shoe and bag designs in textured leathers and bold printed fabrics featuring geometric motifs and graphic flowers have taken the brand to new heights. Helpful assistants will escort you to the rear of the store to view a range of Sixties-style women's separates with fabrics and finishes that cleverly complement the shoes. Downstairs holds the younger sportier styles—like motorbike racing leathers and baseball sneakers plus clothes with strong colours and cuts—along with a classic men's range which also includes rtw, bags and belts. When you think about just how far down the fashion path this label has come, it's hard not to yodel with delight. *bally.com*

Expensive	*Amex/MC/V*
Via Montenapoleone 8	**02 760 08406**
20121 Milan	Mon-Sat 10-7

☆ Banner

In a city packed with one-label flagship stores from its homegrown global fashion brands, you may have to walk a long way to find a store that carries a mix of the biggest cutting-edge international designers. Fortunately for those-in-the-know (including you, now), this centrally located boutique fills the gap. Here you'll find clothes by Stella McCartney, Dries Van Noten, Marc Jacobs, Viktor and Rolf, Pucci, Yohji Yamamoto, Junya Watanabe's Comme des Garçons, Rick Owens, John Galliano, Tod's shoes and bags and Zucca watches all displayed under a single roof. And what a roof it is! This amazing Dali-esque boutique was designed by Gae Aulenti—the architect behind Paris's Gare d'Orsay museum and another stellar resident of Milan. Owned by the Biffi family (of Biffi boutique fame), it's no wonder that this store has become one of the main attractions of Milan's golden fashion shopping rectangle. Beat back the fashion crowd, and march right in.

Expensive to luxury	*Amex/MC/V*
Via Sant'Andrea 8/A	**02 760 04609**
20121 Milan	Mon 3-7:30, Tues-Sat 10-7:30

Barbara Bui

You'll find this modern label by Franco-Vietnamese designer Barbara Bui situated right next to one of Milan's two remaining medieval gates, the Archi di Porta Nuova. But there's nothing even faintly retro about this clean, almost clinical store. Two huge floor-to-ceiling mirrors dominate the entrance to show off the sharply tailored, urban-savvy clothes, bags and shoes. Though the designer's favourite colour palette is white, grey and black, you'll find the occasional splash of colour. The long cut of the trousers and skirts is a favourite with models—but not to worry, an alteration service is available for those of us who don't top six feet. *barbarabui.com*

Expensive to luxury *Amex/MC/V*
Via Manzoni 45 **02 290 60216**
20121 Milan Tues-Sat 10-1:30, 2:30-7

☆ Basement 🧍

Opened in November 2003, this is the latest of a growing number of discount designer stores in the city centre, which means you no longer have to travel a zillion miles out of Milan to pick up to last season's looks at friendly prices. Still, the tricky entranceway means that unless you've got your wits about you, you may never make it inside this fabulous store. So, follow these easy instructions: go to the left of the main entrance at Number 15, head down the red-carpeted stairs to the basement, and you should be one of the lucky few who make it though the door. Once inside, you'll be confronted with a bewildering array of bargains from D&G, Gucci, Armani, Prada, Blumarine, Valentino, JPG, Moschino, YSL and many others, all at discounts of 50-70%. Sizes are generally on the small side, but there are three associated stores in Florence, and the assistant is happy to phone them to see if your chosen item is available in a larger size; if they do, it will be sent to the Milan store. This is a modern-day bargain basement with old-fashioned service: they'll even do alterations if you ask.

Affordable to moderate *Amex/MC/V*
Via Senato 15 **02 763 17913**
20121 Milan Mon 3-7, Tues-Sat 10:30-7

Benetton 🧍🧍🧍

Just because you have a Benetton just around the corner at home doesn't mean you should give Milan's numerous branches a miss. You know what to expect from this Italian low-cost chain and their trousers, jeans, T-shirts and sweaters are still worth checking out (though in recent years, quality has suffered at the cost of chasing trends). For the widest variety of men's, women's and children's wear, head to Corso Vittorio Emanuele, Corso Buenos Aires or Corso Vercelli. The stores are brightly lit without being oppressive and the garments are neatly displayed, making shopping surprisingly pleasant. The 012 stores have a wide selection of bright, affordable clothes for kids aged 0-12. *benetton.com*

Affordable *Amex/MC/V*
Piazza 5 Giornate 10 **02 541 08410**
20129 Milan Mon 10:30-2:30, 3:30-7:30
  Tues-Sat 10-7:30

Corso di Porta Romana 23 **02 584 30710**
20122 Milan (opening hours as above)

Via Dante 4 **02 805 7404**
20121 Milan (opening hours as above)

Corso Vittorio Emanuele II 9 **02 771 2941**
20122 Milan Daily 10-8
(Benetton 012/Sisley)

Corso Buenos Aires 19
20124 Milan
(Benetton 012)

02 202 2911
(opening hours as above)

Via Torino 61
20123 Milan
(Benetton 012/Sisley)

02 890 12908
(opening hours as above)

Corso Vercelli 8
20145 Milan
(Benetton 012)

02 433 51121
Mon 3-7:30, Tues-Sat 10-7:30

Viale Corsica 45
20135 Milan

02 711 832
(opening hours as above)

B-Fly

Customers who haunt this store say you'll find vintage Levi's here that you won't find anywhere else. Jeans from the classic American label are piled up all over the shop, with the really special finds displayed along the walls like paintings in an exhibition. You won't be bothered by over-helpful sales staff; instead you'll be left to yourself to get on with trying things on. You'll find vintage leather pieces and a range of T-shirts too.

Affordable to moderate   *Amex/MC/V*

Corso di Porta Ticinese 46
Milan 20123

02 894 23178
Mon 3-7:30, Tues-Sat 11-2, 3-7:30

☆ Biffi

For the last 40 years this bright, cream-painted store under fashion doyenne Rosi Biffi has been one of Milan's best sources for both established and emerging labels. It's a great place to find the best clothes and bags from top labels like Prada, Gucci and Marni, and there are cutting-edge brands like Yohji Yamamoto and Helmut Lang alongside more obscure names. You will also find menswear with staples from Dior, Gucci and Tod's, plus Rogan Jeans and Brooks Brothers shirts. If you can't decide between the Fendi and the Gucci, the very friendly staff are always willing to help. There's a branch with sportier styles across the street at Corso Genova 5.   *biffi.com*

Luxury   *Amex/MC/V*

Corso Genova 6
20123 Milan

02 831 16052
Mon 3-7:30, Tues-Sat 9:30-1:30, 3-7:30

Corso Genova 5
20123 Milan

02 831 16044
(opening hours as above)

Bipa

This pretty pink boutique at the edge of the Brera area is a good place to track down the latest pieces from hip international names. It's also one of the few places that carry slightly larger sizes—up to continental 46, an uncommon sight in Milan. Start checking out the labels as you enter down the windowed passageway, then take turns at sinking into the sofas while you and your friends try things on. Among the clothing and shoes stocked here, you'll find feminine dresses from Philosophy by Alberta Ferretti, Cheap & Chic from Moschino, D&G, Cacharel, Joseph and Vanessa Bruno. Assistants can be a little off-hand—but don't let that put you off.

Expensive to luxury   *Amex/MC/V*

Via Ponte Vetero 10   **02 878 168**
20121 Milan   Mon 3-7, Tues-Sat 10-7

Blunauta

As you cross over the threshold of this store, the unmistakable aroma of raw silk fills the air. This Italian company offers a wide variety of apparel in silk and other natural fibres, made in China but nattily designed in Rome. The label has a handful of stores in Milan, but the widest variety is available at the three-story Via Dante location, not far from the Renaissance Castello Sforzesco. It's a good place to find an all-purpose dress for the office or some comfortable clothes for travel at prices that won't break il banco. You might even pick up some reasonably priced eveningwear—we recently spotted a black silk wraparound top studded with diamanté droplets that wouldn't have looked out of place on Marilyn Monroe. Men will find a small selection of informal jackets, pants, shirts and sweaters upstairs. *blunauta.com*

Affordable to moderate   *Amex/MC/V*

Via Dante 11   **02 864 54266**
20123 Milan   Mon-Sat 9:30-7:30

Corso Indipendenza 10   **02 700 06575**
20129 Milan   Mon 3-7:30, Tues-Sat 9:30-1:30, 3-7:30

Via Zenale 11   **02 480 00873**
20123 Milan   Mon 2:30-7, Tues-Sat 10-7

Boggi

Ever wondered how so many of Milan's males managed to look so impeccably dressed? One of their secrets is Boggi, whose good quality and fair prices have long been appreciated by discerning locals. Businessmen come here to snap up tailored jackets and trousers with crisp cotton shirts in every conceivable colour and weave. While though those in the know say there are better sources for knitwear, you'd be hard pushed to find a larger selection of ties anywhere on the planet. Tiny Boggi concession stores dedicated to shirts and ties dot Milan's fashion centre, while the larger spaces offer the wider business selection in addition to sportswear. *boggi.it*

Moderate to expensive   *Amex/MC/V*

Largo Augusto 3   **02 760 01489**
20122 Milan   Mon 3-7:30, Tues-Sat 10-7:30

Corso Buenos Aires (corner Via Caretta 1)   **02 295 26458**
20124 Milan   (opening hours as above)

Piazza San Babila 3   **02 760 00366**
20122 Milan   (opening hours as above)

Corso Vercelli 23-25
20144 Milan

02 433 19501
(opening hours as above)

Via Dante 3 (shirts only)
20121 Milan

02 875 258
Mon 1:30-7:30, Tues-Sat 10-7:30

Bonpoint

Mothers, grandmothers and devoted aunts and uncles should steer well clear of this store—unless their bank manager has given them carte blanche. The Liberty-style print tops, pretty smocked dresses and pastel knits will have you stocking your favourite child's wardrobe until he or she is in his teens. (If your favoured one is a boy, you're on slightly safer ground: the girl's collection goes up to 16, while the boyswear stops at 12). As with all Bonpoint boutiques, the Milan store resembles an elegant but comfortable reception room. The two floors are stuffed with crystal chandeliers, rugs, velvet sofas and faded prints with teddy bears piled everywhere. In keeping with the old world atmosphere, purchases are carefully wrapped in tissue paper, and the counter is stacked with glass jars full of coloured sweets that match the carefully chosen packaging. Just make sure your toddler doesn't send them flying while you're still rhapsodising over the clothes.   *bonpoint.com*

Expensive to luxury   *Amex/MC/V*

Via Manzoni 15
20121 Milan

02 890 10023
Mon 3-7, Tues-Fri 10-7, Sat 10-2, 3-7

Borbonese

You may not have heard of this old-school accessories brand but the Arpels family, who bought the company in 2000 and hired Alessandro Dell'Acqua to dream up a ready-to-wear line, has set out to change that. With Arpels signing the cheques and Dell'Acqua sketching the sizzle, the rest of the world will soon join the Italians in coming to know and covet Borbonese's signature bird's-eye print. The unmistakable spotted suede fabric, which became a Seventies icon, covers all the house's best accessories like the 'sexy bag' (the mini version is an obligatory purchase), wallets, key chains, travel cases and even the linings of stiletto sandals and teddy bears. In the Milan store—with its dark wooden floor and light, airy ambience—it also covers a crazily shaped sofa head-to-toe. Dell'Acqua has ensured that the famous deconstructed bags get a makeover in the hottest colours, details and fabrics each season, and has whipped up a collection of sexy but very wearable clothing to cap the jet-set look.   *borbonese.it*

Expensive to luxury   *Amex/MC/V*

Via Santo Spirito 26
20121 Milan

02 760 17202
Mon 3-7, Tues-Sat 10-7

Borsalino

There can't be many accessories companies that have had a film named after them, but this top-class milliner is one. Honoured by the classic Franco-Italian spoof-gangster film

Borsalino (1970) starring Alan Delon and Jean-Paul Belmondo, this tiny shop on the corner of Milan's glamorous 19th-century arcade is typically packed with well dressed Milanese ladies and gents trying on everything from berets to panamas. The store is piled to the ceiling with headgear—from the over-the-eye style worn by Humphrey Bogart in *Casablanca* to the wide-brimmed version worn by Ingrid Bergman in a range of colours and fabrics. Other standouts include pork-pie hats, baker-boy styles and fine straw hats in basic shapes for women. Think of it, you're just one purchase away from looking like the legendary film star of your choice…   borsalino.it

Expensive   *Amex/MC/V*

Galleria Vittorio Emanuele II 92   **02 890 15436**
20121 Milan   Mon 3-7, Tues-Sat 10-2, 3-7

Via Verri 5 (corner Via Bigli)   **02 763 98539**
20121 Milan   Tues-Sat 10-2, 3-7

Bottega Veneta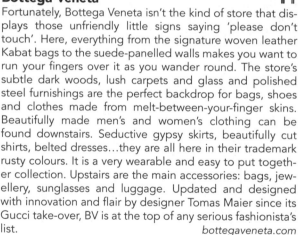

Fortunately, Bottega Veneta isn't the kind of store that displays those unfriendly little signs saying 'please don't touch'. Here, everything from the signature woven leather Kabat bags to the suede-panelled walls makes you want to run your fingers over it as you wander round. The store's subtle dark woods, lush carpets and glass and polished steel furnishings are the perfect backdrop for bags, shoes and clothes made from melt-between-your-finger skins. Beautifully made men's and women's clothing can be found downstairs. Seductive gypsy skirts, beautifully cut shirts, belted dresses…they are all here in their trademark rusty colours. It is a very wearable and easy to put together collection. Upstairs are the main accessories: bags, jewellery, sunglasses and luggage. Updated and designed with innovation and flair by designer Tomas Maier since its Gucci take-over, BV is at the top of any serious fashionista's list.   bottegaveneta.com

Luxury   *Amex/MC/V*

Via Montenapoleone 5   **02 760 24495**
20121 Milan   Mon-Sat 10-7

Boule de Neige

Boule de Neige ('snowball') seems an appropriate name for this white-walled store, whose snowballing stock of designer collections has grown so large that the owners have had to open a new outpost (next door to legendary shopping emporium 10 Corso Como) at #8, just down the street. As befits a boutique on this increasingly hip fashion strip, the walls at the older store (#3) provide a brief history of fashion, with illustrations and texts in English: it's an essential stopover for the fashion globetrotters who frequent this corner of Milan. Combining its own label range with a handful of Italian, British and American brands, the store forms the perfect backdrop for soft dresses and suits from

Michael Kors and Calvin Klein, cashmere by Fissore and a new range from Narciso Rodriguez. There are also stylish shoes from Edmundo Castillo and L'Autre Chose, along with English classics from Emma Hope and Anya Hindmarch. To browse La Boule de Neige's own designs, pop across the street to #8 for the fresh young range of co-ordinated trousers, skirts and crisp tailored suits. They stock more shoes by L'Autre Chose, plus ladylike heels by Boccaccini.

Expensive to luxury *Amex/MC/V*

Corso Como 3 **02 629 10777**
20154 Milan Mon 2:30-7:30, Tues-Sat 10-7:30

Corso Como 8 **02 655 1933**
20154 Milan Mon 3-7:30, Tues-Sat 10-2, 3-7:30

Braccialini

If subtle just ain't your thing, this is the place to buy accessories. You'll find this bright little shop down a narrow gallery off the main Via Montenapo shopping drag. Braccialini's quirky, amusing bags are designed to make you smile. Flowers, ships, houses, gardens and graffiti are just some of the motifs favoured by Tuscan founder Carla Braccialini and her son Massimo, who use embroidery, patchwork, appliqué, punched detailing and every other technique they can think off to make their accessories stand out from the crowd. As well as designing their signature collections, the exuberant pair create accessories for British fashion designers Vivienne Westwood and Patrick Cox—a true meeting of eccentric minds. *braccialini.it*

Expensive *Amex/MC/V*

Via Montenapoleone 19 **02 760 18162**
20121 Milan Mon 3-7, Tues-Sat 10-1:30, 2:30-7

Brioni

This Roman tailor has been putting suits on the backs of film stars and big shots (including Kofi Annan and the biggest big shot of all, 270-kilo sumo wrestling champion Konishiki) since 1945. But what makes these get-ups so special? Even if you pick them off the rack, the impeccable tailoring, super-luxe fabrics and tireless attention to detail make them stand out from the crowd. And there's always the possibility of having an extraordinary suit made-to-measure (see Brioni Bespoke, below). Women were finally inducted into the club in 2001, with their own store, complete with a huge glass ceiling so that you can gaze up to and into the Four Seasons Hotel above. Here, you'll find luxurious suits and separates powerful enough for a CEO but posh enough for cocktails. The men's and women's stores in Milan—both of which also offer sportswear, accessories and small leather goods—sit opposite one another in Via Gesù and along the street from the new Brioni Bespoke, allowing for simultaneous his-and-hers power-suiting. *brioni.it*

Luxury   *Amex/MC/V*
Via Gesù 4 (W)   **02 763 94019**
20121 Milan   Mon-Sat 10-7
Via Gesù 3 (M)   **02 763 90086**
20121 Milan   (opening hours as above)

☆ Brioni Bespoke

Opened at the end of 2003 beneath the Four Seasons Hotel, Brioni Bespoke handstitches some of the best suits available in the world today. At the appointed time (you must telephone beforehand), ring the doorbell and an impressively suited tailor will whisk you into the fitting rooms reminiscent of an English gentlemen's club. Comfortable leather armchairs, wood panelling and Persian rugs will put you immediately at your ease—which is just as well when you realise the customer dedication required to create the perfect suit. First, you'll need to check out a vast selection of fabrics, then undergo a preliminary fitting. Three weeks later, you'll be called back again to see if the suit is starting to suit. Another three weeks, and at last it's time for the final fitting (at which point you'll probably need to request a celebratory whisky and cigar). Thankfully, once your personal pattern has been created, you can have repeat orders made up over the phone. The fabulous quality and secret detailing (like the extra buttonhole for the carnation) mean that suits from this venerable label could become an expensive habit.   *brioni.it*

Luxury   *Amex/MC/V*
Via Gesù 2/A   **02 763 18718**
20121 Milan   Mon-Sat 10-7 (by appointment only)

Bruno Magli

When it was taken over by Bulgari-backed investment company Opera in 2001, it looked like the king of hide was on the up and up. But over the past year, the 69-year-old shoe, clothing and accessories brand has hit a rough patch. In 2004 its US wing was forced to file for bankruptcy under chapter 11—sending stateside lovers of quality leather into a state of permanent shock. Fortunately, there's no sign of such worries in Milan. You'll spot the entrance to the Via Manzoni store—with its spanking new cream-and-beige interior—in the elegant courtyard to the left of the boutique. Inside, you'll find the Bologna-based company's handcrafted shoes, bags, coats and jackets—all in the lushest of leathers and suedes. This season, there are slim, classic moccasins, Audrey Hepburn-style ballet pumps and towering stilettos with bags to match. For men, there are classic styles mixed with a sportier range and some belts and wallets. The old Via San Paolo store has closed, but a more convenient replacement has opened up on the thronging Corso Vittorio Emanuele.   *brunomagli.it*

Expensive   *Amex/MC/V*
Via Manzoni 14   **02 763 17478**
20121 Milan   Mon 10:30-7:30, Tues-Sat 10-7

Corso Vittorio Emanuele
(corner Via San Paolo)
20121 Milan

02 865 695
Mon-Sat 10-7

Burberry

Since 2003 Milan's many lovers of classic British style have been able to pick-up their essential check-lined raincoats directly from this outpost in the city's heart. But traditional fans may be shocked as they walk into this sharp, sassy store. All the frumpiness of this classic London label got swept right out the door when Saks exec Rose Marie Bravo took charge and hired former Gucci designer Christopher Bailey to inject some authentic street edge. These days, Thomas Burberry's world-renowned trench coat (now happily available in custom-made formats) hangs rack-by-rack with the latest catwalk looks from Burberry's top line, Prorsum. Other shocking newcomers include bright sporty trousers and jackets from the affordably tagged London line, plus accessories including watches, ties, scarves, cufflinks and wallets. Die-hard Burberry fans needn't despair: those can't-live-without check umbrellas are still available.   *burberry.com*

Moderate to luxury   *Amex/MC/V*

Via Verri 7
20121 Milan

02 760 8201
Daily 10:30-7:30

Byblos

Byblos went all quiet for a while, but thankfully it has made a comeback with a bang and moved into a chic new space-age store on Via Spiga. Upstairs is a burst of bright colour, the womenswear summer collection a silky swirl of yellows and oranges, peaches and purples. Winter promises a tone down in colour, but Byblos collections are not for the black/brown/blue brigade. Downstairs is where the less experimental menswear range hangs; a good selection of accessories is by the till.   *byblos.it*

Expensive to luxury   *Amex/MC/V*

Via della Spiga 33
20121 Milan

02 798 358
Mon 3-7, Tues-Sat 10-7

Cacharel

This French label is alive and kicking up its hip heels again thanks to the design ingenuity of British husband-and-wife team Suzanne Clements & Ignacio Ribeiro. Back in the Sixties the brand made a big splash with colourful Liberty-print dresses, which Clements Ribeiro have revived with a 21st-century twist. Its girly eccentricity makes it a favourite with trendy types who snap up the pretty dresses and tops in thin translucent cotton with intricate pleating, reminiscent of antique christening gowns. Other hot looks include appliquéd skirts with bold ethnic shapes worn with army-green cargo pants and military-style skirts, floaty dresses and blouses in coffee, and a powder-pink rose print by Corinne Sarrut. Cacharel's knack for the sweetly stylish also plays out in a perfectly charming line of children's clothing featuring navy and white batik-printed cotton and gingham check dresses. *cacharel.fr*

Moderate to expensive *Amex/MC/V*

Via San Paolo 1 **02 890 11127**
20121 Milan Mon 3:30-7:30, Tues-Sat 10-7:30

Camper

Milan may be land-locked, but as you step into this Spanish footwear company's Via Montenapoleone store, you could almost swear you were walking onto a beach. A curved seating area with circular beach mats encourages you to sit down and try on the quirky shoes set all around. It's like picking pebbles off the shore. Everything about this store says casual comfort but with a tongue-in-cheek design twist. There are the well-known 'twin' sets of oddly paired shoes, with fun embroidered or printed flowers or plants squiggling unevenly from the left foot to the right. Then there are the famous bowling shoes for men and women with the bubble soles that leave unmistakable footprints— if you ever risk wearing them on actual sand. The young assistants will be only too pleased to find a style to suit. Before you know it, you'll be walking out of the store clutching the company's signature red bag. Bet your old shoes are in the shopper—and your new purchases already twinkling brightly on your feet. *camper.com*

Moderate *Amex/MC/V*

Via Montenapoleone 6 **02 799 015**
20121 Milan Mon-Sat 10-7

Via Torino 15 **02 805 7185**
20123 Milan Mon 3:30-7:30, Tues-Sat 10-7:30

Canali

When Giovanni and Giacomo Canali started this family tailoring business back in the 1930s, the two brothers couldn't have imagined stitching 1,400 suits a day, but that impressive volume is now standard. Canali's look has always been rooted deeply in classic, formal suiting. For die-hard traditionalists, there are rows and rows of beautifully finished, impeccable suits, all boasting A-grade natural fabrics. Casual sportswear also makes it in the mix, but for Canali's core customer—the gentleman who turns up his nose at the concept of dress-down Friday—the sporty pieces are hardly what we'd call relaxed. The store recently underwent a major refurbishment, and re-opened with a snazzy (though not too snazzy) new look.

Expensive *Amex/MC/V*

Via Verri 1-3 **02 763 90365**
20121 Milan Mon-Sat 10-7

Canziani

You'll be surprised to find this old-fashioned men's outfitters slap-bang in the middle of Milan's designer triangle.

This tiny shop caters to gentlemen who prefer to purchase their wardrobe essentials in an atmosphere more tradition-al than cutting-edge. Beat the best-dressed Milanese at their own game, and snap up a couple of classic Italian shirts from over the polished wood counter while you're in town. Better still, have them made to measure. From cash-mere to fine cottons, men will find everything they need folded neatly on the wall-to-wall shelving. Underwear and traditional pyjamas, ties and cravats, socks and sweaters...they're all here.

Moderate to expensive   *Amex/MC/V*

Via Montenapoleone 26   **02 760 22076**
20121 Milan   Mon 2:30-7, Tues-Sat 9:30-1, 2:30-7

Carhartt/Stussy

Carhartt couldn't have found a happier home than Corso di Porta Ticinese with its crowds of cool young lads and lasses and skateboarders zipping up and down. Keeping to its original American principals of simple functional design, Carhartt Europe is equally popular with earnest teenagers and sporty types looking for minimal styling and reliability without losing that essential street cred. With European-cut shapes, comfortable fabrics and a minimal colour palette, it's a great place to pick up reasonably priced jackets, jeans, sweatshirts and tees. Carhartt's slightlier trendier sibling, Stussy, recently opened up right next door.   *carhartt-europe.com*

Affordable to moderate   *Amex/MC/V*

Corso di Porta Ticinese 103   **02 894 21932**
20123 Milan   Mon 3-7:30, Tues-Fri 10:30-1, 3-7:30
                                      Sat 10:30-1:30, 3-7:30

Corso di Porta Ticinese 103 (Stussy)   **02 832 41803**
20123 Milan   Mon 3-7:30, Tues-Fri 10:30-12:30, 3-7:30
                                         Sat 10:30-1, 3-7:30

☆ Carla Sai Bene

Carla's white and grey striped shop is about as big as a walk-in cupboard. The look is Provencal shabby chic, though more chic than shabby especially when she lets on that her clothes sell both in St Barts and Club 55 in St Tropez. Her look is very feminine, with a wonderful attention to detail, whether it be the lace trimming lining the inside of a jacket or the one-off designs of her own pretty floral fabrics. Sai Bene creates a very personal and wearable look while refusing to be a slave to trends, which is a refreshing find.

Expensive   *Amex/MC/V*

Via San Maurilio 20   **02 874 008**
20123 Milan   Mon 3-7,Tues-Sat 10-2, 3-7

Car Shoe

If you like your creature comforts you will love this store. Walk in to discover a fabulous array of casual footwear, all designed with the driver in mind. There'll be no more scuffed heels when revving up the accelerator in a pair of these no-nonsense shoes. And fortunately, there are styles and colours to suit every taste—so there's no need for practical to mean dull. Lace-ups, slip-ons and sandals (for both men and women) come in bright green and orange—though there are some more neutral tones as well. The company was taken over by Prada three years ago, and with only two shops in Italy (Milan and Capri) you can feel confident that you won't bump into anyone wearing your shoes when you head out on the school run. As you might expect with leather of such fine quality, the shops also stock a good selection of casual bags (the in-store video shows you just how the craftsmen make these unique goods). At the cash desk, try and nab a couple of the Fifties-style promotional postcards—they'll look great tucked into a mirror back home.

Expensive   *Amex/MC/V*
Via della Spiga 50   **02 760 24027**
20121 Milan   Mon-Sat 10-7:30

Casadei

You have a film premiere to appear at this evening? A VIP-splattered opening to attend? Head to the colourful Milan branch of Casadei for the kind of shoes that beg to be taken off the shelves and placed on the feet of the most glamorous girls about town (and, ideally, forced to saunter down a red carpet). The assistants do their utmost to show this high-octane footwear at its best, by wearing the boldest shoes as they teeter expertly between the customers. Bright colours, sparkling textures, and heels from kitten to skyscraper are just some of the details that catch the eye. This season, there are shoes the colour of boiled sweets and sparkly pink peep-toe sandals that would make Barbie proud. Founded in the Fifties by Quinto Casadei, the company remains firmly independent, even though it has been in the sights of many a famous-name buyer over the years. The menswear collection was introduced two years ago and is expanding every season.   *casadei.com*

Luxury   *Amex/MC/V*
Via Sant'Andrea 17   **02 763 18293**
20121 Milan   Mon 3-7, Tues-Sat 10-7

☆ Casa Del Bianco

This unassuming store can make your dreams of having your children look like those *Sound of Music* Von Trapps come true (we are obviously talking of the period before they got hold of those gaudy curtains). It has perfectly pleated flannel shorts for boys, and pretty floral Liberty-print puffed-sleeved shirts for girls, not to mention those famously durable classic shoes made by Pepe. Nothing here is made for a rumble in the sandpit, but it will impress the other mums.

Moderate to expensive   *Amex/MC/V*

Corsa Magenta 2 **02 864 51471**
20123 Milan   Mon 3-7, Tues-Sat 9:30-12:45, 3-7

☆ Cavalli e Nastri

Born in the days when vintage was still called secondhand, Cavalli and Nastri are one of the oldest vintage outfits in Milan. Their two very different stores are both worth a lengthy browse. The well-organized shop in the artsy Brera area doesn't look like your average vintage store. But venture inside and you'll find rails stacked with choice pieces from the turn-of-the-last-century to the 1970s with tags spanning the whole gamut from affordable to top-of-the-range. These days, though, this small boutique is also a showcase for one-of-a-kind pieces by young, local designers, as well as a few, choice ethnic imports (loose, embroidered ethnic shirts and trousers; Turkish sandals daubed with glitter paint). If you've got a passion for fashions past, you'd best head to their other store on Via de Amicis in the Navigli (Canal) area where you're more likely to find exquisite pieces by Gucci, Pucci et al. In true secondhand style, you'll find hatboxes piled up on shelves, vintage Vogues and fabrics strewn across chairs and old-fashioned chests of drawers. There are also glass-fronted cabinets stuffed full of hats, gloves, jewellery, bags, frocks, suits, blouses and skirts —couture, handmade—all in good condition and dating back to the beginning of last century.   *italianvintage.com*

Moderate to expensive   *Amex/MC/V*

Via Brera 2 **02 720 00449**
20121 Milan   Mon 3-7:30, Tues-Sat 10:30-7:30

Via de Amicis 9 (entrance Via Arena 1) **02 894 09452**
20123 Milan   (opening hours as above)

Celine

Not so very long ago, no fashionista worth her salt would have given this tired French label the time of day. Then along came Michael Kors, the man credited with bringing the Miami South Beach look to Paris, to revive Celine's classic clothes, bags and accessories with a colourful tropical island-style stamp. He has now moved on and a new designer was about to be announced as we went to press. But you can still grab the hottest accessories (including the popular Boogie bag whose roomy cut makes it an ideal repository for endless clutter) and the metallic, buckled Chouquette in everything from hot pink to soft-as-butter tan. Take the spiral staircase up to the newly refurbished VIP area, to discover the perfect backdrop for the label's conservative luxurious style. Plonk yourself down on the plush ecru seating, and watch the assistants put together a personalised total look. Contemplate the parade of goodies— yes, that funky sandal in metallic leather with the new logo really is a re-interpretation of a Scholl, and for summer there is a version in a stream of fluorescent colours.   *celine.com*

Luxury   *Amex/MC/V*

Via Montenapoleone 25/2   **02 760 15579**
20121 Milan   Mon-Sat 10-7

Celio

Begun in the Eighties with 'men's needs in mind, the right products at the right price at the right time,' this extremely friendly priced casual menswear chain from France is one of few which appeals to the masculine fashion-haters in our midst. Yes, they exist in Milan, too, and many of them make a beeline for this store. The clothes are designed in-house and production is closely monitored. The guy who thinks clothes are just for wearing will find everything here—from pants to pac-a-macs, socks to shirts and even caps and coats. Look out for VIPs, not Very Important People (you won't find any of them in here) but Very Important Products. Opening his wallet won't cause your fashion-hater too much pain, and he'll come out looking far more stylish than when he walked in.   *celio.com*

Affordable   *Amex/MC/V*

Corso Vittorio Emanuele II 5   **02 869 95293**
20121 Milan   Mon 11-9, Tues-Sun 9:30-9

Via Dante 14   **02 869 15490**
20121 Milan   Mon-Fri 9:30-7:30, Sat 9:30-8

Galleria Buenos Aires 42-9   **02 295 37367**
20124 Milan   Mon-Fri 10-8, Sat 10-7:30

Cerruti

Despite much business uncertainty, Cerruti's aura still survives in their sharply cut suits in luxurious fabrics, accessorised with high-quality leather, belts, bags, wallets, briefcases, holdalls and silk ties, or more casual punched suede zip-up jackets and casual trousers—all for men. Well-heeled women will find their needs satisfied with a small but stylish range of tailored suits in natural fabrics highlighted with apricot, and gorgeous blouses in soft pink silk. Down in the basement are men's shirts, jackets, knitwear and coats, and even a new fragrance—in case your admirers need any more convincing that they're looking at a perfect gent.

Expensive to luxury   *Amex/MC/V*

Via della Spiga 20   **02 760 09777**
20121 Milan   Mon-Sat 10-2, 3-7

Cesare Gatti

Looking for authentic Italian cashmere at prices that won't make you swoon? Cesare Gatti could be the answer to your dreams. Tucked down a narrow gallery off the Via Montenapoleone, you'll find this intimate, wood-panelled store and one of Italy's premier cashmere manufacturers, best known as a producer for the likes of Dior, Gucci, Valentino and Fendi. Luckily for you, Gatti also manufactures its own collection of silk and cashmere classics—including suits, coats, wraps and sweaters in a myriad of colours—which comes straight to Milan from the factory in

Biella. You'll also find some fine cottons in spring and summer and a selection of pretty sandals and slippers.

Moderate to expensive   *Amex/MC/V*

Via Montenapoleone 19   **02 796 860**
20121 Milan   Mon 3-7, Tues-Sat 10-1:30, 2:30-7

Cesare Paciotti

With their seriously pointy toes, these shoes should come with a dangerous weapons warning. The distinctive silver dagger logo is found on everything from the door handles to the jewellery. The two boutiques sit next to each other, stocking men's and women's day and evening footwear plus sports shoes—you'll even find some children's styles. From outrageous designs in funky leathers with towering heels, buckles and fringing, to green crocodile loafers and a sporty sneaker range, these shoes are a must for anyone who loves to walk on the wilder side of life. Distinctive bags and jewellery from the independent, Marche-based designer are also available.   *cesare-paciotti.com*

Expensive   *Amex/MC/V*

Via Sant'Andrea 8 (W)   **02 760 01338**
20121 Milan   Mon-Sat 10-7

Via Sant'Andrea 8/A (M)   **02 760 01164**
20121 Milan   (opening hours as above)

Chanel

Milan may be home to Armani, Prada and a host of other top-notch designers, but the famous double 'C' logo is guaranteed to send even the most Italophile fashion fan into raptures of near-religious awe. The grey panelled walls, deep reds and metal-framed mirrors of the Milan boutique show off the latest collections in an atmosphere of rarefied reverence, where assistants shadow your every step. Design meister Karl Lagerfeld continues to interpret Coco's spirit, producing collections of elegance and style. You'll find the quintessentially Chanel wool jackets, gilt chains and quilting, but you will also find a surprising range of sportswear: wetsuits, golf bags, tennis dresses, rollerblades…all adorned with the double C. Best of all is Chanel's version of Dr Scholl's wooden-soled flip-flop. There is a good selection of 'bijoux' (paste jewellery) but if you really have the urge to splurge, just a little way down the road towards Via Montenapoleone at number 3 you'll find Chanel's haute joaillerie collection (not paste), cushioned within a jewel-box of a shop.   *chanel.com*

Luxury   *Amex/MC/V*

Via Sant'Andrea 10/A   **02 782 514**
20121 Milan   Mon-Sat 10-7

Chicco

Children's chain Chicco (pronounced Keeko) is an institution among new (and expecting) Italian parents, providing every basic bit for babes, from bibs to bottles to bath tubs. For older children, there's an extensive range of toys and clothing up to age 8 and for mums there's some maternity gear. The clothes are usually nicely made and fun—from cute little red cotton dresses with studded collars to tropical-hued beachwear. *chicco.com*

Moderate *Amex/MC/V*

Corso Matteotti 10 **02 760 08399**
20121 Milan Mon-Sat 10-7:30

Corso Buenos Aires 75 **02 671 00853**
20132 Milan Mon-Sat 10-7:30

Via Paolo Sarpi 1 **02 331 06879**
20154 Milan Mon 3:30-7:30, Tues-Sat 9:30-1, 3:30-7:30

Largo Settimio Severo (Corso Vercelli) **02 480 18533**
20144 Milan Mon 10-7:30, Tues-Sat 9:30-7:30

Christian Dior

John Galliano continues to stamp his personality on the house of Dior, with a distinctly fetish feel to the latest collection. Trousers and skirts have corset lacing, T-shirts and evening gowns have straps and buckles, and just about everything in the store has a punky, bondage edge. Look out for the small but interesting new range of Dior baby and children's wear, under the label Miss Dior. Then check out the fine jewellery collection. They may look a little like novelty items, but be prepared for the prices: it's real gold and diamonds, not paste, that you're dealing with here. Their famous creator, Victoire de Castellane, was stolen from Chanel, and her daring 'more is more' flamboyance in jewellery design is a perfect match for Galliano's creations. *dior.com*

Luxury *Amex/MC/V*

Via Montenapoleone 12 (W) **02 763 17801**
20121 Milan Mon-Sat 10-7

Via Montenapoleone 14 (M) **02 763 98530**
20121 Milan (opening hours as above)

Christian Dior Homme

There can be nothing more different than Christian Dior women and Gucci-sleek Dior men. The ground floor of this shop is devoted to accessories and has a backdrop of steel, chrome, cement and Perspex. The large central staircase swoops you up to the first floor and the menswear collection, which is very much made for the blue/black/brown crowd. There is a whiff of pastel and pinstripe but the focus is on 'less is more'. There is a strong feel of the institutional, with military khaki, plimsolls and satchels. The cut is fine and looks best on small-boned men like Dior's impish designer Hedi Slimane.

Expensive *Amex/MC/V*

Via Montenapoleone 12 **02 763 17801**
20121 Milan Mon-Sat 10-7

Christies

From seamless super-smooth silhouettes to ooh-la-la frills, here you'll find all the seductive lingerie you need to indulge your fantasies. Gorgeous lace bustiers, delicate bras, sheer stockings and teasing knickers—from sexy shorts to tangas—are some of the styles tucked away in drawers in the mostly white interior with just one stunning red wall. There's also some over-the-top swimwear with beading and embroidery, though we're not sure how it would do if you actually went swimming in it. While you're deciding what to buy, enjoy a coffee or a prosecco at the small bar at the rear of the store. Friendly assistant Luana will help you decide.   *christieslingerie.it*

Expensive   *Amex/MC/V*

Corso Vercelli 51   **02 480 22152**
20144 Milan   Mon 3-7, Tues-Sat 10-2, 3-7

Church's

Stand in this intimate, wood-panelled store for a moment—and it becomes obvious that while the owners (Prada) may be Italian, Church's style remains resolutely English. Though the shoes—classic wingtips, oxfords, lace-ups, loafers and brogues—are distinctly Brit, the shop assistants are dressed in natty Prada uniforms rather than the traditional tailored suits of Jermyn Street you might expect. But this cross-cultural marriage appears to be thriving: the venerable British shoemaker has found a happy home-away-from-home here, under the watchful eye of its parent company.   *churchshoes.com*

Expensive to luxury   *Amex/MC/V*

Via Marino 7   **02 720 94454**
20121 Milan   Mon-Sat 10-7:30
Via Sant'Andrea 11   **02 763 18794**
20121 Milan   Mon-Sat 10-7:30

Civico 82

This small boutique concentrates on dressy casualwear for women looking to get in touch with their feminine side. You'll find jeans, flirty dresses and plunging tops in pretty colours like pink, silver and white, plus an array of sexy-sporty shoes and jewellery. Owner Manuela Menaldo—a former fashion designer for Harley-Davidson—scours the hippest rtw shows in search of clothes by upcoming Italian labels, such as Unisa, Blay and Catrin Cortes, all at moderate prices. She'll help you put together a look (like low-cut one-shoulder tops paired with combat pants)—so that the girly thing doesn't become too much.

Moderate   *Amex/MC/V*

Corso di Porta Ticinese 82   **02 894 23810**
20123 Milan   Mon 3-7:30, Tues-Sat 10:30-1:30, 3-7:30

Clan Pontaccio

Clean, sleek walls and a fashionable staff serve as a cool backdrop for this multi-brand outpost. The brands, almost all homegrown, are on the small side, with a strong push towards fashionable urbanwear. It's sporty, it's cool and it attracts a youthful crowd. Guys will find John Richmond jackets to pair with hip Frankie Morello or Diesel pants and bright casual footwear by Viadora. Cool young women in search of the miniest miniskirts venture toward hard-core Rose D leather jackets, Jean Paul Gaultier and Guess jeans and sexy tops or dresses by Philosophy or Kristina T paired with Pollini shoes. The offering is mixed, the pieces are often original and the prices never reach levels of absurdity.   *clan-pontaccio.com*

Moderate to expensive   Amex/MC/V

Via Pontaccio 15   **02 875 759**
20121 Milan   Mon 3-7:30, Tues-Sat 10-7:30

☆ Coccinelle

Got a handbag fetish? Put this store on your list. Here handbags come simple and, above all, safe—as in, a bank robbery is not necessary to exit with something special. Aimed at the high-end younger market and with a wide range of both colourful and neutral leather goodies to drool over, you may go through agonies of indecision before walking out with a big smile on your face. Find apple-green patent handbags, pale blue leather shopping bags, shoulder bags, beach bags, travel cases, make-up bags in every shape, size and colour…all made from quality materials and many complemented by a selection of trendy shoes. *coccinelle.it*

Moderate   Amex/MC/V

Via Bigli 28   **02 760 28161**
20121 Milan   Mon-Sat 10-7

Corso Buenos Aires 16   **02 204 04755**
20124 Milan   Mon 3-7:30, Tues-Sat 9:30-7:30

Corso Genova 6   **02 894 21347**
20123 Milan   Mon 3-7:30, Tues-Sat 10-1:30, 3-7:30

Via Statuto 11   **02 655 2851**
20121 Milan   Mon 3:30-7:30, Tues-Fri 9:30-7:30
                                                  Sat 10:30-7:30

☆ Co-Co

Located in Milan's scruffy China Town (around Via Paolo Sarpi), this super-chic store is one of the best-kept secrets in town. It's tucked away in an inner courtyard and takes a while to find; only the truly determined make it through the doors. Inside is a treasure-trove of great-looking, affordable pieces by Nicoletta Ceccolini and Maretta Toschi who create the kinds of clothes they know their stylish friends want to wear. You'll find dresses, cute car coats and perfectly cut skirts and trousers in interesting fabric combinations. Most of Co-Co's own designs fall into the 'cheeky classic' category: trousers and jackets have linings in unexpected, clashing fabrics; Audrey Hepburn-style raincoats are made from waterproofed silk. Trousers are craftily designed to fit real women, and Nicoletta and Maretta will advise on which suit your figure best. Upstairs, the pair have an extensive collection of vintage clothing, which they rent out to TV and theatre companies on demand. But if you have a special event to go to, they'll let you hire that perfect Twenties beaded hat.

Moderate   *MC/V*

Via Giannone 4   **02 336 06356**
20154 Milan   Mon-Fri 10-7, Sat 11-5

Coin

One of four branches of the Veneto-based chain in Milan, this flagship department store on the corner of Piazza 5 Giornate has nine floors of classic, mostly good quality, good value clothing, accessories, make-up and home collections. Start by taking a cappuccino in the basement café and then browse round the colourful housewares, from chunky glasses to ethnic cushions. Next head to the ground floor for a wide selection of mid-priced accessories, shoes, perfumes, cosmetics, jewellery and sunglasses. On the first and second floors is menswear, with suits by Fascino, Professione, Luca D'Altieri and Tombolini and casuals by Timberland, Dockers and Fred Perry. The next four floors are dedicated to women. For classics and casuals, look on the third and fourth for Leiluna, Trussardi Jeans, Marina Yachting, Misstridd and Donna Ennra; for young, trendier labels go to the fifth: Diesel, Guess, Levi's, Miss Sixty and Killah. The sixth floor has a surprisingly luscious selection of lingerie and nightwear, and the seventh is for kids. When you finally reach the eighth, take time out to look at the panoramic views over Milan. The Globe restaurant, with its free buffet snacks, has become a popular venue for aperitifs.   *coin.it*

Affordable to moderate   *Amex/MC/V*

Piazza 5 Giornate 1/A   **02 551 92083**
Milan 20129   Mon-Sat 10-8:30, Sun 11-8

Corso Vercelli 30-32   **02 439 90001**
Milan 20144   Mon-Sat 10-7:30

Piazzale Loreto 15   **02 261 16131**
Milan 20131   (opening hours as above)

Piazzale A Cantore 12   **02 581 04385**
Milan 20123   (opening hours as above)

Combo

Every time you walk down this street, it seems that a hip new streetwear brand has opened up. Among the latest is Combo, owned by the brother of the proprietor of Fornarina (across the road) and offering young, casual looks for cool teenagers who don't want to be seen trying too hard. For guys, there are slouchy jeans, sweatshirts, baseball trainers and hats, and the girls get the same urban styling but with a girly hint. Both can buy the T-shirts with cool prints inspired by the Japanese comic book illustrations which also cover the boutique's walls.   *combo.it*

Affordable to moderate   *Amex/MC/V*

Corso di Porta Ticinese 62   **02 832 42047**
20123 Milan   Mon 3:30-7:30, Tues-Fri 10:30-1:30, 3-7:30
Sat 10:30-7:30

Corneliani

With its red marble floor and a huge steel table holding a profusion of flowers, this store is the epitome of elegance. Hailing from Mantua, this high-quality tailor offers classic single or double-breasted suits (with sewn rather than fused interlinings), crisp shirts, ties and accessories for every occasion. For made-to-measure suits walk to the back of the store to a wood-panelled room where'll you'll be fitted and advised by the in-house tailor amid black-leather-and-steel sofas. A vast choice of 150 top-notch fabrics is available, and a suit will typically take three to four weeks to make. If you prefer ready-to-wear, Corneliani offers alterations at no extra cost. For fashionable casuals, like hip leather jackets, you can browse the rails for the Trend Corneliani line.   *corneliani.com*

Expensive to luxury   *Amex/MC/V*
Via Montenapoleone 12   **02 777 361**
20121 Milan   Mon-Sat 10-7

Costume National

Popular with lovers of the minimalist look, this much sought-after Italian label, headed by designer Ennio Capasa, has a reputation for uncluttered design and clever cuts. The basic colour palette (mostly black, white and brown) and modern fabrics brings out the graphic styling—though you will find the occasional nod towards this season's colours and a touch of femininity. This small shop houses both the men's and women's ranges along with accessories, including shoes (always fabulous), bags, sunglasses and perfumes.   *costumenational.com*

Expensive to luxury   *Amex/MC/V*
Via Sant'Andrea 12   **02 760 18356**
20121 Milan   Mon-Sat 10-7

Custo Barcelona

Spanish brothers Custodio and David Dalman have been turning out their distinctive quirky designs since 1996. Starting with T-shirts, they went from strength to strength and now produce a full collection of colourful designs. In 2004 they opened their first Milan store, raising cheers from the model set. Not for shrinking violets, the tops, trousers and skirts, jackets and bags are all emblazoned with colourful illustrative prints, designed to stand out in a crowd. The store is always buzzing with shoppers, trying to decide which print to buy. Most give in and buy several at once—a fate you too will probably meet with, if you set foot in this store.   *custo-barcelona.com*

Moderate to expensive   *Amex/MC/V*
Corso di Porta Ticinese 58   **02 581 04853**
20123 Milan   Mon-Sat 11-8

☆ Cut

Before the streetwear brands moved in, Corso di Porta Ticinese was known for small, artisan boutiques and this handmade leather company run by brothers Luciano and Germano Peragine is a survivor from those days. They use the front of the store to display their small ready-to-wear leatherwear line; in the back, they design and make up made-to-measure leather garments for a discerning clientele. They'll make anything from slim jackets to sharp tailored skirts and trousers—even a pair of shorts, if you insist. With family members running in and out all day, the atmosphere couldn't be more relaxed.

Moderate to expensive   *Amex/MC/V*

Corso di Porta Ticinese 58   **02 839 4135**
20123 Milan   Mon 3-7:30, Tues-Sat 10:30-1:30, 3-7:30

☆ DAAD Dantone

This tourist-laden corner of Milan isn't the first place you'd head to track down one of the city's most directional stores, but take one step into the oddly named DAAD and all misgivings about the un-cool surroundings will disappear. Where else in Milan will you find deconstructed intellectual rags by Antonio Marras thrown together with Dsquared's sex-bomb sportswear? Trust us, you won't any place else. Inside, cool T-shirts, sexy evening dresses and funky shoes from overexposed but must-have brands like Roberto Cavalli, Yohji Yamamoto, Commes des Garçons and Jean Paul Gaultier hang temptingly from the racks. But there are also unique finds to be had at every glance for hip guys and girls on the scout for something new from the likes of Andrew McKenzie or Roberto Cavalli.   *daad.dantone.com*

Expensive to luxury   *Amex/MC/V*

Corso Matteotti 20   **02 760 02120**
20121 Milan   Mon 3-7:30, Tues-Sat 10-7:30

D&G

The Corso Venezia home of Dolce & Gabbana's diffusion line is often packed to the door jambs with Milan's trendy young things searching among the racks and between the gilded columns for a piece of D&G action. The duo certainly know how to have fun with fashion and keep it sexy, and you'll find bright printed shirts, sexy denim miniskirts, tiny cropped vests and well-cut trousers in this store. In the back is the cute D&G Junior line with everything from lace-trimmed denims to cycling hats.   *dolcegabbana.it*

Expensive   *Amex/MC/V*

Corso Venezia 7   **02 760 04091**
20121 Milan   Mon-Sat 10-7

David Mayer

Are you a Hollywood star? A famous sports personality? Or do you just like to stand out from the crowd? If so, Rome-based designer David Mayer may have just the flashy-cool look you're seeking in his three Milan shops. Hanging from the racks, you'll find shirts with floral prints or in canary yellow linen, glitter T-shirts and cargo pants in dusty pinks. If this sounds like your scene, you're in some suave company—football star Francesco Totti and actor Leonardo DiCaprio is among Mayer's fans. Other DM merchandise such as underwear, lotions and deodorants is also available. *davidmayer.com*

Moderate to expensive *Amex/MC/V*

Corso Vittorio Emanuele II 22 **02 877 655**
20121 Milan Mon 11:30-7:30, Tues-Sat 10-7:30
Sun 11-7:30

Corso Buenos Aires 66 **02 295 20134**
20124 Milan Mon 3-7:30, Tues-Sat 10-7:30

Via Meravigli 16 **02 869 84075**
20123 Milan Mon 3:30-7:30, Tues-Sat 10:30-2, 3-7:30

Davide Cenci

Whether you're shopping for business or pleasure, the brands in this small boutique on the burgeoning fashion street of Via Manzoni tend towards the classic so you'll never be taken for a trend chaser. Polo shirts, long-pleated skirts, tailored jackets, Malo knitwear and Burberry's classic trench coats are complimented by footwear from Hogan, Tod's, Car Shoes and Pirelli sneakers. The selection is slightly more male-oriented, particularly the beautiful suits, though you'll find casual linen outfits for both sexes with a classy sporty look. An added bonus is the attentive service, in perfect harmony with the store's restrained image. *davidecenci.com*

Expensive to luxury *Amex/MC/V*

Via Manzoni 7 **02 864 65132**
20146 Milan Mon 3:30-7:30, Tues-Sat 10-7:30

Decathlon

This no-frills store is a good address to pocket, not just for its extended shopping hours but because it's a one-stop shop for anything related to sport. Whether you're into team sports, tennis, golf, cycling, water sports or mountaineering, Decathlon offers value for money. And that goes for their casual clothes too, right down to newborns. *decathlon.it*

Affordable to moderate *Amex/MC/V*

Via Foro Bonaparte 74/76 **02 805 09755**
20129 Milan Mon-Fri 10-9, Sat 9-8, Sun 10-8

DEV

The jewels of Diego Della Valle's empire—Tod's, Hogan, Fay and Acqua di Parma—are neatly wrapped into one shop on the out-of-the-way Corso Vercelli, which is rapidly becoming a valid alternative to Milan's main designer drags. One of eleven DEV shops in Italy and the only one in Milan, this quiet, refined store caters to the Milan bene, the city's conservatively stylish middle classes, who trickle in to purchase a Tod's Capri or Sofia bag or a quilted Fay jacket. But Diego Della Valle plans to open 100 DEV stores in Italy and internationally—so watch out, DEV may soon be coming to a street corner near you. Meanwhile, dive into the Milan branch for a Fay overcoat with a retractable quilted vest either in camel hair or herringbone, or a pair of elevated Hogan lace-ups—both must-haves if you want to look suave the Italian way.

Expensive   *Amex/MC/V*

Corso Vercelli 8   **02 480 28848**
20145 Milan   Mon 3-7:30, Tues-Fri 10-2, 3:30-7:30
                                               Sat 10-1, 3-7:30

☆ **Diesel**   👫👨

Opened in spring 2004, Diesel's new three-floor flagship/concept store is more like a home—filled with chillout Sixties and Seventies furniture—than anything as commercial as a boutique. That's all part of the streetwear label's ironic marketing ploy of course, but why not have some fun? The staff seem genuinely enthusiastic, and will lead you on a tour of the 'Diesel lifestyle' on display. Follow the spiral staircase to the first-floor denim bar which carries the main jeans lines plus womenswear, then wind your way up to the second floor for menswear in high-tech fabrics and experimental prints. Walk through a wood-panelled tunnel to the shoes and accessories where you'll find goldfish swimming with watches, and Seventies garden furniture to relax upon. On the third floor, step into a wardrobe to try on the latest women's collection (don't worry, you won't find Narnia on the other side). For more of the same kind of thing—only downsized—head a few stores along and you'll find Diesel Kids, with clothes for hip young street dudes ages three months to 14 years. Diesel hasn't abandoned its old haunts on Corso di Porta Ticinese, either. At #44, filled with funky furniture and Fifties memorabilia, you'll find prototype designs for the customer on the lookout for something that absolutely nobody else has; the price tags are higher than the main line collections, but many of the pieces are unique. The 55DSL store is a hangout for skateboarders, snowboarders and surfers, and specialises in casual pieces for streetwise sporty types.   *diesel.com*

Moderate   *Amex/MC/V*

Corso Venezia 7   **02 760 06233**
20121 Milan   Mon-Sat 10-7:30, Sun 3:30-7:30

Corso Venezia 11 (kids)   **02 760 11701**
20121 Milan   Mon-Sat 10:30-7:30

Corso di Porta Ticinese 44   **02 894 20916**
20123 Milan   Mon 3:30-7:30, Tues-Sat 11-1:30, 3-7:30

Corso di Porta Ticinese 60 (55DSL)   **02 832 00500**
20123 Milan   Mon 3:30-7:30
                                    Tues-Sat 10:30-1:30, 3:30-7:30

Diffusione Tessile

Tucked at the end of Galleria San Carlo, off the Corso Vittorio Emanuele, is one of the many bargain basements that are increasingly taking over locations close to the revered Golden Rectangle. Diffusione Tessile has been here longer than most, and sells last season's collection from all the MaxMara group labels at an excellent discount. You'll find bargains from MaxMara, Max & Co, Sportmax, Marella, Penny Black and even Marina Rinaldi, the group's label for plus-size women. The range is enormous, including everything from silky knits or crumpled linen skirts and trousers to business basics and eveningwear. There are also plenty of lovely classic coats as well as shoes, bags and other accessories. *diffusionetessile.it*

Moderate   *Amex/MC/V*

Galleria San Carlo 6   **02 760 00829**
20122 Milan   Mon 3:30-7:30, Tues-Sat 10-7:30

Dimensione Danza

When you get back to the gym to burn off the pounds you've put on eating pasta and pastries, make sure you have the ultimate in Italian gym attire. Spot yourself in the mirror wearing a pair of Danza odalisque pants and a pink relax singlet and you'll power through to the end of your workout. Besides dance and gym clothes, they stock bags, shoes and plenty of relaxed sportswear. There is much to choose from for girls as well, from adorable tutus and tights for ballet school to more edgy cropped cotton pants and halterneck T-shirts. *dimensionedanza.it*

Moderate   *Amex/MC/V*

Corso Vercelli 31   **02 480 22215**
20144 Milan   Mon 3-7:15, Tues-Sat 10-1:30, 2:30-7:15

Corso Europa 2   **02 760 04020**
20122 Milan   Mon 3-7:15, Tues-Sat 10-7:15

Corso Vittorio Emanuele II 9   **02 760 14874**
20122 Milan   Mon 3-7, Tues-Fri 10-7, Sat 10-7:30

D-Magazine Outlet

D-Magazine used to be called El Dorado, and it's not hard to see why. Located on Via Montenapoleone in the midst of some of the most luxurious stores on the planet, this designer discount store is a bargain hunter's delight. The bland entrance—up a short walkway past a lengthy window display—is hard to spot. But that doesn't deter the hordes of low-earning label lovers, who come here to hunt down last season's Prada, Miu Miu, Yves Saint Laurent, Marc Jacobs, Gucci, Jean Paul Gaultier, Costume National, Marni and more. If you're in the mood for some digging there may be treasures to be found but keep your expectations in check: clothes that were extremely expensive to begin with will not necessarily come cheap. Still, the sharpest eyes will find some great buys on occasion. Check out the stock of beautiful (and fabulously low-priced) designer leather belts.

Affordable to expensive   *Amex/MC/V*

Via Montenapoleone 26   **02 760 06027**
20121 Milan   Daily 9:30-7:45

☆ Docks Dora

If you are into retro and revival, it's worth making the extra effort to find this roomy store packed with new and secondhand clothing, much of it with Sixties and Seventies panache. Located just beyond the beaten fashion path at the northern end of the artsy Brera district, it houses a seemingly endless selection of jeans by offbeat labels like Seven, G-Star, Re-hash and Indian Rose, as well as skirts, trousers, shirts, jackets, coats and dresses all made from original Seventies fabrics. Upstairs, there's a wide range of handpainted and slogan-emblazoned T-shirts, swimwear with matching plastic beach shoes and a selection of lingerie. The psychedelic changing-room curtains are also on sale, as part of the new Docks Dora home collections, whose furniture and household objects again have a Sixties-Seventies beat. The latest addition to the expanding Docks Dora empire is a small range of children's clothes in the store's typical style. As we went to press the Viale Crispi store was about to be renamed Nolita Loft, so this looks like becoming Milan's Manhattan Central.   *docks-dora.com*

Moderate   *Amex/MC/V*

Viale Crispi 7   **02 290 06950**
20121 Milan   Sun-Mon 3-8, Tues-Sat 11-8

Via Toffetti 9   **02 552 13641**
20139 Milan   Sun-Mon 2:30-7:30, Tues-Sat 10:30-7:30

Docksteps

If you're a sneaker maniac on the lookout for a reason to snap up your tenth pair, stop by this store. As the official suppliers to the Juventus football team, Docksteps has a range of seriously kicky styles in breathable leather. But the real thrills come with the brightly coloured sneakers, from the likes of Merrell, Cult, Bikkemberg and Armando D'Alessandro. Among the most-desired looks this season are the Pony sneakers in metallic pink, lilac, blue, silver or gold. And you get a choice of heels, too—from pointy stilettos by Miss D to football-inspired flats and kitten-heel pumps.   *docksteps.com*

Moderate to expensive   *Amex/MC/V*

Via Cusani 10   **02 869 15563**
20121 Milan   Mon 3-7, Tues-Fri 10-7, Sat 10-1, 3-7

Dolce & Gabbana (women)

Commanding a grand corner position at the top of one of Milan's most exclusive streets, it's hard to miss this store. And that's as it should be from this northern Italian/Sicilian design duo who made their name on Milan's runways in the mid-Eighties and haven't looked back since. Elegant assistants in their razor-sharp regulation black buzz around between the baroque throne-like chairs and huge, cacti-filled urns. They'll advise you as you try on Domenico and Stefano's sexy-chic outfits—from fabulous silk and satin separates to sparkling black lace skirts and side-laced va-va-voom dresses, all with a dash of Sicily-meets-Madonna panache. Step out in one of their more outré creations and don't be surprised if passers-by ask for your autograph as you sashay down the street. *dolcegabbana.it*

Luxury *Amex/MC/V*

Via della Spiga 26 **02 760 01155**
20121 Milan Mon-Sat 10-7

Via della Spiga 2 **02 795 747**
20121 Milan Mon-Sat 10-7

☆ Dolce & Gabbana (men)

The Milan-based design duo inaugurated this historic 18th-century palazzo as a stage set for their sizzling menswear in 2003. Walk through the black marble interior to the tranquil courtyard and discover a Sicilian barbershop, a full-service spa and a super-hip martini bar serving light lunches and pre-dinner drinks. Yes, there are three beautifully furnished floors of Dolce and Gabbana's menswear—closely cut fashion on the ground, super-dude accessories on the first and gangster-worthy tailoring on the second—but the real joy is being able to relax with a hot-towel shave or an olive-studded martini in the private courtyard to stave off a wave of shopping fatigue. *dolcegabbana.it*

Luxury *Amex/MC/V*

Corso Venezia 15 **02 760 28485**
20121 Milan Mon-Sat 10-7

☆ Domo Adami

The unusual wedding dresses designed by Mauro Adami at this by-appointment-only store could set you back anywhere from $2,000 to $10,000—not bad if you're only going to do it once. Located in a charming pebbled courtyard off Via Manzoni, the Domo Adami studio also lends a hand with accessories, make-up, hair, wedding albums and a host of other essentials for the Big Day. There are plenty of traditional gowns available, but for the less conventional bride Adami likes to experiment with pale colours and fitted, rather than frothy, cuts. He makes much use of taffeta, organza and antique lace in delicate, transparent layers. For the bride who insists on making an alternative statement, there's a hippy-dippy gypsy bridal gown that makes subtle references to Flower Power. *domoadami.com*

Luxury *Amex/MC/V*

Via Manzoni 23 **02 805 7207**
20121 Milan (by appointment only)

Du Pareil au Même

If you haven't yet stumbled across this cute French childrenswear label, and have kids aged 0-14, pay a quick visit while you're here. At times, you have to fight through mothers and pushchairs to lay your hands on the choicest pieces—from bright corduroy pinafores with fun appliqués to sweet velvet jackets and coats. But the best thing here is the prices: they're as affordable as they come. The Buenos Aires store is the larger of the two and has much key equipment like strollers, high chairs and stuffed toys. Still, the smaller store has the advantage of flanking the pedestrian-only Via Dante, so your toddler can have a fine time chasing pigeons as you leave the store.   *dpam.fr*

Affordable   *Amex/MC/V*

Corso Buenos Aires 49   **02 294 11607**
20124 Milan   Mon 12-7:30, Tues-Sat 10-7:30

Via Dante 5 (corner Largo Cairoli)   **02 720 94971**
20123 Milan   (opening hours as above)

Elena Mirò   ♀

Just when you've lost hope of squeezing into those teensy fashions in the stores along the designer drag, help is at hand in the shape of Elena Mirò. The quality might not be the finest but the styles and prices here are great—and best of all, everything is available in continental sizes 37-51. The Via Dante store is the largest of the three Milanese boutiques, offering everything from ethnic shirts and floaty skirts to generously cut trousers in silk, cotton and linen. There's also a fun Miami Beach range, with bright cotton and jersey tops combined with striped cropped trousers. Treat yourself to some sexy lingerie, also available in sensible sizes.   *elenamiro.com*

Affordable to moderate   *Amex/MC/V*

Via Dante 4   **02 864 55016**
20121 Milan   Mon 3-7:30, Tues-Sat 10-7:30

Corso Buenos Aires 15   **02 295 37347**
20124 Milan   (opening hours as above)

Corso XXII Marzo 7   **02 540 90094**
20124 Milan   Mon 3:30-7:30
                              Tues-Sat 9:30-1:30, 3:30-7:30

Eleonora Scaramucci   ♀

Sexy pink walls and jigsaw mirrors entice young gals-about-town and their mothers into this youthful-looking store, with clothes by Eleonora Scaramucci or her other brands, Fatalità and Elisir. But it may be the mothers rather than the gals who walk out swinging their purchases in a paper bag. The racks are lined with raw silk two-piece suits in delicate pastel shades or, for the more adventurous, acid green, orange or lemon yellow. Team these with knitwear and a modest selection of silk scarves by Fatalità, or spend time sifting through the hats, belts and bags. For a smart statement, try the range of black linen tailored dresses, cropped jackets, skirts and trousers all precision top-stitched in contrasting white. Still, daughters won't have to spend all their time admiring their mothers as they march in and out of the changing-rooms in an endless parade of clothes—Scaramucci also stocks jeans and brightly printed T-shirts from an ever-changing roster of upcoming labels such as Huevo Blanco, Creola or Nickel & Dime.

Moderate   *Amex/MC/V*

Via Dell'Orso 1   **02 805 2216**
20121 Milan   Sun-Mon 3:30-7:30, Tues-Sat 10-7:30

E.Marinella   ♟

Anyone who has the remotest interest in ties will have heard of E. Marinella. Based in Naples, this purveyor of luxury neckwear has supplied everyone from Luchino Visconti to Tony Blair. So when gents who still get excited about ties heard that the legendary company was opening an outpost (the only one outside Naples) in Milan, there were quite a few suppressed whoops of delight. To join Marinella's exclusive roster of clients, ring for admittance at the discreet entrance to the palazzo that houses the store. Inside, besuited assistants will help you create the perfect made-to-measure tie, while doling out advice on the garment's history, the most suitable fabrics and the best way to tie the perfect knot. Fabrics are draped across glass-topped teak cabinets, so you can touch as well as see them while you're making your choice. All exclusively woven from English silk, each tie is handmade in the small workroom in Naples. There are also ready-to-wear ties, scarves, perfumes and a range of watches—mostly housed in cabinets that wouldn't disgrace a museum.   *marinellanapoli.it*

Expensive   *Amex/MC/V*

Via Santa Maria alla Porta 5   **02 864 67036**
Milan 20123   Mon 3-7, Tues-Sat 10-7

Emilio Pucci   ♀

Unless you've been in a deep snooze for several seasons, you know that this legendary Sixties label from Florence has made a comeback. Now overseen by Christian Lacroix, Pucci is part of the French-owned LVMH stable of luxury goods companies. At the end of a covered passageway just off the designer strip, you'll find the bright swirling signature prints on dresses, tops, trousers, scarves, swimwear, bags, belts, hats, sunglasses, towels, wallets, purses and shoes. If all that colour is too much for you, try the new make-up range from Stephane Marais available in Pucci cosmetic cases.   *emiliopucci.com*

Luxury   *Amex/MC/V*

Via Montenapoleone 14   **02 763 18356**
20121 Milan   Mon-Sat 10-7

Energie   ♟♀♟

This street-cred store with its thumping music is a great source for girly brands like Killah Babe and Miss Sixty, plus more macho streetwear from Energie and Sixty Pro-Tec. It may not look like much from the outside, but all five floors of Energie are packed with the latest in Italian streetwear, from tiny T-shirts to long, low-waisted flared jeans and platform shoes—alongside the company's own new range of footwear. There's a lot here to sift through, but when your own energy starts to flag, take our advice and head into the San Satiro church right next door to get an eyeful of its fabulous false apse. From fashion to spirituality: what more could you ask for from a trip to Milan?   *energie.it*

Moderate   Amex/MC/V

Via Torino 19   **02 720 20077**
20123 Milan   Mon-Fri 10-7:30, Sat 9:30-8

Eral 55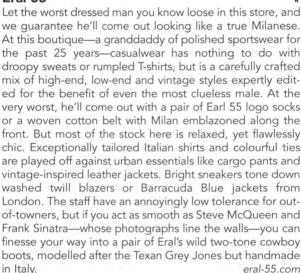

Let the worst dressed man you know loose in this store, and we guarantee he'll come out looking like a true Milanese. At this boutique—a granddaddy of polished sportswear for the past 25 years—casualwear has nothing to do with droopy sweats or rumpled T-shirts, but is a carefully crafted mix of high-end, low-end and vintage styles expertly edited for the benefit of even the most clueless male. At the very worst, he'll come out with a pair of Earl 55 logo socks or a woven cotton belt with Milan emblazoned along the front. But most of the stock here is relaxed, yet flawlessly chic. Exceptionally tailored Italian shirts and colourful ties are played off against urban essentials like cargo pants and vintage-inspired leather jackets. Bright sneakers tone down washed twill blazers or Barracuda Blue jackets from London. The staff have an annoyingly low tolerance for out-of-towners, but if you act as smooth as Steve McQueen and Frank Sinatra—whose photographs line the walls—you can finesse your way into a pair of Eral's wild two-tone cowboy boots, modelled after the Texan Grey Jones but handmade in Italy.   *eral-55.com*

Moderate to expensive   Amex/MC/V

Piazza XXV Aprile 14   **02 659 8829**
20124 Milan   Mon 3-7:30, Tues-Sat 10:30-7:30

Ermenegildo Zegna

The first thing that most people still remember about this brand is that it's where Monica bought that tie for Bill. But to limit this label to the gossip columns is to do a serious disservice to both of them, to Zegna—and to you. Set out over four floors there is something for every guy of every age in this store on Via Verri (a street rapidly becoming the best menswear shopping drag in Milan). On the ground floor you can browse through the ties artistically arranged in drawers or try on a pair of stylish leather brogues. Climb the stairs to the first floor for chic sportswear, then to the second for the company's younger, casual fashion line. On the third floor, you'll find ready-to-wear suits in a wide choice of fabrics. But the fourth floor is the most glorious: this is where Milan's well-heeled gents come to be fitted for the company's fabulous custom-made suits. The store promises to ship your purchases home for you within four weeks. *zegna.com*

Expensive to luxury Amex/MC/V

Via Verri 3 **02 760 06437**
20121 Milan Mon-Sat 10-7

Ethic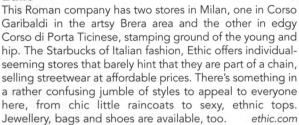

This Roman company has two stores in Milan, one in Corso Garibaldi in the artsy Brera area and the other in edgy Corso di Porta Ticinese, stamping ground of the young and hip. The Starbucks of Italian fashion, Ethic offers individual-seeming stores that barely hint that they are part of a chain, selling streetwear at affordable prices. There's something in a rather confusing jumble of styles to appeal to everyone here, from chic little raincoats to sexy, ethnic tops. Jewellery, bags and shoes are available, too. *ethic.com*

Affordable MC/V

Corso di Porta Ticinese 50 **02 581 05669**
20123 Milan Mon 3-7:30, Tues-Sat 10:30-2, 3-7:30

Corso Garibaldi 34 **02 805 2284**
20121 Milan Mon 3-7:30, Tues-Sat 10:30-2:30, 3:30-7:30

Etro

Fashionistas fanatical about wearing only black might change their minds after visiting this men's and wom-enswear boutique. Beautifully made suits, shirts, scarves and accessories in ethnic Mexican/Indian prints or with geometric appliqués in a rainbow of colours leap off every rack. The brilliant colour palette has spilled over onto chairs, sofas, candles, vases…and even fabric-lined baskets for your dog. Select something spectacular to spice up your wardrobe from the ready-to-wear range or splash out on a made-to-measure outfit from the wood-panelled Etro su misura, which is on the ground floor as you enter the Montenapo store. The best looks are men's jackets with lin-ings in bright fuchsia or turquoise—for those who like to play their subversive sides close to their chests. A few years ago the womenswear got an extra infusion of Etro blood with the arrival of Etro Snr's daughter, Veronica. She has been successful in making the line even more youthful and trendy and, best of all, she is completely uninhibited in her use of design and pattern mixes. For Etro perfumes and beauty products, head around the corner to the Via Bigli store. Also check out their website—it's very informative and full of fun Etro alchemy. (p.s. If you're a serious bargain hunter, there's a discount outlet at Via Spartaco 3. Tel: 02 550 20218.) *etro.it*

Expensive to luxury Amex/MC/V

Via Montenapoleone 5 **02 760 05049**
20121 Milan Mon-Sat 10-7

Via Bigli 2 (corner Via Verri) **02 760 05450**
20121 Milan Mon 3-7, Tues-Sat 10:30-1:30, 2:30-7

Exté

Unless you are tall and lean, you might have a few problems finding anything to fit you in this store. The skirt hems are itty-bitty, tops come cropped and with vampish necklines, and pulling on a pair of trousers is often a two-person undertaking. The logo-splashed bags and the big belts with Exté buckles say it all: this is a brand that's shouting to be noticed. That's as maybe—but until they settle for a single, longish-term designer (until now they've dropped designers faster than a fashion editor dismisses last season's accessories, though they have recently appointed Sergio Ciucci)—they're unlikely to make it into the big league. Still, you'll find some subtler looks (jeans, cotton trousers, wearable tops) in here as well, and the prices are a bit lower than most designers. *exte.it*

Expensive   *Amex/MC/V*

Via della Spiga 6   **02 783 050**
20121 Milan   Mon 3-7, Tues-Sat 10-7

Fabi

Established in 1965 this Italian shoe brand has stores in Italy, Moscow and Lisbon. Its first Milan store opened on funky Corso di Porta Ticinese in February 2004, then a sister store opened on smart Via Montenapoleone in June of the same year. In the Via Montenapoleone store, green, blue and grey lights cast an eerie, moonlight glow over the shoes, displayed on white and metallic shelves. Though the styles are mostly classics with a twist, recent ads have given the brand a killer edge. A black men's lace-up with a pointed toe was shot in place of a dagger sticking into a 'murdered' girl's wound; high white courts with flower details were positioned at police 'crime' scenes. But head to Fabi anyway: in real life, the shoes aren't as scary as the ads make out. *fabishoes.it*

Expensive to luxury   *Amex/MC/V*

Corso di Porta Ticinese 84   **02 832 41355**
20123 Milan   Tues-Sat 10-1, 2-8

Via Montenapoleone 17   **02 760 16413**
20121 Milan   Mon 3-7, Tues-Sat 10-7

Fabrizio Corsi

Tuscan producer Corsi began making leatherwear back in the Fifties, and over the years has supplied or acted as licensee for trendsetting names from Antonio Marras to Alessandro dell'Acqua and Stefano Guerriero. Then the brand's dynamic manager, Fabrizio, had the brilliant idea of appointing upcoming Anglo-Italian talent Riccardo Tisci as designer, creating a range of chic, modern leatherwear under Corsi's own name. In February 2004, Corsi opened its first-ever own-brand store in Milan's Golden Rectangle—on the same street as John Richmond and Jil Sander. The tiny entrance is easily missed, but those who persist will be well rewarded. Follow the tunnel-like entrance, then head up the stairs to see the main collection. Most of the clothes (leather skirts, suede dresses and trousers, crumpled shirts in subtle colours) are for women but there is a smaller selection of beautifully tailored jackets and shirts for men. Don't be afraid to try things on—the assistants are very friendly. *fabriziocorsi.it*

Expensive   *Amex/MC/V*

Via Verri 7   **02 760 21502**
20121 Milan   Mon 3-7, Tues-Sat 10-1, 2-7

Fatto a Mano

Fatto a Mano ('handmade') was one of the first shops to bring Asian fusion style to this area, and it's full of iridescent colours, rich silks and embroideries on clothes and accessories that the owner picks up on his trips to Thailand and China. Styles are simple and formal with longer skirts and semi-fitted jackets and shirts, and there are origami pleating details on everything from clothes to cushions. Finish off your outfit with some of the ethnic jewellery or the hundreds of silk scarves. Stock flows in and out rapidly, so there's something new to be found every week.

Affordable   *Amex/MC/V*

Corso di Porta Ticinese 76   **02 894 01958**
20123 Milan   Mon 3-7:30, Tues-Sat 10-7:30

Fay

These are clothes that keep Italy's population—the impeccably dressed half—looking photo-grade in all their luxury time. With only two stores in Italy (here and Naples)—this is one of the few places where the elite can check out the entire collection from quilted jackets to smart shirts to well-pressed pants. The look here is chic and preppy—which is as you'd expect from the brand's owner Diego Della Valle, who also owns bourgeois-shoes-du-jour lines Hogan and Tod's. On entering the store you'll see a huge selection of smart/casual clothes that will please any multi-tasking woman and are ideal for fun family days out. Hang around for just a moment and you'll have a choice of assistants offering to lend a hand. The menswear section at the back of the store contains row upon row of finely stitched jackets scattered around a huge metal sculpture resembling car engine pistons which dominates the room. Solid wooden wardrobes—each housing pristine shirts and trousers—add a homely touch. If you can't tear the man in your life away from the rails, fill in time by taking junior off to try on a trendy outfit from the small selection of children's wear. *fay.it*

Expensive   *Amex/MC/V*

Via della Spiga 15   **02 760 17597**
20121 Milan   Mon-Sat 10-7

Fedeli Red and Blue

Traditional gents head to this small store—with its outsized, antique chandelier—on Via Montenapoleone for classic menswear. It belongs to the Fedeli family and has been here for more than 50 years, and their shirts, sweaters, socks and ties are as good as ever. A great place to pick up a birthday present for Dad.

Expensive   *Amex/MC/V*

Via Montenapoleone 8   **02 760 23392**
20121 Milan   Mon 3-7, Tues-Fri 10-1:30, 2:30-7
Sat 10-1, 2:30-7

Fendi

The brand responsible for the worldwide baguette epidemic dishes out cult items season after season. Take the latest disco and radio bags—all in gorgeously worked leathers and fabrics that take your breath away. Or marvel over this year's bag of choice—the Compilation, a glitzy little number with an out-sized buckle. You can finger all these bags and more on the ground floor of this smoky grey store in the Golden Rectangle, which seems packed with just about every bag or accessory the house has ever dreamed up. Upstairs, you'll find the men's and women's ready-to-wear collections alongside a small home collection of luxe cushions and throws. And don't forget that Fendi was first known for its fabulous furs—look for the small fur room on the first floor where (if this is what fires you) you can slip on one of their coats.   *fendi.it*

Luxury   *Amex/MC/V*

Via Sant'Andrea 16   **02 760 21617**
20121 Milan   Mon-Sat 10-7

Fila

If you are the sporty type, or just want to look cool in the latest sporty gear, this well-known Italian label is a good bet. Fila has collaborated with Ferrari on a line of mod sportswear, including red patent-leather shoes, polo shirts and other items embellished with the signature galloping horse. It has worked with Ducati on an equally hip line of motorbike gear, including the ultra-light Ducati Desmo shoes in cherry red that you'll have a hard time taking off between rides. For those who prefer their sport a little calmer, there's the Beyond Yoga range, with spaghetti-strapped camisole tops and capri pants in breathable Lycra in a range of colours. Add shorts, sweats, swimsuits, T-shirts, running shoes and other athletic gear, watches, duffel bags and sunglasses, and you're almost bound to find something to please you here.   *fila.com*

Moderate   *Amex/MC/V*

Centro Commercial, Viale Umbria   **02 551 5603**
20135 Milan   Daily 9-9 (Thurs 9-10, Sun 9-8)

Fornarina

This sexy, youth-infused Marche-based label offers fashion-conscious streetwear for girls who just want to have fun. You'll find daring denim, flirty skirts, slinky dresses and jersey tops in the latest shapes, eye-catching colours and prints. Funky footwear and accessories are available too, and all at high street prices. Friendly staff will give you space to browse, and the boyfriend can chill out on comfy seating while you decide what to wear for your next night out. Ask for Denise. *fornarina.com*

Affordable to moderate   *Amex/MC/V*

Corso di Porta Ticinese 78   **02 832 00759**
20123 Milan   Mon 2:30-7:30, Tues-Sat 10-1:30, 3-7:30

☆ Francescatrezzi

Ever noticed how the little dogs attached to Milan's smartest signoras always have leads that match their owners' coats? Or that the pooches' collars usually tone with the signoras' shoes? You too can now join the smartest doggy-owner brigade—by heading to young Milanese designer Francesca Trezzi's store. Inside the long, narrow space, skip over the Jack Russells and chihuahuas who come here with their owners to lather over harnesses, leashes, doggy-coats (in sizes 24-60), travelling pouches and collars. You and your pet will be spoilt for choice: the canine wardrobe comes in everything from turquoise calfskin to polka-dotted fabric and elegant faux croc. Once you've selected a look you both like, treat yourself to the matching weekend bags, shopping bags and clutches, classic stilettos and sensible, flat pumps, as well as evening styles (in silver calf). Then step outside and blend right in with all those other signoras walking Fido round the block. *francescatrezzi.com*

Moderate to expensive   *Amex/MC/V*

Corso Garibaldi 44   **02 869 15103**
20121 Milan   Mon 3:30-7:30
                              Tues-Sat 10:30-2:30, 3:30-7:30

Francesco Biasia

Pushed out by an invasion of furniture design stores, this long, thin boutique with its cool blue-lit interior has relocated to Via Montenapoleone from Via Durini (now the hub of interior and homewares shopping in Milan). Here you can feast your eyes on a range of trendsetting leather and fabric handbags by the Vicenza-based company in bright eye-catching colours and styles. Looking for something that even the fashion-blind couldn't miss? Take a look at the satin drawstring bags enclosed in an outer layer that resembles a leather fishing net—available in turquoise, bright red, dusty pink and clean crisp white. You're the sort of girl who likes to shout—but not too loud?

Examine the black handbags with top stitching and large buckle fastenings—their exaggerated classic features will never quite disappear in a crowd. If you've already reached your handbag quota on this trip, focus on the unusual watches, sunglasses, wallets, belts and gloves—all in bright colours and stylish designs.   biasia.com

Moderate   *Amex/MC/V*

Via Montenapoleone 1   **02 760 05436**
20121 Milan   Mon 3-7, Tues-Sat 10-7

☆ Franco Jacassi

Hidden in the right hand corner of a cobbled inner court-yard, this secret boutique is Milan's top vintage store. You'll find more stuff here than in a costume museum—and most of it is for sale. Jacassi doesn't encourage casual shop-pers—his rambling archive is aimed at fashion designers and cool hunters who come here to seek out choice pieces as inspiration in seasons to come. But brazen your way through the door anyway for an experience you'll never for-get. In the first room, you'll find mannequins wearing pieces from Pucci or Yves Saint Laurent that Jacassi may or may not auction off. Further down the passageway are moun-tains of vintage bags, scarves, belts and shoes. Further still is an Aladdin's cave of fabrics, braids, lace, ribbon, buttons, buckles and trimmings…true haberdashery heaven. At the very back of the shop, past towers of faded cardboard boxes, you'll spy an iron spiral staircase leading up to yet more clothes. Here you can find everything from a Fifties Pucci bikini to a heavily beaded Dior evening gown. There's even a selection of Victorian pieces, including those frilly, white cotton underclothes if you're looking for a new night-gown. And the name of the website couldn't be more expressive…   vintagedelirium.com

Moderate to expensive   *MC/V*

Via Sacchi 3   **02 864 62076**
20121 Milan   Mon-Fri 10-1, 2-6:30 (by appointment only)

Fratelli Rossetti

Based just outside Milan in the upmarket shoe-making town of Parabiago (even Manolo produces here), this 52-year-old footwear company inspires a loyalty among its clients of which bigger brands can only dream. Lovers of hard-wearing, classic yet stylish footwear come to this store time and time again, hoping to pick up the same designs they bought here several seasons back. Sadly (for some), time doesn't stand still and they may not find them. But they'll soon be balancing on the soft brown leather cubes in this airy store, trying to find a replacement among the latest collection of traditional looks—all updated with of-the-moment twists. More fashion-conscious types will also find satisfaction here. Besides the legendary soft leather moccasins in light tan and rich natural browns, men will find the bestselling Flexa Active comfort range employing the latest footwear technologies. Women can choose between gold metallic leather slingbacks with matching handbags, brilliant white leather flat sandals decorated with appliqué flowers, very flat flip-flop sandals in a wide variety of metallic leathers and two-tone oxfords trimmed with medal ribbons. Also worth checking out are the beautiful soft suede and leather jackets for both men and women, plus handbags, belts and wallets. The kids get off to a running start with a small range of children's shoes on the first floor.   *rossetti.it*

Expensive   *Amex/MC/V*

Via Montenapoleone 1   **02 760 21650**
20121 Milan   Mon-Sat 10-8, Sun 10-2, 3-7

Corso Magenta 17   **02 864 54284**
20123 Milan   Mon 3-7:30, Tues-Sat 10-7:30

Frette

For Frette Milan is unique, in that the customer can choose between the ultra expensive Haut label, in the Via Montenapoleone store, or go to the other three shops for much more moderate prices. All the stores have the same name, but the lines inside are very different. Everything in the Montenapo store breathes luxury. Displayed among the original Deco furniture are the famed bed linens on which the world's richest and most decadent have demanded to lay their heads for well over a century. Alongside sheets with stratospheric thread-counts and silk duvets, you'll find a full line of homewear that will make you want to stay locked behind closed doors for the next century. Over the past few years, designer Cristina Azario has done a marvellous job of conjuring up delicate, beautifully crafted silk and lace nightgowns, French knickers and pastel-coloured piped satin pyjamas for both men and women. You can retreat to bliss in cashmere or velvet robes lined in heavy satin, warm up in a fur-trimmed wrap sweater, or trollop around your boudoir in a pair of mink-lined crocodile or delicate silk mules. The spectacle doesn't come cheap, but if Frette is good enough for the Pope, you better believe it's worth the tag.   *frette.com*

Moderate to luxury   *Amex/MC/V*

Via Montenapoleone 21   **02 783 950**
20121 Milan   Mon 3-7, Tues-Sat 10-7

Via Manzoni   **11 02 864 433**
20121 Milan   Mon 3-7, Tues-Sat 10-1:30, 3-7

Corso Buenos Aires 82   **02 294 01072**
20124 Milan   Mon 3:30-7:30
          Tues-Fri 9:30-12:30, 3:30-7:30, Sat 9:30-1:30, 3-7:30

Corso Vercelli 23/25   **02 498 9756**
20144 Milan   Mon 3:30-7:30, Tues-Fri 9:30-12:30
                                    Sat 9:30-1, 3-7:30

☆ Frip

Forget the name, there's definitely no frippery here. Run by DJ Marcello and design researcher Ana, this low-profile store favours equally low-profile Scandinavian fashion with design details so minimal they're barely there. Scandinavian designers featured here include Rodebjer and Pour, paired with French Schmoove shoes for men. Britain is also represented with designs by Kulture, Michael Keller, Umbro and You Must Create, and there are some exclusive designs usually only found in Japan. The clothes are urban contemporary casuals with a strong Eighties influence and there are absolutely no frills or pretty colours; there's also a range of jewellery with some quirky original ideas. The backdrop to all of this is a clean white space, with all-white walls, floors, lamps and shelves. When he's not filling you in on the background to the designers, you'll find Marcello behind his music deck getting into his collection of house, drum and base, new jazz, tech and broken beats. There's a big selection of LPs and CDs to flip through in this offbeat store.

Moderate to expensive   Amex/MC/V
Corso di Porta Ticinese 16   **02 832 1360**
Milan 20122   Mon 3:30-7:30, Tues-Sat 11-2, 3:30-7:30

Fuerteventura

Looking for a cute souvenir to remind you of a great vacation? Head to this tiny store, the brand's first in Milan. You'll find jersey separates inspired by the colours of the Italian flag. If they don't please, choose a T-shirt or fitted sweater splashed with 'I ❤ Italy'—just so that your friends back home will be in no doubt about where your true sentiments lie. The store does also have lines without a specifically Italian theme—among them are casual bags, funky belts and hats logo'd with badges and prints. There's also a small range of microminis, jersey pants with ribbed cuffs, graphic print tops, Seventies-inspired jackets and pants—all with the bright colours and funky sports styling that are the hallmark of this brand.   *fuerteventura.it*

Affordable   Amex/MC/V
Corso di Porta Ticinese 46   **02 581 08388**
Milan 20123   Mon-Sat 11:30-8:30

Furla

Like so many established Italian brands, this Bologna-based leather accessories company has kept things in the family since its foundation back in 1927. Today Giovanna Furlanetto spins boatloads of calfskin or glossed leather bags in bright red, acid green or citrus yellow with clever contrasting handles in beige. Everything from super shiny patent leather to soft hole-punched suede is used to make shoulder bags, shoppers, clutches, handbags, purses, wallets and shoes. The same no-nonsense approach goes into the brand's other accessories: jewellery, watches, small leather goods, scarves and T-shirts to match the colours and print designs on the bags. In Milan, you'll find the best choice at the busy Corso Vittorio Emanuele store, though the other, smaller boutiques are also worth a visit. Once you've fallen in love with a Furla bag, you may be tempted to tell the world, in a T-shirt with 'I love Furla' emblazoned on it. *furla.com*

Moderate	*Amex/MC/V*
Corso Vittorio Emanuele II 2	**02 796 943**
20122 Milan	Mon-Sat 10-7:30
Corso Vercelli 11	**02 480 14189**
20145 Milan	Mon 3-7:30, Tues-Sat 10-7:30
Corso Buenos Aires 18	**02 204 3319**
20124 Milan	Mon 2:30-7:30, Tues-Sat 10-7:30

Gallo

Gallo is targeted at conservative people, or conservative people who urge to be edgy. Started as a sock company, Gallo has come up with a quality sock that is both long lasting and comfortable (retailing at around 15-20 euros). What sets them apart from the rest of the sock pack are the graphics and colours printed on their socks. Discreet darker shades are always in store, but Gallo is constantly experimenting with bold colours and graphics, which are now frequently seen around Milan both in and out of offices. Their popularity has encouraged the company to experiment with other accessories: cashmere ties, scarves, boxers, swimwear and underwear. Many of the lines also come in mini sizes for kids.

Moderate	*Amex/MC/V*
Via Manzoni 16b	**02 783 602**
20121 Milan	Mon-Sat 10-7

Gas

Scrawl your name on the downstairs wall of this recently opened store from the Veneto-based streetwear label to get yourself in the mood. Then head downstairs for an overwhelming range of jeans, denimwear, chinos, T-shirts and funky, sexy jersey tops. There's also a great surfing and beachwear collection, and (a must, with all those low-rise jeans around) underwear lines for both boys and girls. There is plenty of colour and print on everything including the shoes, trainers, belts and bags. All the shop fittings are made from recycled materials, including a cash desk made from beer cans. *gasjeans.com*

Affordable	*Amex/MC/V*
Corso di Porta Ticinese 53	**02 894 27776**
20100 Milan	Mon 3-7:30, Tues-Sat 10:30-7:30

Gemelli

Grandmothers have been shopping here alongside their granddaughters for over 50 years. The shop's façade and first floor are not greatly appealing but inside, you'll find an endless range of chic appealing attire. Upstairs, there is a wide array of knits (Malo, Fissore and Napoleonerba), linen pashminas in bright colours, coats (Ermanno Scervino, Moncler, Ramosport and Aspesi) and swimsuits (Eres). Across the street is a store housing Gemelli's sportswear and children's collection by the likes of Vintage, Lamartina and Ralph Lauren.

Expensive to luxury   *Amex/MC/V*

Corso Vercelli 16   **02 480 00057**
20145 Milan   Mon 3-7:30, Tues-Sat 9:30-1, 3-7:30

☆ Gentucca Bini

Young, innovative designers with their own shop are a rarefied breed in Milan. Gentucca's place is a little off the beaten track, but for those who are looking for something a bit different it's worth the visit. After her studies Gentucca's genius was quickly picked up by the big fashion houses. She has made inox (that's brillo pad wire) webbed hats for Chanel, and flowered hair appliqués out of antique glass. During the last few years she has been experimenting with the construction and deconstruction of clothing, a little in the vein of Yohji Yamamoto. It's a risky look: cloth is shorn, shredded and pleated in various ways. She also tries out interesting combinations, such as a Fifties themed satin dress with a mohair crocheted petticoat peeping through underneath. The shop carries the equally original children's clothing line Melameli, by Mela Melazzi, another unrestricted creative genius.

Expensive   *Amex/MC/V*

Via Pantano 17   **02 583 15434**
20122 Milan   Mon 3-7, Tues-Sat 10-2, 3-7

Geox

Mario Moretti Polegato, founder of Geox, seems intent on quietly taking over the world. The company's entire raison d'être is founded on letting feet breathe, through a patented sole that releases moisture through the tiny perforations in the bottom of the shoe without letting water seep back in. In 2002, the company opened a huge boutique in Piazza San Carlo, just off Corso Vittorio Emanuele, and they opened another shiny new outlet (their first in the US) in New York last year too. Polegato knows that he's doing the world a favour—his shoes are comfortable and affordable, and many of them are reasonably stylish. You'll find heels for the office, summer flats, classic loafers for kicking around on the weekend, kids' shoes—all with the famous breathable sole. Though bright and cheery, the Corso Vittorio Emanuele store tends to get a bit busy, with assistants who are always slightly hurried…which is good news for Polegato, if not always for us. *geox.com*

Affordable *Amex/MC/V*

Via Montenapoleone 26 **02 760 9372**
20121 Milan Mon 3-7, Tues-Sat 10-7

Piazza San Carlo 2 **02 760 28217**
20122 Milan Mon 3-7:30, Tues-Sat 10-7:30

Corso Buenos Aires 2 **02 295 31626**
20124 Milan (opening hours as above)

Via Speronari 8 (corner Via Torino) **02 869 95608**
20123 Milan Mon 11-7:30, Tues-Sat 10-7:30

Corso Buenos Aires 42 **02 204 01189**
20124 Milan Mon 3-7:30, Tues-Sat 10-7:30

Corso Vercelli 9 **02 469 4742**
20144 Milan (opening hours as above)

Via Rovello 1 (opposite Via Dante) **02 890 11481**
20121 Milan (opening hours as above)

Via Manzoni 20 **02 760 0372**
20121 Milan (opening hours as above)

Germano Zama

This new store on the increasingly hip Via Solferino stocks casual classics for twenty and thirty-somethings with an artsy edge. It's a great place to pick up officewear that will have your colleagues begging you to spill the secrets of your Little Black Shopping Book. But the Bologna-based company also designs and manufactures everything from casual jeans to cropped T-shirts with bold abstract prints to knee-length trousers with sexy side-laces. Add to these a mix of suede and leather jackets, high-heeled shoes and accessories—belts, jewellery, bags—and you'll see that Zama is really going for what the Italians call the 360° look. Men won't feel left out here either—there are nicely cut white shirts and pinstriped jackets with unexpected details on the back. *germanozama.com*

Moderate *Amex/MC/V*

Via Solferino 1 **02 878 740**
20121 Milan Mon 3-7, Tues-Sat 10-2, 3-7

Giacomelli Sport

The giant action photo of Paolo Maldini, Milan's football star, is reason enough to visit this one-floor sportswear shop. Other sporting greats, like Boris Becker and Michael Jordan, get face time too. Among the brands on sale you'll find the latest models from Nike, Adidas, Asics, Diadora, Arena, Lotto and Reebok alongside sporty clothes by Fila, Ellesse and Garman. Beware of visiting during the sales when the competition can get tougher than any international football match. *giacomellisport.com*

Moderate *Amex/MC/V*

Piazza Argentina 4 **02 294 09806**
20124 Milan Mon 2:30-8, Tues-Sat 9:30-8

☆ Gianfranco Ferré

As if being a first-rate couturier and top of the line ready-to-wear designer weren't enough, maestro Gianfranco Ferré also has an architectural degree which he put to work in his recently opened store and adjoining day spa. The boutique's rich red interior of dupion silk walls and lacquered floors declares that this is a designer who doesn't just flirt with clothes. Amongst the glitter and luxe, you'll find fabulous sculptural creations which could stand up by sheer design force alone. Ferré's designs appeal greatly to the heavily bejewelled ladies-who-do-nothing-but-lunch set—they love the structured silhouette and dramatic eveningwear with heavy detailing. But the younger crowd will also find something to please, not least the beautifully cut shirts. There's also a beachwear collection and a range of fabulous bags and perfumes. When they've finished browsing, classic customers and sweet young things alike will find consolation in a post-shopping hot stone facial or detoxification at the adjoining spa—an immediate antidote to post-spending woes. *gianfrancoferre.com*

Luxury *Amex/MC/V*

Via Sant'Andrea 15 **02 794 864**
20121 Milan Mon-Sat 10-7

☆ Gianni Campagna

It's a very long walk down Corso Venezia to this elegant top-of-the-range store in a majestic 19th-century building near Milan's public gardens. In fact, it's far better to take the Metro to Palestro or arrive in style by taxi—a more acceptable form of transport for Campagna's regular clientele. Sharon Stone, Pierce Brosnan and Jack Nicholson are among the many who have commissioned Campagna to drum up one of his famous precision-tailored, silk-lined suits. Trained under legendary Milan-based tailor Domenico Caraceni (whose label he recently bought) Campagna still personally measures and cuts all his custom-made suits, limiting them to just 700 a year. There's not much point asking for innovation here: Campagna believes he's come up with the perfect proportions—men's trousers, for instance, always have legs with bottoms 22.5cm wide. These days, he also offers 6,000 suits a year in the financially friendlier ready-to-wear collection, all in the same rich fabrics (Super 150 and Super 180 wools, vicuña, and guanaco). *sartoriacampagna.it*

Expensive to luxury *Amex/MC/V*

Via Palestro 24	**02 778 811**
20100 Milan	Mon-Sat 9:30-7

Gianni Versace

Even those whom Donatella has never entirely convinced would do well to put aside their prejudices and step through the door to this surprisingly clean-lined, five-storey temple to over-the-top style. On the ground floor, make your way past shoes, perfumes, make-up, skincare products and other accessories—not all of which will send your eyeballs into a spin. But take the in-store lift to womenswear on the first and second floors—and there'll be no mistaking that you've stepped into Versaceland. Dresses, shirts and skirts in shocking colours and vibrant patterns hang from every rack, and on the second floor, you'll also find the jewellery (bling! bling!) to complement the pieces you've picked up en route. If all this luxurious vulgarity makes you shudder, check out the eveningwear for turtleneck sweaters and beautifully cut pants (they're hung, of course, next to the sexily cut evening frocks with slits right up the thigh). Men will find everything from vibrant print shirts to pure simple black knitwear on the two floors above. Head to nearby Via San Pietro all'Orto for the younger, slinkier and more affordable Versus label (see separate entry). *versace.com*

Luxury *Amex/MC/V*

Via Montenapoleone 11	**02 760 08528**
20121 Milan	Daily 10-7:30 (Sun 10-7)

☆ Gibo

One fine day designer Julie Verhoeven popped into Milan's recently opened Gibo shop, decided it needed a statement and gave it one on the spot. Check out the shop's floor for the subversive, punky line drawings from this multi-talented British designer for proof of her quirky talent. Chosen by manufacturing giant Gibo to design its own-label collection, Verhoeven had previously worked for John Galliano, Martine Sitbon and others, before creating the young, decadent look for Gibo—in her own inimitable style. Her clothes use jersey printed with graphic checks and stripes, and clever cuts to create sporty separates and some more grown-up, sophisticated looks. Her best-selling printed T-shirts (with drawings similar to those on the shop's floor) storm out of the shop.

Moderate to expensive *Amex/MC/V*

Via Sant'Andrea 10/A	**02 799 988**
20121 Milan	Mon-Sat 10-2, 3-7

☆ Gio Moretti

This fun store—from one of the doyennes of the Milanese fashion scene—is among the best shopping experiences in the city. The bright lights, colour-splashed walls and huge, mismatched vases filled with orchids lift your spirits the moment you step inside. The assistants are plentiful and actually seem to enjoy what they do—even making pulling out your credit card a real pleasure. What's more, Moretti's immaculate taste means that her editing is perfect, saving you masses of wasted time sorting through the no-nos (yes, they do exist) in the city's endless designer stores. Look no further for the best pieces by John Paul Gaultier, Ralph Lauren, Roberto Cavalli, Jil Sander, DKNY or Chloé. Downstairs, a sporty yet chic collection of menswear is enlivened with funky home objects, cameras, art books and obscure CDs. For the time-conscious guy who wants to combine a fitness regime with shopping there is even a techno-gym complete with treadmill, cycle and weights.

Expensive to luxury   *Amex/MC/V*

Via della Spiga 4   **02 760 03186 (W)/02 760 02172 (M)**
20121 Milan   Mon 3-7, Tues-Sat 10-7

Gio Moretti Baby

To cap off an envy-evoking family portrait, head just a few doors down the street from the main Gio Moretti store— and scoop up some of the most adorable (and pricey) children's clothes in Milan. Just like the store for grown-ups, this much smaller place offers an impeccable selection from top designers, including Simonetta, BluMarine, Ralph Lauren and Sophie Petit; there are also a couple of slightly more affordable lines by streetwear brands like Replay. As in the parent store, the staff are extremely helpful and attentive.

Moderate to luxury   *Amex/MC/V*

Via della Spiga 9   **02 780 089**
20121 Milan   Mon 3-7, Tues-Sat 10-7

Giorgio Armani

As the door is swept open by one of Armani's legion of good-looking personnel, you are welcomed into the world of understated elegance that Giorgio does so well. Like the other Giorgio Armani stores in Italy, the interior is by Claudio Silvestrin—and there's an atmosphere of a Roman bathhouse here, between the sand-coloured walls and the cool water pool. The walls form the perfect backdrop for the fine fabrics, subtle colours and textures of Armani's stylish classics. The women's day and eveningwear is on the ground floor along with accessories; menswear is downstairs. You'll find a dedicated accessories boutique around the corner at Via della Spiga 2.   *giorgioarmani.com*

Luxury   *Amex/MC/V*

Via Sant'Andrea 9   **02 760 03234**
20121 Milan   Mon-Sat 10:30-7:30

Via della Spiga 19 (accessories)   **02 783 511**
20121 Milan   (opening hours as above)

Gucci

Gucci may not strictly be a Milanese brand—but where else would it choose to locate its largest outlet, if not Via Montenapoleone in the heart of Milan? An endless labyrinth with neutral walls and glass-and-chrome display cases it features more product than any Gucci addict could possibly hope for—and much, much more than they could ever possibly buy. Rows and rows of Gucci's sexed-up ready-to-wear in cool creams and essential black—highlighted with bright green and canary yellow—grace almost the entire basement, though rails of itsy-bitsy underwear, including some of the tiniest Gucci knickers ever, take up what space remains. And amidst the stacks of sexy women's footwear you'll find delights like the baby shoes, so that you can start 'em young. The ground floor is packed with every coveted bag on the planet. If you're feeling snooty about seeing your same croc clutch in the hands of your best friend, do what any proper slave to statement would do and snag a limited-edition piece or whip up your own personalised delight from the made-to-order collection. Be sure to bring your man along for the eye-popping ride to test out the made-to-measure men's shoes which will have him looking like a slick Forties gangster in no time. Gucci's newest baby is the store in the Galleria which focuses on accessories. The tight little box hedges and steely plant pots do look a little out of place, but they point you in the right direction. They hide the café, which flanks the shop, where you can get pick-me-up juices or patisseries. *gucci.com*

Luxury *Amex/MC/V*

Via Montenapoleone 5-7 **02 771 271**
20121 Milan Mon-Sat 10-7

Galleria Vittorio Emanuele II **02 859 799**
20123 Milan (opening hours as above)

☆ Guess?

It's hard to miss this store, prominently located in San Babila, and the American label continues to have a surprisingly strong presence on the Milanese fashion scene. But examine the clothes and you'll soon see why that might be. There's no hint of the baggy, one-size-fits-all look often associated with mid-range American casualwear. Instead, you'll find tighter-fitting, European cuts in T-shirts, jeans, jackets and tops in fun styles and funky colours. This season, there are even striped ankle socks to be worn with strappy sandals—an outrageous look in conservative Milan. *guess.com*

Moderate *Amex/MC/V*

Piazza San Babila 4/B **02 763 92070**
20122 Milan Mon-Sat 10-7:30, Sun 2:30-7:30

Guja

Yeow! Pink floor, pink walls…not to mention shoes with ribbons, shoes with studs, shoes with buckles, shoes with appliqués, shoes with silk flowers. There's not a single dull shoe in the house. Sit down on one of the stainless-steel chairs and take it all in. Among the adorable girly shoe brands you'll find Pedro Garcia, Kalisté, Janet & Janet,

Lolita, Sinela, Alima and (of course) Sexy Kiss. Most shoes run between 100 and 200 euros. *guja.it*

Moderate   Amex/MC/V

Galleria di Corso Vercelli 23   **02 498 6429**
20145 Milan   Mon 3:30-7:30, Tues-Sat 10-7:30

Via San Giovanni sul Muro 13   **02 874 344**
20121 Milan   (opening hours as above)

H&M

You'll need lots and lots of energy as you slog around this over-lit, over-trafficked store. It's a huge space on three floors with cluttered rails, head-throbbing music and people milling everywhere. However, as in any of this Swedish chain's stores around the world, you never know what you might turn up. It's disposable fashion of course, but they certainly have their finger on the pulse. Choose from a wide range of T-shirts, trousers, dresses, shoes, lingerie, jewellery, accessories...all reflecting the latest runway trends. The emphasis is on a quick turnaround of goods so they keep lowering the prices until the stock has gone. The lengthy queues for dressing-rooms and check-outs are proof that the younger generation adore this store—but when it opened last year in the historic Fiorucci space many Milanese were furious, and we don't entirely disagree. *hm.com*

Affordable   Amex/MC/V

Galleria Passerella 2   **02 760 17222**
20122 Milan   Mon-Sat 10-8, Sun 12-8

Helmut Lang

Minimalist, cutting-edge, experimental are just a few of the words that spring to mind when thinking of this king of cult. Unfortunately, the king himself has left and Prada, the brand's majority owner, is in the doldrums. Still, there are the futuristic space-age materials hanging next to punkish cotton trousers and quirky tailored suits in a concrete warehouse. This two-floor store is far too scary to be seen in—unless you're dressed to the über-cool nines. Lang himself designed the decor—including the neon light exhibits and the dark wooden monoliths that double as stair rails. As well as an artfully constructed ready-to-wear selection, you'll find a small offering of offbeat shoes, accessories and own-brand perfume. *helmutlang.com*

Luxury   Amex/MC/V

Via della Spiga 11   **02 763 90255**
20121 Milan   Mon-Sat 10-7:30

Henry Béguelin

The subtle scent of expensive leather wafts over you as you open the door of this intriguing store. Inside is an open space with natural whitewashed walls with a rusty finish, lots of gnarled driftwood decorations and natural wood surfaces. Mouth-watering shoes and bags sit on benches;

clothes hang from wooden beams. You won't find this season's hottest style or standard city classic—these are pieces with a casual, hippy chic all their own (even though the line's original creator, Henry Béguelin, is no longer there—see Henry Cuir, below). Quality leathers and fabrics are carefully selected and dyed in natural colours; nothing is mass-produced. You'll find cotton kaftans with leather detailing, butter-soft leather trousers, skirts and jackets, and shoes with original designs. You may be staggered by the prices, but you're paying for craftmanship and exclusivity. And if that's not enough, there's a new service for customised bags and shoes. *henrybeguelin.com*

Luxury *Amex/MC/V*

Via Caminadella 7 **02 720 00969**
20123 Milan Mon 3-7, Tues-Sat 10-2, 3-7

☆ Henry Cuir

Swiss artisan Henry Béguelin began making leather shoes back in the Seventies on the island of Elba. Later he moved to Milan, where his comfortable, chic designs became the favoured footwear of the kind of signoras who flit between homes in Portofino and Courmayeur. Then in the Nineties he had an acrimonious, Jil Sander-like split with his business partner and was forced to abandon his label, Henry Béguelin. But Henry is never happy unless he's working his beloved leather, and soon he'd created a new label, Henry Cuir, with a workshop in the footwear-producing town of Vigevano. He also opened a store in Via Arena (near Corso di Porta Ticinese), with rust-coloured walls, a leather-tiled floor, ethnic furniture and an old piano—which clients are free to play. Inside the store, Henry's bags and shoes are displayed on wooden tables. There are cream-coloured camel leather ankle boots, low-heeled peep-toe sandals and brown riding boots, all with secret details—like an encased amber bead, or a tiny, handstitched dog motif. Henry's shoes are never tottering, but they're always stylish—and they often have bags to match. This is not a place for the latest runway crazes—you'll just find handcrafted pieces that you'll wear for years and years. *henrybeguelin.com*

Luxury *Amex/MC/V*

Via Arena 19 **02 832 41740**
20123 Milan Mon 3-7, Tues-Sat 10-1:30, 3-7

Hermès

Amid prints of bucolic hunting scenes and saddles tacked to the walls, this lofty French house delivers all the luxe you can lap up. From the famous Kelly Bag to the bold-printed silk scarves, you'll find those Fifties classics alongside more modern designs for both men and women. Recently, Jean Paul Gaultier has brought his own brand of Parisian style to the women's collection which is upstairs along with the luxurious home collection of throws, bed linens, dressing-gowns and a small children's line. The ground floor is devoted to the exquisitely made bags, scarves, perfumes and other accessories. There's a colourful array of ties, and the growing menswear collection all waiting to be wrapped and boxed in that famous orange box. And these days you don't need a horse to mount a Hermès saddle—you can invest in a bicycle signed 'Hermès'.   *hermes.com*

Luxury   *Amex/MC/V*

Via Sant'Andrea 21   **02 760 03495**
20121 Milan   Mon 3-7, Tues-Sat 10-7

Hogan

Instantly recognisable, Diego Della Valle's Hogan shoes are regularly spotted on celebrity feet—from Sharon Stone's to Tom Cruise's. In the much-frequented Milan branch, they (the shoes, not the celebrities) are displayed in suspended boxes above the smart wooden floor. Look out for this season's bestseller shown against a startling bright red wall as you walk in—and then explore the rest of the stock in this long, narrow, clean-lined boutique. The great thing about Hogans is that they come in every colour. So if you're looking for elegant, comfortable footwear to go with your brand-new outfit in red, green, beige, black or brown—this is the place to come. This season, there's also a smart range of kitten-heel sandals in green and white with matching bags trimmed with leather rope and tassels in bright pink. Finally, there are shoes for children, if your offspring could do with a style fix.   *todsgroup.com*

Expensive   *Amex/MC/V*

Via Montenapoleone 23   **02 760 11174**
20121 Milan   Mon-Sat 10-7

Host

Managed by the son of Pupi Solari (one of Milan's longest-reigning fashion retail empresses who has a boutique next door), this classic men's shop has everything for a tried and true ageless look, lifted with modern pieces such as sea-blue corduroy jackets and lilac cashmere V-necks. The typical client is part of Milan's alta borghesia and aged 35-50. The shop has beautiful window displays that invite passers-by in for a further look. Lines include knits by Ballantyne and William Lockie; jackets by Caruso and Piombo; trousers by Incotex; shirts by Hartford and Conte; shoes by John Spencer and Car Shoe; and coats by Alberto Aspesi.

Expensive to luxury   *Amex/MC/V*

Piazza Tommaseo 2   **02 436 085**
20145 Milan   Mon 3-8, Tues-Sat 10-8

Hugo Boss

Hugo Boss is known for its well-cut, well-made garments at better prices than many labels. This airy store is mostly dedicated to menswear: tailored suits, crumpled leather bikers' jackets and white striped trousers abound. But unlike the poor Florentines, the lucky Milanese have recently been treated to a small selection of womenswear—from silk trouser suits to fine knitwear and smart bags and shoes. Good news: the great prices and smart fits mean the range has taken off and there are plans to extend it very soon.   hugoboss.com

Moderate to expensive   *Amex/MC/V*

Via Matteotti 1   **02 763 94667**
20121 Milan   Mon 3-7:30, Tues-Sat 10-7:30

Iceberg

An automatic door opens onto a mass of multicoloured, patterned garments in this spacious welcoming store. Animal and jungle prints shout from the surrounding brightness, competing for your attention with fun dresses, tops and skirts in everything from fuchsia to citron yellow. Set out over two floors with the men's selection downstairs, there is plenty to choose from here. A little-known fact: the original store design is by Vincenzo De Cotiis (the designer behind the hot new Milan design hotel, Straf). Staff repaint the display benches and the odd wall each season, to reflect the colours of the new clothes.   iceberg.com

Luxury   *Amex/MC/V*

Via Montenapoleone 10   **02 782 385**
20121 Milan   Mon-Sat 10-7

Imarika

This discreet little shop on the corner of out-of-the-way Viale Piave stocks beautifully crafted pieces from Jil Sander, Mira Mikati and Jean Paul Gaultier; there are also pieces from upcoming designers like Monika Varga, including white silk or cotton jacquard dresses with colourful laser-printed patterns. To complement them, there's a range of perfectly chic accessories—from embroidered hats to beaded bags and shoes from Emma Hope—all displayed on the pristine white shelves. The mature staff just love telling you how beautiful everything is and fuss around adjusting here, there and everywhere. Lovely.

Expensive to luxury   *Amex/MC/V*

Via Morelli 1 (corner Viale Piave)   **02 760 05268**
20129 Milan   Mon 3-7:30, Tues-Sat 10-1:30, 3-7:30

I Pinco Pallino

If your little cherubs deserve a treat, bring them straight to this store, for kids aged 2-14. Once here, though, you may forget whether the treat was supposed to be for them, or for you. Strategically placed opposite what must be one of Milan's best-positioned schools, this wonderland of finery is popular with well-heeled Italian mamas. Be wowed by the giant chandelier made from shapes of stars, birds, flowers and hearts in Moreno glass (one client was so impressed, he tried to buy it, but it's not for sale). Have fun dressing your little girl up like Cinderella on her way to the ball in the extravagantly designed dresses made from silk with layers of frothy underskirts. There are also loads of fun styles for boys (sailor suits etcetera), if you can persuade your son to try them on. If you're looking for clothes for kids aged 0-2, try the nearby sister shop, in Via Borgospesso. *pincopallino.it*

Expensive *Amex/MC/V*

Via della Spiga 42 **02 781 931**
20121 Milan Mon 3-7, Tues-Sat 10-7

I Pinco Pallino Baby

Via Borgospesso 25 **02 781 356**
20121 Milan (opening hours as above)

I Pinco Pallino 1950

Galleria Manzoni 40 **02 760 08682**
20121 Milan (opening hours as above)

Isabella Tonchi

Upcoming designer Isabella Tonchi worked for Fiorucci, Miu Miu, Calvin Klein and Versace before branching out with her own collection of sporty-sexy clothes. Her first Milan store (there are several in the USA) opened in December 2003 on the new fashion strip of Via Maroncelli, right next to Agatha Ruiz de la Prada—although her creations are far more understated than those of her Spanish neighbour. The clothes are displayed inside antique pine wardrobes or on pine tables, creating a simple, uncluttered feel. Take time to look at the huge fashion storyboard on the wall which explains Isabella's design philosophy and inspirations. Quality and exclusivity are the key points: top-notch Swiss cotton, French jersey and Japanese silks are draped into sexy knee-length pleated skirts, rollneck sweaters and lightweight bomber jackets—all made in or near Milan. This season, there are clever pieces like shirts made from Palestinian keffiyehs (traditional head scarves) and stretchy tops in smocked Japanese silk—used as exclusive gift-wrap in Japan. *isabellatonchi.com*

Moderate to expensive *Amex/MC/V*

Via Maroncelli 5 **02 290 08589**
20154 Milan Tues-Sat 10:30-1, 2:30-7

JDC—Urban Store

Known simply as JDC, this den of denim bang in the middle of the city attracts a generally young and trendy crowd. As well as JDC's own collection, there are labels like Dolce & Gabbana, Guru (known for its bright floral designs), Pepe Jeans, Nickel & Dime, Le Coq Sportif, Levi's, Lonsdale and Diesel, plus the bags from sportswear companies that have been sweeping streetwear for a year or two. Avoid the weekends, when the colourful funky store with its fringed yellow and orange lampshades in Piazza Duomo seems to draw in half Milan's youth. *jdc-milano.it*

Affordable to moderate *Amex/MC/V*

Piazza Duomo 31 **02 864 61737**
20122 Milan Daily 10-7:30

Corso Buenos Aires 1 **02 295 34043**
20124 Milan Mon 12-7:30, Tues-Sat 10-7:30

☆ Jil Sander

There has been a double tragedy at Jil Sander. The downhill run began when Prada snapped up a majority stake in the German minimalist label. Jil just couldn't get on with Patrizio Bertelli, CEO of Prada, so she left. Then she swallowed her pride and returned, only to leave again. A company spokesperson has said that 'a team of studio designers, many of whom trained directly under Sander, have continued to interpret her pure and unflinching vision and are now in charge of the look.' The future may be uncertain, but for fall/winter 2006 there is a range of beautiful belted coats, soft but slick. The focus is definitely on the cut and cloth quality, keeping it simple. White, grey and black predominate, in contrast to the golden-toned store with floors in Spanish Arria limestone, African ebony display tables and silver-coloured wickets. *jilsander.de*

Luxury *Amex/MC/V*

Via Verri 6 **02 777 2991**
20121 Milan Mon-Sat 10-7

☆ Jimmy Choo

Nothing arouses unadulterated passion more consistently than a set of Jimmy Choo's stiletto heels. This cult British label, founded out of a couture shoe business by former British *Vogue* accessories editor Tamara Mellon, is now required foot candy for uptown ladies and red-carpet divas alike. Designer Sandra Choi consistently whips up colourful strappy sandals, elegant pumps and sexy slingbacks that elongate the leg like no other. These towering pieces of foot-art don't come cheap, but the surge of instant glamour is worth every last penny. The small but beautifully formed Milan boutique also features the new line of ladylike but very modern leather bags to complete your well-heeled look. *jimmychoo.com*

Luxury *Amex/MC/V*

Via San Pietro all'Orto 17 **02 454 81770**
20121 Milan Mon-Sat 10-7

John Richmond

Milanese kids in their teens and 20s have adopted the blaring crystal-encrusted logo 'Rich' and wear it splayed across their bosoms and butts. They are not referring to their healthy bank balances (though you need them, to buy this brand), but paying homage to the English designer John Richmond. His stuff is hugely popular in the multibrand shops down by Porta Ticinese, but for the complete experience take a trip to his Via Verri shop. Over three floors you'll find everything from jackets with huge emblems splashed on the back to killer-heel shoes, big bouncy bags and a range of sunglasses, underwear and beachwear. Fancy a black T-shirt with silver-painted George Cross motifs, and multi-strapped sandals, all held together by safety-pins? There's also a selection of English and French magazines so that the multinational clientele who frequent this store can try out their language skills.

Expensive   *Amex/MC/V*

Via Verri (corner Via Bigli)   **02 760 28173**
20121 Milan   Mon 3-7:45, Tues-Sat 10-7:45

☆ Joost

The name may take its inspiration from German architect Joost Schmidt, teacher of the Bauhaus movement—but not everything is rigorously functional in this fabulous men's store. As well as the Joost range there's a revolving door of trendsetting labels—currently the popular G-Star denim collection, the individualist's favourite Michiko Koshino, plus shoes by Henderson and Buttero. There's also the full range of Acqua Di Genova cologne, body and bath creams and oils. You'll find it difficult not to confuse the super-cool assistants with the super-cool customers (hint: the customers are the ones with the girl/boyfriend or pooch attached). If in doubt, ask for the fabulous Fabrizio. You can't miss him: he'll be the hippest guy in the place. *joost.it*

Moderate to expensive   *Amex/MC/V*

Via Cesare Correnti 12   **02 720 14537**
20123 Milan   Mon 3-7, Tues-Sat 10-2, 3-7

☆ Just Cavalli

Imagine Kubrick's space ship from *2001—A Space Odyssey* crashing into the Amazon jungle and the two fusing together. It sounds crazy, but it's the closest way to describe this outrageous store. Huge tanks of tropical fish, walls of orchids and even a cloud-shaped elevator lined in white leather and mink are only the beginning. The animal prints and glitter we have come to adore in Cavalli's clothes peep out from the rails, and the good news is that the 'Just' in Just Cavalli means that this is his younger diffusion range, so a few zeros have been knocked off the price tags. And for time out after shopping, the store comes equipped with DJ and fully stocked bar which also serves light lunches.   *robertocavalli.it*

Expensive to luxury   *Amex/MC/V*

Via della Spiga 30   **02 763 16566**
20121 Milan   Mon-Sat 10-7

Kallisté—Un Dimanche à Venise

At first glance the shoes in this small shop look pretty ordinary, but look harder and you'll find shoes under the label Un Dimanche that deserve a try-on or two. Like all the brands in this shop, they're by the Italian producer Kallisté and are very nicely made indeed. Check out the wide range of strappy sandals in bright colours and metallic leathers with intricate woven insoles. Then slip into the comfortable flats in soft pastel leather that have natty Kallisté-made leather jackets to match. Prices stay relatively reasonable even for the glamorous stiletto sandals in bright colour combos.

Moderate   *Amex/MC/V*

Corso Matteotti 22   **02 763 17447**
20121 Milan   Mon 3-7, Tues-Sat 10-7

Kenzo

You'll still find the original Kenzo Asian folk style at this Japanese-Parisian label, though the current womenswear designer—Sardinian Antonio Marras—has brought a wider range of cultural influences to the brand. Strong in colour and pattern, the collections include the first, more sophisticated lines, plus the younger, funkier lines, Jungle for Women and Kenzo K for men. Check out the latest looks—most pieces for 2006 are made up of bright florals, paisleys or tartans going right down to the minutest geometric prints. The joy of Kenzo is that it's often all thrown together in one look, with a good helping of pompoms, fur collars and tassels on the side. Ask for Matteo, who'll give you excellent advice on all the ranges.   *kenzo.fr*

Expensive to luxury   *Amex/MC/V*

Via Sant' Andrea 11   **02 760 20929**
20121 Milan   Mon 3-7:30, Tues-Sat 10-7:30

Killah

Like many of the streetwear brands on this buzzing street, Killah opened its doors here in March 2004. Part of the same group as Miss Sixty and Energie, this is the company's first store in Italy, selling disposable fashion at friendly prices. The label's look is a smart take on the Fifties—seen in everything from the pink Chevy in the window to the bright interior with the music pumping out from the open doors. Inside, bright, loud colours and prints with bold messages blaze across everything from T-shirts and sexy, figure-hugging dresses to vests, bags and belts. There's a denim line with jeans in a variety of styles and cuts, fitted jackets and short, short skirts. Trainers and strappy sandals complete the look. The sales team always look incredibly busy but they will stop to help and advise.   *killah.it*

Affordable   *Amex/MC/V*

Corso di Porta Ticinese 58-60   **02 894 20577**
20123 Milan   Mon 3:30-7:30, Tues-Sat 10:30-7:30

Kristina Ti

Turin-based designer Cristina Tardito's soft approach to lingerie design has helped her earn the nickname 'designer of the invisible'. Invisible, because of the careful attention she pays to even the smallest details, and because her clothing is often hidden under other layers. Nowadays, she also applies her delicate touch to the creation of ready-to-wear, which you'll find hanging from the rails alongside her better-known lingerie line in this tiny boutique. And she is less invisible than before: many of the fresh, feminine styles she comes up with now are in transparent layers, so you can see that all-important lingerie underneath. The shop also showcases her swimwear and a new accessories line including belts and French handbags. *kristinati.it*

Expensive	*Amex/MC/V*
Via Solferino 18	**02 653 379**
20121 Milan	Mon 3-7, Tues-Sat 10-7

Krizia

Mariuccia Mandelli's style hasn't changed a huge amount since she founded her company almost 50 years ago. Though the Milan-based designer has updated regularly over the years, her collections still focus on soft, deconstructed day and eveningwear for women, such as a cream silk evening gown with low-cut back. Using natural materials—including mixtures of silk and cashmere—this is elegance at its best. These days the store also carries the label's less expensive diffusion lines—including Krizia Poi and Krizia Jeans with similar sleek styles and subtle colours. All of this is accompanied by accessories: bags, jewellery, shoes and perfume. The biggest news is that there's now a free café/bar for customers. If you need to unwind after too long in the changing-rooms, the bar—with its rows of cacti on shelves—is the perfect place to relax. *krizia.net*

Moderate to expensive	*Amex/MC/V*
Via della Spiga 23	**02 760 08429**
20121 Milan	Mon-Sat 10-7

☆ Laboratorio Italiano

Five well-heeled and well-groomed Milanese gentlemen got together to offer the wider public their own personal style: timeless elegance of the highest quality. Their store is principally a sartoria, i.e. a bespoke tailor. A made-to-measure suit needs two to three fittings and about a month to complete. Il Laboratorio also offers other men's necessities, such as ties, socks and shirts, also made-to-measure. The shop is just a stone's throw from the bustle of Via Montenapolenone, but its sea-grass floors, taffeta-lined walls and conservatory make it a wonderful refuge of sophistication with a cosy clublike atmosphere. The look is conservative but with a touch of the dandy in some of the colour waves.

Expensive to luxury	*Amex/MC/V*
Via Borgonuovo 12	**02 290 60953**
20121 Milan	Mon-Fri 9-1, 2-7

Laltramoda

This Roman label hit the jackpot with its first store 11 years ago and continues to produce clothes that are good quality, well cut, sensibly priced and with a fashion edge. The whole idea back then was to produce several collections a season, so they could keep abreast with fashion's inconstant trends. This they have continued to do, and with three stores in Milan they are well established with the sassy girl-about-town set. The simply decorated store in Corso Venezia is the best, though with just one piece on the rails from each collection you have to ask the ever-helpful assistants for your size—which can be a little intimidating if you happen to be over British size 8. Recently, these reverentially treated garments have included floaty chiffon dresses and blouses in bright bold floral prints, ethnic embroidered tops and sexy tailored suits in delicate silks.   *laltramoda.it*

Affordable to moderate   *Amex/MC/V*

Corso Venezia 5   **02 760 21117**
20121 Milan   Mon 3-7, Tues-Sat 10-7

Corso Vercelli 20   **02 469 9248**
20145 Milan   Mon 3:30-7:30, Tues-Sat 10-2, 3:30-7:30

Via Solferino 2   **02 653 362**
20121 Milan   Mon 3-7, Tues-Fri 10-7, Sat 10-1, 3-7

La Perla   ♀

Spending so much money on something that few people are ever likely to catch more than a fleeting glimpse of may seem like a contradiction to many women, especially if their mind-set happens to be Anglo. But style-conscious Italian females know that their look won't convince unless they're kitted out in the very best from top to toe—including all the barely visible bits in between. Take a leaf out of their book, and head to this haven of luxury Italian lingerie, offering everything from embroidered lace bustiers and seamless bias-cut full-length nightgowns in pure white, to the teensiest of sex-kitten panties in strawberry pink. If you still can't persuade yourself to take the plunge, go for the much more visible ranges of swimwear, ready-to-wear or shoes, from delicately frosted satin slippers to sashaying mules. La Perla's ready-to-wear designer is Alessandro Dell'Aqua and his collection for 2006 is delicate, with ultra-feminine micro-pleated and corseted chiffon dresses. Many are designed with lingerie peeping through, but it all looks sultry rather than slutty. Finally, to ensure your total irresistibility, try the new Shiny Creation and Blu perfumes available in 50ml or 100ml sprays. Who knows what might happen later on?   *laperla.com*

Expensive to luxury   *Amex/MC/V*

Via Montenapoleone 1   **02 760 00460**
20121 Milan   Mon 3-7, Tues-Sat 10-7

Corso Vercelli 35   **02 498 7770**
20144 Milan   Mon 3:30-7:30, Tues-Sat 10-7:30

La Rinascente   ♂♀♂

Unlike branches in other cities, Milan's La Rinascente is a major fashion destination, packed with mid and upper-range brands for adults and children. That's as it should be at this city institution, which has been at this address, right opposite the Duomo, since 1865. As in every self-respecting department store, the ground floor is mostly filled with cosmetics, but head up the escalators to the mezzanine and you'll soon be rhapsodising over teensy undies from labels like La Perla and D&G. The mezzanine also carries 'alternative toiletries', from labels like Lush, Nuxe and Perlier. The higher floors are mostly dedicated to clothing for the entire family by everyone from Nike and Adidas to Dockers and Diesel, Missoni and Moschino. At the top you'll find an Estée Lauder spa, an Aldo Coppola hairdressing salon and a café with a view of the Duomo's spikes and gargoyles, so close you could almost tickle their chins. The biggest news is the addition of linked passageways on the second and fourth floors to La Rinascente's sister store, the teenage trendoids' favourite, Jam. Spread over two floors are 75 brands, including Diesel, Calvin Klein, Miss Sixty, Guess, French Connection, Levi's, Replay and the Italian retro label Docks Dora. Whoever said that Italy's department stores were stuck in their ways? *rinascente.it*

Affordable to luxury   *Amex/MC/V*

Via Santa Radegonda 3   **02 885 21**
20121 Milan   Mon-Sat 9-10, Sun 10-8

L'Armadio di Laura

Laura has been in the fashion business longer than most of us have been alive. She was the first signora to set up a secondhand shop in Milan, much to the horror of the by-the-book fashionistas at the time. Since then attitudes concerned 'used' clothing have relaxed and Milan does have its vintage community, in which Laura and her courtyard boutique flourish. Her take on the vintage phenomenon, however, is extremely broad and encompasses the big business of recent designer good at heavy discounts. With last season's Prada and Dolce & Gabbana at 50% off, Laura's closet is like one big outlet store. But you'll also find thrift variety (soccer shirts and beat-up cords) as well as more classic vintage items like beaded dresses from the Forties.

Moderate   *MC/V*

Via Voghera 25   **02 836 0606**
20125 Milan   Tues-Sat 10-6

Larusmiani

Smart city gents head to this newly revamped store for sportswear, casual cotton classics, linen and wool fabrics all manufactured and tightly quality-controlled by textile manufacturers Larusmiani. It's the ideal place to go shopping on a very hot day. Inside, a cascading waterfall flows from the ground floor to the basement, offsetting the natural dark wood and cool cream marble of the walls and fittings. Although we don't advise your diving under it, just looking at this water feature is guaranteed to make the most exhausted shopper feel refreshed. Once you're in the mood, work your way through the racks of well-styled clothes—from smart tailored pinstriped business suits to crumpled linen co-ordinates. You'll also find toning knitwear and shirts in pastel shades, dark tan leather gloves, shoes and all the accessories a guy about town could ever need. *larusmiani.it*

Expensive to luxury   *Amex/MC/V*

Via Montenapoleone 7   **02 760 20470**
20121 Milan   Mon-Sat 10-7:30, Sun 10:30-1:45, 2:45-7

Laura Biagiotti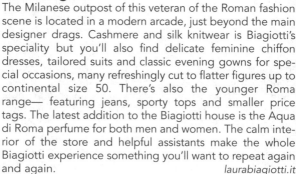

The Milanese outpost of this veteran of the Roman fashion scene is located in a modern arcade, just beyond the main designer drags. Cashmere and silk knitwear is Biagiotti's speciality but you'll also find delicate feminine chiffon dresses, tailored suits and classic evening gowns for special occasions, many refreshingly cut to flatter figures up to continental size 50. There's also the younger Roma range— featuring jeans, sporty tops and smaller price tags. The latest addition to the Biagiotti house is the Aqua di Roma perfume for both men and women. The calm interior of the store and helpful assistants make the whole Biagiotti experience something you'll want to repeat again and again. *laurabiagiotti.it*

Expensive   *Amex/MC/V*

Via Borgospesso 19   **02 799 659**
20121 Milan   Mon 3-7, Tues-Sat 10-1:30, 2:30-7

Laura Urbinati

Just off the buzzy Corso di Porta Ticinese, this small elegant shop looks out onto a small tree-lined square packed with people taking a shopping break or enjoying an ice-cream from the gelateria across the street. With only two other stores (in Rome and Los Angeles) it offers contemporary feminine pieces which your friends back home are unlikely to have. Most of the customers are classy Italian women who come here for the delicate flower-patterned dresses and skirts and trousers in bright colours. There are also bright patterned knits, tees in scrummy colours and cute swimwear—just the thing for cocktails in Capri. To complete your outfit, there's a small selection of bags in all shapes and colours, plus sunglasses and shoes by Rose's Roses and Miki Thumb; in between, there are a few pieces by Martin Margiela and Antik Batik. The cheerful staff are helpful and not pushy. But alas, sizes only go up to 44. *lauraurbinati.com*

Expensive   *Amex/MC/V*

Piazza Sant'Eustorgio 6   **02 836 0411**
20122 Milan   Mon 3:30-7:30
                            Tues-Sat 9:30-1:30, 3:30-7:30

☆ La Vetrina di Beryl

The store may not look much from the outside, but when you look into this window you are gazing on the hottest shoe kingdom in Milan. Siblings Barbara Beryl and Norman Villa have presided here for more than 20 years and they have few challengers. Their cleverly balanced stock features a mix of established names, lesser-known brands and emerging designers—many of whom they also represent as agents. This is the place for the latest footwear candy from Miu Miu, Costume National, Christian Lacroix, Marc Jacobs, Amaterasu, Cazabat, United Nude, Elman, Hinfray, L'Autre Chose, Ras, Y3…plus hard-to-find, handmade paint-splattered Granny boots by Paul Harnden. For men there is a small range of casual shoes from some of the same names. Barbara also designs her own moderately priced footwear and clothes under the label Ordinary People. From the footwear store, walk into the duo's clothing boutique stocking men's and women's ready-to-wear by offbeat labels like Coast and Webber and Yanuk (jeans). There's not a well-pressed Milanese suit in the house—instead you'll find crumpled linen shirts, crushed velvet coats, jackets and skirts, ethnic prints and embroidered fabrics and customized military jackets, all accessorized with ethnic bags and jewellery.

Moderate to luxury   *Amex/MC/V*

Via Statuto 4   **02 654 278**
20121 Milan   Mon 3-7:30, Tues-Sat 10:30-7:30

Les Chaussures Mon Amour

Open since September 2003, this raspberry and bubblegum-pink store is where all the local girls stock up on the latest shoe styles at prices that won't max out the parents' credit cards. Les Chaussures' funky own-brand designs, made in the nearby footwear-making town of Vigevano, are the best bargains. You'll find ice-cream-coloured Robin Hood boots, sparkly glitter flats and bright ballerinas. There is also a selection from Fornarina and Irregular Choice. Accessories include some vintage Sixties jewellery and bags from D-Squared and hip Milanese label Frank Morello.

Moderate to expensive   *Amex/MC/V*

Via Cherubini 3   **02 480 00535**
20144 Milan   Mon 3-8, Tues-Sat 10:30-8

Les Copains

On the upcoming Via Manzoni, this futuristic store beckons you in with multi-toned wood-panelled walls and misty Perspex and chrome fittings. Inside, you'll find that the Italian brand's designs are classic with a twist rather than avant-garde. Even the fashion-forward Trend Les Copains line—by hot Sardinian designer Antonio Marras—is more cocktails-on-a-yacht than Costa Smeralda club, though there are a few vampy evening options along the racks. But the best thing here is the sexy knitwear, made from beautiful wools, cashmeres and silk blends. Undoubtedly, you'll walk away with a great V-neck something, whether it's in spider's-web weight silk or a chunky fabric rag knit. For guys, the offering is less fashion-oriented, but a crisp polo or a wool sweater can't be beat. There is a slight lack of coherence, but the very fair prices make small sins forgivable.

Expensive   *Amex/MC/V*

Via Manzoni 21   **02 720 80092**
20121 Milan   Mon 3-7, Tues-Sat 10-2, 3-7

☆ Le Solferine/Le Vintage

Run by sisters Silvia and Paola Bertolaya, this funky little shoe store in the Brera area is one of the best footwear boutiques in Milan. You'll find armchairs shaped like jester caps by Edra, flaking gold-leaf lights, and a selection of shoes that would have had Carrie from *Sex and the City* calculating just how many pairs she could carry home. Towering stilettos, simple slingbacks, funky sandals and cool boots crowd the window and the display shelves, with ultra-feminine looks by Emilio Pucci, Rene Caovilla, Kate Miller and Gianni Barbato prominently on display. Recently, the sisters have begun designing their own simply styled lines; check out Silvia's round-toed courts, and Paola's leather clothes—like silver, ruched shirts—all at prices you can afford. If you're looking for something really special, ask to see the limited-edition evening shoes made from vintage fabrics by Roman designer Angelica Discacciati for her own label ADD. And finally, the sisters sell last season's stock alongside vintage clothes at Le Vintage in the upcoming Isola area…it's well worth the trip.

Moderate to luxury   *Amex/MC/V*

Via Solferino 2   **02 655 5352**
20121 Milan   Mon 11-1, 3-8, Tues-Sat 10-8

Le Vintage

Via Garigliano 4   **02 693 11885**
20159 Milan   Mon 3-8, Tues-Fri 11-2, 3-8
          Sat 11-1:30, 2:30-6:30, Sun 1-7

☆ Les Tropeziennes

Shoe designer Tania Ercoli is rarely seen in anything less than an 8cm heel—and her own footwear label, Les Tropeziennes, displays her ultra-feminine vision of what a woman looks best in. This boudoir-like store is the brand's first own-brand store on the planet. Inside, gold strappy sandals perch on pink satin cushions, while Swarovski-encrusted heels swirl on a revolving plinth alongside sprays of tropical flowers (also on sale). The decor has a touch of Marilyn Monroe-style glamour with its pink carpets, fabulous Murano glass chandeliers, mirrors designed by Philippe Starck, pink and gold shoe boxes, and private fitting-room complete with chaise longue. Ercoli has also designed a range of bags and lingerie, to complement the shoes.   *lestropeziennes.it*

Luxury   *Amex/MC/V*

Corso di Porta Ticinese 107   **02 894 23109**
Milan 20123   Mon 3-7, Tues-Sat 10:30-7:30

Lorella Braglia

This store on the corner of Via Solferino and Via Ancona is a haven of feminine chic. Soft, subtle touches and the occasional departure from standard tailoring render these easy-to-wear pieces unique. Braglia's clothing is made by Dielle, a knitwear company she founded in the mid-Eighties before starting to design her own ready-to-wear. Recent collections have focused on floaty, romantic skirts and dresses in soft silk or chiffon with drapes, ruffles and pleats. She teams these with tailored jackets that have unexpected details like smocked backs or pleated-elbow sleeves. Rust red, burnt orange and tan are combined with cream and beige, while fabrics have abstract shapes printed over stripes to give even the simplest pair of trousers an original twist. *lorellabraglia.com*

Moderate to expensive *Amex/MC/V*

Via Solferino (corner Via Ancona) **02 290 14514**
20121 Milan Mon 3-7, Tues-Sat 10-2, 3-7

Lorenzo Banfi

You know a store means to stay exclusive when the only way to get in is by ringing a bell. And with clients like Sylvester Stallone, Harrison Ford, Eddie Murphy and Tom Cruise on this shoemaker's roster, maybe the apparent pretension is justified. Milan's top footballers also flock to this store, now the only Banfi store still trading in Milan. With a wide range of tasselled loafers, two-tone lace-ups and classic ankle boots to choose from, it's easy to see why A-listers like it, though it's certainly not innovation that draws them in. Banfi also sells stylish briefcases and wallets and some ultra-traditional women's loafers, leather jackets and bags. *lorenzobanfi.com*

Expensive to luxury *Amex/MC/V*

Via Sant'Andrea 1 **02 760 01529**
20121 Milan Mon 3-7, Tues-Sat 10-2, 3-7

Loro Piana

Breathe in deep as you enter this three-floor temple to all things soft and cuddly—even the air has a cashmerey feel. The women's silk scarves in every imaginable colour (cashmere knitwear that co-ordinates with luxurious trousers), plus skirts, blouses and jackets crafted in top-notch fabrics all speak of a padded world with no worries except, maybe, how the stock market is going to turn. Men will also find classic suits in cashmere and more casual linen shirts and trousers. The family-owned Piedmontese company makes all its clothes from the finest natural materials and this is reflected in the wooden flooring and natural cream carpets at the Milan store. If you venture down to the basement, there's a small range of children's clothes for the next generation of Loro Piana fans.

Luxury *Amex/MC/V*

Via Montenapoleone 27 **02 777 2901**
20121 Milan Mon-Sat 10-7

☆ Louis Vuitton

Perhaps it's their Gallic charm, or their long years of experience (Louis Vuitton founded his company in the 1840s), but Louis Vuitton's stores are often as stylish as their beautiful goods, far outshining those of rivals. Like the other stores in Italy, the latest Milan boutique in the Galleria Vittorio Emanuele does not disappoint. Inside, pillars, arches and a glass dome add a touch of aristocratic class to the spacious main floor. Sunlight glances off a huge display of trunks and suitcases along the whole of the back wall, beckoning you inside. Rows of counters packed with top-notch accessories and stationery line each side of the room. The LV-monogrammed bags are constantly morphing—this season there is plenty of fluorescence and denim, while the classic brown/beige has got a cherry/LV combo. And there is a danger of being sidetracked to the accessories because Marc Jacobs, Louis Vuitton's ready-to-wear designer, creates delightful minxy collections on Fifties themes.   *vuitton.com*

Luxury   *Amex/MC/V*

Via Montenapoleone 2   **02 777 1711**
20121 Milan   Mon-Sat 9:30-7:30, Sun 11-7:30

Galleria Vittorio Emanuele II   **02 721 47011**
20121 Milan   (opening hours as above)

Love Therapy (by Elio Fiorucci)

Die-hard Fiorucci fans have gone into mourning. Forced to move out of its old digs by the Swedish H&M, the Milan outlet for the iconic brand is a sad vestige of its former self. Now housed in a teensy two-story boutique around the corner from its previous spacious location, the store continues to stock a nifty (though limited) selection of kitsch gifts. You'll find soaps, candles, books, hair accessories—many modelled in pink plastic—and angels still abound on T-shirts and notepads. The children's clothing is particularly cute, if a bit overpriced, and there are jeans and skirts for teenyboppers. If you are looking for a memento of Milan as classic as a panetone or a Prada key ring, a Fiorucci T-shirt should be on your list. They come in cute baby blue and pink tin boxes, and are printed with graphics as famous at the Fiorucci name itself.   *eliofiorucci.it*

Moderate   *Amex/MC/V*

Corso Europa 1   **02 760 91237**
20122 Milan   Mon 12-8, Tues-Sat 10-8, Sun 1-8

Luciano Barbera

If you're determined to be the chicest golfer on the course, this is the place to come. Company founder Carlo Barbera was passionate about golf and his influence remains to this day: the cavernous store, opened in September 2003, has a whole area for smart golfing clothes. Luciano Barbera is a family-run business and still produces all its own fabric—so your chic new outfit will feel as good as it looks. But avowed golf-haters will find something here too: Barbera does classic and formal wear for men and women aged 30 and up, from country chic to day and nightwear for urbanites.   *lucianobarbera.it*

Expensive   *Amex/MC/V*
Via Santo Spirito 22   **02 760 08499**
20121 Milan   Mon 3-7, Tues-Sat 10-2, 3-7

Luisa Beccaria

Designer Luisa Beccaria would seem to lead a very charmed life indeed, retreating when she pleases from the hustle and bustle of Milan to her family's Sicilian estate. No wonder the clothing in this pretty little store reverberates with old-fashioned romanticism, from the exquisite tailleurs to the flowing dresses in delicate soft pink floral-print chiffons. While many of the styles look great on more mature figures, there are also some slightly more youthful lines, such as Fifties-style halterneck prom dresses in polka-dotted cream and shimmering shirts in petrol-blue silk. Beccaria also has a choice of bridal gowns and an adorable selection of classic children's clothes.   *luisabeccaria.it*

Expensive   *Amex/MC/V*
Via Formentini 1   **02 864 60018**
20121 Milan   Mon 3-7, Tues-Sat 10-7

Luisa Spagnoli

Along with Marina Rinaldi and Elena Mirò, this store offers some of the most stylish outfits for generously proportioned women. With Italian sizes from 40-52 (52 is equivalent to English 20 and American 22) there is no need to be frumpy in what granny used to wear. Spagnoli offers silk trouser suits, beaded tops, floaty dresses and accessories for work, weddings or special evenings out. Check the ornate balcony upstairs for a truly inspiring collection.

Moderate to expensive   *Amex/MC/V*
Corso Vittorio Emanuele II   **02 795 064**
20122 Milan   Mon-Sat 10-7:30, Sun 11-1, 3-7

Corso Buenos Aires 39   **02 295 37033**
20124 Milan   Mon 3-7:30, Tues-Sat 10-7:30

Malo

The tiny entrance gives little hint of the vast Aladdin's cave filled with leather and cashmere that lies beyond. Two floors filled with luscious goodies will have luxury lovers in raptures of delight. Also unexpected is the large rear window on the first floor, looking out over a Zen-pebbled roof terrace and tall trees: somehow, you don't expect to see so much greenery in the centre of Milan. But the window is functional as well as beautiful: the natural light shows the top-quality knitwear, casual trouser suits, beachwear, accessories and scarves at their very best. Finger one of the creamy sweaters, or the butter-soft leather jackets and you'll fall instantly in love. These days, though, there are some funkier, lower-priced items, too. Don't miss the Velvet bags with velvet-braided handles; some designs are exclusive to this store.   *malo.it*

Expensive to luxury   *Amex/MC/V*

Via della Spiga 7	**02 760 16109**
20121 Milan	Mon-Sat 10-7

Mandarina Duck

The innovative brand is almost as well known for its outré store designs as its punch-packing luggage—though when we last checked, the Milan stores were still lagging behind. Still, the white, sporty style of the Corso Europa store forms an undistracting backdrop for the 'Duck's' futuristic suitcases, rucksacks, briefcases, messenger bags and wallets—all in soft leather and durable high-tech fabrics. They also have sportswear and casualwear for men and women, much of it in the same high-tech fabrics.   *mandarinaduck.com*

Moderate   *Amex/MC/V*

Galleria San Carlo (Corso Europa)	**02 782 210**
20122 Milan	Mon-Sat 10-7:30
Via Orefici 10	**02 864 62198**
20121 Milan	(opening hours as above)
Corso Buenos Aires 3	**02 295 30520**
20124 Milan	(opening hours as above)
Corso Vercelli 27	**02 480 07264**
20144 Milan	Mon 3-7:30, Tues-Sat 10-7:30

Mango

This recently opened store is yet another outpost for the sassy Spanish label—though you might think you've discovered a new Metro stop in bustling Via Torino as you enter the store. The cavernous entrance and wide black marble steps sweep down to the basement, while black Perspex walls give the boutique a real underground feel. Add to that the rush of Mango commuters—all buzzing with excitement and energy—and you'll find yourself looking round for the platform where your train draws in. But no, the real reason why all these people are swarming in are the fabulous products at equally fabulous prices. It's all a bit of a novelty for the Milanese, who had never discovered the beauty of the bargain high-street chain until Mango's rival Zara moved in only three years ago. This store has everything you'd expect to find in any Mango, with its signature bright T-shirts, crotch-gripping cotton trousers, short short skirts and MNG bags. If you don't mind looking like a billboard, pick up a Mango Addict T-shirt: they come in every colour under the sun.   *mango.es*

Affordable   *Amex/MC/V*

Via Torino 21	**02 869 90288**
20123 Milan	Mon 2-7:30, Tues-Sat 10-7:30
	Sun 2:30-7:30

☆ Mariella Burani

Women who crave the seductive glamour of historic Hollywood will find plenty to please them here. Burani's designs include romantic feminine dresses in silk, trimmed with antique lace and sequins in soft brown and dusty pinks. But she also knows how to do smart—with handkerchief-cut skirts, tailored jackets, Fifties-style dresses in bright, bold jazz prints, metallic leather studded shoes and bags. In Milan to shop for your Big Day? Then you really should head upstairs to check out the designer's very special collection of evening and bridal wear. *mariellaburani.it*

Expensive *Amex/MC/V*

Via Montenapoleone 3   **02 760 03382**
20121 Milan   Mon 3-7, Tues-Sat 10-7

Marilena

The daughter of the luxury Vergelio group, these stores are the place to head when you're sick and tired of dropping shedloads of dosh at Prada and Gucci. Few places make a better stab at offering this wide a range of up-to-the-minute shoes at prices that barely cause your bank balance to blip. For an idea of what's on offer, browse the corridor windows of the Vittorio Emanuele flagship. You won't be alone: this store manages to cater to women of all ages and styles, drawing them in with high-quality, totally modern looks that have enough personality not to be labelled knock-offs. In the basement you can see the entire collection, and will soon be trying on everything from strappy stilettos to knee-high boots.

Moderate *Amex/MC/V*

Corso Vittorio Emanuele II 15   **02 760 00665**
20122 Milan   Mon 3:30-7:30, Tues-Sat 10-7:30

Via Torino 13   **02 864 60732**
20123 Milan   Mon 3-7:30, Tues-Sat 10-7:30

Corso Buenos Aires 25   **02 201 251**
20124 Milan   (opening hours as above)

Marina Rinaldi

'Style is not a size…it's an attitude,' scream the clothes at Marina Rinaldi—and don't we wish that more clothing manufacturers would follow their lead? Part of the MaxMara empire, the brand's three Milan stores cater for those who need more breathing room than most Italian fashion affords, with sizes starting at an American 12. The aesthetic is mostly classic: suits, knits, and tailored basics for day, with some bolder bits for the evening and a sporty selection of casualwear—appealing to a demographic that is typically 30 plus. The biggest store (all three floors of it) is on the corner of Galleria Passarella (entrance on Corso Vittorio Emanuele). Start with the sporty and classic range on the ground floor, then take the stairs to the eveningwear department where you are bound to find that sophisticated black party dress you've been looking for. Pretty shoes and handbags are also available to give your outfit some edge.

Moderate *Amex/MC/V*

Corso Vittorio Emanuele   **02 782 065**
(corner Galleria Passarella)   Daily 10-7:30
20122 Milan

Corso Buenos Aires 77	**02 669 2691**
20124 Milan	Mon 3:30-7:30
	Tues-Sat 10-2, 3:30-7:30
Corso Vercelli 3	**02 481 00433**
20144 Milan	Mon 3:30-7:30
	Tues-Sat 10-7:30

Marisa

Along with Rosi Biffi, Gio Moretti and Pupi Solari, Marisa Lombardi is one of the longest-reigning dames of Milanese retail. But you won't find off-the-wall experimental designs in her boutique—though she maintains a healthy roster of top designers, she's edited out all the absurd skirt lengths and skin-tight ensembles that are best left to young things. The main store at 10/A has selections from Alexander McQueen, Balenciaga, Rochas, Pleats Please by Issey Miyake and Comme des Garçons. There are also evening-wear ranges from Escada and Alessandro dell' Acqua with fabulous evening shoes from American designer Stuart Weitzman. The della Spiga boutique holds the casual/sporty ranges…jeans, T-shirts and the like; while Via Sant'Andrea 1 specialises in Zoran, Sonia Rykiel, Cividini and Paco Rabanne.

Luxury	*Amex/MC/V*
Via Sant'Andrea 10/A	**02 760 00905**
20121 Milan	Mon 3-7, Tues-Sat 10-1:30, 3-7
Via Sant'Andrea 1	**02 760 01416**
20121 Milan	(opening hours as above)
Via della Spiga 52	**02 760 02082**
20121 Milan	(opening hours as above)

☆ Marni

Before you even think of setting foot inside this store, stand back and admire the space. Designed by architects Future Systems, this space-age boutique has one of the funkiest interiors in Milan. With its pink colouring and the clothes suspended—seemingly at random—from curved steel rails, the shop looks more like a contemporary art gallery than a fashion shop. By contrast, the clothes have a retro bohemi-an feel—but look closer at the floaty floral dresses and bal-looning chiffon skirts and you'll see clever cuts and modern fabrics and prints. Consuelo Castiglioni's inspirational designs have a following of ultra-hip devotees, and prom-ise you will never be missed in a crowd.

Expensive to luxury	*Amex/MC/V*
Via Sant'Andrea 14	**02 763 17327**
20121 Milan	Mon-Sat 10-7

Martin Luciano

If you're into military styling, vintage or modern, take a stroll down one of Milan's canals in the Naviglio district to this warehouse filled with original military vintage clobber from the Italian, American and German armed forces. The giant space offers wall-to-wall stalls of flight suits, bomber jackets, trench coats, padded sweaters—some battered and abused, other hauled out of storage in spanking new condition. Best is the large variety of fatigues and cargoes. There's enough here to put an entire brigade in the trenches—or send a fashion-hungry pack off in ruggedly authentic style. Access to the warehouse is through the shop on the right which carries a wide range of new and used jeans by Levi's and Wrangler.

Affordable	*Amex/MC/V*
Alazaia Naviglio Grande 58	**02 581 01173**
20143 Milan	Tues-Sat 9-12:30, 3-7:30

Martino Midali

Milanese designer Martino Midali is best known for his stylish and affordable knits. You'll find well-constructed pieces like cross-over cardigans in dark tones from black to burgundy—all at reasonable prices. He also conjures up tailored and casual clothing under the Midali Toujours label—which offers everything from printed vests which are then sprinkled with glitter to tailored cotton jackets emblazoned with bold number motifs in black and white. On a recent visit we also spotted wacky chiffon skirts covered in tiny elastic bands. More generously proportioned women may strike it lucky here: sizes go up to continental 48. The Porta Ticinese store moved to a smaller boutique across the street last year, but still contains a wide selection from the range.

Moderate	*Amex/MC/V*
Corso di Porta Ticinese 87	**02 894 06830**
20123 Milan	Mon 3-7:30, Tues-Sat 10-7:30
Via Ponte Vetero 9	**02 864 62707**
20121 Milan	Mon 3-7:30, Tues-Sat 10-2, 3-7:30
Via Marghera 22	**02 469 5191**
20149 Milan	(opening hours as above)
Via Mercato 6	**02 801 295**
20121 Milan	(opening hours as above)

Mauro

There's hardly room to swing a stiletto in this recently opened, tiny shoe shop at busy times. All the styles are out on show, on tables and shelves and in every nook and cranny—while floor-to-ceiling piles of boxes use up any spare corners. Part of the same family who run the successful Vanilla boutique over the road, Mauro Leone's secret is his ability to create funky, up-to-the-minute styles at affordable prices. You'll find everything here from ballerinas in funky shades of pink, blue and apple to killer stilettos and suede pixie boots. If you do manage to sit down, make sure you don't get up again until you're really ready—you're sure to lose that seat to the next barganista in the queue.

Affordable to moderate	*Amex/MC/V*
Corso di Porta Ticinese 60	**02 894 29167**
20123 Milan	Mon 3-7:30, Tues-Sat 10-7:30

Max & Co

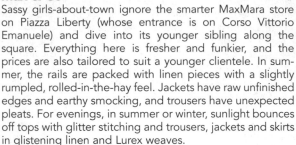

Sassy girls-about-town ignore the smarter MaxMara store on Piazza Liberty (whose entrance is on Corso Vittorio Emanuele) and dive into its younger sibling along the square. Everything here is fresher and funkier, and the prices are also tailored to suit a younger clientele. In summer, the rails are packed with linen pieces with a slightly rumpled, rolled-in-the-hay feel. Jackets have raw unfinished edges and earthy smocking, and trousers have unexpected pleats. For evenings, in summer or winter, sunlight bounces off tops with glitter stitching and trousers, jackets and skirts in glistening linen and Lurex weaves.

Moderate   *Amex/MC/V*

Piazzale Liberty 4   **02 780 433**
20121 Milan   Mon-Sat 10-7:30, Sun 10:30-2, 3-7:30

Via Dante 7   **02 861 504**
20121 Milan   Mon 3:30-7:30, Tues-Sat 10-7:30

MaxMara

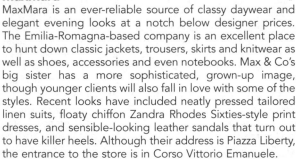

MaxMara is an ever-reliable source of classy daywear and elegant evening looks at a notch below designer prices. The Emilia-Romagna-based company is an excellent place to hunt down classic jackets, trousers, skirts and knitwear as well as shoes, accessories and even notebooks. Max & Co's big sister has a more sophisticated, grown-up image, though younger clients will also fall in love with some of the styles. Recent looks have included neatly pressed tailored linen suits, floaty chiffon Zandra Rhodes Sixties-style print dresses, and sensible-looking leather sandals that turn out to have killer heels. Although their address is Piazza Liberty, the entrance to the store is in Corso Vittorio Emanuele.

Moderate to expensive   *Amex/MC/V*

Piazza del Liberty 4   **02 760 08849**
20121 Milan   Mon-Sat 10-7:30, Sun 10:30-2, 3-7:30

Via Orefici 1   **02 890 13509**
20121 Milan   (opening hours as above)

Mazzini—Shop in Progress

A newcomer to Via della Spiga, Tuscany-based Mazzini sells some of the most affordable bags in the designer quad. Taking its inspiration from New York's Fifth Avenue in the Fifties, the 'Shop in Progress' currently features sketches on the wall that have something of the look of last year's Prada city prints. The bags are all cleverly designed to suit the needs of a busy 21st-century woman-about-town. If you're the type who's always rooting around for a ringing mobile, take a look at the unique big bag with inside straps. The straps have handy fasteners to keep your mobile, keys, mineral water, lipsticks etcetera in place, so you need never lose them again.   *mazzini.com*

Affordable to moderate   *Amex/MC/V*

Via della Spiga 52   **02 782 246**
20121 Milan   Mon 3-7, Tues-Sat 10-2, 3-7

Mila Schön

Yugoslavian aristocrats' daughter Mila Schön came to Italy as a child and fell in love with the world of haute couture. In particular she became a devotee of Dior and Balenciaga, and her label's clothes—currently designed by Marc Helmuth—still reflect her admiration for classic structures. As you push open the heavy glass doors and enter her spacious, uncluttered store, your eyes will be attracted by the carefully crafted suits, dresses and eveningwear displayed reverently around the room. Individual garments hang sparsely around the gallery-like store—each one deserving its individual space so that you can admire the work of a perfectionist. These days, Mila Schön goes for sophisticated chiffon dresses in bright bold prints and dramatic black crêpe eveningwear. For tailored daywear, head up the sweeping marble staircase to the first floor where, from among the pillars, you can also pick a sophisticated soft leather bag to complete your outfit.   *milaschon.com*

Expensive to luxury   *Amex/MC/V*
Via Manzoni 45   **02 653 354**
20131 Milan   Mon 3-7, Tues-Sat 10-2, 3-7

☆ Miss Ghinting

If you want to look like Marilyn Monroe—or like Olivia Newton-John before the makeover in *Grease*—head to this store. Owned by young boho chicks Elena Migliorati and Nicoletta Canu, Miss Ghinting is the best Fifties vintage store in town. Against walls papered with original Sixties Sanderson wallpaper, you'll find racks packed with swirling New Look skirts, boxy, tailored suits from Milan's best sartorie, and fitted evening dresses from the Sixties and Seventies by the likes of Pucci and Dior. Recent finds have included a black sleeveless satin-silk dress with a crimson flap detail by Milanese tailor Tezzoli-Cecchini, and a black and cream trouser suit by Dior. If you've always liked that Fifties vibe on the beach, Elena and Nicoletta have a trunk full of vintage bikinis and swimsuits tucked away: just ask. There are also racks and boxes stuffed with hats, bags, shoes and jewellery. But be warned: most pieces don't go beyond size 44.

Moderate to expensive   *Amex/MC/V*
Via Borsieri, opposite number 16   **02 668 7112**
20159 Milan   Tues-Sat 10-1, 3-7:30

Missoni

Think Italian knitwear and Missoni's colourful zigzags invariably come to mind. Ottavio and Rosita started the business in the late Fifties, and now daughter Angela heads the design team that has helped the zigzag to evolve. From fine cobweb scarves to dresses and many-coloured shirts, there's an endless choice in this brightly lit store by hot architect Matteo Thun, whose mirrors magnify the collection on and on and on. Missoni now extends beyond men's and womenswear to gorgeous beachwear, accessories and a home collection of cushions, crockery, glassware and throws. You'll find all of them here. *missoni.com*

Luxury *Amex/MC/V*

Via Sant'Andrea 2 **02 760 03555**
20121 Milan Mon 3-7, Tues-Sat 10-7

Miss Sixty 👤

With its acid-yellow plastic floor and walls covered in shag-pile carpet, Miss Sixty's new shop looks slightly out of place in sophisticated Via Montenapoleone. Still, it's a welcome change from the nondescript all-white stores that line much of the rest of the street. The fun, youthful clothes—and the reasonable prices—are other reasons why the weary high-fashion shopper will soon be sighing with relief. This is the place for minis or large full skirts in vivid Fifties-style prints, tight-fitting bodices and halterneck tops, jeans in every type of denim and bold floral acid house prints. There are also cheeky T-shirts and sexy dresses, accessorised with bright plastic handbags, and heavy plastic bangles. To complete your outfit, don't forget the new range of Miss Sixty shoes in vibrant colours and bold patterns. Understated it is not. *misssixty.com*

Moderate *Amex/MC/V*

Via Montenapoleone 27 **02 763 90698**
20121 Milan Mon-Sat 10-7:30, Sun 10-1, 2-7:30

Via Torino 10 **02 860 246**
20123 Milan Mon-Fri 10-7:30, Sat 9:30-8

Miu Miu 👤👤

By choosing a play on her own name—meaning 'meeow'—for her second, younger label, Miuccia Prada indicated that she meant to have fun. And fun she has had with this whimsical line, whose designs—from gold ra-ra skirts to jewelled platform sandals—are funkier and cheaper than the more serious bourgeois-ironic looks she dreams up for Miu Miu's big sister, Prada. At this large open-spaced shop with its white, silver and red interior, you'll find a pretty complete selection of pieces from her latest collection. The space stretches back to a small courtyard, which on sunny days brings a welcome breeze wafting through the store. There's a small selection of womenswear at the front, flanked by bags and shoes, while at the back are the main men's and women's collections, with yet more bags and shoes, and lingerie. The assistants wander back and forth dressed in variations of the latest collections and are only too happy to help you get the look too. *miumiu.it*

Expensive *Amex/MC/V*

Corso Venezia 3 **02 760 01799**
20121 Milan Mon-Sat 10-7:30

Mortarotti 👤

Arranged over three floors, this multi-brand clothing store offers designer selections for those who eschew the sexed-up, vampy looks that so often plague today's runways. From the outside the Montenapo store resembles a very chic townhouse; inside, you'll find clothing, shoes and accessories from Missoni, Hugo Boss, Roberto Cavalli and Sonia Rykiel that could happily hang in the closet of an elegant lady living in such a house. Colours are bright (but never brash) and subtle; cuts are of the type that women of all ages can wear. The comfy chairs, piles of magazines and friendly assistants make the whole experience very pleasant indeed. *mortarotti.com*

Expensive to luxury *Amex/MC/V*

Via Montenapoleone 24 **02 760 03839**
20121 Milan Mon 10:30-7:30, Tues-Sat 10-7:30

Corso Magenta 29 **02 864 52253**
20123 Milan Mon 3-7:30, Tues-Sat 10-7:30

Via Belfiore 6 **02 480 00021**
20145 Milan Mon 10:30-7:30, Tues-Sat 10-7:30

Moschino

It's worth pushing open the gold heart door handles of this Sant'Andrea store just to look at the witty interior decorations. As at the Rome store, you'll find a chandelier made of glass slippers, a sculptural wall constructed from dressmakers' pins and a children's version of The Emperor's New Clothes scribbled over the walls. The clothes and accessories are faithful to Franco Moschino's quirky spirit. Classic designs are given an irreverent twist with prints, beading and appliqués; fun, witty bags are modelled on cottages or jam jars. The Via Sant'Andrea store carries the women's first line, while round the corner in Via della Spiga you'll find the Cheap and Chic collection for men and women along with jeans, children's clothes and swimwear. As you leave don't forget to take a look at the latest window display—it's bound to make you smile. *moschino.it*

Luxury *Amex/MC/V*

Via Sant'Andrea 12 **02 760 00832**
20121 Milan Mon-Sat 10-7

Via della Spiga 30 **02 760 04320**
20121 Milan (opening hours as above)

Nadine

This friendly priced chain has everything you need to inject some colour into your life. You'll find bright abstract print jackets, sexy fitted dresses, full flowery skirts and whole basements full of accessories and gorgeous little shoes. The stores are favourites with style-savvy thirty-somethings who come for fashionable wardrobe staples. We suggest you join the crowd. *nadinefashiongroup.com*

Affordable to moderate *Amex/MC/V*

Corso Vittorio Emanuele II 34 **02 760 09028**
20122 Milan Mon-Sat 9:30-8, Sun 10-8

Corso Buenos Aires 38 **02 202 41642**
20124 Milan Mon-Sat 9:30-7:30

Via Dante 16	**02 869 15906**
20121 Milan	Mon 1-7:30, Tues-Sun 10-7:30
Corso Genova 1	**02 894 09421**
20123 Milan	Mon 1-7:30, Tues-Sat 9:30-7:30
Via Marghera 18	**02 480 05729**
20149 Milan	Mon 11-7:30, Tues-Sat 9:30-7:30

Naj-Oleari

Way back when, Naj-Oleari was a top brand name with its own stores dedicated to its earthy, feminine wares. We're not exactly sure what caused it to fall off the fashion radar, but this store in Via Brera has been transformed to sell a hodge-podge of clothing, accessories and novelty items, all in the brand's original bohemian spirit. On a recent visit, we found the boutique bursting with Indian leather sandals paired with flowing cotton trousers and fitted, cap-sleeved blouses in delicate floral prints in silk and cotton. It's also one of the few places in Milan where you can find the cute children's clothing from the French bohemian line Antik Batik, plus Simply Kids. An impossible-to-resist line of baby-wear in undyed, unbleached cotton and calico by Emilia will have you fantasising about which of your best friends might decide to have a baby soon. Continuing the bohemian ethos, half the store is now a herbalist's, with cosmetics and body products all made from natural ingredients such as flowers and fruit. *najoleari.com*

Moderate to expensive *Amex/MC/V*

Via Brera 8	**02 805 6790**
20121 Milan	Mon 3-8, Tues-Sat 10-8

Napapijri

Located on the same street as Armani, Les Copains and Mila Schön, this store—stocking garments for extreme sports—comes as something of a shock. These are the clothes that keep hot-looking geologists and nature-loving mountain men in stylish form for their treks across the Himalayas or their navigation through Alaskan waters. But Napapijri, whose name means 'arctic polar circle' and whose Norwegian flag logo is a symbol of the men who first took part in polar expeditions, doesn't dabble in fluffy fashion land. This is the real stuff—high-performance jackets, waterproof pants, snow-climbing boots and fleece apparel—and luckily it also happens to look great. Non-adventurous types need not fret—there is also a substantial collection of nylon jackets, cotton trousers, fleece vests and utilitarian duffels that will be perfect for a danger-free weekend outing. If you're planning your great escape, pick up a utility kit-bag big enough to take all you need for a year-long expedition.

Moderate to expensive *Amex/MC/V*

Via Manzoni 46	**02 782 413**
20121 Milan	Mon-Sat 10-7:30

Nara Camicie

If you're looking for an affordable white shirt with interesting tucks, pleats, smocking or embroidery—or a cotton shirt in a particular shade—the chances are you'll find it in the smart Via Montenapoleone branch of this popular chain. Fancy something a bit wilder? The store also stocks bright printed shirts and T-shirts with matching watches—which make great birthday gifts for have-it-all teenagers who, with any luck, won't have seen this one before. Guys aren't forgotten here either: a few classic men's shirts and ties can be found at the back of this very reasonably priced boutique. *naracamicie.com*

Affordable   *Amex/MC/V*

Via Montenapoleone 5	**02 799 622**
20121 Milan	Mon 11-7, Tues-Sat 10-7
Piazza Duomo 31	**02 805 2362**
20122 Milan	Mon 11-7:30, Tues-Sat 10-7:30
Corso Vittorio Emanuele 4	**02 864 61806**
20122 Milan	Mon 11-7:30, Tues-Sat 9:30-7:30

☆ Narciso Rodriguez

Rodriguez has been on the fashion radar for some time but is still best known for designing the late Carolyn Bessette's wedding dress. With a design education that includes stints at Calvin Klein, Cerruti and Loewe, he has cultivated a look that tends towards chic minimalism. In the taverna-like interior of his Milan store—complete with arched pillars, wooden stairs and exposed wood-beam ceiling—his fabulously cut and constructed clothes are displayed on dark wooden tables. But despite the publike setting, these clothes are more suited to sipping tea and nibbling at cucumber sandwiches than to swigging back pints of beer. Heavy linen suits and jackets with beautifully piped seams harmonise with delicate peach and cream silk blouses, while elegant dresses have matching shoes and bags. Colours are generally neutral and styles fashionably restrained. *narcisorodriguez.com*

Luxury   *Amex/MC/V*

Via Montenapoleone 21	**02 763 17072**
20121 Milan	Mon 3-7, Tues-Sat 10-7

Nero Giardini

The Marche-based producer opened its first store in Milan in 2003, and aren't your poor shopping-weary feet glad? Sink into the seats at this monochrome shop—with walls in black Perspex and padded white leather—and try on the shoes: most cradle your tootsies like new-born babes. Women will find trainers and low platform sandals, while men can choose between everything from smart business shoes to soft leather sandals perfect for the beach. Most are so neutral that they'll go with most outfits—and we guarantee you'll wear them into the ground. There's also a small selection of bags and belts in leather, snake or faux croc. Prices seem so low after the designer drags, that clients almost faint with the shock. *nerogiardini.it*

Affordable *Amex/MC/V*

Corso Venezia 9 **02 760 17351**
20121 Milan Mon 2-7, Tues-Sat 10-7

☆ No Season

Judging from this store's name, you'd think it didn't give a fig for fashion's fickle seasons but, in fact, it prides itself on only stocking the magazine editors' designers du jour. Though it's in a street full of hip teenage wannabes, you'll find only fully-fledged fashionistas here—and, as is only right and proper in a place that takes its fashion this seriously, brands change every season. Last time we browsed the labels, we spotted Marc Jacobs, Viktor and Rolf, John Richmond, Givenchy, Lanvin, Juicy Couture and Pucci hanging from the racks. They also love to pick up on the hottest emerging designers: this season, it's Maria Intsher, ex-assistant to McQueen, and new Italian label Golden Goose. Accessories include hats from Philip Treacy and Jas-M&B bags. Womenswear is on the ground floor, menswear in the basement; in the shop next door you'll find the footwear collections with the latest in trendy trainers and girly shoes. There's a range of lounge, house, nu-house and garage CDs and the latest designer coffee-table books. *noseason.com*

Expensive to luxury *Amex/MC/V*

Corso di Porta Ticinese 77 **02 894 23332**
20123 Milan Mon 3:30-7:30, Tues-Sat 10:30-1, 3-7:30

Onyx Fashion Store

Exasperated parents park their grumpy teenagers here for hours at a time, knowing they'll be entertained without too much damage to the credit cards. Mothers, incognito, sometimes pop in too. The emporium in the centre of Milan is a temple to streetwear the Italian way—which means with reasonable style. There's a great choice of casuals for young trendsetters, from jeans, coats and mini-minis to T-shirts with 'Onyx' emblazoned with sequins and glitter. There is even a section for the younger crowd aged 5-11. *onyx.it*

Affordable *Amex/MC/V*

Corso Vittorio Emanuele II 24 **02 760 16083**
20122 Milan Daily 10-8 (Sun 12-8)

☆ Outlet Matia's

If you're in Milan with limited time and money, make sure this outlet store is on your list. Conveniently located in the Brera area in an airy basement, its well-organised layout and fabulous prices make it a joy to shop. Everything is arranged by type and colour, so if you're desperate for a pair of red trousers or a white shirt, it shouldn't take too long to hunt one down. From simple jeans to glittery evening gowns, the discount is 50-70%. You'll find all the big names: jackets by Moschino, Valentino men's shirts at 50 euros, Gucci suits, Blumarine dresses and Prada skirts as well as little gems by Aspesi, Ralph Lauren, Moncler and Fay. To add a touch of refinement to your outfit, pick up a pair of shoes by Tod's or L'Autre Chose.

Moderate	*Amex/MC/V*
Piazza Mirabello 4	**02 626 94535**
20121 Milan	Mon 10-2, Tues-Sat 10-2, 3:30-7

Parisi

Over the road from Via Spiga is Parisi, the shop for brand-weary people. Just removing those Gs, Hs, Cs and LVs means an instant reduction of around 50%, even though the quality is still the same. The friendly and helpful owner Cinzia is always ready to assist you sifting thorough the familiar styles until you find what suits you. The shop also stocks a comprehensive range of Hervé Chapelier. These inexpensive, light and durable bags are easy to fold up and tuck away, and come in handy when you're guilty of over-shopping and extra luggage space is needed to lug your new purchases home.

Moderate	*Amex/MC/V*
Via Turati 3	**02 290 02229**
20121 Milan	Mon 3-7, Tues-Sat 10-7

Patrizia Pepe

Patrizia Pepe has one of the best pricing to quality to style ratios in Milan. The store has high ceilings and bright lighting, and the walls are signed over and over again by Patrizia (the label's name comes from one of its two Florentine creators, Patrizia Bambi and Claudio Orrea). A glass walkway leads to the stylish fitting rooms where you can try on whatever is hot for the season—a feminine dress, a sharp pair of trousers, the perfect belt, a slouchy sweater, the shortest of miniskirts. This is a great place to pick up a stylish suit for a wedding (a killer sexy dress can cost as little as 120 euros), though you may risk outshining the bride. Easy-to-wear pieces include thigh-length jackets with hipster belts and a distinctly Jackie O feel. If you've always had trouble finding trousers that flatter, try on a pair here. This company may specialise in knocking out speedy reinterpretations of the latest looks from the runways, but their cuts sometime out-do the labels they take their inspiration from.   *patriziapepe.com*

Moderate	*Amex/MC/V*
Via Manzoni 38	**02 7601 4477**
20121 Milan	Mon-Sat 10-7:30

Paul & Shark

Don't let the very English name throw you off the scent: this is an Italian label specialising in hi-tech sailing clothes tested by the company's own sailing team in the harshest of conditions. But anyone without sea-legs will also find plenty to please in this wood, white marble and blue lacquer store, including pullovers, windbreakers, jackets, turtlenecks, corduroy pants, ties, shoes, bags and umbrellas. An added bonus: many of the clothes come in large sizes to accommodate those burly sailors. *paulshark.it*

Moderate to expensive *Amex/MC/V*

Via Montenapoleone 15 **02 760 08565**
20121 Milan Mon 3-7, Tues-Sat 10-7:30

☆ Paul Smith

The British fashion knight has planted his feet firmly in Via Manzoni with this salmon-pink store designed by Sophie Hicks. You'll find men's, women's and children's clothes on the ground floor mixed with vintage finds, amusing toys, classic books and a small homeware collection. Upstairs is the main women's range—a cocktail of classic English tailoring and colourful kitsch—along with jewellery, shoes and bags. If you're only going to invest in a single item, make it one of Sir Paul's bestselling, colourful stripey shirts. *paulsmith.co.uk*

Expensive to luxury *Amex/MC/V*

Via Manzoni 30 **02 763 19181**
20121 Milan Mon-Sat 10-7

P-Box

It's well worth braving the heavy traffic on Via Manzoni to experience this amazing emporium of shoes and bags created by Italian clothing manufacturer Aeffe and produced by legendary leathergoods maker Pollini. Besides Pollini's impeccably crafted, classic pumps you'll get a flirty dose of Alberta Ferretti and Philosophy's strappy sandals, an irreverent kick from Moschino's creative designs and plenty of sexy, mile-high slingbacks by Narciso Rodriguez, the new poster boy of minimalism. High-end product placed sparsely around the dark room creates a moody, artistic ambience that makes dropping piles of cash a calming, almost Zen-like experience.

Expensive to luxury *Amex/MC/V*

Via Manzoni 13 **02 890 13000**
20121 Milan Mon 3:30-7:30, Tues-Sat 10-2, 3:30-7:30

Via Pontaccio 19 **02 864 64991**
20121 Milan (opening hours as above)

Peter Pan

The walls of this inviting children's shoe emporium are covered in phrases about Neverland and boys (and girls) who would not grow up. The store is every mother's dream, with footwear for every occasion. Two-tone Mary Janes, ballerinas in the palest of pinks and robin's-egg-blue, rosy Pumas with a fuchsia swirl, lavender lace-up Hogans, and Giesswein slip-on cotton slippers are just the beginning. Down below are shelves dotted with tiny trainers by Tod's,

Hogan, Puma, Adidas and Birkenstock, alongside impeccable classics from Eureka, Galluci, Equerry, Mirella and Start-Rite. And the best news is that many models are available in sizes up to 39 or 41—for sports shoes—so that Mums can match their offspring. To make sure legs look really stylish, Peter Pan also sells Gallo socks in gorgeous stripes and solids. Besides footwear there is a small selection of seasonal clothes: brightly coloured knit hats and scarves, and raincoats for example. The service is very personal and attentive: shoes are gift-wrapped and younger customers always receive a candy treat.

Moderate to expensive   *Amex/MC/V*

Via Mascheroni 12   **02 480 16205**
20145 Milan   Mon 3-7, Tues-Sat 10-7

Philosophy

If you've always wanted to own a Ferretti outfit but have never quite managed to find the cash, this somewhat quirkier and younger diffusion line by Alberta Ferretti has lots of designs at slightly more affordable prices that the main collection. Especially covetable are the interestingly cut silk crêpe dresses in typical Ferretti colours: chocolate brown with icy blue, muted pinks and cool greens. Climb the elegant spiral staircase (with the shop assistant breathing down your neck) to find more of the gathered, pleated, embroidered, lace-covered, fresh, sexy feminine details that give this designer's clothes their unmistakable stamp.   *philosophy.it*

Moderate to expensive   *Amex/MC/V*

Via Montenapoleone 19   **02 796 034**
20121 Milan   Mon-Sat 10-7

Plus

The name doesn't refer to the store's sizing policy (which ranges from the usual skinny-fitting to Milan's version of medium-large) but to the very large choice of labels: you'll find something of everything here. Recently updated in a sassier, more contemporary style, the roster currently includes Jean Paul Gaultier, Philosophy by Alberta Ferretti and Marithé et François Girbaud, plus younger labels like Antoni & Alison, All in All, Stella Forest, Fuzzi and Tasha. The owner's clever selection will save you miles of legwork as you complete your spree. Just a hop, skip and jump from Piazza Duomo, it's well worth straying just beyond the fringes of the Golden Rectangle to see what lies in store.

Moderate to expensive   *Amex/MC/V*

Piazza Missori 2   **02 864 61820**
20121 Milan   Mon 3-7, Tues-Sat 10-7

Pollini

Pollini's Piazza Duomo store couldn't be in a better location. Right opposite the gothic cathedral, there's no excuse for not popping into this boutique—even if your 'real' reason for being in Milan is sightseeing. Think of it as cultural research…into just how Italy's leather brands always manage to get it right. With over 100 years of cobbling practice, the Pollini family certainly knows a thing or two about putting together a well-crafted shoe. Their highly polished footwear and leather goods are only shown to the world after a painstaking process of modelling, cutting, stitching and hand-finishing high-grade hides from the Pollini factories in the Emilia-Romagna region. The result is top quality and (unfortunately) the prices tend to swing right alongside. Some of the styles tiptoe towards fashion-forward, but the majority are in the safe zone that helps Italy's well-heeled, conservative set maintain their style status quo. Pollini recently hired Rifat Ozbek to design their new clothing line; head upstairs for a neat range of leather and fabric jackets, cardigans and trousers, all just as well made as the luscious shoes. *pollini.com*

Expensive *Amex/MC/V*

Piazza Duomo 31 **02 875 187**
20122 Milan Mon 2:30-7:30, Tues-Sat 10-7:30

Corso Vittorio Emanuele II 30 **02 794 912**
20122 Milan (opening hours as above)

☆ Prada

Founded in 1913 by Miuccia Prada's grandfather Mario, the world's first-ever Prada store in the glass-roofed Galleria Vittorio Emanuele arcade retains much of its former glory. Upstairs, this evocative old shop still has wooden shelving, glass display cabinets, a black and white checkerboard floor…and even the original cashier's desk. Nowadays, it's mostly given over to bags and small leather goods, whose bright contemporary hues contrast stylishly with the olde worlde charm. When you've take in the goodies on the first floor, follow the grand marble spiral staircase down, past the Twenties-style cruise liner travel trunks, to the light and spacious basement. The full range of men's and women's shoes is on display and the helpful but not overpowering assistants are happy to help you try on as many pairs as you wish. Once you've picked out the perfect pair, you can browse the clothes racks for perfectly cut skirts and trousers, soft silk shirts, appliquéd T-shirts and belted coats before swooshing back up the stairs, proudly clutching your purchases in a Prada carrier bag. *prada.com*

Luxury *Amex/MC/V*

Galleria Vittorio Emanuele II 63-65 **02 876 979**
20121 Milan Mon-Sat 10-7:30, Sun 10-7

Prada (shoes, accessories, lingerie)

For years Milan's well-dressed signore had bought their handbags from the Galleria Vittorio Emanuele store. Then along came Miuccia, with her black nylon knapsacks with the triangular brand label, and Prada exploded onto the world. There can be few fashion victims left in the universe who don't have several covetable Prada pieces hanging in their closets, and Prada continues to surprise with innovative wearable designs. This huge new corner shoe and accessories store bang in the middle of Milan's swishest street is a mecca for those still adding to their Prada collections. Sink your feet into the magnificent mauve carpet, then flop into one of the lush seats and have an assistant bring you heaps of flats and other casual shoes, which this season are on the bulky side; wacky wedges are also here in a multitude of colours and shapes. You'll find everything from Miuccia's famous square toes to the rounded pumps in vogue this season, from elegant boots to strappy sandals with jewelled wedge heels—all in fabulous suedes, fabrics and leathers. Once you've made the agonising decision of which pair (or pairs) to buy, match them with a bag or purse from the large array on display. If the urge to splurge is still not sated, there is a multitude of key rings made from workshop oddments, or belts with bright resin buckles. Next, pop along the street to the smaller lingerie store. The delicious silk underwear and nightwear is guaranteed to make you feel like a million dollars—and you can even buy undies to match your Prada bag.   *prada.com*

Luxury	*Amex/MC/V*
Via della Spiga 18 (shoes, accessories)	**02 780 465**
20121 Milan	Mon-Sat 10-7:30
Via della Spiga 5 (lingerie)	**02 760 14448**
20121 Milan	Mon-Sat 10-2, 3-7:30

Prada (men)

This spacious clothes and accessories store gives guys the opportunity to browse or shop at their own pace—without wives, female friends or girlfriends distracting them from the serious job in hand. Full-on concentration is required to sort through the racks of gorgeous suits, shirts and casualwear that fill this store. If you don't have the time, the inclination (or the cash) to try anything on, focus on the smaller stuff from leather stationery to Miuccia's ultra-cool sunglasses. Don't forget to check out the fabulous suitcases which are far too beautiful to be battered about in an airplane hold.   *prada.com*

Luxury	*Amex/MC/V*
Via Montenapoleone 6	**02 760 20273**
20121 Milan	Mon-Sat 10-7:30

Prada (women)

This labyrinth of corridors and rooms stuffed with Miuccia's creations on two floors on Via Montenapoleone is better than Paradise for Prada fans. Like Alice in Pradaland, they wander through room after room, gaping open-mouthed at racks, shelves and cabinets displaying clothes, shoes and accessories, all with the unmistakable Miuccia stamp. Try on one of the fine knits and your skin will tingle with excitement. Or slip on a pair of satin pumps—and one of the new

bubble-shaped skirts, with rolled-under hems—and feel like
Cinderella heading for the Ball. *prada.com*

Luxury *Amex/MC/V*

Via Montenapoleone 8 **02 777 1771**
20121 Milan Mon-Sat 10-7:30

Prada (sport)

There seems to be a Prada store, if not two, on every street
in Milan's Golden Triangle, but this one is dedicated solely
to sportswear. Dark wood-panelling is a low-key background to stylish but functional clothes from swimwear to
skiwear. Accessories include bags, wallets, sunglasses, hats
and gloves, while at the rear there are the popular trainers
(thankfully, not all of them in the ubiquitous Prada silver)
plus sporty shoes and boots for men, women and children.
Prada have combined their ultra-chic styling with modern
technical design so these clothes are definitely not just for
show. *prada.com*

Expensive *Amex/MC/V*

Via Sant'Andrea 21 **02 760 01426**
20121 Milan Mon-Sat 10-7:30

ProMod

This trendy chain can sometimes resemble a jumble sale on
a Saturday afternoon, with so many devotees checking out
the goods, and indeed the merchandise moves fast
through these two stores which is one reason why the fans
keep coming back. It has been called a supermarket of
fashion, but it does stand out for the relative durability of its
designs. From little vast tops to silk two-piece suits, linen
shirts, tailored jackets and funky accessories, this is a great
place to pick up fashions you can wear for at least two seasons at prices similar to those in other high street chains.
The Via Mazzini location is the more convenient—it's on a
corner of the Piazza Duomo so you can sightsee as well as
shop. *promod.com*

Affordable to moderate *Amex/Mc/V*

Via Mazzini 2 **02 890 14745**
20123 Milan Mon-Sat 10-8, Sun 11-8

Corso Buenos Aires 41 **02 295 20575**
20124 Milan Mon 10-8, Tues-Sat 9:30-8, Sun 10-7:30

Puma Concept Store

Tucked away in a cobblestoned ochre courtyard off Corso
Vercelli, Puma's only Milan store opened in April 2002. A
huge white leaping cat on a crimson background greets the
visitor, giving way to two floors of sportswear for men,
women and children. This is the place to pick up a pair of
Puma's sizzling hot trainers (among the latest are
Speedcats, R & B Streets and Mostros, if you really want to
know). Then there's the usual array of T-shirts, sweats, skirts,
bags, backpacks and even a bustier for that must-have sexy
gym look. Kids' clothes are sized from 0 to 16 years, and

there are more than 25 trainer options just for children. If the price tag is too high, try the discount outlet on Viale Monte Nero.

Moderate

puma.com
Amex/MC/V

Corso Vercelli 29
20144 Milan

02 469 0150
Mon 3-7, Tues-Sat 10-7

Viale Monte Nero 22 (outlet)
20135 Milan

02 599 02227
Mon 3-7, Tues-Sat 10-1, 3-7

☆ Pupi Solari

If you only visit a single shop outside Milan's centre, it should be this lovely multi-brand boutique overlooking the Piazza Tommaseo. Fashion doyenne Pupi Solari's six windows are hung with the most gorgeous handmade Japanese blinds, framing displays that are works of art in themselves. Flowers from Tea Rose (the hip florist in Via Santo Spirito) give the sun-filled space an elegant and welcoming atmosphere. The store simply oozes good taste. Mixed with must-have classic pieces such as Ballantyne cashmere V-necks, Alberto Aspesi trousers and pink Car Shoes are handmade coats by Kiton, deconstructed knits by the Serbian Dusan, and to-die-for knits by Matilde; also, this is the only shop in Milan to carry Lambertson Truex bags. One third of the store is devoted to children sizes 0-12, much of it under Pupi Solari's own label. Even if you don't have children you won't be able to resist perusing the classic smock dresses, overcoats and baby-soft knitwear. All shopping should be this good.

Expensive to luxury

Amex/MC/V

Piazza Tommaseo 2
20145 Milan

02 463 325
Mon 3-7:30, Tues-Sat 10-7:30

☆ Purple

It may sit opposite the Roman columns of San Lorenzo, Milan's anointed gathering place for scruffy teenagers, but only the most stylish of the tattooed and lip-pieced crowd venture in here. Purple stock Evisu jeans, Puma, Morella clothing and the latest cutting-edge labels. It's one of few spots in the city offering a healthy mix of underground, smaller design labels, which is refreshing. Their success is such that in 2004 they opened a women's store called Pur5 right opposite the first boutique, selling funky feminine pieces with handcrafted details from labels like No Name, Traffic People and Super Luxury Cat. You'll find none of the pomp or attitude that is obligatory in the boutiques which line the luxury thoroughfares.

purpleshop.it

Moderate to expensive

Amex/MC/V

Corso di Porta Ticinese 22
20122 Milan

02 894 24476
Mon 3-7:30, Tues-Fri 10:30-1:30, 3:30-7:30
Sat 10:30-1:30, 3:30-8

Pur5

Via Pio IV, 1
20122 Milan

02 581 03812
(opening hours as above)

Ralph Lauren

Across the Atlantic he may have to share the limelight with the likes of Calvin and Donna, but here in Italy Ralph's reign as the king of American casualwear goes undisputed. This store is Lauren's first free-standing venture in Italy. The locals had been kept drooling for what seems like years in anticipation of the four floors filled with sporty prepster classics ablaze with American flags and polo shirt tailoring. With the complete offering of Ralph's luxury apparel and accessories, including all the top labels and the coveted home line, no one will be going back to the casa empty-handed. *polo.com*

Expensive to luxury   *Amex/MC/V*

Via Montenapoleone 4   **02 778 8721**
20121 Milan

☆ René Caovilla

If you have the lifestyle and stamina for heels up to 5 inches, René Caovilla is the store for you. After years of collaborations with the likes of Valentino, Dior and Chanel, Caovilla decided to go it alone and bring a touch of his Venetian heritage to Milan with his flowered, fur-lined and jewelled creations, which are already on the red carpet and snapping at the heels of those Blahniks and Choos. His baroque Grand Canal palazzo-styled shop has its own special atelier for VIP clients, and for those who are hard to please Caovilla also offers made-to-measure jewelled shoes. *renecaovilla.com*

Expensive to luxury   *Amex/MC/V*

Via Bagutta 28   **02 763 19049**
20121 Milan   Mon 3-7, Tues-Sat 10-7

Replay

Too cool for school? This is your place. At the entrance, an illuminated sign in numerous languages 'Welcomes' teenagers to this flagship of the Italian streetwear brand. Denim jeans, jackets, miniskirts, teensy shorts and other essential pieces of the universal young hipster's uniform hang on racks above the pebble-covered floor. You'll also find tanks, sweatshirts, fitted blouses and patchwork tops with frayed edges and cap sleeves. Follow the wide punctured-metal stairs to the basement to discover more streetwise clothes, this time for men. *replay.it*

Affordable   *Amex/MC/V*

Largo Corsia dei Servi 11   **02 763 10196**
20122 Milan   Mon 3-7:30, Tues-Sat 10-7:30

Roberto Cavalli

Cavalli's trademark blown-up animal prints, feathers, beading and diamanté-studded jeans and tops dress up even the dullest occasion—not that his devotees would consider any of their 'occasions' dull. These days, the Florentine designer spends much of his free time at his home on the glitzy Costa Smeralda on Sardinia, and most of his extravagant creations seem designed for the party, party, party scene that takes off there every summer. This boutique has two floors, mainly filled with womenswear (ground floor) though there's a smaller selection for men (downstairs). Cavalli extends his reputation for excess to a rich range of shoes and accessories—so you'll find everything you need if Sardinia's on your itinerary this year. *robertocavalli.it*

Luxury   *Amex/MC/V*

Via della Spiga 42   **02 760 20900**
20121 Milan   Mon 3-7, Tues-Sat 10-7

Ruffo

If the pungent aroma of leather does it for you, soak up the smell at these stores. Set out in two separate shops for men and women, next door to each other, is a huge display of the softest leather you could ever wish to wear. Well known in the industry as suppliers to Versace, Prada and Jil Sander, this master of tanning also has its own label to boast its high-quality hides. The jackets, tops and trousers show off all the company's techniques—they pleat, burn, wash and smash leather into inconceivable states. You'll find hides transformed into looks that are both edgy and classic. Sprinkled throughout are non-leather pieces like cotton shirts and jersey sweaters. *ruffo.it*

Luxury   *Amex/MC/V*

Via della Spiga 48   **02 760 15523**
20121 Milan   Mon 3-7, Tues-Sat 10-7

☆ Sadogy

This unusual store is for those who are tired of global copy-cat fashions: there's not a branded tailored suit or miniskirt in sight. Instead, the spacious and simply furnished interior showcases Sadogy's own line, featuring handprinted silks and cottons from India and Japan, handmade shoes in unusual materials from Israeli designer Joseph Debach (each signed and dated), and hats from Milan-based Japanese designer Keiko Suganuma. Everything has a distinctly ethnic feel; the shapes are easy and comfortable and the fabrics and earthy colour palette reflect the natural theme. You'll also find the French label (but made in Italy) Marithé et François Girbaud, Hood and upcoming Italian designers A.T.Shirt and Franco Armilla Studio. To complete the look, try shoes by Moma, bags by Franco Orciani and leather by Spanish designer Sominemi. Most of the exclusive pieces stocked here come at a price, but you may find some more reasonably tagged goodies tucked away along the rails.

Moderate to expensive   *Amex/MC/V*

Corso Como 2   **02 654 735**
20154 Milan   Mon 3-7, Tues-Sat 10:30-7:30

☆ Il Salvagente/Salvagente Bimbi

It's a bus/taxi ride away from the main shopping drags, but this long-established designer discount store is always packed with fashionistas screaming with delight over their latest finds. To join them, walk through the basement entrance in the parking area of the residential block that houses the store, then leave your bags in one of the lockers at the entrance next to the cash desk on the left. On the ground floor, you'll find women's designer labels including Prada, Gucci, Antonio Fusco, D&G, Blumarine and Alberta Ferretti. Amble through the maze of rooms and you'll find bargain jeans by Diesel, Gas and Armani. Head upstairs to menswear, where you'll have to squeeze past Milanese Matrons on a Mission to find the best shirts and trousers. The lowest-priced womenswear is upstairs, too. If you're in the mood for more bargains there's a childrens outlet, Salvagente Bimbi, about 10 blocks away. *salvagentemilano.it*

Moderate to expensive | *MC/V*

Il Salvagente

Via Fratelli Bronzetti 6	**02 761 10328**
Milan 20129	Mon 3-7, Tues, Thurs-Fri 10-12:30, 3-7
	Wed, Sat 10-7

Salvagente Bimbi

| **Via Balzaretti 28** | **02 266 80764** |
| 20133 Milan | Mon 3-7, Tues-Sat 10-7 |

Salvatore Ferragamo

High-quality leather shoes and accessories from the Florence-based legend are exactly what you'd expect to find inside this long thin cream marble store with inviting white leather cube seating. And though they are expected, somehow this company's exquisite products never disappoint. At the women's store – and Salvatore is the saviour of all narrow-footed women – you'll find a range of comfort sandals in ultra-soft leathers and delicate colours with matching handbags, alongside sporty shoes, purses, wallets, sunglasses, scarves and belts—all discreetly embossed with the Ferragamo logo. There's also a range of ready-to-wear and a small display of men's ties and gift items along with the Ferragamo perfumes for both sexes. Though known for conservative and classic collections, the company recently brought in some new young blood, so more original finds now exist among the tried and tested styles. For a more extensive choice, male customers should head down the street to the dedicated branch. *salvatoreferragamo.com*

Expensive to luxury | *Amex/MC/V*

| **Via Montenapoleone 3 (W)** | **02 760 00054** |
| 20121 Milan | Mon 3-7, Tues-Sat 10-7 |

| **Via Montenapoleone 20 (M)** | **02 760 06660** |
| 20121 Milan | (opening hours as above) |

Samsonite

Although some of the initial buzz has died down, there are still plenty of high-quality creative finds for a globetrotting fashion nomad in this light and airy store. In addition to the tried and true luggage—including those black suitcases, now so popular that fights regularly break out amongst owners of identical pieces at the airport conveyor belt—there are streamlined sporty clothes, comfortable shoes and sandals, wallets, bags, and even travel games for guys and dolls always on the run. With this super-sleek line in accessories and travel-inspired clothing, Samsonite has made Sixties 'flight attendant chic' something to talk about again. *samsonite.com*

Moderate *Amex/MC/V*

Corso Matteotti 12 **02 760 20264**
20121 Milan Mon 3-7:30, Tues-Sat 10-7:30

Via Belfiore 6 **02 480 12452**
20145 Milan Mon 3-7:30, Tues-Sat 10-1, 3-7:30

☆ Sebastian

Sebastian is as near to perfect as a shoe store can get. In this small branch, you can indulge in everything from 'art for the feet' by eccentric Swiss-born footwear legend Andrea Pfister, to quirky fashion shoes from Sebastian and sensible everyday shoes from The Saddler, all made in Parma by Calzaturificio Mafra. For an elegant occasion, try their stilettos in startling black and white with matching bags or, for a more low-key feminine look, the pretty floral embroidered mesh shoes in bright fresh colours. If comfort and a more traditional look is what you are after, The Saddler range is for you. For men, The Saddler has a few classic business shoes in brown, black and tan, plus some more casual soft leather slip-ons for those times when you don't need to be quite so tight-laced. *sebastianmilano.com*

Moderate to expensive *Amex/MC/V*

Via Montenapoleone 25 **02 760 02036**
20121 Milan Mon 3-7, Tues-Sat 10-7

Sergio Rossi (women)

Sexy stilettos dominate this feminine range from master shoe designer Sergio Rossi, whose brand is now part of the Gucci stable. Glam up your life in a pair of these lovingly made creations and feel an instant surge of power. Pointed toes, towering heels and streamlined shapes are the basic ingredients of Rossi's magic: they'll turn you into a femme fatal—without the blistered feet. These shoes are far too beautiful to tuck away in your wardrobe—you'll want to display them on a bedside cabinet, or even the windowsill, when you can bear to take them off. *sergiorossi.com*

Luxury *Amex/MC/V*

Via della Spiga 15 **02 760 02663**
20121 Milan Mon 3-7, Tues-Sat 10-7

Via Montenapoleone 6/A **02 760 06140**
20121 Milan (opening hours as above)

Sergio Rossi (men)

Designed to resemble a gentleman's club, with wood-panelled walls, ponyskin armchairs and a table stacked with coffee-table books, this is the only dedicated Sergio Rossi men's boutique in the world. The store was created to show off Rossi's ever-growing men's collection. With styles spanning everything from classic Oxfords to white leather beach flip-flops finished with a between-the-toe knot, well-dressed men will be hard-pressed to put a foot wrong. *sergiorossi.com*

Luxury *Amex/MC/V*

Via della Spiga 5 **02 763 90927**
20121 Milan Mon 3-7, Tues-Sat 10-7

Sermoneta Gloves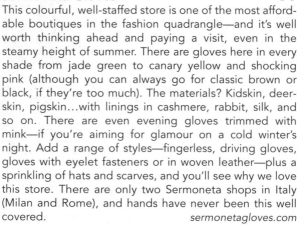

This colourful, well-staffed store is one of the most afford-able boutiques in the fashion quadrangle—and it's well worth thinking ahead and paying a visit, even in the steamy height of summer. There are gloves here in every shade from jade green to canary yellow and shocking pink (although you can always go for classic brown or black, if they're too much). The materials? Kidskin, deer-skin, pigskin…with linings in cashmere, rabbit, silk, and so on. There are even evening gloves trimmed with mink—if you're aiming for glamour on a cold winter's night. Add a range of styles—fingerless, driving gloves, gloves with eyelet fasteners or in woven leather—plus a sprinkling of hats and scarves, and you'll see why we love this store. There are only two Sermoneta shops in Italy (Milan and Rome), and hands have never been this well covered. *sermonetagloves.com*

Affordable to moderate *Amex/MC/V*

Via della Spiga 46 **02 763 18303**
20121 Milan Mon-Sat 10-7

Shabby Chic

This fabulous shop is run by Graziana Biagini, who likes nothing better than helping you find a style that suits. On the ground floor, there's a huge selection of Lacoste polo shirts in every colour possible, cashmere from Pringle and Ballantyne, and racks of pretty skirts and dresses from the Fifties and Sixties. In the basement, there are trench coats from labels such as Burberry and Aquascutum, fantastic Irish tweeds, sports jackets and suits, suede and leather coats—all in excellent condition and kept in air-conditioned luxury. Shabby Chic is next to one of Milan's best (though not prohibitively priced) fish restaurants, Da Giacomo. So splurge the euros you've saved on some salt-crusted branzino—and you may find yourself sitting next to Madonna or Bill Clinton, both of whom dine here when in town. *shabby.it*

Moderate *MC/V*

Via B.Cellini 21 **02 760 18149**
Milan 20129 Mon 3-7:30, Tues-Sat 10:30-7:30

☆ Silvano Lattanzi

This Roman shoe designer is a legend among the best-shod Milanese men, so the opening of this Milan outpost last year was greeted with a sigh of relief. Now, the city's gents can choose from the classic ready-to-wear collection from the comfort of the store's cream leather armchairs, thus saving themselves a lengthy journey to the Eternal City. Or they can be measured for a pair of made-to-measure shoes. Lattanzi spends so much of his time trotting the globe to take the measure of illustrious feet that he doesn't actually have time to make the shoes himself. Instead, his expert artisans craft them to perfection at his workshops in the shoe-producing Marche region of central Italy. But wielding a pen is more in keeping with his designer role, and each pair carries his personal signature inside.   *zintala.it*

Luxury   *Amex/MC/V*

Via Borgospesso 25   **02 763 17711**
20121 Milan   Mon 3-7, Tues-Sat 10-1, 3-7

Simonetta Ravizza by Annabella

Real fur may not be to everyone's taste but there's little doubt that, like so many things in the fashion world, Italians are among those who do it best. If your stomach is strong enough, climb the beautiful white marble staircase to this store, to find a capsule selection of fashion fur from Annabella—the furrier whose boutique fills almost an entire side of the main piazza in the historic town of Pavia, not far from Milan. Not to be missed is the Simonetta womenswear collection of leather and suede jackets in young fashionable shapes and fresh bright colours, complemented by linen and cotton trousers, shirts and skirts. They also carry a few leather accessories, shoes, bags and belts in bright spring shades.   *annabella.it/simonetta*

Expensive to luxury   *Amex/MC/V*

Via Montenapoleone 1   **02 760 12921**
20121 Milan   Mon 3-7, Tues-Sat 10-1:30, 2:30-7

Sisley

Sisley began back in 1968 as a Parisian denim manufacturer before being acquired by Benetton in 1974. Thirty years later, they're ready to branch beyond clothing to housewares and have sponsored a young French ceramics designer, Sam Baron, to produce plates and tableware for the Design Slices label under Sisley's wing. But the unpretentious Via Dogana store on the corner of Piazza Duomo is mainly devoted to the affordable brand's young classics, with the occasional kooky garment breaking up the rails. Youngsters, tourists and Milanese, come here to rummage through the shelves for the best pieces—including business basics and sleek eveningwear.   *sisley.com*

Affordable   *Amex/MC/V*

Piazza Duomo **02 869 96191**
20123 Milan Mon 2-7:30, Tues-Sat 10-7:30

Galleria Passarella 1 **02 763 881**
20122 Milan Daily 10-8

Corso Buenos Aires 3 **02 204 6446**
20124 Milan Mon-Sat 10-8

Benetton/Sisley

Corso Buenos Aires 19 **02 202 29111**
20124 Milan (opening hours as above)

Corso di Porta Romana 54 **02 583 26441**
20122 Milan Mon 10:30-2:30, 3:30-7:30
Tues-Sat 10-2:30, 3:30-7:30

Benetton/Sisley

Corso Vercelli 8 **02 433 51121**
20145 Milan Mon 3-7:30, Tues-Sat 10-7:30

☆ Sportmax

If MaxMara and Max & Co were mother and daughter respectively, Sportmax would be a distant relative on the family tree stylewise. Fun, wearable and affordable, though certain items are now getting pricey, every season Sportmax takes its trend-savvy customers on a rollercoaster ride of fashion ecstasy. Sportmax is boho chic—tans, brown denims, studded low-slung belts, lace and layers create the look that litters the store, and you can guarantee there will be a dangerously short hipster skirt. It's good to find a store in this street that lets you go home feeling like a trendsetter without melting your credit card. This is one of only three free-standing stores in existence, the others being in Paris and Tokyo. With its vast entrance and no doors, the Milan boutique is one of the least intimidating on Via della Spiga—a street which may irritate shoppers but is especially irritating for the poor shop assistants who also have to deal with a zillion lost tourists asking for directions.

Moderate to expensive *Amex/MC/V*
Via della Spiga 30 **02 760 11944**
20121 Milan Mon-Sat 10-7:30

Stefanel

Count on this Treviso-based label for separates that are easy, wearable, affordable and of acceptable quality. The clothes are designed with an eye to the latest trends but without overdoing it. You are guaranteed to find all your basic wardrobe essentials here. Jeans, sweaters, T-shirts, shoes and a full range of accessories are neatly displayed and the ambience is laid-back. The styles are decidedly cool and well within most people's budgets. Browse at your leisure: if you have any questions, you'll probably be able to get the strategically placed assistants to help. *stefanel.it*

Affordable *Amex/MC/V*
Corso Vittorio Emanuele II 28 **02 763 18722**
20122 Milan Mon-Sat 10-8, Sun 10:30-7:30

Corso Buenos Aires 77   **02 667 12234**
20124 Milan   Daily 10-8

Corso XXII Marzo 4   **02 541 08555**
20124 Milan   Mon 3:30-7:30, Tues-Sat 10-7:30

Via San Gregorio 1   **02 295 15564**
20124 Milan   Mon-Sat 9:30-7:30

Stone Island and CP Company

It may be Italian-owned, but Stone Island's head and heart are stuck smack dab in the Australian outback. The sporty, highly utilitarian clothing for men is perfect for a swift dismount from a mud-splattered 4X4, but the exceptional fabrications, the result of astute research by its Italian factories, will have you looking just as good strutting the streets of the concrete jungle. Joining the rugged linen shirts and washed cotton trousers is dressier fare from CP Company. Soft button-down sweaters and crews are a bonus, but the tour de force is the impressive selection of high-tech outerwear: check out the extra-light, breathable jackets with hideaway hoods, elasticised internal windproof cuffs, chest level and underarm air vents. Take a moment to look at the innovative store design: those tiny circles in the floor are there so that the display units can be moved into new configurations as the collections demand.   *stoneisland.com*

Moderate to expensive   *Amex/MC/V*

Corso Venezia 12   **02 760 01409**
20121 Milan   Mon 3-7, Tues-Sat 10-7

Strenesse

German designer Gabrielle Strehle's streamlined designs are as rigorously pared-down as the bare bones architecture of this Milan store. Raw wood and cement give the space an industrial feel, playing off the absolute simplicity of the clothes. Strehle's a purist at heart and leans toward the cerebral. One look at the clean lines on the suits, the relaxed cut of the pants and the simplicity of flowing dresses and you'll see that selling sex is not on her agenda—but that doesn't mean that the clothes are dull. Now in its fourth season, the menswear range livens up natural colours and fabrics with splashes of bright purple. There are more good finds in the basement, where the young, casual, sporty Blue line hangs out. Fortunately, this once greenhouse-like store now has air conditioning so that summer shopping is a cool experience in more ways than one.   *strenesse.com*

Expensive to luxury   *Amex/MC/V*

Via Manzoni 37   **02 657 2401**
20121 Milan   Mon-Sat 10-2, 3-7

Tanino Crisci

As the mounted horse logo suggests, this family-owned northern Italian company may have its roots in riding boots, but these days its fashion lines are off to a racing start. Alongside the traditional leather shoes in black, brown and tan for men, you'll find women's slingbacks and sandals in everything from tan to fuchsia pink and acid green. There are also classic belts, wallets, bags, briefcases, soft leather jackets and men's woven silk ties. Crisci can certainly hold its head up high on Milan's most fashionable street. *taninocrisci.com*

Expensive *Amex/MC/V*

Via Montenapoleone 3 **02 760 21264**
20121 Milan Mon 3-7, Tues-Sat 10-2, 3-7

☆ Tim Camino

Be warned. Small girls regularly rush out of this shop in floods of tears—having discovered that the clothes featuring their favourite cartoon, Power Girls, don't come in pint-pot sizes. In fact the embroidered, printed and patchwork jeans, tees, bags and cushions—splashed with Warner Brothers characters—are strictly aimed at grown-up lasses. Though the company's designers have recently gone overboard with the Power Girl theme (they now have a contract with Warner Brothers), you'll still find the downtown New York streetwise vibe in the cult jeans and the cute mismatched T-shirts and vests. There's also a range of little girl shoes (in adult sizes) with round toes—including Mary Janes in pink, black or yellow patent leather. The staff are great to talk to and love to get the chance to practise their English. Ask for fashion-mad Mirella.

Moderate to expensive *Amex/MC/V*

Via de Amicis 3 **02 836 0124**
20123 Milan Mon 3-7:30, Tues-Sat 10-7:30

Tod's

Drift in here and you'll find yourself drawn, as if by a magnet, to view everything in the store. This magical pull is less mysterious than it seems: the store's layout is a giant square, taking you up the stairs by the left-hand entrance, past all the luscious products on the first floor, and back down the right-hand staircase to end up back on the ground floor. Of course you'll see several variations on the famous pebble-soled driving shoe, which comes out in several new materials each season. But you'll also find the red Ferrari driving shoes, a few heels, a Junior Tod's collection and some beautiful bags. Don't miss the limited-edition collection of bags and shoes, exclusive to this store. *todsgroup.com*

Expensive *Amex/MC/V*

Via della Spiga 22 **02 760 02423**
20121 Milan Mon-Sat 10-7:30

Trussardi

If you're only in Milan for a short time, make sure you pop into the roomy Trussardi lifestyle store, next door to La Scala. The home collection of exclusive linens, towels and other goods is on the ground floor, together with a large cache of bags and accessories, and upstairs are a restaurant and café, ideal for a pre-opera dinner. It's also a great place for truly stylish gifts—from Trussardi-embossed trinkets to top-notch leather accessories. For Beatrice Trussardi's ready-to-wear, you'll have to go to Via Sant'Andrea. *trussardi.com*

Moderate to luxury *Amex/MC/V*

Piazza della Scala 5 **02 806 88242**
20121 Milan Mon-Sat 10-7

Via Sant'Andrea 3-7 **02 760 20380**
20121 Milan Mon-Sat 10-7

T' Store

If the main Trussardi store is for 'lifestyle', those seeking a more casual lifestyle should check out this store, a showcase for the Trussardi Jeans and Sports ranges. With three floors and an impressive clear Perspex spiral staircase linking them together, it contains all the leather and fashion house's most reasonably priced lines, for both men and women. For menswear, dive into the basement where you'll find jeans and the casual sports range including sweatshirts, denim jackets, T-shirts and crisp cotton shirts with snazzy top-stiching in contrasting colours. The other two floors are devoted to young, sporty womenswear, from glazed cotton trousers and printed T-shirts to baggy jeans and a few sexy dresses. *trussardi.com*

Moderate to expensive *Amex/MC/V*

Corso Europa (corner Galleria San Carlo) **02 783 909**
20122 Milan Sun-Mon 3-7, Tues-Sat 10-8

Urrah

If you're looking for a place to kit out the entire family, Urrah could be worth a try. In the women's and children's store, the cool white-washed interior sets off the bright and bubbly clothes. This place is more about casual, good-looking comfort than about competing in the high-fashion stakes. While Mum tries on the loose-fitting dresses, drawstring trousers, flowing skirts and large shirts in natural cotton, linen and silk by Mia Zia, teenagers can squeeze into jeans, cotton miniskirts and bright printed T-shirts by Kookaï. Mothers may choose sensible flats and sandals from Birkenstock while their daughters try to persuade them to buy them a pair of Sketchers sneakers—actually, Mum will probably look better in these, too. Meanwhile, Dad and the boys can head to the menswear store next door, whose look is more understated. If you have a keen sailor in the family, check out the nautical print shirts and T-shirts and the obligatory deck shoes.

Moderate to expensive *Amex/MC/V*

Via Solferino 3-5 **02 864 385**
20121 Milan Mon 10:30-2, 3-7, Tues-Sat 10-7

☆ **Valentino**

As you'd expect from the Roman, Milan's recently revamped Valentino store is one of the chicest boutiques on this very chic street. Walk in through the wide corridor lined with magnificent lamps with Valentino's signature 'V' stamped big and loud on the shades. Glance into the various rooms leading off the corridor to see flawlessly cut men's suits and glamorous womenswear artistically displayed (only the strongest will resist the flowered lace shawls). At the end of the hallway you'll reach a wide, sweeping staircase, where you will find the finest examples of the designer's haute couture dresses protectively displayed behind glass cases at the top of the stairs. Nearby, the bride-to-be can choose from the small, newly introduced selection of simple bridal gowns. The designer truly deserves the accolades lavished upon him. *valentino.it*

Expensive to luxury | *Amex/MC/V*

Via Montenapoleone 20 | **02 760 06182**
20121 Milan | Mon-Sat 10-7

Valextra

The label may not be widely known beyond these shores, but utter the word 'Valextra' to a group of Italians and they'll pause in communal tribute to give this A-list Milanese brand its due respect. These top-notch leather goods of incomparable quality and style have been accessorizing Europe's elite since 1937. Valextra's signature cross-hatched leathers, which come in light tan and rich cream in addition to more traditional blacks and mahoganies, are so smooth, so delightful, that you'll find yourself caressing your purse or wallet more often than your mate. Handstitching featuring impeccable seams and Sherlock Holmes-style locks are an added bonus on beautifully crafted canvas and deep black leather weekend bags, shoppers, small box bags, document cases and wallets. The Via Cerva location also offers made-to-measure. *valextra.it*

Expensive to luxury | *Amex/MC/V*

Piazza San Babila 1 | **02 760 05024**
20122 Milan | Mon 3-7, Tues-Sat 10-7

Via Cerva 11 | **02 760 00103**
20121 Milan | Mon 3-7, Tues-Sat 10-1:30, 2:30-7

Via Manzoni 3 | **n/a at press time**
20121 Milan

☆ **Vanilla**

Upcoming designers on this street come and go as fast as the skateboarders whizzing past outside. But there's often a queue of young girls waiting to get into this tiny, recently opened shop. Once in, they squeeze into designer Matteo Leone's sporty pieces—like sweat-material miniskirts and jersey jump suits. Casual shoes and a small selection of accessories are available too. But take note: the range is as small as the sizes.

Affordable   *Amex/MC/V*

Corso di Porta Ticinese 103   **02 581 05041**
20123 Milan   Mon 3-7:30, Tues-Fri 10:30-1:30, 3-7:30
                                                      Sat 10:30-7:30

Vergelio

If you're looking for a wide selection of designer shoes, Vergelio offers just about the best in Milan. In the flagship store on Corso Vittorio Emanuele, you'll find something from everyone: Tod's, Costume National, Cesare Paciotti, Armani, Casadei, Roberto Cavalli, Dolce & Gabbana, Hogan and Sergio Rossi. While brands do overlap between stores, we'd suggest you head towards Buenos Aires if your aim is to find reasonably priced top-quality shoes. The Buenos Aires store also shares space with Timberland— walk in one side, it's Vergelio; walk through to the other, it's Timberland—so you can also find those walking shoes for trekking round the sights.

Moderate to luxury   *Amex/MC/V*

Corso Vittorio Emanuele II 10   **02 760 03087**
20122 Milan   Mon 3-7:30, Tues-Sat 10-7:30

Corso Buenos Aires 9   **02 294 06272**
20124 Milan   Mon 3-7:30, Tues-Sat 9:30-7:30

Via Vitruvio 3   **02 295 31208**
20124 Milan   Mon 3-7, Tues-Sat 10-7:30

Via dell'Unione 2   **02 860 901**
20122 Milan   (opening hours as above)

Corso Vercelli 2   **02 498 608**
20145 Milan   (opening hours as above)

Verri

Verri has been on this street (now the best menswear street in Milan) since the Eighties, but with a planned move to bigger premises and a new designer from Holland (Martin Bal) it's about to update its styles and target a younger, more fashionable audience. The fabulous selection of sharp suits, crisp shirts, leather wallets, belts and sunglasses ensures that the discerning buyer can be fitted out with a whole new wardrobe in one go.   *verriuomo.com*

Expensive   *Amex/MC/V*

Via Verri (corner Via Bigli)   **02 760 20355**
20121 Milan   Mon-Sat 10-7

Versus

Versace fans will delight at this buzzing store offering three whole floors of the younger, sportier and more affordable Versus label. If you're young and skinny enough, check out the men's jeans and wild printed T-shirts in the basement, or the sexy and often very short womenswear on the ground floor. But if you can't quite squeeze into anything here, you can always indulge your passion for Versace by kitting out the kids. A mother herself, Donatella has made sure that no one is left out: she's designed cute little all-in-ones and the teensiest of booties for newborn Versace babes, plus bright, lively, logo-covered outfits for kids aged 2 to 14. For the colourful Versace home collection, head across the street to the separate store. *versace.com*

Moderate   *Amex/MC/V*

Via San Pietro all'Orto 10   **02 760 14924**
20121 Milan   Mon-Sat 10-7

Versace (home collection)

Via San Pietro all'Orto 11   **02 760 14544**
20121 Milan   Mon-Sat 10-7

Vicini

Everything about this Emilia-Romagna-based label is on the up-and-up, from its skyscraping list of clients (including plenty of Hollywood stars) to its high-rise heels. Unlike the footwear, designed by Giuseppe Zanotti, the store is small and unobtrusive—forming a wonderful backdrop for the multitude of colourful party shoes. Thin straps, diamanté buckles, glittering flowers, candy-coloured leathers—and those high, high heels—all add up to create the ultimate escape from reality. We especially liked the stiletto sandals with sparkly green and blue butterfly motifs. *vicinishoes.com*

Expensive   *Amex/MC/V*

Via della Spiga 1   **02 760 02828**
20121 Milan   Mon-Sat 10-7

☆ Vierre

You'll notice the crowds buzzing round the window long before you get a chance to peek inside this hip shoe boutique. Marc Jacobs, Miu Miu, Givenchy, John Galliano, Ann Demeulemeester and Michael Perry are only some of the designers whose footwear all those curious folk outside are craning their necks to see. Styles go all the way from teetering Cesare Paciotti stilettos to the latest Puma trainers. Inside, relax on the plush velvet seating while you choose a pair of the latest designs. And remember to swing your Vierre carrier bag proudly (the Milanese will all take note) as you walk back down the street.

Expensive to luxury   *Amex/MC/V*

Via Montenapoleone 29   **02 760 01731**
20121 Milan   Mon 3:30-7, Tues-Sat 10-7

☆ Viktor & Rolf

This quirky duo from the Netherlands specialise in putting a twist on the classics, and their newly opened Milan boutique is a case in point. At first glance it looks conservative. The symmetrical store with its dove-grey boiserie-lined walls and standard chandeliers and fireplace at first conceals its true strangeness. But if you linger a little longer, you will realise that everything is upside down. The chandeliers which spring from the floor are complete with crystals which hang up rather than down. The ceiling is covered with parquet with chairs stuck to it. After this shock, it's a relief to find that Viktor and Rolf decided not to hang their clothes in this inverse fashion but in the normal way. So without breaking your neck you can appreciate their eccentric, yet classic clothing. *viktor-rolf.com*

Expensive   *Amex/MC/V*
Via Sant'Andrea 14   **02 796 091**
20121 Milan   Mon-Sat 10-2, 3-7

Vilebrequin

Milan may be landlocked but that has not stopped Vilebrequin from giving the city a splash of its signature bold tropical colours. The company has kept things simple. There are limited collections of general beachwear and sunglasses, but the key item is men's swimming trunks in four basic shapes and made from the same sort of fast-drying fabric as spinnakers are made from. It's easy to spot proud father and son teams hanging out in the ritziest seaside resorts in their matching sets, confident that even though they may look the same, with around 500 different graphic designs to choose from they will all in fact be slightly different from each other, and therefore stylishly unique. *vilebrequin.com*

Expensive   *Amex/MC/V*
Via della Spiga 46   **02 780 984**
20121 Milan   Mon-Sat 10-7

☆ Vintage 55

Its hard not to be spellbound by the huge flashing Las Vegas-style Vintage 55 sign, and before you know it, you are hypnotically drawn into their black lair. Vintage 55 is the nighly successful American-retro brand, designed and produced by Italians. They bought the 'look' rights from all-time style god Steve McQueen, so now you can now buy the exact T-shirt Steve wore in *Bullitt*, the only change being Vintage 55 written somewhere on the piece. Deep thought has gone into this shop. Experts have been sent out to scour the world and bring home all the Adidas and Nike trainers that came out in the Seventies and Eighties. These are displayed along with Marc Jacobs' limited-edition Vans, vintage glitter helmets, and Oyster Rolexes.

Moderate   *Amex/MC/V*
Via Ponte Vetero 1   **02 805 4823**
20121 Milan   Mon 1-7:30, Tues-Fri 10:30-2, 3:30-7:30
                                              Sat 10-7:30

☆ Vivienne Westwood

When the British queen of eccentricity opened her first Milan store during the runway shows in September 2003, it was the highlight of the party-goers' week. That night, many of Westwood's fans didn't make it through the crush, but you shouldn't run into any such problems now that the initial burst of excitement has died down. Push open the glass doors with the large gold Westwood logo, and prepare to be propelled into a world of precision pattern cutting and innovative colour and fabric combinations. Westwood's creations may be a little wild but they are beautifully made, some of them here in Italy. Her fans will reel with delight over everything—from the plain white cotton shirts to the complicated and sometimes confusing silk jersey evening gowns. This store carries all the ranges, from Gold Label, Red Label and Anglomania (men's and women's) to Vivienne Westwood Man. There's also a generous selection of goods from other brands—including Wolford tights, Libertine and Boudoir perfumes and Coalport by Wedgwood ceramics. With showrooms and offices filling the floors upstairs, this is a little piece of London in Milan. *viviennewestwood.com*

Expensive to luxury   *Amex/MC/V*

Corso Venezia 25   **02 760 80222**
20122 Milan   Mon-Sat 10-7

Von Dutch

How did a brand started by a motorcycle mechanic called Kenny end up on a street as posh as Via Spiga? Kenny was famous in the Fifties for customizing bikes and cars with his signature graphics (the most famous being the Flying Eyeball). After his death in the Nineties, a Frenchman decided to turn his legacy into a fashion label. Via Spiga locals might call it sacrilege, turning a 19th-century building into a garage, but it's been done, complete with tire tracks and graffiti on the walls. The shop stocks men's women's and children's clothes, along with a wide range of accessories from knuckledusters and numberplate frames to G-strings and sweatbands—all very hard core but missing the greasepaint. *vondutch.com*

Moderate   *Amex/MC/V*

Via della Spiga 46   **02 760 17087**
29121 Milan   Mon 3-7, Tues-Sat 10-7

Yamamay

This tiny cupboard of a store is crammed full of all the sexy lingerie you'd expect to find in a Milanese intimo boutique, and you can also pick something from the to-be-seen-in beachwear range—if you can stretch it over your frame. The boutique has thought of everything you might possibly need on a beach, from itsy-bitsy bikinis to matching shorts, from pareos to T-shirts—plus beach bags to carry it all in. Guys can pick up some fun stuff here, too, like the bold print shorts from the beach boy range. *yamamay.it*

Affordable   *Amex/MC/V*

Via Dante 16   **02 720 93876**
20121 Milan   Daily 9:30-8 (Sun 11-8)

Yves Saint Laurent

The Milanese outpost of this über-chic French brand resembles a black-lacquered wooden labyrinth that winds and twists its way through a display of essential Yves Saint Laurent goodies. Tom Ford may have been replaced by his former deputy, Stefano Pilati, but everything here still oozes the sophisticated glamour that is the hallmark of this label. Men's and women's ready-to-wear, watches, eyeglasses, jewellery, shoes and make-up, plus a vast selection of hit-list handbags, fill every corner of this 850 square metre boutique—Europe's largest YSL outpost. Just when you think that the store's deep, dark interior has swallowed you whole, the shoe department at the back bursts out onto a cobbled courtyard flooded with daylight so that you just have time to readjust your eyesight before stepping out onto Via Montenapoleone.   *ysl.com*

Luxury   *Amex/MC/V*
Via Montenapoleone 27   **02 760 00573**
20121 Milan   Mon-Sat 10-7
(Mon 3-7, Tues-Fri 10-7, Sat 10-2:30 in summer)

☆ Zap!

This is a young, flirty, girly store for saucy girls about town who like their teensy T-shirts covered in glitter. Beneath giant chandeliers in a funky bazaar-like setting, this multi-brand boutique currently offers DKNY Jeans, Blumarine, Laltramoda, Chloé, Tarina Tarantino, Playboy (underwear only), Roberto Cavalli and many more. The roster of labels changes pretty frequently so the customers keep going back to see what's new. As well as the two floors of clothes, there are accessories, bags, jewellery, books, gadgets and even collectors' Barbie dolls. Upstairs you'll find an Aldo Coppola hair salon so you can shop and style in the same place.

Moderate to expensive   *Amex/MC/V*
Galleria Passarella 2   **02 760 67501**
20122 Milan   Mon-Sat 10-7

Zara

Walking into Zara's fabulously glitzy entrance off the sombre Corso Vittorio Emanuele II, you may think you have made a wrong turn into a glamorous Forties movie theatre. Gilt mosaics of fairytale scenes cover the walls and are a refreshing backdrop to the up-to-the-minute catwalk styles. The huge store covers four floors with a daunting array of clothes, shoes and accessories for the entire family at knockdown prices. Be ready to scramble for sizes, especially smaller ones: the Spanish chain only landed in Milan three years ago, but judging by the interminable wait for dressing-rooms and check-out assistance, Zara's Latin flair and low prices are being hungrily devoured. Bestsellers like white faux-Chanel bouclé suits or the faux-Prada fur stoles disappear at the blink of an eye. To get around this, local aficionados only shop on Thursdays or Saturdays when new stock comes in. The service tends to be on the grumpy side; sales assistants are so pressed for time that folding your purchases before stuffing them into the trademark blue paper bag can be optional. Still, Milan's countless Zara fans were thrilled when a second branch opened in Corso Buenos Aires. *zara.com*

Affordable *Amex/MC/V*

Corso Vittorio Emanuele II 11 **02 763 98177**
20122 Milan Mon-Sat 10-9, Sun 10-8

Corso Buenos Aires 54 **02 295 33238**
20124 Milan Mon-Sat 10-8

Zeus

Though the cream interior of this hip boutique could do with a lick of paint, the designer brands it showcases couldn't be smarter. Head here for feminine romantic styles from Blumarine, Blugirl and Plein Sud, swimwear by body-conscious Italian brand Fisico, plus sexy, sparkly stilettos, bags and accessories to match. The slightly dippy assistants flutter round the customers admiring and advising, and will disappear down the cream iron circular staircases to bring up new stock and sizes. Sadly, the cute poodle in the window is not for sale.

Moderate to expensive *Amex/MC/V*

Corso Genova 24 **02 894 08267**
20123 Milan Mon 3:30-7:30, Tues-Sat 9:30-1, 3:30-7:30

The Last Good Buy

You no longer have to wait for the sales to pick up affordable designer clothing in Milan. Over the past few years, a host of designer discount outlets have opened around the city—and now whole purpose-built villages are popping up only a short drive away. Here we list two of the best, so hire a car or catch a train and a taxi—just make sure the boot is big enough to get all your loot back home.

Serravalle Scrivia

There's more than a touch of Las Vegas about the faux 18th-century Ligurian village that houses this massive designer discount shopping centre (80 kilometres from Milan on the A7), but since its opening in 2000 and extension in 2002 Sunday afternoon excursions here have become a Milanese habit. For this reason it's best to avoid the weekends, but during the week the 150 stores here shouldn't be missed. Most of the big brands have outlets here, and discounts hover at around 30-70%. You'll find Versace, Dolce & Gabbana, Roberto Cavalli, Etro, Bulgari, La Perla, Trussardi and Prada, as well as virtual give-aways from middle-market brands like Diesel and Furla. Whatever the time of year, the place is so vast you're bound to find something to suit you.

mcarthurglen.it

Moderate to expensive   *Amex/MC/V (at most stores)*

Via della Moda 1   **0143 609 000**
15069 Serravalle Scrivia   Daily 10-8

Franciacorta Outlet Village   👦👧👦

Opened in September 2003 in yet another purpose-built faux village, this discount shopping centre is the latest to open within a 100-kilometre radius of Milan. With discounts at 30-70%, it's worth the hour-long drive along the A4. Some of the best bargains we saw were at shoe producer Vicini, with bright red stilettos at 139 euros and blue and orange sneakers at 99. Also worth checking out are the bed sets by Frette, and Franciacorta is always a great place to pick up a pair of reasonably priced designer jeans.   *franciacortaoutlet.it*

Moderate to expensive   *Amex/MC/V (at most stores)*

Piazza Cascina Mole 1   **030 681 0364**
25050 Rodengo Saiano   Sun-Thurs 10-7
                    Fri-Sat 10-8 (Oct-Mar), Sun-Thurs 10-8
                                       Fri-Sat 10-9 (Apr-Sept)

Milan Stores by District

Brera/Corso Garibaldi/Corso Como

Corso Buenos Aires

Corso di Porta Ticinese/Corso Genova

Via Montenapoleone & neighbourhood

Corso Vittorio Emanuele/Duomo/Via Torino

Corso Vercelli/Magenta

Piazza 5 Giornate and outwards

Isola

Beyond Milan

Milan—City Centre

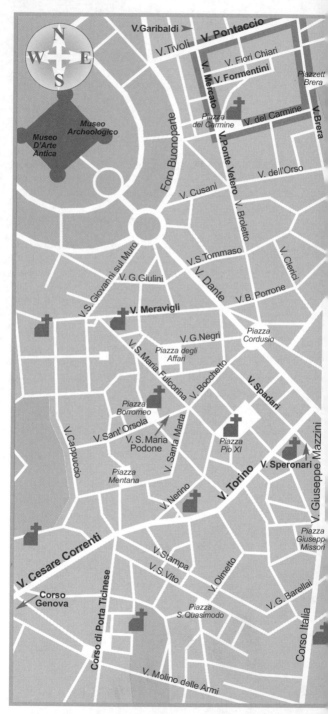

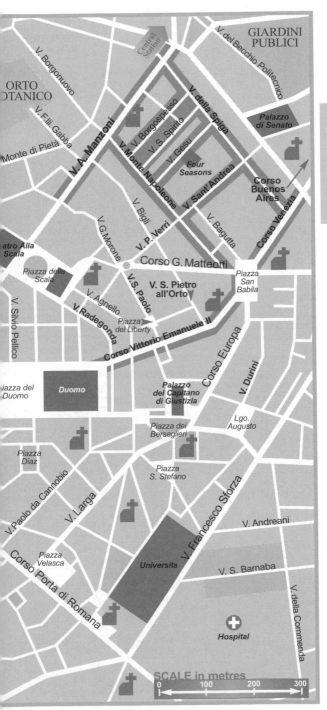

341

Milan—Largo La Foppa

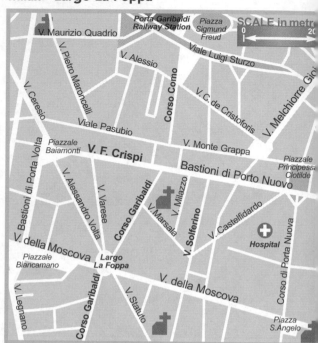

Milan—Corso Buenos Aires

Brera/Corso Garibaldi/Corso Como

See map page 340

10 Corso Como	Corso Como 10
10 Corso Como Outlet Store	Via Tazzoli 3
Agatha Ruiz de la Prada	Via Maroncelli 5
Alfonso Garlando	Via Madonina 1
Alibi	Via Broletto 43
Anteprima & Anteprima Plastik	Corso Como 9
Antonia & Antonia Accessori	Via Ponte Vetero 1
Bagutta	Via Fiori Chiari 7
Bipa	Via Ponte Vetero 10
Boule de Neige	Corso Como 3 & 8
Cavalli e Nastri	Via Brera 2
Chicco	Via Paolo Sarpi 1
Clan	Via Pontaccio 15
Clan Pontaccio	Via Pontaccio 15
Coccinelle	Via Statuto 11
Co-Co	Via Giannone 4
Custo Barcelona	Largo La Foppa 4
Decathlon	Foro Bonaparte 74/76
Docks Dora	Viale Crispi 7
Eleonora Scaramucci	Via dell'Orso 1
Eral 55	Piazza XXV Aprile 14
Ethic	Corso Garibaldi 34
Francescatrezzi	Corso Garibaldi 44
Franco Jacassi	Via Sacchi 3
Germano Zama	Via Solferino 1
Kristina Ti	Via Solferino 18
Laltramoda	Via Solferino 2
La Vetrina di Beryl	Via Statuto 4
Le Solferine	Via Solferino 2
Lorella Braglia	Via Solferino (corner Via Ancona)
Luisa Beccaria	Via Formentini 1
Martino Midali	Via Ponte Vetero 9
Martino Midali	Via Mercato 6
Nadine	Corso Genova 1
Naj-Oleari	Via Brera 8
Outlet Matia's	Piazza Mirabello 4
P-Box	Via Pontaccio 19
Sadogy	Corso Como 2
Urrah	Via Solferino 3-5
Vintage 55	Via Ponte Vetero 1

Corso Buenos Aires

See map page 342

Benetton	Corso Buenos Aires 19
Boggi	Via Caretta 1
Celio	Galleria Buenos Aires 42-9
Chicco	Corso Buenos Aires 75
Coccinelle	Corso Buenos Aires 16

Milan Districts

Coin	Piazzale Loreto 15
David Mayer	Corso Buenos Aires 66
Du Pareil Au Même	Corso Buenos Aires 49
Elena Miró	Corso Buenos Aires 15
Frette	Corso Buenos Aires 82
Furla	Corso Buenos Aires 18
Geox	Corso Buenos Aires 2 & 42
Giacomelli Sport	Piazza Argentina 4
Henry Béguelin	Via Caminadella 7
Henry Cuir	Via Arena 19
JDC—Urban Store	Corso Buenos Aires 1
Luisa Spagnoli	Corso Buenos Aires 39
Mandarina Duck	Corso Buenos Aires 3
Marilena	Corso Buenos Aires 25
Marina Rinaldi	Corso Buenos Aires 77
Nadine	Corso Buenos Aires 38
ProMod	Corso Buenos Aires 41
Sisley	Corso Buenos Aires 3 & 19
Stefanel	Corso Buenos Aires 77
Stefanel	Via San Gregorio 1
Vergelio	Via Vitruvio 3
Zara	Corso Buenos Aires 54

Corso di Porta Ticinese/Corso Genova

See map page 340

Alberto Guardiani	Corso di Porta Ticinese 67
Anna Fabiano	Corso di Porta Ticinese 40
Anna Ravazzoli	Corso Genova 13 & 16
Antonioli	Via Pasquale Paoli 1
Armani Jeans	Corso di Porta Ticinese 60
B-Fly	Corso di Porta Ticinese 46
Biffi	Corso Genova 5 & 6
Carhartt	Corso di Porta Ticinese 103
Cavalli e Nastri	Via de Amicis 9
Civico 82	Corso di Porta Ticinese 82
Coccinelle	Corso Genova 6
Coin	Piazzale Cantore 12
Combo	Corso di Porta Ticinese 62
Custo Barcelona	Corso di Porta Ticinese 58
Cut	Corso di Porta Ticinese 58
Diesel	Corso di Porta Ticinese 44 & 60
Docks Dora	Via Toffetti 9
Ethic	Corso di Porta Ticinese 50
Fabi	Corso di Porta Ticinese 84
Fatto a Mano	Corso di Porta Ticinese 76
Fornarina	Corso di Porta Ticinese 78
Frip	Corso di Porta Ticinese 16
Fuerteventura	Corso di Porta Ticinese 46

Gas	Corso di Porta Ticinese 53
Joost	Via Cesare Correnti 12
Killah	Corso di Porta Ticinese 58-60
L'Armadio di Laura	Via Voghera 25
Laura Urbinati	Piazza Sant'Eustorgio 6
Les Tropeziennes	Corso di Porta Ticinese 107
Martin Luciano	Alzaia Naviglio Grande 58
Martino Midali	Corso di Porta Ticinese 87
Mauro	Corso di Porta Ticinese 60
No Season	Corso di Porta Ticinese 77
Pur5	Via Pio IV 1
Purple	Corso di Porta Ticinese 22
Stussy	Corso di Porta Ticinese 103
Tim Camino	Via de Amicis 3
Vanilla	Corso di Porta Ticinese 103
Zeus	Corso Genova 24

Via Montenapoleone & neighbourhood

See map page 341

Acqua di Parma	Via Gesù 3
Agnona	Via della Spiga 3
Alan Journo	Via della Spiga 36
Alberta Ferretti	Via Montenapoleone 21
Alberto Guardiani	Via Montenapoleone 9
Alexander McQueen	Via Verri 8
Alviero Martini	Via Montenapoleone 26
Angelo Fusco	Via Montenapoleone 25
Anna Molinari Blumarine	Via della Spiga 42
Antonio Fusco	Via Sant' Andrea 11
Armani Collezioni	Via Montenapoleone 2
Armani Junior	Via Montenapoleone 10
Armani/Via Manzoni 31	Via Manzoni 31
Ars Rosa	Via Montenapoleone 8
Atelier Aimée	Via Montenapoleone 29
A.Testoni	Via Montenapoleone 19
Bagutta	Via San Pietro all'Orto 26
Baldinini	Via Montenapoleone 15
Baldinini	Piazza Meda 3
Bally	Via Montenapoleone 8
Banner	Via Sant' Andrea 8
Barbara Bui	Via Manzoni 45
Basement	Via Senato 15
Bonpoint	Via Manzoni 15
Borbonese	Via Santo Spirito 26
Borsalino	Via Verri 5 (corner Via Bigli)
Bottega Veneta	Via Montenapoleone 5
Braccialini	Via Montenapoleone 19
Brioni	Via Gesù 3 & 4
Brioni Bespoke	Via Gesù 2/A

Milan Districts

Bruno Magli	Via Manzoni 14
Burberry	Via Verri 7
Byblos	Via della Spiga 33
Camper	Via Montenapoleone 6
Canali	Via Verri 1-3
Canziani	Via Montenapoleone 26
Car Shoe	Via della Spiga 50
Casadei	Via Sant' Andrea 17
Celine	Via Montenapoleone 25/2
Cerruti	Via della Spiga 20
Cesare Gatti	Via Montenapoleone 19
Cesare Paciotti	Via Sant' Andrea 8
Cesare Paciotti	Via Sant'Andrea 8/A
Chanel	Via Sant' Andrea 10/A
Christian Dior	Via Montenapoleone 12 & 14
Christian Dior Homme	Via Montenapoleone 12
Church's	Via Sant' Andrea 11
Coccinelle	Via Bigli 28
Corneliani	Via Montenapoleone 12
Costume National	Via Sant' Andrea 12
Davide Cenci	Via Manzoni 7
Diesel	Corso Venezia 7 & 11
D-Magazine Outlet	Via Montenapoleone 26
Dolce & Gabbana	Via della Spiga 2 & 26
Dolce & Gabbana	Corso Venezia 15
Domo Adami	Via Manzoni 23
Emilio Pucci	Via Montenapoleone 14
Ermenegildo Zegna	Via Verri 3
Etro	Via Montenapoleone 5
Etro	Via Bigli 2 (corner Via Verri)
Exté	Via della Spiga 6
Fabi	Via Montenapoleone 17
Fabrizio Corsi	Via Verri 7
Fay	Via della Spiga 15
Fedeli Red and Blue	Via Montenapoleone 8
Fendi	Via Sant' Andrea 16
Francesco Biasia	Via Montenapoleone 1
Fratelli Rossetti	Via Montenapoleone 1
Frette	Via Montenapoleone 21
Frette	Via Manzoni 11
Gallo	Via Manzoni 16b
Geox	Via Montenapoleone 26
Geox	Via Manzoni 20
Gianfranco Ferré	Via Sant' Andrea 15
Gianni Versace	Via Montenapoleone 11
Gibo by Julie Verhoeven	Via Sant' Andrea 10/A
Gio Moretti	Via della Spiga 4
Gio Moretti Baby	Via della Spiga 9
Giorgio Armani	Via della Spiga 19

Giorgio Armani	Via Sant' Andrea 9
Gucci	Via Montenapoleone 5-7
Helmut Lang	Via della Spiga 11
Hermès	Via Sant' Andrea 21
Hogan	Via Montenapoleone 23
Hugo Boss	Via Matteotti 1
Iceberg	Via Montenapoleone 10
I Pinco Pallino	Via della Spiga 42
I Pinco Pallino	Via Borgospesso 25
I Pinco Pallino	Galleria Manzoni 40
Jil Sander	Via Verri 6
Jimmy Choo	Via San Pietro all'Orto 17
John Richmond	Via Verri (corner Via Bigli)
Just Cavalli	Via Della Spiga 30
Kenzo	Via Sant' Andrea 11
Krizia	Via della Spiga 23
Laboratorio Italiano	Via Borgonuovo 12
La Perla	Via Montenapoleone 1
Larusmiani	Via Montenapoleone 7
Laura Biagiotti	Via Borgospesso 19
Les Copains	Via Manzoni 21
Lorenzo Banfi	Via Sant'Andrea 1
Loro Piana	Via Montenapoleone 27
Louis Vuitton	Via Montenapoleone 2
Luciano Barbera	Via Santo Spirito 22
Malo	Via della Spiga 7
Mariella Burani	Via Montenapoleone 3
Marisa	Via Sant' Andrea 1 & 10/A
Marisa	Via Della Spiga 52
Marni	Via Sant' Andrea 14
Mazzini	Via delle Spiga 52
Mila Schön	Via Manzoni 45
Missoni	Via Sant' Andrea 2
Miss Sixty	Via Montenapoleone 27
Mortarotti	Via Montenapoleone 24
Moschino	Via della Spiga 30
Moschino	Via Sant' Andrea 12
Napapijri	Via Manzoni 46
Nara Camicie	Via Montenapoleone 5
Narciso Rodriguez	Via Montenapoleone 21
Parisi	Via Turati 3
Patrizia Pepe	Via Manzoni 38
Paul & Shark	Via Montenapoleone 15
Paul Smith	Via Manzoni 30
P-Box	Via Manzoni 13
Philosophy	Via Montenapoleone 19
Prada	Via della Spiga 1 & 18
Prada	Via Montenapoleone 6 & 8
Prada	Via Sant' Andrea 21

Milan Districts

Ralph Lauren	Via Montenapoleone 4
René Caovilla	Via Bagutta 28
Roberto Cavalli	Via della Spiga 42
Ruffo	Via della Spiga 48
Salvatore Ferragamo	Via Montenapoleone 3 & 20
Sebastian	Via Montenapoleone 25
Sergio Rossi	Via della Spiga 5
Sergio Rossi	Via Montenapoleone 6/A & 15
Sermoneta Gloves	Via della Spiga 46
Silvano Lattanzi	Via Borgospesso 25
Silvano Lattanzi	Via Gesù 11
Simonetta Ravizza by Annabella	Via Montenapoleone 1
Sportmax	Via della Spiga 30
Stone Island & C.P.Company	Corso Venezia 12
Strenesse	Via Manzoni 37
Tanino Crisci	Via Montenapoleone 3
Tod's	Via della Spiga 22
Trussardi	Piazza della Scala 5
Trussardi	Via Sant' Andrea 3-7
Valentino	Via Montenapoleone 20
Valextra	Via Manzoni 3
Verri	Via Verri (corner Via Bigli)
Versace	Via San Pietro all'Orto 11
Versus	Via San Pietro all'Orto 10
Vicini	Via della Spiga 1
Vierre	Via Montenapoleone 29
Viktor & Rolf	Via Sant'Andrea 14
Vilebrequin	Via della Spiga 46
Vivienne Westwood	Corso Venezia 25
Von Dutch	Via della Spiga 46
Yves Saint Laurent	Via Montenapoleone 27

Corso Vittorio Emanuele II/Duomo/Via Torino
See map page 341

Benetton	Corso Vittorio Emanuele II 9
Benetton	Via Dante 4
Benetton	Via Torino 61
Blunauta	Via Dante 11
Blunauta	Corso Indipendenza 10
Boggi	Piazza San Babila 3
Boggi	Via Dante 3
Boggi	Largo Augusto 3
Borsalino	Galleria Vittorio Emanuele II 92
Bruno Magli	Corso Vittorio Emanuele II (corner Via San Paolo)
Cacharel	Via San Paolo 1
Camper	Via Torino 15
Carla Sai Bene	Via San Maurilio 20

Celio	Corso Vittorio Emanuele II 5
Celio	Via Dante 14
Chicco (Tuttochicco)	Corso Matteotti 10
Church's	Via Marino 7
DAAD Dantone	Corso Matteotti 20
D&G	Corso Venezia 7
David Mayer	Via Meravigli 16
David Mayer	Corso Vittorio Emanuele II 2
Diffusione Tessile	Galleria San Carlo 6
Dimensione Danza	Corso Europa 2
Dimensione Danza	Corso Vittorio Emanuele II 9
Du Pareil Au Même	Via Dante 5
Elena Miró	Via Dante 4
Energie	Via Torino 19
Furla	Corso Vittorio Emanuele II 2
Gallo	Via Durini 26
Geox	Via Speronari 8
Geox	Piazza San Carlo 2
	(corner Corso Vittorio Emanuele II)
Geox	Via Rovello 1
Gentuccia Bini	Via Pantano 17
Gianni Campagna	Via Palestro 24
Gucci	Galleria Vittorio Emanuele II
Guess?	Piazza San Babila 4/B
H&M	Galleria Passerella 2
Jam	Via Santa Radegonda 8
JDC—Urban Store	Piazza Duomo 31
Kallisté—Un Dimanche à Venise	Corso Matteotti 22
Laltramoda	Corso Venezia 5
La Rinascente	Via Radegonda 3
Le Solferine	Via Meravigli 16
Louis Vuitton	Galleria Vittorio Emanuele II
Love Therapy	Corso Europa 1
Luisa Spagnoli	Corso Vittorio Emanuele II
	(corner Galleria San Carlo)
Mandarina Duck	Galleria San Carlo
	(corner Corso Europa)
Mandarina Duck	Via Orefici 10
Mango	Via Torino 21
Marilena	Corso Vittorio Emanuele II 15
Marilena	Via Torino 13
Marina Rinaldi	Galleria Passerella 2
Max & Co	Piazza Liberty 4
Max & Co	Via Dante 4
MaxMara	Piazza Liberty 4
MaxMara	Via Orefici 1
Miss Sixty	Via Torino 10
Miu Miu	Corso Venezia 3
Nadine	Corso Vittorio Emanuele II 34

Nadine	Via Dante 16
Nara Camicie	Piazza Duomo 31
Nara Camicie	Corso Vittorio Emanuele 4
Nero Giardini	Corso Venezia 9
Onyx Fashion Store	Corso Vittorio Emanuele II 24
Plus	Piazza Missori 2
Pollini	Piazza Duomo 31
Pollini	Corso Vittorio Emanuele II 30
Prada	Galleria Vittorio Emanuele II 63-65
ProMod	Via Mazzini 2
Replay	Largo Corsia dei Servi 11
Samsonite	Corso Matteotti 12
Sisley	Piazza Duomo (corner Via Mazzini)
Sisley	Galleria Passarella 1
Stefanel	Corso Vittorio Emanuele II 28
Stefanel	Via Spadari 1
T'store (Trussardi)	Corso Europa (corner Galleria San Carlo)
Valextra	Piazza San Babila 1
Valextra	Via Cerva 11
Vergelio	Corso Vittorio Emanuele II 10
Yamamay	Via Dante 16
Zap!	Galleria Passarella 2
Zara	Galleria Vittorio Emanuele II 11

Corso Vercelli/Magenta

Benetton	Corso Vercelli 8
Blunauta	Via Zenale 11
Boggi	Corso Vercelli 23-25
Casa Del Bianco	Corso Magenta 2
Chicco	Largo Settimio Severo
Christies	Corso Vercelli 51
Coin	Corso Vercelli 30-32
DEV	Corso Vercelli 8
Dimensione Danza	Corso Vercelli 31
Docksteps	Via Cusani 10
E.Marinella	Via Santa Maria alla Porta 5
Fratelli Rossetti	Corso Magenta 17
Frette	Corso Vercelli 23-25
Furla	Corso Vercelli 11
Gemelli	Corso Vercelli 16
Geox	Corso Vercelli 9
Guja	Galleria di Corso Vercelli 23
Guja	Via San Giovanni sul Muro 13
Laltramoda	Corso Vercelli 20
La Perla	Corso Vercelli 35
Les Chaussures Mon Amour	Via Cherubini 3
Mandarina Duck	Corso Vercelli 27
Marina Rinaldi	Corso Vercelli 3
Martino Midali	Via Marghera 22

Mortarotti	Via Belfiore 6
Mortarotti	Corso Magenta 29
Nadine	Via Marghera 18
Peter Pan	Via Mascheroni 12
Pupi Solari	Piazza Tommaseo 2
Puma Concept Store	Corso Vercelli 29
Samsonite	Via Belfiore 6
Sisley	Corso Vercelli 8
Vergelio	Corso Vercelli 2

Piazza 5 Giornate and outwards

Benetton	Piazza 5 Giornate 54
Benetton	Viale Corsica 45
Benetton	Corso di Porta Romana 23
Coin	Piazza 5 Giornate 1/A
Elena Miró	Corso XXII Marzo 7
Fila	Viale Umbria (corner Via Colletta)
Host	Piazza Tommaseo 2
Il Salvagente	Via Fratelli Bronzetti 6
Imarika	Via Morelli 1
Puma Outlet	Viale Monte Nero 22
Salvagente Bimbi	Via Balzaretti 28
Shabby Chic	Via B. Cellini 21
Sisley	Corso di Porta Romana 54
Stefanel	Corso XXII Marzo 4

Isola

Le Vintage	Via Garigliano 4
Miss Ghinting	Via Borsieri (opposite #16)

Beyond Milan

Franciacorta Outlet Village	Piazza Cascina Mole 1 Rodengo Saiano
Serravalle Scrivia	Via della Moda 1, Serravalle Scrivia

Milan Districts

Milan Stores by Category

Women's

Men's

Unisex

Children's

Women's Accessories

10 Corso Como
Acqua di Parma
Antonia Accessori
Anteprima Plastik
Armani/Via Manzoni 31
Borbonese
Bottega Veneta
Boule de Neige
Burberry
Byblos
Coccinelle
Coin
Dolce & Gabbana
Etro
Francescatrezzi
Frette

Gallo
Giorgio Armani
Gucci
Hermès
Jam
Kristina Ti
La Rinascente
Louis Vuitton
Love Therapy
Malo
Prada
Samsonite
Sermoneta Gloves
Trussardi
Valextra
Zap!

Bridal

Alfonso Garlando
Atelier Aimée
Domo Adami

Luisa Beccaria
Mariella Burani

Women's Career

Antonio Fusco
Brioni
Coin
Davide Cenci
Emporio Armani
Germano Zama

Giorgio Armani
Jil Sander
Laboratorio Italiano
La Rinascente
MaxMara

Women's Cashmere/Knitwear

Agnona
Cesare Gatti
Fedeli Red and Blue
Gemelli
Krizia
Laura Biagiotti

Laura Urbinati
Les Copains
Loro Piana
Malo
Martino Midali
Missoni

Women's Casual

Armani Jeans
Armani/Via Manzoni 31
Benetton
Blunauta
Co-Co
Coin
Decathlon
Diesel
Eleonora Scaramucci

Emporio Armani
Energie
Fay
Fornarina
Germano Zama
Guess?
JDC – Urban Store
La Rinascente
Mandarina Duck

Women's Casual *(continued)*

Max & Co
Nadine
Nara Camicie
Onyx Fashion Store
Paul & Shark
Prada
ProMod

Replay
Sisley
Stefanel
T'Store
Urrah
Von Dutch

Women's Classic

Agnona
Bagutta
Brioni
Coin
Davide Cenci
Fay
Gemelli

Gianni Campagna
Laboratorio Italiano
La Rinascente
Loro Piana
Luciano Barbera
Luisa Beccaria
Nara Camicie

Women's Contemporary

10 Corso Como
Alibi
Anna Fabiano
Anna Ravazzoli
Antonia
Antonioli
Banner
Biffi
Bipa
Boule de Neige
Carhartt
Carla Sai Bene
Civico 82
Clan Pontaccio
Coin
Combo
DAAD Dantone
Ethic
Fornarina
Frip
Fuerteventura
Gas
Gio Moretti
H&M
Imarika
Jam
Killah

Laltramoda
La Rinascente
Laura Urbinati
La Vetrina di Beryl
Lorella Braglia
Mango
Marisa
Martino Midali
MaxMara
Miss Sixty
Mortarotti
Nadine
Naj-Oleari
No Season
Patrizia Pepe
Plus
Pupi Solari
Purple
Sadogy
Samsonite
Sportmax
Tim Camino
Vanilla
Zap!
Zara
Zeus

Women's Designer

Agatha Ruiz de la Prada
Alan Journo
Alberta Ferretti
Alexander McQueen
Anna Molinari Blumarine
Anteprima
Armani Collezioni
Armani/Via Manzoni 31
Barbara Bui
Borbonese
Burberry
Byblos
Cacharel
Celine
Cerruti
Chanel
Christian Dior
Costume National
Custo Barcelona
D&G
Dolce & Gabbana
Emilio Pucci
Etro
Exté
Fendi
Gianfranco Ferré
Gianni Campagna
Gianni Versace
Gibo
Giorgio Armani
Gucci
Helmut Lang
Hermès
Iceberg
Isabella Tonchi

Jil Sander
John Richmond
Just Cavalli
Kenzo
Kristina Ti
Krizia
La Perla
Laura Biagiotti
Les Copains
Louis Vuitton
Mariella Burani
Marni
MaxMara
Mila Schön
Missoni
Miu Miu
Moschino
Narciso Rodriguez
Paul Smith
P-Box
Philosophy
Pollini
Prada
Ralph Lauren
Roberto Cavalli
Ruffo
Salvatore Ferragamo
Strenesse
Trussardi
T'Store
Valentino
Versus
Viktor & Rolf
Vivienne Westwood
Yves Saint Laurent

Women's Discount

10 Corso Como Outlet
  Store
Antonio Fusco Outlet
Basement
Diffusione Tessile
D-Magazine Outlet

Franciacorta Outlet Village
Il Salvagente
Outlet Matia's
Parisi
Puma Outlet
Serravalle Scrivia

Women's Ethnic

Fatto a Mano

Women's Eveningwear & Special Occasions

Alexander McQueen
Christian Dior
Coin
Giorgio Armani
Gucci
Krizia

La Rinascente
Mila Schön
Prada
Valentino
Versace
Yves Saint Laurent

Women's Furs

Fendi
Simonetta Ravizza by
  Annabella

Women's Handbags

Alan Journo
Alviero Martini
Anteprima Plastik
A.Testoni
Baldinini
Bally
Biffi
Borbonese
Bottega Veneta
Boule de Neige
Braccialini
Bruno Magli
Celine
Cesare Paciotti
Chanel
Christian Dior
Coccinelle
Coin
DEV
Etro
Fendi
Francescatrezzi
Francesco Biasia
Furla
Gucci

Henry Béguelin
Henry Cuir
Hermès
Hogan
Imarika
John Richmond
Kristina Ti
La Rinascente
Les Tropeziennes
Louis Vuitton
Malo
Mandarina Duck
Mazzini
Mila Schön
Miu Miu
Moschino
Nero Giardini
No Season
Prada
Sadogy
Salvatore Ferragamo
Sebastian
Tod's
Trussardi
Valentino

Women's Hats

Alan Journo
Borsalino
Imarika

La Rinascente
No Season

Women's Hosiery

Coin

La Rinascente

Women's Leather

Bruno Magli
Cut
Fabrizio Corsi
Fendi
Henry Béguelin

Le Solferine
Pollini
Ruffo
Trussardi

Women's Lingerie

Christies
Coin
Frette
John Richmond
Kristina Ti

La Perla
La Rinascente
Les Tropeziennes
Prada
Yamamay

Maternity

Chicco

Women's Plus Sizes

Elena Mirò
Laura Biagiotti
Luisa Spagnoli

Marina Rinaldi
Martino Midali

Women's Shirts

Coin
Fedeli Red and Blue

La Rinascente
Nara Camicie

Women's Shoes

Agatha Ruiz de la Prada
Alberto Guardiani
Alfonso Garlando
Anna Ravazzoli
Antonia
A.Testoni
Baldinini
Bally
Barbara Bui
Bottega Veneta
Boule de Neige
Bruno Magli
Camper
Car Shoe
Casadei
Celine
Cesare Paciotti
Civico 82

Coccinelle
Coin
Costume National
Davide Cenci
DEV
Docksteps
Fabi
Fornarina
Francescatrezzi
Fratelli Rossetti
Furla
Geox
Gucci
Guja
Henry Béguelin
Henry Cuir
Hogan
Imarika

Women's Shoes *(continued)*

Jimmy Choo
Kallisté—Un Dimanche à Venise
Killah
La Rinascente
La Vetrina di Beryl
Les Chaussures Mon Amour
Le Solferine
Les Tropeziennes
Lorenzo Banfi
Louis Vuitton
Marilena
Mauro
Miu Miu
Nero Giardini
No Season
P-Box
Peter Pan
Pollini
Prada
Puma Concept Store
Rene Caovilla
Roberto Cavalli
Sadogy
Salvatore Ferragamo
Sebastian
Sergio Rossi
Silvano Lattanzi
Tanino Crisci
Tod's
Vergelio
Vicini
Vierre

Women's Swimwear

Christies
Coin
Decathlon
Fila
Gallo
Gemelli
Giacomelli Sport
John Richmond
Kristina Ti
La Rinascente
Laura Urbinati
Malo
Yamamay

Women's Vintage & Retro

B-Fly
Cavalli e Nastri
Co-Co
DAAD Dantone
Docks Dora
Franco Jacassi
L'Armadio di Laura
Martin Luciano
Miss Ghinting
Shabby Chic
Vintage 55

Women's Young & Trendy

Armani Jeans
Carhartt
Combo
Diesel
Energie
Fornarina
Fuerteventura
Gas
Gentucca Bini
H&M
Jam
JDC – Urban Store
Just Cavalli
Killah
Love Therapy
Mango
Max & Co
Miss Sixty
Onyx Fashion Store
ProMod
Replay
Sportmax
Tim Camino
T'Store
Vanilla
Von Dutch
Zara

Men's Business Apparel

Angelo Fusco
Biffi
Boggi
Brioni
Brioni Bespoke
Canali
Coin
Corneliani
Davide Cenci
E.Marinella
Ermenegildo Zegna
Etro
Germano Zama
Gianni Campagna
Laboratorio Italiano
La Rinascente
Larusmiani
Loro Piana
Prada

Men's Cashmere/Knitwear

Cesare Gatti
Fedeli Red and Blue
Gemelli
Les Copains
Loro Piana
Malo
Missoni

Men's Casual

Armani/Via Manzoni 31
Armani Jeans
Benetton
Biffi
Blunauta
Celio
Coin
Decathlon
Diesel
Energie
Ermenegildo Zegna
Fay
Germano Zama
Guess?
H&M
JDC – Urban Store
La Rinascente
Larusmiani
Mandarina Duck
Napapijri
Paul & Shark
Prada
Replay
Sisley
Stefanel
Stone Island &
   C.P.Company
T'Store
Urrah
Vilebrequin
Von Dutch

Men's Classic

Brioni
Canziani
Davide Cenci
Ermenegildo Zegna
Gemelli
Gianni Campagna
Host
Laboratorio Italiano
Larusmiani
Loro Piana
Luciano Barbera
Silvano Lattanzi

Men's Contemporary

10 Corso Como
Antonioli
Biffi
Carhartt
Clan Pontaccio
Coin
Combo
DAAD Dantone
David Mayer
Eral 55
Frip
Fuerteventura
Gas
Gio Moretti
Hugo Boss
Jam
Joost
Killah
La Vetrina di Beryl
La Rinascente
Mango
No Season
Purple
Samsonite
Verri

Men's Designer

Alviero Martini
Antonio Fusco
Armani Collezioni
Burberry
Byblos
Cerruti
Christian Dior
Christian Dior Homme
Costume National
Custo Barcelona
D&G
Dolce & Gabbana
Etro
Exté
Fendi
Gianfranco Ferré/GFF
  Gianfranco Ferré
Gianni Versace
Giorgio Armani
Gucci
Helmut Lang
Hermès
Iceberg
Jil Sander
John Richmond
Just Cavalli
Kenzo
Krizia
Les Copains
Louis Vuitton
Missoni
Miu Miu
Moschino
Paul Smith
Pollini
Prada
Ralph Lauren
Roberto Cavalli
Ruffo
Salvatore Ferragamo
Strenesse
Trussardi
T'Store
Valentino
Versus
Vivienne Westwood
Yves Saint Laurent Rive
  Gauche

Men's Discount

D-Magazine Outlet
Franciacorta Outlet Village
Il Salvagente
Outlet Matia's
Parisi
Serravalle Scrivia

Men's Hats

Borsalino	La Rinascente

Men's Leather & Leather Goods

A.Testoni	La Rinascente
Baldinini	Lorenzo Banfi
Bally	Louis Vuitton
Bottega Veneta	Pollini
Bruno Magli	Prada
Coin	Ruffo
Cut	Salvatore Ferragamo
Fabrizio Corsi	Trussardi
Gucci	Valextra
Hermès	

Men's Shirts

Bagutta	DEV
Boggi	Fedeli Red and Blue
Brioni	La Rinascente
Canziani	Nara Camicie
Coin	Paul Smith
Corneliani	

Men's Shoes

Alberto Guardiani	Fratelli Rossetti
A.Testoni	Geox
Baldinini	Hogan
Bally	La Vetrina di Beryl
Bottega Veneta	Lorenzo Banfi
Bruno Magli	Nero Giardini
Camper	Pollini
Car Shoe	Prada
Casadei	Puma Concept Store
Cesare Paciotti	Sebastian
Christian Dior Homme	Sergio Rossi
Church's	Silvano Lattanzi
Davide Cenci	Tanino Crisci
DEV	Tod's
Docksteps	Vergelio
Fabi	Vierre

Men's Swimwear

Coin
Decathlon
Fila
Gallo

Gas
Giacomelli Sport
La Rinascente
Vilebrequin

Men's Undergarments

Coin
D&G

Gallo
La Rinascente

Men's Vintage & Retro

B-Fly
Docks Dora
Franco Jacassi

Martin Luciano
Shabby Chic
Vintage 55

Men's Young & Trendy

Armani Jeans
Carhartt
Combo
DAAD Dantone
Diesel
Energie
Fuerteventura
Gas
H&M

Jam
JDC – Urban Store
Just Cavalli
Killah
Mango
Replay
Von Dutch
Zara

Unisex Athletic

Decathlon
Dimensione Danza
Giacomelli Sport

La Rinascente
Puma Concept Store

Unisex Outdoor Sports Apparel

Decathlon
Luciano Barbera
Napapijiri

Paul & Shark
Prada
Samsonite

Children's Clothing

Agatha Ruiz de la Prada
Armani Junior
Ars Rosa
Benetton
Bonpoint
Burberry
Cacharel
Casa Del Bianco
Chicco
Christian Dior
Coin
D&G
Decathlon
Diesel
Dimensione Danza
Docks Dora
Du Pareil Au Même
Fay
Fila
Fuerteventura
Gallo
Gemelli
Gentucca Bini
Giacomelli Sport
Gio Moretti
Gucci
Il Salvagente Bimbi (discount)
Imarika
I Pinco Pallino
La Rinascente
Loro Piana
Love Therapy
Luisa Beccaria
Moschino
Naj-Oleari
Napapijri
Onyx Fashion Store
Paul Smith
Prada
Pupi Solari
Replay
Urrah
Versus
Vilbrequin
Von Dutch
Zara

Children's Shoes

Casa Del Bianco
Cesare Paciotti
Fila
Fratelli Rossetti
Geox
Gucci
Hogan
Peter Pan
Prada
Puma Concept Store
Tod's

Dogs

Francescatrezzi
Gucci

Milan Restaurants

Milan In-Store Restaurants

10 Corso Como Caffè   02 290 13581
Corso Como 10
fusion food in Milan's most
famous shopping emporium

360°   02 835 6706
Via Tortona 12
creative buffet lunches inside a
designer housewares store

Armani Caffè   02 723 18680
Corso Europa 2/corner Via dei Giardini
Mediterranean and fusion

Bistrot (in La Rinascente)   02 877 120
Via San Raffaele 2
salads and sandwiches with a fabulous
view; not for those in a hurry

Globe Restaurant (in Coin)   02 551 81969
Piazza 5 Giornate 1/A
Italian, international and ethnic

Marino Alla Scala Ristorante (in Trussardi)   02 806 88201
Piazza della Scala 5
Italian food in an elegant ambience
overlooking Piazza della Scala

Martini Bar at Dolce & Gabbana   02 760 11154
Corso Venezia 15
sandwiches, drinks and snacks

Nobu (in Armani)   02 623 12645
Via Pisoni 1
sushi in Armani-style minimalist surroundings

Milan Restaurants

BRERA/CORSO GARIBALDI/CORSO COMO

Alla Cucina delle Langhe   02 655 4279
Corso Como 6
Piedmontese delicacies; a fashion haunt

Bento Bar   02 659 8075
Corso Garibaldi 104
elegant Japanese

Brick Oven   02 290 15281
Via Marsala 2
off-beat pizzeria serving
wafer-thin, crunchy pizza

Bushido   02 657 0565
Corso Como 6
the models' favorite sushi bar;
also does take-aways

Grand Italia 02 877 759
Via Palermo 5
busy, basic pizzeria; grab a triangle
of pan-cooked pizza for lunch

La Briciola 02 655 1012
Via Solferino 25
traditional Italian restaurant; spot the photos
of your favourite celebrity-customers as you eat

La Torre di Pisa 02 874 877
Via Fiori Chiari 21
Tuscan

Light 02 626 90631
Via Maroncelli 8/corner Via Tito Speri
minimalist restaurant and lounge bar
popular with footballers and fashion types

Pottery Caffè 02 890 13660
Via Solferino 3
soups, sandwiches, desserts,
herbal teas…and pottery!

Radetzky Caffè 02 657 2645
Corso Garibaldi 105
best for coffee and aperitivi

Santini 02 655 5587
Via San Marco 3
…for a touch of Venice

Topkapi 02 864 63708
Via Ponte Vetero 21
restaurant/pizzeria with fabulous selection
of antipasti; not for avowed seekers of style

ISOLA

Corso Buenos Aires Asmara 02 295 22453
Via Lazzaro Palazzi 5
no-frills Eritrean

Da Giannino l'angolo d'Abruzzo 02 294 06526
Via R. Pilo 20/corner via Nino Bixio
homely, no-frills restaurant with generous
helpings of Abruzzese cuisine

Ditirambo 02 690 06955
Via Garigliano 12
creative cuisine in a relaxed, contemporary
ambience; service can be painfully slow

Joia 02 295 22124
Via Castaldi 18
stylish restaurant serving haute vegetarian
cuisine, and a bargain lunch (on Saturdays,
open for dinner only)

Pizza OK   02 294 01272
Piazza 8 Novembre/corner Via Lambro 15
as it says, pizzas only

Rosy & Gabriele   02 295 25930
Via Sirtori 26
Excellent fish

CORSO DI PORTA TICINESE/CORSO GENOVA/NAVIGLI

Exploit   02 894 08675
Via Pioppette 3
buzzy restaurant with a popular happy hour

La Hora Feliz   02 837 6587
Via San Vito 5
buzzy Mexican restaurant and cocktail bar

Le Biciclette   02 581 04325
Via Torti l/corner Corso Genova
trendy cocktail bar/restaurant, known for Sunday brunch

Rita   02 837 2865
Via Fumagalli 1
*small bar/restaurant with refined cuisine
and outstanding cocktails*

Sushi Koboo   02 581 10956
Viale Col di Lana 1
sushi

Viola   02 894 21529
Via Pavia 6/2
*elegant wine bar with endless selection
of wines and cheeses; excellent service*

MONTENAPOLEONE & SURROUNDINGS

Al Girarrosto   02 760 00481
Corso Venezia 31
*Tuscan specialities, popular with
businessmen and the fashion elite*

Bagutta   02 760 02767
Via Bagutta 14
*Tuscan and international cuisine,
with a literary tradition*

Bice   02 760 02572
Via Borgospesso 12
*Tuscan comfort food for the fashion crowd—
impossible to get a table during fashion week*

Caffè Cova   02 760 05599
Via Montenapoleone 8
charming turn-of-the-century tea room; fabulous cakes!

Il Baretto al Baglione   02 781 255
Via Senato 7
*gentleman's club-like restaurant—
where the smart set lunch*

Il Salumaio di Montenapoleone　　02 784 650
(La Corte di Montenapoleone)
Via Montenapoleone 12
for local specialities, e.g. risotto with
saffron; sit in the hidden garden

Paper Moon　　02 760 22297
Via Bagutta 1
trendy pizzeria and restaurant

CORSO VITTORIO EMANUELE/DUOMO

Alla Vecchia Latteria　　02 874 401
Via dell'Unione 46
crowded vegetarian

Café Real　　02 763 16505
Via Merlo 1
over-the-top baroque restaurant
with a great location

Da Giacomo　　02 760 23313
Via Sotto Corno 6/corner via Cellini
serious specialists in fish, porcini, white
truffles—adored by the fashion crowd

La Bruschetta　　02 869 2494
Piazza Beccaria 12
osteria/pizzeria—every meal starts
with complimentary bruschetta

Luini　　02 864 61917
Via Santa Radegonda 16
panzerotti, standing only

Sant Ambroeus　　02 760 00540
Corso Matteotti 7
exceptional espressos, pastries and
salads in one of the city's oldest cafés

Santa Lucia　　02 760 23155
Via San Pietro all'Orto 3
authentic Neapolitan pizzas, delicious pasta,
and the company of numerous stars whose
photographs grace the walls

Taverna Morigi　　02 864 50880
Via Morigi 8
wine, cheese and cold cuts in
a lovely old Milanese tavern

Victoria Cafè　　02 805 3598
Via Clerici 1
pizzeria/bar, serving crispy pizza, salads and
sandwiches in a stylish, curtain-swathed setting

Milan Restaurants

CORSO VERCELLI/MAGENTA

Bar Magenta   02 805 3808
Via Carducci 13
another favourite turn-of-the-last-century
place, for sandwiches and aperitivi

La Cantina di Manuela   02 439 83048
Via Raffaello Sanzio 16
great wines, cheeses and salads

Orti di Leonardo   02 498 3197
Via Aristide de Togni 6-8
a favourite with everyone from businessmen to footballers—
fried shrimp and zucchini flowers a speciality

VIA ARIOSTO/VIA VINCENZO MONTI/PARCO SEMPIONE

Just Cavalli   02 311 817
Via Luigi Camoens at La Torre Branca
Roberto Cavalli's fashionable eatery in the
middle of Parco Sempione

Leonardo   02 439 0302
Via Saffi 7
cute café serving coffee, snacks, ice-cream
and cakes, owned by the Pupi Solari family

Noy   02 481 10375
Via Soresina 4
intimate minimalist bar/restaurant

Milan Services

Beauty Salons

Hairdressers

Make-up Artists

Skin Treatments

Manicures

Day Spas

Fitness Studios

Dry Cleaners

Mending & Alterations

Shoe & Leather Repairs

Trimmings (fabric, ribbons, buttons etc)

Personal Shopper

Drivers

Taxis

Beauty Salons

Aldo Coppola　　　　　　　　　　**02 655 2144**
Corso Garibaldi 110　　　　　　　　　Tues-Sat 9-6
aldocoppola.it

Aldo Coppola　　　　　　　　　　**02 864 62163**
Via Manzoni 25　　　　　　　　　　　Tues-Sat 9-6

Aldo Coppola　　　　　　　　　　**02 760 07299**
Piazza San Babila 1　　　　　　　　　Tues-Sat 9-6

Aldo Coppola　　　　　　　　　　**02 541 16026**
in Coin (7th floor), Piazza 5 Giornate 1/A　　　Mon 1-8
　　　　　　　　　　　Tues-Fri 10-8, Sat 10-6

Aldo Coppola　　　　　　　　　　**02 798 464**
in Zap!, Galleria Passarella 2　　Mon 3-7:30, Tues-Sat 10-7

Aldo Coppola　　　　　　　　　　**02 890 59712**
in La Rinascente (8th floor)　　　　　Mon-Sat 10-9
Piazza del Duomo　　　　　　　　　　Sun 10-8

Aldo Coppola　　　　　　　　　　**02 608 1171**
Via Borsieri 29　　　　　　　　　　　Tues-Sat 9-6

Downtown　　　　　　　　　　　　**02 760 11485**
Piazza Cavour 2　　　　　　　　Mon-Fri 7-midnight
downtownpalestre.it　　　　　　　　Sat-Sun 10-9

Intrecci　　　　　　　　　　　　　**02 720 22316**
Via Larga 2　　　Mon 11-8, Tues-Fri 10-11, Sat 10-9

Orea Malià　　　　　　　　　　　**02 469 4976**
Via Marghera 18　　　　　Tues-Wed, Fri 9:30-7:30
oreamalia.it　　　　　　　　　Thurs 11-10, Sat 9-7

Orea Malià　　　　　　　　　　　**02 204 6584**
Via Castaldi 42　　　　　　　　Tues-Thurs 9:30-7
　　　　　　　　　　　　　Fri 9:30-8, Sat 9:30-7

Tony & Guy　　　　　　　　　　　**02 480 27137**
Via Vincenzo Monti 27　　　　　　　Mon 9:30-6:30
　　　　　　　　　　Tues-Wed, Fri-Sat 9:30-7:30
　　　　　　　　　　　　　　　Thurs 9:30-8:30

Tony & Guy　　　　　　　　　　　**02 760 18360**
Galleria Passarella 1 (1st floor)　　　Tues-Sat 10-7:30
　　　　　　　　　　　　　　　　(Thurs 10-10)

Hairdressers

Aldo Coppola　　　(as in the 7 beauty salons listed above)

Antica Barbieria Colla　　　　　　**02 874 312**
Via Gerolamo Morone 3　　Tues-Fri 8:30-12:30, 2:30-7
　　　　　　　　　　　　Sat 8:30-12:30, 2:30-6)

Intrecci　　　　(as in the beauty salon listed above)

Jean Louis David　　　　　　　　**02 202 41065**
Via Plinio 5　　　　　　　　　　　　Tues-Sat 9:30-7

Jean Louis David
Via S.Marco/corner Via Moscova 29

02 659 9993
Mon-Sat 9-7

Jean Louis David
Passaggio Duomo 2

02 720 02912
Tues-Sat 9-7

Metodo Rossano Ferretti
Via Turati 30

02 290 60017
Tues-Sat 9:30-6:30

Orea Malià   (as in the 2 beauty salons listed above)

Rolando Elisei
Via Manzoni 31
rolandoelisei.com

02 655 1527
Tues-Sat 9-7

Piergiuseppe Moroni
Via S.Pietro all'Orto 26
piergiuseppemoroni.com

02 760 21631
Tues-Sat 9:30-6

Tony & Guy
Via Vincenzo Monti 27

02 480 27137
Mon 9:30-6:30
Tues-Wed, Fri-Sat 9:30-7:30
Thurs 9:30-8:30

Tony & Guy
Galleria Passarella 1 (1st floor)

02 760 18360
Tues-Sat 10-7:30
(Thurs 10-10)

Make-up Artists

Diego Dalla Palma Make Up Studio
Via Madonnina 15
diegodallapalma.it

02 876 818
Mon 3:30-7:30
Tues-Sat 10-1, 2:30-7:30

MAC
Via Fiori Chiari 12
maccosmetics.com

02 869 95506
Mon-Sat 10-8

Madina
Corso Venezia 23
madina.it

02 760 11692
Mon 3:30-7:30, Tues-Sat 10-7:30

Madina
Via Tivoli 8

02 860 746
(opening hours as above)

Madina (showroom too)
Via Meravigli 17/
corner Via Magenta

02 869 15438
(opening hours as above)

Shu Uemura
Via Brera 2

02 875 371
Mon 3-7, Tues-Sat 10:30-2, 3-7

Skin Treatments

Estée Lauder Skincare Center
in La Rinascente (7th floor),
Piazza del Duomo

02 801 480
Mon-Sat 9:30-6:30

Manicures

Enhancements   **02 626 94537**
Via Solferino 46   Mon-Sat 10-8
enhancements.it

Just Nails   **02 463 498**
Via G.Washington 76   Tues-Sat 9-7

Day Spas
(all provide massages, facials and other treatments)

Arte del Benessere   **02 290 62000**
Via Moscova 24   Mon-Fri 10-8, Sat 9-3:30
(ayurvedic treatments)

Blissful Club   **02 890 12820**
Via dell'Unione 1   Mon-Sat 9-8
blissfulclub.com   (Sundays by appointment)

Centro Benessere (in Jean Louis David)   **02 659 9993**
Via S.Marco/corner Via Moscova 29   Mon-Sat 9-7

Club 10   **02 623 01**
Hotel Principe di Savoia   Mon-Fri 7-10
Piazza della Repubblica 17   Sat-Sun 9-8

E'Spa @ Gianfranco Ferré   **02 760 17526**
Via Sant' Andrea 15   Mon-Fri 10-10, Sat 10-9, Sun 11-8
gianfrancoferre.com

Grooming Dolce & Gabbana   **02 764 08888**
Corso Venezia 15   Mon 2-7, Tues, Fri 10-9
                                        Wed, Thurs, Sat 10-7

Habits Culti   **02 485 17286**
Via Angelo Mauri 5   Daily 10-10
habitsculti.it

Hammam della Rosa (women only)   **02 294 11653**
Viale Abruzzi 15   Tues-Fri 12-10, Sat-Sun 11-7
hammamdellarosa.com

Moresko Hammam Café   **02 404 6936**
Via Rubens 19   Mon, Wed, Thurs 12-11
(Turkish spa for men and women)   Fri 12-midnight
moresko.it   Sat- Sun 10-10

Navigli Beauty Center   **02 835 6601**
Via Mortara 5   Mon-Sat 10-8

Fitness Studios

Cairoli Health Club   **02 760 28517**
Via Senato 11   Mon-Fri 7-11, Sat 9-9, Sun 10-7

Club 10   **02 623 01**
Hotel Principe di Savoia   Mon-Fri 7-10
Piazza della Repubblica 17   Sat-Sun 9-9

Downtown   **02 760 11485**
Piazza Cavour 2   Mon-Sat 7-12, Sun 6-9
downtownpalestre.it

Downtown   **02 863 1181**
Piazza Diaz 6   Mon-Fri 7-11, Sat-Sun 10-8

Dry Cleaners

Antonina Campista   **02 655 2201**
Via Moscova 15   Tues-Fri 8-7, Sat 8-12

Lavasecco Fontana   **02 545 7934**
Via Fontana 5   Mon-Fri 8-12:30, 3-7:30
     Sat 8-12:30

Lavasecco Santa Croce   **02 832 2471**
Via Santa Croce 1   Mon-Fri 8-12:30, 2:30-7
     Sat 8:30-12:30

Rinnovapel   **02 506 5321**
Via degli Umiliati 7   Mon-Fri 9-7
(cleaning and repair of leather clothing)

Tintoria Alberti   **02 890 17677**
Piazza Castello 2   Mon-Fri 8:30-12:30, 1-7
     Sat 8:30-12:30

Via Visconti di Modrone 40   **02 890 17677**
     (opening hours as above)

Tintoria De Leo   **02 864 61931**
Via Rovello 8   Mon-Fri 9:15-7

Tintoria D'Elite   **02 782 333**
Viale Piave 12   Mon-Fri 9-12:30, 3-7:30
(general dry cleaning, also bridal,   Sat 9-12:30
eveningwear and leather)

Mending & Alterations

Bottega Artigianale di Rimedi e Stile   **02 480 12026**
Via Ruggiero Settimo 4   Mon-Fri 3:30-7
(specialist in vintage and bridal)   (Sat by appointment)

Carabella   **02 659 2790**
Corso Garibaldi 93   Mon-Fri 8:30-12:30, 3-7:30

Nicoletta Colella   **02 295 14699**
Viale Regina Giovanna 28   Mon 2-6, Tues-Fri 9-1, 2-6
     Sat 9-1

Sartoria Tosini   **02 312 018**
Via Poliziano 8   Mon-Fri 7:30-12:30, 2:30-7:30

Te lo 6 Rotto   **02 545 8089**
Via della Commenda 28   Mon 3:30-7
     Tues-Sat 9:30-12:30, 3:30-7

Milan Services

Shoe & Leather Repairs

Alvisi Milano **02 740 413**
Via Mameli 24   Mon 3-7:30, Tues-Sat 8:30-12:30, 3-7:30
alvisimilano.it

Artigianoteca **02 551 92855**
Viale Premuda 1   Mon-Fri 8-12:30, 2:30-7
Sat 8-12:30

Calzoleria Valentini **02 864 52589**
Corso Italia 14   Mon-Fri 10-2:30, 3:30-7
valentinicalzature.it   Sat 10-12:30, 4-7

Giuseppe Milito **02 836 1149**
Piazzale Cantore Antonio 5   Mon-Fri 8:30-12:30, 3-6
Sat 8:30-12:30

La Rinnova Scarpe **02 864 53020**
Via Meravigli 18   Mon-Fri 9-1, 3-7, Sat 9-12:30

Margarita Vincenzo Calzolaio **02 583 10161**
Corso Italia 46   Mon-Fri 8-1, 2:30-7:30

Trimmings
(fabrics, buttons, ribbons, cross stitch and embroidery kits, etc)

Franco Jacassi **02 864 62076**
Via Sacchi 3   Mon-Fri 10-1, 2-7
vintagedelirium.com

Gandini Tessuti Alta Moda **02 760 08641**
Via Gesù 21   Mon, Fri 9-1, 2-5
gandinitessuti.it   Tues-Thurs 9-1, 2-6

Ida del Castillo Tessuti **02 581 12137**
Corso di Porta Ticinese 105   Mon 3:30-7:30
Tues-Sat 10:30-1, 3:30-7:30

Il Mondo di Alice **02 540 50066**
Via Orti 4   Mon 3-7:30, Tues-Sat 10-7:30
ilmondodialice.it

Le Mercerie **02 864 54338**
Via San Vittore 2   Mon 3-7, Tues-Fri 9:30-1:30, 3-7
Sat 9:30-1, 3-7

Le Mercerie di Miriam Bonetti **02 864 376**
Via Arco 1, corner Via Pontevetero 23   Mon 3-7
Tues-Sat 10-2, 3-7
(in July, closed Sat afternoon)

Ottolenghi **02 760 01622**
Piazza San Babila 3 Galleria Del Toro   Mon 2-7
Tues-Sat 10-1, 2-7

Tessuti Mimma Gini **02 894 00722**
Via Santa Croce 21   Mon 3-7, Tues-Sat 10-7
tessutimimmagini.it

Tuttomoda **02 290 03718**
Via Statuto 18   Mon 2:30-7, Tues-Fri 9-1:30, 2:30-7

Personal Shoppers

Alessia Geraci   **339 414 8072**
alessia.geraci@tin.it

Jasmine Serrurier   **338 671 5867**
jasmineserrurier@hotmail.com

Drivers

Autonolo Milano   **335 600 0927**
Via Carlo De Cristoforis 5   (available 24 hours)
autonolomilano.it

Taxis

02 4040

02 6969

Avant-garde: forward-thinking or advanced. When referring to art or costume, sometimes implies erotic or startling. Derived from the French for 'advance guard'.

Bridge collection: a collection that is priced between designer and mass market.

Couture: French word used throughout fashion industry to describe the original styles, the ultimate in fine sewing and tailoring, made of expensive fabrics, by designers. The designs are shown in collections twice a year—spring/summer and fall/winter.

Custom-made/tailor-made, also called bespoke: garments made by tailor or couture house for an individual customer following couturier's original design. Done by either fitting a model form adjusted to the customer's measurements or by several personal fittings.

Diffusion line: a designer's second and less expensive collection.

Ensemble: an entire costume, including accessories, worn at one time. Two or more items of clothing designed and coordinated to be worn together.

Fashion trend: direction in which styles, colours and fabrics are moving. Trends may be influenced by political events, films, personalities, dramas, social and sporting events or indeed any human activity.

Faux: false or counterfeit, imitation: used in connection with gems, pearls and leathers. Faux fur (fake fur) is commonplace today, as is what is sometimes known as 'pleather' (plastic leather). Artificial gems, especially pearls, are often made from a fine kind of glass known as 'paste', and are accordingly sometimes called 'paste' for short.

Haberdashery: a store that sells men's apparel and furnishings.

Knock-off: trade term for the copying of an item of apparel, e.g. a dress or a coat, in a lower price line. Similar to piracy.

Made-to-measure: clothing (dress, suit, shirt etc) made according to individual's measurement. No fittings required.

One-off: a unique, one-of-a-kind item that will not be found in any other store or produced again in the future, e.g. a customized denim skirt or a rare vintage cocktail dress. Can also refer to made-to-measure and couture garments designed for a particular person and/or event, such as a dress for the Oscars.

Prêt-à-porter: French term which literally means ready-to-wear, i.e. to take (or wear) straight out of the shop.

Ready-to-wear (rtw): apparel that is mass-produced in standard sizes. Records of the ready-to-wear industry tabulated in the U.S. Census of 1860 included hoop skirts, cloaks, and mantillas; from 1890 shirtwaists and wrappers were added; and, after 1930, dresses.

5 very good reasons why you should become a *Where to Wear* online subscriber

1. Access the guide online from wherever you are.

2. Take the guide on a laptop or CD ROM.

3. Find a particular designer, type of clothing or boutique easily by just typing in what you want and seeing the result.

4. Results printed out to show information and location, member concessions, special offers and promotions from stores.

5. Exclusive seasonal offers available to *Where to Wear* members only from selected stores.

Visit our new exclusive members website at

www.wheretowear.com/member.htm

How to order *Where to Wear*

Where to Wear publishes guides to the following cities: London, New York, Paris, Los Angeles, San Francisco and Las Vegas. In addition, there is *Where to Wear Italy*, *Where to Wear Florida* and *Where to Wear Australia*. Each edition retails at £9.99 or $14.95.

There is also a gift box set, *Shopping Guides to the World's Fashion Capitals*, available for £29.99 or $49.99 which includes the London, New York, Paris and Italy guides (four books for the price of three).

If you live in the UK or Europe, you can order your copies of *Where to Wear* by contacting our London office at:

10 Cinnamon Row
Plantation Wharf
London SW11 3TW
TEL: 020 7801 1381
EMAIL: uk@wheretowear.com

If you live in the USA, you can order your copies of *Where to Wear* by contacting our New York office at:

666 Fifth Avenue
PMB 377
New York, NY 10103
TEL: 212-969-0138
TOLL-FREE: 1-877-714-SHOP (7467)
EMAIL: usa@wheretowear.com

Or simply log on to our website: www.wheretowear.com
Where to Wear delivers worldwide.

Where
Wear to

ITALY

PLACE YOUR
CORPORATE LOGO
HERE

FASHION SHOPPING FROM A-Z

CUSTOMIZE TO MEET YOUR OBJECTIVES

Where to Wear, the only recognized brand name in fashion shopping guides, is an effective marketing tool for your business. *Where to Wear* can customize any of its city guides to reflect your company's brand identity. Our corporate clients have used *Where to Wear* in a variety of different ways: subscription renewals, hotel in-room gift, magazine cover mount, event or holiday gift, or a much needed thank-you to key clients.

Where to Wear has its own in-house design team who will work with you to co-brand our guides:

- Stamp your corporate logo onto the *Where to Wear* front cover
- Create co-branded covers with additional pages detailing your important information
- Offer mini guides with specially selected stores to your demographic profile
- Design leather pocket-size agenda books for men and women
- Cover full-size editions of *Where to Wear* in beautiful leather or suede in a variety of colors
- Create a box set, including different cities, with a co-branded cover